Community Banking
from
Crisis to Prosperity

Timothy W. Koch

Makawk Books
A Division of TWK Strategies
Irmo, SC

Copyright © 2014 by TWK Strategies
Published by Makawk Books
126 Blackburn Road, Irmo, SC 29063

TWKstrategies.com

All Rights Reserved. No part of this publication may be reproduced, stored in a retrieval system, or transmitted, in any form or by any means without the prior permission in writing of Makawk Books, or as expressly permitted by law.

ISBN: 978-0-9899003-0-0

First Edition 2014
Cover design and printing by Stan Sands, Creative Agents, Irmo, SC
Printed in the United States of America

To Susan, Michala and Andy
For making my journey fascinating and enjoyable

Acknowledgments

I have had the opportunity to work with outstanding academics, bankers and bank consultants throughout my career. The ideas and recommendations that I offer in this book reflect my interpretations and biases from numerous conversations and debates with many of these individuals. I am particularly grateful to the following individuals who contributed directly to this book via their insights and observations; Donna de St. Aubin, Sue Evans, Charlie Funk, Jeff Gerrish, Scott Hein, Glen Jammaron, Nick Ketcha, Ed Krei, Don Musso, Karl Nelson and Mike Stevens. I want to especially thank Ed Krei for his insights on bank investments and Don Musso, Nick Ketcha and the Managing Directors of FinPro for extensive analysis and discussions regarding enterprise risk management, value creation and regulation. Finally, I end the book with an analysis of First Community Bank's organizational structure, strategy and performance throughout the recent financial crisis. Mike Crapps was instrumental in clarifying details related to the bank's strategic objectives and response to regulatory issues.

In 1980, I was offered the opportunity to teach at the Stonier Graduate School of Banking and at one point thereafter I taught at each of the six general graduate schools of banking offered throughout the United States. In 2001, I was named President of the Graduate School of Banking at Colorado (GSBC) in which capacity I continue to serve. In this role, I have the opportunity to visit with GSBC trustees, faculty and students whenever I need an expert on topics beyond my comfort zone, for which I am especially grateful. In addition, during the early stages of the financial crisis, I served on the FDIC's Advisory Committee on Community Banking along with 13 presidents and CEOs of community banks and was thus introduced to the regulatory view of key issues affecting community banks and the associated reactions from senior managers of community banks. In 2010, I became a director of TIB, a bankers bank headquartered in Dallas, Texas. Finally, I also serve as Professor of Finance at the Moore School of Business, University of South Carolina having previously taught at Texas Tech University and Baylor University. The basic idea for the book originated when I was on sabbatical from the University of South Carolina.

The views expressed in this book are mine and are not necessarily those of the trustees or representatives of the Graduate School of Banking at Colorado or the University of South Carolina. Any errors are my responsibility.

Timothy W. Koch
Professor of Finance, University of South Carolina
President, Graduate School of Banking at Colorado

Table of Contents

Introduction 1
- Types of Banks
- Introduction to Some Dodd-Frank Provisions
- Objective of the book

Overview of Community Banking and the Regulatory Environment

Chapter 1
The Community Banking Model 9

    Core Attributes of Traditional Community Banks
    Ownership
    Organizational Structure
    Bankers Banks and Community Banking
    Executive Compensation

Chapter 2
How Community Banks Can Survive and Thrive 25

    Koch's Ten Prescriptions for Community Bank Financial Health
    Positive Aspects of the Future Banking Environment
    Strategic Checklist

Chapter 3
Bank Regulation and Regulatory Reform 41

    Structure of Bank Regulation
    Deposit Insurance
    Federal Government Liquidity Programs
    Regulation of Community Banks
    Problem Banks and Regulatory Enforcement Actions
    Factors Associated with Recent Failures
    Key Regulatory Issues
    Dodd-Frank Wall Street Reform and Consumer Protection Act
    Qualified Residential Mortgages and the Borrower's Ability to Pay
    Community Reinvestment Act and Fair Lending

Understanding Community Bank Performance

Chapter 4
Basic Financial Statements & Key Risk Ratios 65

Financial Statements for Community Banks
Fundamental Risks in Community Banking
Maintaining Adequate Capital to Ensure Solvency

Chapter 5
Earnings & Shareholder Value Analysis 95

Profitability Analysis Using Financial Ratios
Strategic Performance Objectives
Value Creation at First Community Corporation

Strategies for Improved Risk Management

Chapter 6
Funding the Bank 113

Alternative Business Strategies & Implications for Funding
Core Deposits Drive Franchise Value
What is a Core Deposit?
Deposit Service Charges
Wholesale Funding
Government Liquidity Programs
Liquidity Planning
Contingency Funding Planning

Chapter 7
Capital Protects and Provides Opportunities 135

Capital Protects Against Failure
What Counts as Bank Capital?
Regulatory Capital Requirements
Capital Ratios at Community Banks Versus Larger Banks
Basel III Capital Proposals
Capital Planning for Community Banks

Chapter 8
Lending: We Eat Our Own Cooking 155

Credit Risk
Recent Loan Problems
Know Your Borrower
Loan Portfolio Credit Risk Analysis
Loan Workouts

Chapter 9
Managing the Investment Portfolio 179

- Introduction to Bond Ratings
- Characteristics of Investment Instruments
- Objectives of the Investment Portfolio
- Accounting for Securities Holdings
- Types of Securities Owned
- Factors Affecting the Size and Composition of the Portfolio
- Portfolio Strategies

Chapter 10
Asset and Liability Management 205

- Interest Rate Risk at Community Banks
- 2010 Regulatory Guidance on Interest Rate Risk
- Asset & Liability Management Committee Agenda
- GAP Analysis
- Earnings Sensitivity Analysis
- Economic Value of Equity Sensitivity Analysis
- Managing the Bank's Interest Rate Risk Profile
- Community Banks and Derivatives

Strategies for Achieving Competitive Advantage

Chapter 11
Taking Advantage of Competitive Opportunities 237

- Strategies to Enhance Shareholder Value
- The U.S. Retail Payments System
- Financial Targets

Chapter 12
Building Value in Difficult Times: One Bank's Story 249

- A Brief History of First Community Bank
- Financial Results for 2007
- Problems with the Investment Portfolio
- Capital Strategy
- Building Shareholder Value
- Positioned for Prosperity
- Value-Enhancing Actions

Abbreviations and Acronyms

AFS	Available for Sale
ALCO	Asset & Liability Management Committee
ALLL	Allowance for Loan and Lease Losses
ALM	Asset & Liability Management
AML	Anti-Money Laundering
ARM	Adjustable Rate Mortgage
ATM	Automated Teller Machine
BAB	Build American Bond
BQ	Bank Qualified Municipal
BSA	Bank Secrecy Act
C&D	Cease & Desist
CAMELS	Capital, Asset quality, Management, Earnings, Liquidity, Sensitivity
CCAR	Comprehensive Capital Analysis and Review
CD	Certificate of Deposit
CDARS	Certificate of Deposit Accounts Registry Service
CDI	Core Deposit Intangible
CDO	Collateralized Debt Obligation
CDS	Credit Default Swaps
CEO	Chief Executive Officer
CFO	Chief Financial Officer
CFP	Contingency Funding Plan
CFPB	Consumer Financial Protection Bureau
CMO	Collateralized Mortgage Obligation
CMP	Civil Money Penalty
CPP	Capital Purchase Program
CPR	Constant Prepayment Rate
CRA	Community Reinvestment Act
CRE	Commercial Real Estate
CSBS	Conference of State Bank Supervisors
DDA	Demand Deposit Account
DDoS	Distributed Denial of Service
DFA	Dodd-Frank Act
DIF	Deposit Insurance Fund
DOJ	Department of Justice
DUR	Modified Duration
ECOA	Equal Credit Opportunity Act
EPS	Earnings Per Share
ERM	Enterprise Risk Management
FDIC	Federal Deposit Insurance Corporation
FSOC	Financial Stability Oversight Council
EM	Equity Multiplier
EPS	Earnings Per Share
ERM	Enterprise Risk Management
ESOP	Employee Stock Ownership Plan
EVE	Economic Value of Equity
FDICIA	FDIC Improvement Act
FHLB	Federal Home Loan Bank
FHLMC	Federal Home Loan Mortgage Corporation (Freddie Mac)
FNMA	Federal National Mortgage Association (Fannie Mae)
FRB	Federal Reserve Bank
FSOC	Financial Stability Oversight Council

GAAP	Generally Accepted Accounting Principles	
GAP	Rate sensitive assets - Rate sensitive liabilities	
GNMA	Government National Mortgage Association (Ginnie Mae)	
GSE	Government Sponsored Enterprise	
HELOC	Home Equity Line of Credit	
HMDA	Home Mortgage Disclosure Act	
HTM	Held to Maturity	
IRR	Interest Rate Risk	
LGD	Loss Given Default	
LIBOR	London Bank Offer Rate	
MBS	Mortgage-Backed Security	
MMDA	Money Market Deposit Account	
MMMF	Money Market Mutual Fund	
MRA	(Regulatory) Matter Requiring Attention	
MVA	Market Value of Assets	
MVL	Market Value of Liabilities	
NCFD	Net Non-core Funding Dependency	
NIM	Net Interest Margin	
NI	Net Income	
NOI	Net Operating Income	
NOW	Negotiable Order of Withdrawal	
NPA	Nonperforming Asset	
NRSRO	Nationally Recognized Statistical Ratings Organization	
OAS	Option-Adjusted Spread	
OCC	Office of the Comptroller of the Currency	
OCI	Other Comprehensive Income	
OLEM	Other Loans Especially Mentioned	
OMB	Office of Management and Budget	
OREO	Other Real Estate Owned	
OTD	Originate to Distribute	
OTS	Office of Thrift Supervision	
PAC	Planned Amortization Class	
PCA	Prompt Corrective Action under the FDIC Improvement Act	
P/E	Price to Earnings or Private Equity (PE)	
PLL	Provisions for loan losses	
PSA	Public Securities Association standard for prepayment speeds	
P2P	Person-to-Person	
QE	Quantitative Easing	
QM	Qualified Mortgage	
QRM	Qualified Residential Mortgage	
REMIC	Real Estate Mortgage Investment Conduit	
ROA	Return on average assets	
ROE	Return on average equity	
RSA	Rate Sensitive Asset	
RSL	Rate Sensitive Liability	
SAFE	Secure and Fair Enforcement for Mortgage Licensing Act	
SBA	Small Business Administration	
SEC	Securities Exchange Commission	
SIFI	Systemically Important Financial Institution	
SIV	Structured Investment Vehicle	
TAC	Targeted Amortization Class	
TAF	Term Auction Facility	
TARP	Troubled Asset Relief Program	
TBTF	Too Big to Fail	
TBVS	Tangible Book Value Per Share	
TCE	Tangible Common Equity	
TDR	Troubled Debt Restructuring	
TEA	Tax-Exempt Adjustment	
TLGP	Temporary Liquidity Guarantee Program	
TRuPS	Trust Preferred Stock	
UBPR	Uniform Bank Performance Report	
UDAAP	Unfair, Deceptive or Abusive Acts and Practices	
VaR	Value at Risk	

Introduction

With the recent financial crisis, many individuals and much of the media view banks and the business of banking negatively. Critics emphasize a broad range of bad practices, such as excessive risk taking, particularly by making subprime loans, confusing borrowers with complex financial products, charging excessive fees, the inappropriate use of derivatives and paying excessive compensation to senior managers. An often-voiced solution to these alleged abuses is additional regulation which will presumably force institutions to treat customers more fairly and better align risk taking with the wishes of stockholders and the federal government, which insures bank deposits and regulates management practices.

However, the casual reference to "banks" and "banking" is imprecise. It is based on the premise that all banks are the same. As demonstrated throughout this book, community banks differ sharply from other financial institutions. There are four different general categories of banks in the United States. They are the (1) Too Big To Fail (TBTF) institutions, (2) large regional banks, (3) community banks and (4) shadow banks that operate in the shadow banking system. Each operate in a different way and serve different clienteles:

- *Too Big To Fail Banks.* These are the largest financial institutions whose primary business may be lending, investment banking (securities underwriting, asset management and proprietary trading), insurance or consumer finance.

- *Large Regional Banks.* These are large financial institutions that operate in regional and national geographic markets and offer fewer banking services than the TBTF institutions. Banking services include deposits, loans, leases, credit cards, securities underwriting and brokerage, market making, asset management and insurance sales. These firms generate substantial revenues from both net interest income and fee income, but typically have little international exposure.

- *Community Banks.* These are smaller commercial banking organizations that typically operate within a relatively small trade area, offer banking services that emphasize loans and deposits, generate the bulk of earnings from net interest income and emphasize personal relationships between customers, stockholders, managers and employees.

- *Shadow Banks.* These are noncommercial bank financial institutions that are actively involved in financial intermediation by which funds are transferred from investors to borrowers. They might originate loans but generally do not want to hold the loans in portfolios. They might securitize loans and place them with investors. They often acquire securities based on the perceived risk versus return as signaled by rating agencies and the security underwriters. They may be insurance companies, pension funds, hedge funds, money market funds, *government-sponsored enterprises* (GSEs), off-balance sheet entities with names such as *structured-investment vehicles* (SIVs), or payday lenders.

Institutions across the four categories have dramatically different business models. Not surprisingly, they contributed differently to the ongoing financial crisis, received different levels of governmental assistance and have performed differently coming out of the economic downturn. One of the principal themes of this book is that the financial crisis was caused largely by the actions of the TBTF Banks and Shadow Banks. Yet, the U.S. government quickly and consistently provided assistance to many of these institutions to keep them from failing. Consider how Fannie Mae and Freddie Mac are currently structured under conservatorship rather than being allowed to fail. Similar assistance has never been available to many large regional banks and community banks. TBTF banks presumably carry systemic risk in that their failure may bring about the collapse of the global financial system.[1] Failures of other institutions are presumably less critical to the smooth functioning of the money and capital markets. We thus saw federal regulators approve bank holding company applications in record (short) time so that Goldman Sachs, Morgan Stanley, American Express and MetLife, among others, could get loan guarantees and access to borrowings from the Federal Reserve Banks. Without access, a liquidity crisis would likely have forced these firms to fail to perform on transactions obligations. Similar holding company requests by community banks typically take months to be processed.

Market participants and bank regulators recognize the discriminatory treatment. It is an advantage of size and a critical benefit from the interconnected relationships between key individuals in government and senior managers and directors of TBTF banks.[2] Community banks are allowed to fail while the federal government protects TBTF banks regardless of the roles played in causing the crisis. In response, the Obama administration proposed substantive changes in regulation to address some of the incentives that managers of TBTF Banks have and to force a fairer treatment of individual consumers. In mid-2010, Congress passed the Dodd-Frank Regulatory Reform Act (DFA) which formalized many game-changing rules. One series of provisions provides for the identification and orderly liquidation of *systemically important financial institutions* (SIFIs) if certain conditions are satisfied.[3] Banks that qualify as SIFIs under current regulation are listed at the end of the chapter. Not all of these organizations are too big to fail, but those subject to stress tests presumably are as well as some of the other large organizations not currently required to conduct annual stress tests. Given the close relationships between government officials and principals of these large firms, many financial experts do not believe that TBTF firms will be liquidated.

As proposed, the profitability and risk-taking activities of the largest institutions will likely decline over time —at least until we forget. Unfortunately, many of the provisions of DFA and additional attention to consumer compliance regulations harm community banks who contributed relatively little to the problems. Owners and managers of many of the smallest banks believe that the administration and regulators are consciously trying to reduce the number of independent banks. These legislative and regulatory reforms follow substantial increases in Federal Deposit Insurance Corporation (FDIC) deposit insurance premiums. While insurance coverage increased to $250,000 per account from the previous $100,000, surviving banks paid a special assessment to supplement the insurance fund which was followed by the prepayment of more than three years of premiums to provide cash for the FDIC to close failed institutions. Premium increases are even greater for banks that the FDIC designates as riskier. For some community banks, the increased deposit insurance premiums wiped out the bulk of 2008 and 2009 earnings.

One of the provisions of DFA created the Consumer Financial Protection Bureau (CFPB). The CFPB's mandate is to protect consumers by ending unfair practices in direct consumer lending and credit card lending. Ominously, many of the rules implementing provisions have yet to be determined. The American Bankers Association identified 30 provisions of the bill that harmed community banks largely by increasing compliance costs.[4] Increased compliance costs may drive some of the smallest banks out of business because they will be unable to cover the costs if revenues do not rise substantially in the near future. If this conjecture is true, small banks may eventually disappear typically by merger or acquisition. Whether intentional or not, it doesn't seem right that small banks that often serve small, rural communities suffer most under the new rules.

Because banks have access to FDIC-insured deposits, excessive risk-taking potentially harms the deposit insurance fund if a bank fails. The new rules are designed to return banking to its core principles and thereby protect the insurance fund. These core principles involve meeting the credit and other financial needs of customers while carefully managing risk. Effective risk management, in turn, focuses on loan diversification, core deposit funding, holding ample liquid assets, having access to wholesale borrowings and operating with large amounts of equity capital. This is the future of community banking.

This book attempts to explain the operations of traditional community banks. While it touches on the causes and consequences of the financial crises that emerged in 2007, it does not try to explain them in detail. Rather, it analyzes a model of community banking which, if followed, will enable community banks to not just survive the difficult regulatory and economic environment, but to thrive. It emphasizes effective risk management practices. Where appropriate, it documents differences between the four categories of banks and offers a critique as to what is appropriate and inappropriate for insured institutions. An appreciation of these differences leads to a recognition of the types of regulation, policies, and practices that will prevent future crises, promote healthy competition and lead to sustained economic growth throughout the country.

Appendix: List of Systemically Important Financial Institutions

RP: Must submit a Resolution Plan
ST: Must conduct annual stress tests

U.S. Headquartered Banking Organizations*

	Resolution Plan	Stress Tests
Bank of America (FIA Card Services)	RP	ST
Bank of NY Mellon	RP	ST
Citigroup	RP	ST
Goldman Sachs	RP	ST
JPMorgan Chase	RP	ST
Morgan Stanley	RP	ST
State Street	RP	ST
Ally Financial		ST
American Express		ST
MetLife**		ST
BB&T		ST
Capital One Financial		ST
Fifth Third Bank		ST
KeyCorp		ST
PNC Financial		ST
Regions Financial		ST
SunTrust Banks		ST
U.S. Bancorp		ST
Wells Fargo		ST

Other U.S. Banks with Total Assets Greater than $50 Billion
TD Bank
HSBC Bank USA
RBS Citizens
The Northern Trust Company
Union Bank
BMO Harris Bank
Charles Schwab Bank
Sovereign Bank

Manufacturers and Traders Trust Company
Discover Bank
Compass Bank
Comerica Bank
Bank of the West
USAA Federal Savings Bank
Deutsche Bank Trust Company Americas
Huntington National Bank

Other U.S. Headquartered Systemically Important Financial Institutions (SIFIs)
Identified by the Financial Stability Oversight Council (FSOC)

AIG
GE Capital
Prudential Financial

*In 2009, the federal government conducted formal stress tests to assess whether these 19 institutions needed to raise additional capital. They are widely presumed to be TBTF.
**In February 2013, MetLife sold its depository business to GE Capital and received official clearance to deregister as a bank holding company.

Overview of Community Banking and the Regulatory Environment

CHAPTER 1
The Community Banking Model

Community banks are the lifeblood of many small towns, cities and states. They are often locally-owned and managed such that customers know their bankers personally. Members of the boards of directors are typically small business owners and public figures with positive reputations in the community. Bank officers serve on many community boards and foundations and banks are important contributors to schools and local nonprofit organizations. Economic growth in the area often varies directly with local community banks' willingness and ability to lend.

Of course, there is no such thing as a standardized community bank that operates in every market. There are, however, attributes that differentiate the best managed banks from those that have recently experienced severe problems. It is these attributes that characterize traditional community banking and serve as a model for financial strength and having growth options going forward.

Core Attributes of Traditional Community Banks

Conventional wisdom defines a community bank as any commercial bank or savings bank with $1 billion or less in total assets.[1] While such a description is useful because it emphasizes institutions of a manageable size, it ignores the importance of organizational structure and business strategy. In this book, I designate community banks as institutions that follow four basic principles. First, management focuses on "high touch" relationships between bank customers, stockholders and employees. Second, management pursues core financial strategies that focus on capital adequacy, a reliance on core deposits, originating loans and holding them in portfolio and holding a minimum amount of liquid assets. Historically, most community banks generate the bulk of earnings via net interest income. Third, there is a strong link between ownership and management. Finally, community banks generally compete in limited geographic markets. While community banks can be any size, these attributes effectively constrain the population of qualifying banks to those that are much smaller than the megabanks that compete in national and international markets.

CHAPTER 1

Relationship Banking

Community banking is about the importance of relationships. Marketing specialists often refer to a "high touch" approach that incorporates a personal element with frequent human interaction.[2] From a banker's perspective, it can be characterized by the phrase "know your customer." Community bank employees generally live in the communities where they work. Their families attend school with their customers' families. They are members of the same civic and religious organizations. They are familiar with the key employers and businesses in the area and they drive by the properties and businesses that they finance. Bank officers generally understand a customer's total banking relationship including deposits, loans, trust services, and the like, along with his or her personal circumstances such as employment status, work history and education. Such "soft knowledge" about customers allows bankers to customize products and services to the specific needs of customers and helps reduce risk associated with making loans and accepting deposits. From the customer's perspective, community banking is characterized by dealing with familiar bank employees year after year. Aunt Martha recognizes the teller when she stops by for coffee and to check her deposit balance. She also recognizes the loan officer who helps finance the working capital needs of the family business. When she requests a loan, she knows that the loan officer understands her company's financial statements and unusual cash flow needs as well as her personal financial condition. She will not have to train another lender each time the company or she needs to borrow. If necessary, she can contact her banker by phone or Internet to request specific services or assistance—and the banker will typically respond quickly and favorably. Importantly, decisions are made by individuals who live locally rather than by individuals living outside the local area.

This focus on relationships has been labeled "relationship banking" as opposed to "transactional banking," which emphasizes the effective completion of repetitive transactions. Whether true or not, most banks claim to focus on relationships, at least in specific departments or divisions. For example, wealth management or private banking departments of the largest organizations offer personal service covering a wide range of financial needs to high-net worth and high-net income customers and often label employees with customer contact as "relationship managers." This is relationship banking offering high-touch service. The largest financial organizations in their entirety, however, are rarely community banks because the corporate focus is on growth obtained via increasing transactions volume. Banks that focus on transactions often use statistical models involving credit scoring to make credit decisions. The financial profile of an individual or small business as demonstrated by key financial ratios determines the customer's credit score. This numerical score, in turn, dictates whether credit is provided and, if available, what the terms are. The mechanical nature of credit scoring allows real efficiencies in the form of fewer employees and fast decision making. It is lower cost, on average, and presumably allows for better risk management because it enables larger, more diversified portfolios. Of course, the expected risk may differ sharply from realized risk if the credit scoring models are poorly calibrated.[3]

The emphasis on transactional banking is also demonstrated by how bank customers interact with their bank when they have questions or problems. For example, suppose that Andy Pedestrian is not a customer of the transactional bank's wealth management (or private banking) group that deals with high-net worth customers. When he calls the bank to discuss a problem with his deposit account, he doesn't speak to an employee of the bank in the community where he lives, but is instead channeled to someone overseas often after waiting a good amount of time on the phone. To lower costs, transactional banks push customers such as Andy to bank online, at kiosks or via mobile devices because this lowers the cost of providing services. Business borrowers with small dollar financing needs are often credit scored rather than having a dedicated loan officer who works directly with them. Given their large size, transactional banks prefer to deal with large dollar loans that potentially impact their bottom line in a meaningful way. It is important to recognize that, if followed appropriately, the transactional model also works. But it has a sharply different emphasis and different risks than a true relationship bank.

The importance of relationships extends to a bank's employees and stockholders. Many community banks are family-owned or operate as S corporations with a limited number of stockholders. Managers thus often need to make decisions that recognize the roles that founders, family members and key stockholders play and their financial circumstances. Many community banks offer Employee Stock Ownership Plans (ESOPs) to provide ownership benefits to long-term employees who are not family members. Similarly, institutions that are organized as mutual savings banks do not have common stock, but are rather "owned" by member depositors. Any profits generated are retained by the institution. Such mutuals typically exhibit the same relationship focus and risk aversion as family-owned banks. Still, one of the key problems and risks facing community banks, particularly those located in rural areas, is that they have difficulty hiring and retaining top talent because they don't pay salaries comparable to those available in larger cities. They typically compete for a smaller pool of talent due to perceived quality of life opportunities, particularly those desired by younger individuals, which are not as readily available in small and rural communities. Community banks must offer their employees growth opportunities via education and increased responsibilities in order to attract and retain the best people.

Core Financial Strategies

Manage the Spread

Community banks generally operate with conservative balance sheets and generate the bulk of earnings from charging more on loans than they pay on deposits. If it sounds simple, it is. This philosophy is a throwback to the highly regulated banking environment evident until the mid-1980s. At that time, banks and savings and loan associations (S&Ls) were limited by regulation on the rates they could pay depositors. In many cases, there were usury restrictions that also limited the rates they could charge on many types of loans. This led to the 3-6-3 rule of banking—pay 3% (maximum allowed) on deposits, charge 6% (maximum allowed) on loans, and hit the golf course at 3 P.M. The 3% spread between the loan and deposit rates was effectively guaranteed on low-risk assets. How times have changed!

Banks that operate with sufficient capital no longer face interest rate restrictions and can charge and pay whatever rates managers want. However, community banks manage this same spread as judiciously today as in the past. They can best control funding costs by attracting and retaining large amounts of low-cost core deposits. Think of the rates that banks pay on demand deposits, interest checking, savings accounts and small-time deposits. They similarly make and price loans to try and achieve a risk-adjusted spread of at least 3%. Core deposits are relatively stable because they are owned by individuals and small business customers who are more concerned about access to and the security of their funds and are relatively insensitive to interest rates.

Originate and Hold Loans

An important component of core earnings is interest earned on loans. Community banks originate loans and generally hold them in portfolio.[4] They often receive an origination fee from the borrower who subsequently makes periodic interest and principal payments. These interest payments represent the bulk of community bank revenue. Not surprisingly, community bank lenders evaluate carefully the borrower's character, capacity, and willingness to repay the loan as scheduled. When necessary, they require the borrower to post collateral as a potential secondary source of repayment. If done well, this credit risk analysis allows the bank to control loan losses. If done poorly, it leads to rising problem loans, increased loan charge-offs and a drop in interest income. Because community banks hold most of the loans they originate in portfolio, they care greatly about the underlying loan's risk and monitor the borrower's performance after granting a loan.

During the years leading up to the recent financial crisis, many institutions, particularly too-big-too-fail (TBTF) banks and shadow banks, pursued business models characterized by the term *originate-to-distribute* (OTD). The OTD model emphasized returns from originating then selling, or securitizing, loans. It relied on credit scoring or ratings of the underlying loans so that investors would readily buy the securities issued that were backed by the loans. Once the loans were sold, the originator no longer bore the risk that the borrower might not make the promised loan payments.[5] The institution would then originate additional loans repeating the process over and over. In retrospect, the obvious problem is that loan originators who plan to sell the loans are willing to extend credit to increasingly risky borrowers who are less likely to pay. After all, loan producers are paid on the basis of how much new loan volume they create. Once the loans are sold, the credit risk is transferred from the originator to the investor. If these increasingly risky loans are not priced substantially higher with the risks accurately estimated, the ultimate holders of the loans will bear significant losses.

Hold Liquid Assets

Banks must balance expected cash outflows with cash inflows so that they can meet payment obligations. For example, when a customer withdraws funds to make a payment, the bank must have access to actual cash or clearing balances to meet the payment request. Cash inflows arise from normal principal and interest payments received from borrowers as well as from new deposits. In the event that cash inflows fall short of expected outflows on any one day, the bank must have access to cash. The more aggressive banks rely on new borrowings to obtain cash as needed. Most community banks hold a minimum amount of liquid assets to cover potential near-term cash needs in the event that such borrowings are not available. As such, the institution can always meet the clearing needs of its customers. Because many bank liabilities are payable on demand (think of checking accounts), banks must monitor their cash outflows carefully and be defensive in their investments. Liquid assets include federal funds sold, Treasuries and short-term, hiqh-quality securities. Unfortunately, these liquid assets do not carry the yields that other, more risky, assets carry.

Maintain Adequate Capital

Banking regulators have long recognized the importance of capital at banks. In fact, a key component of bank regulation requires that banks maintain minimum capital ratios. In a strict mechanical sense, each bank must operate with a minimum amount of equity capital in relation to assets owned as well as a minimum amount of equity and total capital in relation to the amount of risk assets owned. This formal capital requirement is designed to lower the overall risk of the bank.

Think of equity capital as the sum of common stock outstanding and retained earnings (cumulative retained profits over the life of the bank). A bank with $100 million of loans and securities, such as that in Exhibit 1.1, might finance these assets with $8 million in equity capital and $92 million in deposits. This bank's core capital (leverage) ratio is 8% ($8/$100) because equity represents 8% of total assets. If regulators set a minimum capital ratio at 8%, the bank could grow assets only if it could increase equity because it is already at the minimum. Alternatively, the 8% minimum represents a maximum financial leverage ratio (total assets/equity capital) of 12.5×. Thus, the bank's debt could not exceed 92% of assets or assets could not exceed 12.5 times the amount of equity capital. The important point is that setting a minimum capital ratio limits the amount of debt relative to equity that a bank can operate with, which limits a bank's ability to grow.

Exhibit 1.1 Simple Balance Sheet for a Community Bank
Millions of Dollars

Total Assets		Liabilities + Equity	
Loans	$ 70	Deposits	$ 92
Securities	30	Equity	8
	$100		$100

Capital also provides a buffer against loan losses. The bank in Exhibit 1.1 could lose $8 million before its equity is wiped out and the bank is insolvent. The greater is the proportionate amount of capital financing, the greater is the buffer. In this sense, capital protects stockholders and ultimately the FDIC as insurer of banks.

Community banks generally operate with large amounts of equity capital relative to assets compared with other banking organizations. Lower financial leverage is consistent with lower risk tolerance, but this is important for institutions that compete in limited geographic areas. Community banks are less able to diversify their credit risk (default risk on loans) given that many of their loans are to borrowers in the same line of business (think agriculture, commercial real estate or small commercial businesses) and in the same general geographic area such that they are potentially affected by the same economic conditions. Banks with higher capital-to-asset ratios can charge-off proportionately more loans yet remain solvent.[6]

Community bank equity capital ratios are considerably higher than those at TBTF banks and large regional banks. Prior to their demise, investment banks, such as Bear Stearns and Lehman Brothers, routinely operated with capital ratios of 2.5% to 3%, which equates to leverage ratios of 33× to 40×. From 2007 through 2009, Citigroup and Bank of America similarly operated with equity capital ratios around 6% or leverage ratios from 15× to 18×. Small community banks that operate in just a few locations often have capital ratios around 15% or higher (leverage ratios around 5× to 6×). Capital ratios typically decline as asset size increases. Bank regulators monitor capital levels closely to try and ensure that banks with problems obtain additional capital before they realize losses. Over time, banking pundits have frequently interpreted FDIC to stand for "Forever Demanding Increased Capital."[7]

Operate in Limited Geographic Markets

In order to truly offer relationship banking, bankers need to know their customers well. Banks that expand outside their local trade areas often have difficulty enforcing this discipline. Consider the situation faced by many banks in the Midwest in recent years. A bank headquartered in rural Kansas or rural Minnesota that wants to expand might consider opening a branch in Kansas City or Minneapolis, respectively, because growth opportunities in the local community are limited by the declining population and low-growth business activity. While there is opportunity in expansion, there are also considerable risks. Is it likely that the rural bank's owners and managers adequately understand the market in the metropolitan area? Will the bank be able to hire employees with local knowledge and existing customer relationships to mimic the successful community banking model? Will key credit decisions be made locally? If the answer to any of these questions is no, the bank has broken the emphasis on relationships. In fact, many small banks that saw their problem loans jump during the financial crisis can attribute the majority of problems to losses on loans originated in distant trade areas.[8]

Ownership

One of the strengths of community banking is local ownership and control. Decisions are made locally so they can be made quickly. If a customer wants to discuss an issue, he or she can visit with an actual person locally and does not have to call an 800 number or wait for an email response from a remote respondent. The response will be quick. Conducting banking business is more personal. Bankers use soft information about customers to make more informed decisions that may lead to better risk management. Soft information includes knowledge of specific circumstances surrounding a customer's employment and financial history and a familiarity with his or her property—where is it located, what parties have owned it previously and for what purposes has it been used, what are the characteristics of the neighborhood and corresponding growth opportunities, and the viability of performance guarantees.

Local ownership of banks manifests itself in several ways. First, since 1997 commercial banks have had the opportunity to organize and operate as S corporations. Because S corporations do not pay federal corporate income taxes, all income is allocated to stockholders on a pro rata basis (based on percentage of ownership) who pay taxes at their personal tax rates. To qualify for S corporation status, a bank can have no more than 100 shareholders.[9] Thus, S corporation banks are closely-held and represent an attractive organization form for families with a controlling interest in a bank and for community banks in general. Second, due to their small size, local orientation and closely-held status, most community banks do not have publicly-traded stock. The interests of major stockholders are often aligned with management because they are effectively one and the same. In essence, a significant portion of the owners' and managers' wealth is tied to the community bank. If the stock price falls, or worse if the firm fails, both stockholders and managers lose their investment and lifestyle. Limited size carries the additional benefit that if a nonpublic bank has less than $500 million in total assets, it does not have to meet Sarbanes-Oxley financial reporting requirements.

The same basic description applies to mutual savings banks. The first organizations of this type were formed in the early 1800s with the intent of encouraging savings from the poor.[10] These organizations do not have common stock such that they operate more like a cooperative. Depositors have the right to vote, amend bylaws, nominate, elect and remove directors, and the right to share in the assets of the organization when it is dissolved.[11] If a depositor moves her account to another institution, she no longer has any rights. The net result is that mutuals typically follow a conservative business strategy that focuses on residential lending, holding loans in portfolio and funding assets with core deposits.

Exhibit 1.2 documents the ownership of U.S. banks over time. There are several strong trends. First, note the decline in total number of banks from 10,923 in 1997 to 7,083 in 2012, a 34% drop. Second, the number of S Corp banks grew from just 604 in 1997 when the option first became available 2,281 in 2012 where they accounted for more than 30% of all FDIC-insured institutions. Finally, the number of mutuals has steadily declined to where these firms represented just 8% of FDIC-insured institutions in 2012. At the end of 2012, 7,083 FDIC-insured institutions existed with 26% having publicly-traded stock.

The interests of managers and stockholders are not as closely aligned with publicly-traded firms largely because managers own just a small fraction of the company. Large financial institutions, including TBTF banks and large regional

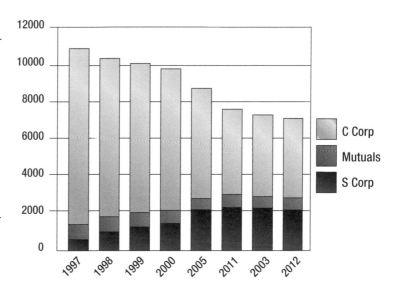

Exhibit 1.2 Ownership of U.S. Banks, 1997–2012 (through June)

Source: Data from FDIC Graph Book, www.fdic.gov and Swift (2009).

banks, generally have publicly-traded stock. Managers of these firms have to answer to a wide range of institutional and individual stockholders who typically focus on quarterly performance results. Investors, stock analysts and bank managers effectively play a game in which analysts forecast quarterly earnings, investors buy or sell stocks based on whether they believe the firm's earnings will exceed or fall short of consensus forecasts, and then all watch as the stock price rises or falls depending on whether the "surprise" at the quarterly earnings announcement is positive or negative. Critics contend that this game leads to excessive risk taking. Managers feel a need to systematically grow earnings in order to meet investor expectations. A significant portion of their compensation is often tied to profitability targets and the firm's stock price. It is not surprising that they may take excessive risks because the upside potential swamps the negatives if bad things happen.

During the period leading up to the financial crisis, many of the largest financial institutions pursued earnings growth by taking greater risks in the areas of creating risky mortgage-related securities and proprietary trading. They followed the OTD model originating loans that went increasingly to high-risk (sub-prime) borrowers. Citibank, among others, created *structured investment vehicles* (SIVs) as off-balance sheet entities to which they 'sold' high risk loans in order to lower their own capital requirements. As a last resort, they held portions of these securitized loans in portfolio because they couldn't sell them to other investors. *Proprietary trading* involves buying and selling assets, businesses and derivatives with the firm's own funds in order to make a profit. The assets and contracts may be stocks, bonds, currencies, futures contracts, credit default swaps, and the like, and even entire companies. Such trading is highly speculative and potentially leads to large losses as evidenced by the collapse in the value of some mortgage-related securities in 2008-2010. It is not surprising that key provisions of the Dodd-Frank Act force large institutions to reduce their exposures to proprietary trading activities.

The role of management compensation in leading to excessive risk-taking cannot be overstated. Annual compensation packages at the largest firms are typically heavily weighted toward stock options and stock grants, such that managers benefit more from increases in firm profits and stock price than their base salaries. It is logical that they might pursue strategies to create short-term stock price gains rather than maximize stockholder value over the longer-term. If the stock price rises, stockholders win and managers gain significant wealth. If the stock price falls, stockholders lose and managers negotiate new compensation agreements with options based on lower stock prices. They effectively reload and start the game anew.

Organizational Structure

Most banking organizations choose to operate as bank holding companies. A holding company is basically a shell organization that gets funding from stockholders and debt holders and uses the proceeds to buy stock in subsidiaries. A *one-bank holding company* (OBHC) owns controlling interest in just one bank while a *multibank holding company* (MBHC) owns controlling interest in more than one bank. Both can own stock in nonbank subsidiaries. Community banks may be either OBHCs or MBHCs and may control both bank and nonbank subsidiaries.

Consider the organization chart for Coastal Bancshares, an OBHC, presented in Exhibit 1.3. Coastal Bank is the community bank owned by Coastal Bancshares. When we mention bank stockholders, we refer to the owners of the holding company because the holding company generally owns 100% of the shares of its subsidiaries. In this instance, Coastal Bancshares also owns 100% of the stock in a leasing subsidiary. Coastal Bank has three divisions including credit, finance & investments and operations. The Board of Governors of the Federal Reserve System must approve all holding company applications and acquisitions.[12] The holding company form of organization is especially useful in raising capital, acquiring other firms, branch expansion and repurchasing stock.

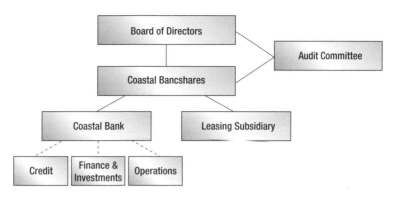

Exhibit 1.3 Organization Chart for a One-Bank Holding Company

Board of Directors

At the top of the organization chart is the Board of Directors. Board members are referred to as inside directors and outside directors depending on whether they are an employee of the holding company or bank (inside director) or employed elsewhere (outside director). Some nonemployees may be designated as insiders if they currently have or have had some strong affiliated relationship with the firm or senior executives. Outside directors are presumably more independent because their livelihood is not dependent on the bank's operations. Generally, a bank's chief executive officer (CEO) and chief financial officer (CFO) are inside directors. Board members elect a chair who leads the board in meeting its responsibilities. Critics of poorly performing boards typically argue that the same individual should not serve as both board chair and CEO of the bank.

One of the common weaknesses of community banks is poor corporate governance practices emanating from boards of directors. At many family-owned banks, corporate governance practices reflect the objectives of the principal owner/manager. Owners who have been in banking for years and who are confident in their knowledge and skills often construct a board comprised of family friends and relatives. Such boards often routinely affirm the owners' decisions and focus on the social benefits of board membership. This leads to board members being underappreciated, underutilized and not fully aware of firm risks and their legal liability. The owner/manager does whatever he or she wants. More progressive boards attempt to fully understand the organization's risks and business strategy and assist in the implementation of the bank's strategic plan.

Effective community bank boards of directors do the following:
- Focus on increasing shareholder value
- Identify and retain the best chief executive officer
- Understand the audit process and have an ability to reasonably interpret bank financial statements
- Regularly assess the key external and internal risks facing the institution
- Remain aware of key policies and practices and revise them as appropriate
- Help provide strategic direction
- Understand the regulatory process and the implications of regulatory enforcement actions
- Demonstrate concern for employees and stockholders and insist on accurate communication of bank objectives and performance

You will know when boards are ineffective if the directors are not fully aware of (1) the bank's strategic plan, (2) CEO compensation and the organization's management succession plan, (3) how to interpret key bank performance ratios and risk measures, (4) the bank's relationship with its primary regulators, and (5) whether the bank's auditors have any issues with management or the reporting of financial information. It is increasingly risky to be a bank director. You must know what your responsibilities are and feel comfortable making decisions for the best interest of stockholders, employees and managers.

Parent Company

The parent company, or bank holding company, is the entity that owns controlling interest in the community bank and any related subsidiaries. Its primary assets are thus equities in its subsidiaries with the primary funding coming from stockholders and debt holders. Importantly, a bank holding company's principal source of revenue is fees charged its subsidiaries and dividend income. If a bank does not generate sufficient earnings to pay dividends upstream to its parent organization, the holding company will have difficulty making principal and interest payments on its debt. Federal legislation determines the types of businesses that bank holding companies can acquire and banks must obtain formal approval for any new acquisitions.

Bank and Nonbank Subsidiaries

Coastal Bancshares in Exhibit 1.3 owns two subsidiaries, Coastal Bank and a leasing company. In this example Coastal Bank is the community bank that is essentially a partner organization with the leasing company. Many bank holding companies use nonbank subsidiaries to provide ancillary banking services which generate fee income and thereby diversify the organization's revenue stream.

As discussed in Chapter 3, the FDIC insures deposits of Coastal Bank, but not the debt of Coastal Bancshares or the leasing company. For this reason, regulators want to control the types of businesses that holding companies acquire. They are also concerned about what types of firms operate as holding companies. Since the onset of the recent financial crisis, regulators authorized several private equity firms to acquire banks.[13] The activities of private equity firms should be carefully scrutinized to prevent abuses of government deposit insurance. For example, it is possible that any holding company could use FDIC-insured deposits to indirectly fund nonbank operations. In such instances, holding companies should provide cross-guarantees of subsidiary debts or the risks to the FDIC are heightened. A real concern with private equity firms is that they focus on short-term returns and thus may be more inclined to use leverage—and thus increased risk—to increase profit potential. Regulators are also concerned that banks not transfer important assets to the holding company without the appropriate disclosures and conditions.

Coastal Bank has separated its business into three divisions; credit, finance and investments, and operations. The credit division focuses on lending activities, finance and investments manages the securities portfolio and firm-wide interest rate risk, and the operations division handles the retail side of the bank including deposit gathering through the branch system, check processing and related operational activities. Individuals who head up each division typically serve as the bank's senior management team along with the chief financial officer (CFO) and others.

Bankers Banks and Community Banking

Bankers banks are firms that provide financial services to community banks. They are owned by the banks that obtain services and thus operate much like a reverse holding company. Typical services include the buying and selling of federal funds (overnight loans of collected balances) and related deposits, loan participations in which individual community banks each take a portion of a large loan to a single entity, and bank stock loans in which bankers banks provide the loans for groups to buy stock in banks. Bankers banks presumably take advantage of economies of scale by which they lower the unit costs of providing these services below that which a single bank would have to pay to obtain the same service. Bankers banks may also offer credit card programs, bond accounting and investment services, cash management services and similar products which smaller institutions do not have the capacity or expertise to run internally.

Bankers banks evolved with the collapse of the correspondent banking system. Historically, large national and regional banks provided the same services that bankers banks now provide. Over time, many community banks viewed these large correspondent banks as competitors because they went after the same customers in local markets that community banks target and often underpriced community banks. Today, the nation's largest bankers banks are TIB, which has operations in 46 states, and PCBB, which operates primarily in the western states. Overall, there are 20 distinct bankers banks that operate throughout the United States.

Two recent events raised serious concerns about the roles that bankers banks will play in the future. In May 2009, bank regulators closed Silverton Bank in Atlanta, Georgia, which had long operated as a bankers bank. In 2007, Silverton essentially became a national correspondent bank by offering a wide range of investment, asset/liability management, capital markets and related financial services. However, it also moved aggressively to originate loans and either held them in portfolio or sold them to member banks as loan participations. During the financial crisis, many of the loans originated by Silverton and loan participations that it purchased from its bank owners went into default. Silverton was in financial distress. Unable to successfully negotiate terms with any potential buyer for Silverton, the FDIC sold off the failed firm's businesses on a piecemeal basis. Market participants became concerned about how the failure affected banks that owned loan participations with Silverton because the FDIC became the lead negotiator with the borrower. The FDIC's interests were not the same as those of the member banks and the members lost control of the decisions involving the loans. Many bankers believed that the FDIC delayed resolutions of distressed loans and ultimately cost their firms a meaningful portion of the value. More generally, Silverton's failure caused the regulators to question the bankers bank model and thus led to increased scrutiny of other bankers banks. The primary issue relates to how bankers banks finance their operations. Historically, they relied on overnight federal funds purchased held by member banks that any member could withdraw at a moment's notice. The concern was that problems with member banks would necessarily lead to liquidity problems at the bankers bank. Most bankers banks restructured their liabilities to rely less on fed funds financing and instituted rigorous interest rate risk strategies to hedge against adverse rate moves.

Executive Compensation

Many analysts and market participants blame bank compensation practices for the recent financial crisis. The argument is that extensive reliance on bonus plans that presumably tie an employee's pay to actual performance creates incentives for risk taking. During the years building up to the crisis, if the risks paid off in the form of rising short-term profits from trading or the overall firm, the employee received a large bonus payment. If the risks led to poor performance, the employee received little or no bonus. In fact, even when the firms did poorly, many employees were paid well though stock grants or other benefits.

Andrew Cuomo, then attorney general for the state of New York, conducted a study of the compensation practices in 2008 of the nine large banks that were the initial recipients of funds under the federal government's Troubled Asset Relief Program (TARP).[14] The analysis confirmed the perception that compensation did not fall even when the banks reported large losses. Incredibly, Citigroup and Merrill Lynch paid their employees cumulative bonuses of $5.3 billion and $3.6 billion, respectively, even though each firm lost almost $28 billion for the year. By the end of 2008, Citigroup had received $45 billion in TARP funds along with a guarantee that the government would absorb losses on over $300 billion of problem assets while Merrill Lynch received $10 billion in TARP funds and was collapsed into Bank of America to prevent its failure. As its performance continued to deteriorate in 2009, Citigroup was contemplating how to pay a "top-performing" employee around $100 million in bonus he was accorded under the bank's prevailing compensation plan. It seems reasonable that such compensation practices drive risk taking.

President Barack Obama reacted to large institution compensation practices by appointing Kenneth Feinberg as the administration's "pay czar." Feinberg was charged with reviewing the compensation practices of 419 firms that got funding under the Troubled Asset Relief Program (TARP) prior to February 2009. In July 2010, he concluded that 17 financial firms paid their executives $1.6 billion more than was reasonable in the five months following the Fall 2008 government assistance, but he indicated that he would not attempt to recover the excess pay on behalf of the government. While Feinberg had limited legal authority to claw back any excessive compensation from affected employees or their firms, his pronouncements on excessive pay received considerable publicity. No firm, particularly a large TBTF firm, wants the headlines this produces in difficult economic times.

It's no wonder that taxpayers are angry at the nation's largest banks that got government assistance when they use the proceeds to pay bonuses in amounts that most Americans cannot fathom. This anger is directed at banks, in general, but again ignores the fact that not all banks are the same. It is the TBTF banks and some shadow banks that caused much of the crisis, yet TBTF firms reaped most of the government assistance. Community banks operate more like traditional small businesses. When they have bonus plans, they are typically tied to the firm's aggregate profits. Key employees may have stock options, but the amounts are relatively small compared to the largest institutions. Can you imagine your local community banker claiming an annual bonus in the $100 million range?

Exhibit 1.4 summarizes key results of the Cuomo analysis. While they are often lumped together, most of the nine firms followed substantially different business strategies. Bank of America, Citigroup and JPMorgan Chase operated as universal banks as they tried to compete in traditional banking and investment banking. Both Bank of America and Citigroup have extensive retail branch networks. Goldman Sachs, Merrill Lynch and Morgan Stanley operated as traditional investment banks, generating earnings not primarily from lending and deposit gathering (net interest income) but instead from asset management, market making, brokerage, underwriting and proprietary trading. Wells Fargo operated as a business and retail commercial bank while Bank of New York Mellon and State Street offered specialized niche services. The first column of data indicates the initial

Exhibit 1.4 Compensation Summary for the Nine Initial TARP Recipient Banks in 2008

Institution	TARP $ (billions)	Net Income (billions)	Total Bonuses (billions)	No. Employees Bonus > $1 million	Personnel Expense Per Employee
Bank of America	$45	$4	$3.3	172	$75,601
Bank of NY Mellon	$3	$1.4	$0.945	74	$119,231
Citigroup	$45	-$27.7	$5.33	738	$100,496
Goldman Sachs	$10	$2.322	$4.82	953	$363,655
JPMorgan Chase	$25	$5.6	$8.693	1,626	$101,111
Merrill Lynch	$10	-$27.6	$3.6	696	$269,542
Morgan Stanley	$10	$1.707	$4.475	428	$262,030
State Street	$2	$1.811	$0.47	44	$134,925
Wells Fargo	$25	$2.655	$0.978	62	$80,976*

*Does not include data for Wachovia which was acquired at year-end.
Source: Cuomo (2009) and 2008 annual reports.

allocation of federal government assistance in terms of the amount of preferred stock that each firm sold to the U.S. Treasury. This program is discussed in detail in the Chapter 3. The next three columns indicate each firm's earnings during 2008 and its bonus payments in dollar terms and per the number of employees who received a bonus of $1 million or more for the year. The final column of data summarizes each firm's total personnel expense, including salaries, bonuses and benefits, per the total number of firm employees.

Several extraordinary facts jump out in this comparison. First, for many of these firms total bonuses paid exceeded net income even when net income was positive. While you may be surprised by the fact that both Citigroup and Merrill Lynch paid large bonuses even though the firms suffered large losses, bonuses were more than twice earnings for both Goldman Sachs and Morgan Stanley. This behavior raises the question of whether the firms are run primarily for the benefit of employees or stockholders. Second, it seems unusual that JPMorgan might have a bonus plan where over 1,600 individuals receive incentive pay of $1 million or more in a year when net income fell by almost two-thirds from $15.4 billion the year before. Finally, total personnel expense per employee varies with different business strategies. Average expense at Wells Fargo and Bank of America is the lowest due largely to their extensive use of branches and loan production offices throughout the U.S. Goldman Sachs, Merrill Lynch and Morgan Stanley have the highest average expense because they engaged primarily in investment banking businesses which require fewer people than traditional commercial banking.

Importantly, these compensation figures, while fairly consistent across large institutions, do not capture compensation practices at community banks where senior managers and owners typically receive much smaller dollar compensation annually. For example, contrast the figures in Exhibit 1.4 with those for small commercial banks. Exhibit 1.5 summarizes average data for FDIC-insured commercial banks with less than $1 billion in assets at the end of 2008 divided into different size institutions. Net income divided by average total assets indicates that the average bank was profitable during the year for all size categories. Personnel expense per employee is remarkably constant across different size banks ranging from $51,250 to just under $61,000. Average compensation is well below that for the nine TARP banks examined previously.

Exhibit 1.5 Profit and Personnel Expense Data for Small Commercial Banks in 2008

Asset Size	Net Income / Total Assets	Personnel Expense / Total Assets	Personnel Expense / No. of Employees
< $50 million	0.89%	1.88%	$57,180
$50 – $100 million	1.11%	1.55%	$54,860
$100 – $300 million	0.93%	1.65%	$51,250
$300 million – $1 billion	0.55%	1.53%	$60,940

Source: Uniform Bank Performance Reports, Peer Group Averages.

The remainder of the book documents the basic strategies pursued by most community banks and documents their subsequent financial performance. The primary objective is to identify key strategies that community banks should follow to be successful. There are three basic themes. First, not all banks are the same. Community banks, in particular, differ substantially from large banks, traditional investment banks, shadow banks and other entities in their overall structure and business strategy. Second, community banks focus on relationships and operate with core financial strategies that allow them to better identify and measure risk. These strategies may take different forms, but follow the same basic tenets. Finally, regulations designed to curb abuses that helped cause the financial crises should be targeted at the institutions responsible for the crisis and not community banks. Current proposals suggest that community banks will bear a disproportionate share of the burden for past problems. Such an outcome is patently unfair.

CHAPTER 2
How Community Banks Can Survive and Thrive

"The report of my death was an exaggeration."
—Mark Twain, *New York Journal*, June 2, 1897

Recent events have led many analysts to forecast the demise of community banking. The large number of small bank failures, the sharp slowdown in new bank charters, commercial real estate woes, economic actions and regulatory pressures that slow lending and the passage of comprehensive regulatory financial reform are viewed as signals that community banks may not be able to compete with their larger brethren and shadow banks. This viewpoint ignores the many successful institutions that remain strong and profitable and continue to serve their communities well. Clearly the rules have changed and the competitive landscape is more treacherous. Community bankers must reassess their business models to ensure that they best position themselves for success. However, if they are proactive in addressing weaknesses and if they pursue reasonable strategies, community banks will not only survive, they will thrive.

This chapter identifies attributes of community banks that will thrive in the future. The attributes are presented as prescriptions for financial health. It describes basic strategies to acquire these attributes if the bank does not already possess them. Still, it is not enough to know the attributes. As owners, managers and employees, you should live them throughout all stages of the business cycle and the pressures of current fads. You are building something long-term that can withstand short-run difficulties. Not surprisingly, the most important factor is people having the appropriate objectives and incentives and displaying the appropriate behaviors.

Koch's 10 Prescriptions for Community Bank Financial Health

Businesses excel when they have a cost advantage or a differentiation advantage.[1] To remain viable and competitive, community banks must continue to differentiate themselves from their competitors. Differentiation requires offering products and services that are unique as perceived by customers. And the list of competitors is long including TBTF firms, large regional banks, finance companies, insurance companies, Edward Jones, Wal-Mart and firms that lend to "high-risk" consumers, such as payday lenders and pawn shops. Can you explain in one minute what is unique and better about your institution?

Following are 10 prescriptions for a community bank's financial health. All are centered on the principle of establishing and maintaining strong personal relationships. After all, the primary reason that individuals and businesses choose to work with community banks is that their banker knows them and their business activity. While there is no particular order of emphasis, it is best to focus on ensuring that you have the right people making the right decisions. To the experts, these prescriptions will seem obvious. So, why did so many community banks forget them or ignore them?

Koch's 10 Prescriptions for Community Bank Financial Health

1. Attract and retain the best customers
2. Attract and retain the best employees
3. Have actively engaged directors who understand corporate governance
4. Build a fortress balance sheet and diversified revenues
5. Have access to liquidity backstops
6. Understand operating costs
7. Integrate risk management into strategic planning and budgeting
8. Conduct own-institution stress tests
9. Enter into partnerships for critical services
10. Work closely with regulators

Attract and Retain the Best Customers

The most valuable and unique attribute of community banking is the emphasis on customer relationships. While most individuals are sensitive to prices, community banks can overcome their cost disadvantages versus other service providers if they successfully personalize their services. Many individuals do not have any real expertise in finance, so they look to their banker for financial assistance. Initially, it is important to have the appropriate package of services and an array of delivery systems. Individuals want different services at different stages of life. They also want to access them at their convenience and via whatever delivery system they choose. Younger customers generally care most about transactions capabilities and often prefer ATMs, mobile banking and Internet-based services. Older customers typically care more about deposit, savings, trust and money management services. Small business customers care about credit availability and deposit services including payroll and remote capture.

As a manager, you should know your bank's customer demographics and target the high-interest services accordingly. Examine your depositor base according to age, gender, geographic location and how the customer accesses most services (branch, kiosk, ATM, online via personal computer or mobile banking). Key questions include (1) Which customers use multiple services offered by the bank (deposit and savings accounts, credit card, consumer loan, business loan, trust, etc.) and what services do they use most frequently? (2) Which customers maintain large deposit balances at the bank? (3) Which customers are profitable? Do the same analysis for loan customers in the event you have some that do not have a deposit relationship. Remember that people like simplicity and convenience. How easy is it for customers to bank with you? Have a strategy to retain younger customers as they leave the local community in search of jobs or quality of life elsewhere. For example, what will happen to your bank when wealthy residents living locally die and their estates are settled? Remember that the next generation will inherit much of the resources currently parked locally at your institution. Do you offer family members an incentive to keep banking with you?

How do you work with your core borrowers? How often do you touch them with a significant business question or idea? Your best customers not only appreciate the constant touches, but will pay for the service. Consider agriculture borrowers as an example. Why not conduct a comprehensive review of the business plan every fall after harvest when production is confirmed? Meet with the principals again in February to review financial statements and expectations for the spring planting. During the summer, visit the operation to review performance relative to plan. These frequent touches will reduce surprises and allow better management of the entire customer relationship. Customers benefit from the consistent communication which will further cement the relationship.

As Goldman Sachs has woefully demonstrated negatively, your bank's reputation is everything. Your current customers' perceptions of the bank and the bank's reputation in the community will attract new customers. Ensure that you have your customers' trust. Live up to your commitments. Support your community's schools and other public organizations. Make the bank an integral part of community events and have your bankers fill key roles in community organizations.

Consistent, quality service drives value for the bank. It involves both tangible elements related to facilities and intangibles related to the human component of relationships.

- *Facilities*: How does the bank physically deliver products and services? Are the main office and branches attractive structures and clean? Do the ATMs work consistently and are they readily accessible? Does the bank's website have the functionality and speed that customers expect? Is the appearance of employees consistent with the level of professionalism expected by customers? Is the bank's mobile app easy to use?

- *Human Element*: Are employees courteous when dealing with customers live, via the phone or electronically? Do employees recognize customers and acknowledge them when they enter the branch or office? Are employees well-trained and competent to perform their responsibilities at a high level in quick-time if necessary? Customers expect employees to understand their financial problems and have the ability to help them find solutions. Are employees empathetic? Most importantly, are the bank's products, services and employees reliable? If employees commit to a response, do they live up to the commitment in a timely fashion?

A bank will likely attract and retain customers who believe that their bank is focused on them and who make them feel good about their banking experience.

Finally, have a good customer profitability analysis system so that you know how profitable different customers are. This will help in pricing by allowing you to incorporate the entire relationship when setting loan and deposit rates. It will also help you identify the attributes of customers who generate the greatest financial value to the organization.

Attract and Retain the Best Employees

It is critical that community banks identify, hire and retain the best talent possible. Given the limited number of employees, it is important that everyone get along as well as understand and fulfill their work responsibilities. It is costly to continually train new employees and high turnover damages reputation. One of the most attractive features of community banking is that customers appreciate being on a first-name basis with the bank's tellers, customer service representatives and loan officers, let alone the bank president. And the best employees are often the first to leave when they have the opportunity if the work environment doesn't meet their expectations.

Donna de St. Aubin has identified "10 Tips for Retaining Top Talent" at community banks.[2] The factors will presumably attract and retain talent as well as provide for a positive work environment. As a manager, you should recognize what is personally important to your employees and have a plan to keep them engaged.

- *Have a retention strategy:* Know the retention drivers, such as the company's reputation as a great place to work, a good relationship with a supervisor and understanding the potential career track within the organization.
- *Emotional intelligence:* Hire individuals who understand and fit the culture of the bank and the job specifications.
- *Opportunities for advancement:* Provide opportunities for individual growth and career development.
- *Recognition and reward system:* Offer competitive compensation and benefits. Ensure equity internally for individuals doing the same type of work and performing at the same level. Consider pay as well as other forms of recognition.
- *Communication:* Keep employees informed. Regularly ask for feedback. Support employees' activities in the community and demonstrate the importance of social responsibility.

- *Retention surveys:* Measure employees' feelings via regular surveys. You will learn of issues prior to the issues becoming serious problems.
- *Company mission and values:* Clarify what you are as a company and where you are headed. Ensure that employees understand and buy into your bank's values.
- *Leadership:* Have a stable senior management team which promotes security, trust and mutual respect. Ensure that the appropriate individuals are promoted and rewarded.
- *Manage accountability for turnover:* An individual's manager has the greatest impact on employee turnover. Hire and train managers who are effective at retaining top talent. Have a mentoring system for managers.
- *Social responsibility:* Provide employees the opportunity to represent the bank as an ambassador to external constituents. Have them serve on community boards, charities or arts organizations. Encourage them to be visible representatives of the bank throughout the community.

Many community banks need to review their compensation practices to ensure that they properly attract and reward key employees. Family-owned banks face the difficulty that nonfamily employees will likely never be controlling owners. If key employees do not have a financial upside, they are more likely to leave for better paying positions. Well-run community banks often put substantive profit sharing plans in place. If designed appropriately, all employees can benefit in the bank's sustained strong earnings performance. Consider establishing an *employee stock ownership plan* (ESOP) in which a bank sets up a trust with shares allocated to employees. The ESOP buys the bank's stock with contributions from the bank or via loans. Either way, employees effectively own shares and benefit when the bank performs well. ESOP ownership rewards employees and improves retention prospects.

The best employees understand people. They pay attention to detail and enjoy working with others. They realize that people are different and make every effort to accommodate differences. You can identify the best employees by whether they consistently do the right things for the right reasons. They also exhibit a balance between work and their life away from work.

Have Actively-Engaged Directors Who Understand Corporate Governance

Directors are legally responsible for the management of the bank. Their most important responsibility is to select and appoint the bank's CEO. They also play a role in confirming the selection of other executive officers. In general, boards have the following responsibilities in performing effective governance of the bank.[3]

- Work with senior management to establish the bank's overall business strategy
- Determine the bank's risk tolerance and appetite
- Ensure that lines of responsibility are clear throughout the firm
- Have compensation policies that are consistent with the bank's long-term objectives
- Provide effective oversight of the bank's risk analysis and controls (safety and soundness, compliance and internal audit)

In the heavily-regulated banking business, directors must ensure that the bank has a full range of sound and prudent policies in place regarding how senior managers conduct operations. Directors have the responsibility to ensure that the bank meets capital requirements and observes all relevant banking regulations and laws. They are effectively responsible for assessing what risks the bank is taking, setting the appropriate risk parameters and then monitoring the bank's risk over time.

Directors are elected by shareholders. Because so many community banks are closely held, the elections are often, in practice, just formalities. Too often, one family or a small block of individuals controls the majority of stock and family or block members comprise the bulk of senior management, such that board members have little influence on strategic decisions. In the past, a CEO might effectively appoint his or her long-time friends as directors and view board meetings as social occasions. This is clearly inappropriate given government deposit insurance and the true responsibilities of directors.[4] Hence, it is important that a well-run bank chooses its directors carefully and actively engages them in the bank's business.

Serving on a bank's board is an honor. But as the preceding discussion suggests, it carries great responsibilities and important risks. Regardless of ownership, a bank needs a cross-section of individuals who will provide consistent guidance and strategic direction. The board represents shareholders, customers and employees and is responsible for hiring competent and trustworthy managers. Directors must understand the critical issues associated with bank activities and regulations, especially in these times of regulatory reform. Each board member is typically labeled as either an inside or outside director. Inside directors are currently senior executives of the bank or members of the family or group who controls ownership in the bank. Outside directors are not employees and do not have any direct affiliation with the bank, except for perhaps being a customer. Corporate governance standards now require boards to have significant representation by outside directors who are, presumably, less dependent on management and thus have fewer conflicts of interest. Given the greater liability associated with serving as a bank director, bank managers should ensure that all directors attend meetings regularly and participate actively. Banks should also compensate directors commensurate with the responsibilities and risks of serving in that role.

Active, engaged directors should have high integrity and exhibit the following attributes:

- *Understanding of the basics of economics and business.* The basic responsibility is to enhance shareholder value at the same time incorporating the interests of customers, employees and the community.

- *Independent thinking.* Offer unbiased opinions when evaluating policies, practices and procedures; ensure that management keeps the board informed and responds quickly to any identified weaknesses; ideally, a board will have more independent outside directors than inside directors. It will also meet in executive session without the CEO and other relevant insiders.

- *Strategic thinking.* Have an awareness of current banking issues and work with management on understanding and directing strategic planning initiatives. The board sets long-term strategy but does not micro-manage the institution.

- *Ownership in the bank.* Individuals with skin in the game, characterized by a reasonable financial interest, will be more engaged; while director compensation is typically modest, offering some compensation in the form of stock grants or options could help align director interests with the bank's performance.

Outside directors should represent the key business and nonprofit interests of the community as well as provide expertise in critical areas such as audit and risk management. Ideally, directors will represent the key demographic groups in terms of race, gender and age. Such a group will better inform management of key issues facing the community and opportunities to expand the bank's business. Diversity in the board members' thinking will enhance customer understanding.

Build a Fortress Balance Sheet and Diversified Revenues

The concept of a fortress balance sheet involves having an efficient operating structure and a balance sheet that is shockproof. In terms of the regulatory and market environment, management must focus on maintaining excellent CAMELS ratings and credit ratings. CAMELS ratings are discussed in the next chapter. Such efforts should support the price of the bank's common stock.

To ensure survival and create opportunities to take advantage of market disruptions, do the following:

- Build a strong capital base
- Have a strong core deposit base
- Have a well-diversified loan portfolio
- Hold short-term, unpledged liquid assets
- Focus on net interest margin
- Manage the investment portfolio, but keep it simple
- Find and grow sources of noninterest income

The starting point to a fortress balance sheet is a strong capital base. Given the current regulatory environment, Tier 1 capital comprised of common equity is the best form of capital. Strong capital allows management to make strategic decisions involving growing the franchise and effectively allocating resources. Should the bank offer new products or services? Should it expand into new geographic markets via branching or acquisition? Without substantial capital, these decisions are moot. All banks must be well capitalized. Beyond this base, target a Tier 1 leverage ratio of at least 8%.

The core business of community banking is accepting deposits and making loans. The best deposits are core deposits from relationship-based customers in the form of noninterest bearing demand deposits, interest-checking accounts, savings accounts, MMDAs and small time deposits. If the deposit holders are local and use multiple bank services, they are likely less sensitive to interest rates. The most valuable and loyal deposit customers:

- Have two or more accounts/services with the bank
- Have been an active customer for three or more years
- Have a primary residence or operate a business within the bank's core trade area
- Have deposit balances that are fully-insured and for which the bank does not pay an above-market rate
- Have active transactions including direct deposit

The bank should not chase deposits by paying the highest rates in the market. The best loans are made in the bank's traditional trade area to businesses, individuals and government units who are also local depositors. To the extent possible, avoid substantive loan concentrations. If your loan portfolio exceeds normal concentration limits, you should have more Tier 1 capital. A fortress loan portfolio will be diversified, with few loans to insiders, few minority participation positions, few loans out of the bank's normal trade area, and will be priced appropriately to reflect true default risk and interest rate risk.

One of the greatest problems facing community banks in the current economic environment is where to find earning assets. Loans still offer the highest promised yields, pre-expense, but in the current low interest rate environment, loan rates are extremely low. It is difficult to maintain net interest margins because most banks have lowered deposit rates to rock bottom levels and don't have much room to lower them more. For banks to maintain their net interest margins, they need to shift their assets more toward loans and less toward investment securities. Such a shift, of course, increases credit risk. Still, community banks must make and price loans proactively to maintain key relationships with business customers over the long haul.

Community banks must have strong net interest margins to cover operating expenses, build capital, pay cash dividends and fund future growth. Fortress banks focus on pricing deposits and loans to ensure a minimum net interest margin. They don't chase loan deals by underpricing and they don't buy deposits by paying above-market rates. Furthermore, they have a good mix of fixed-rate and floating rate loans to take advantage of the rate environment. They also use derivatives judiciously to achieve pricing objectives. In low rate environments, they have floors on loan rates. In rising rate environments, they potentially cap deposit rates and have reasonable early withdrawal penalties.

One of the great lessons of the financial crisis is that liquidity is potentially fleeting. When you most need it, it may be gone. Hold a minimum amount of short-term, liquid assets that you can sell in a crunch. The most liquid assets are federal funds sold and short-term investment securities that are not pledged. While other investments and government-guaranteed loans may also be liquid, short-term marketable securities have the benefit of ready secondary markets with predictable prices. To estimate the minimum amount needed, set up a cash flow worksheet that compares expected cash outflows with expected cash inflows on a daily basis over the next year. The liquidity buffer should be sufficient to cover any gaps.

In terms of the investment portfolio, buy only what you understand and need. Too many banks buy callable agency bonds, step-ups, corporate bonds and a wide range of mortgage-backed securities without knowing the risks they are assuming. Conduct the appropriate analysis to assess whether the underlying credit risk is acceptable and whether the estimated value of the options sold when buying these instruments is appropriate. Do stress testing to fully understand the underlying cash flow you can expect to receive if interest rates rise or fall.[5] Keep your investments simple. Does management fully understand the risk versus return features of asset-backed securities, structured notes and step-ups? Compare the expected total return (from coupon interest, reinvestment income and price moves) from the security being considered with an option-free Treasury or agency bond. Understand extension risk as well as prepayment risk with all mortgage-backed securities.

Typically, noninterest income has contributed relatively little to the bottom line at most community banks. Given the pressure on net interest margins, managers must look to grow noninterest income. Recent regulatory reform legislation makes it more difficult given the opt-in requirement for overdraft privileges and the lowering of interchange fees for debit transactions. However, for long-term viability, community banks must diversify their revenues. It appears that interest rates may remain low in the foreseeable future. Banks that want to increase shareholder value must find new and expanded sources of noninterest income. The choices include imposing new fees on existing products, introducing new products or services that are fee-based or potentially partnering with third-party vendors in offering new services. Until the U.S. economy improves significantly, earnings growth will likely come primarily from such noninterest sources.

Have Access to Liquidity Backstops

Access to liquidity is critical for survival. In addition to maintaining strong cash and equivalent holdings, a bank should maintain borrowing capacity with the Federal Reserve Bank, Federal Home Loan Bank (FHLB) and correspondent banks. The amount of available borrowing depends on the bank's financial condition and available collateral which must be pledged against actual borrowings. To the extent possible, the bank should pledge loans as collateral against all lines so that securities can be available for future pledging. Banks should monitor cash inflows versus cash outflows to better anticipate when liquidity problems might arise. Brokered deposits, rate board deposits and other wholesale funding should be considered potentially "hot" money that will not be available in a crisis. The bank must develop a contingency funding plan which regularly tracks these cash flows, liquid assets and available funds from these borrowing facilities. The contingency funding plan should incorporate high stress scenarios that reveal how much in liquidity might be required in problematic and worst case situations.

Understand Operating Costs

Is there any doubt that a bank's operating costs are going to increase? Examine what your bank paid in FDIC insurance in the years 2007 to 2012, even absent the special assessment. The days of no insurance premiums for well-capitalized banks are gone. Consider also potential compliance costs added to bank operations under the Dodd-Frank Act and rulings coming from the Consumer Financial Protection Bureau (CFPB). In mid-2010, the American Bank Association (ABA) identified 30 areas in which the Dodd-Frank bill would impose new or expanded obligations for community banks. It updated this list with a discussion of 12 critical issues in 2012.[6] Examples include the requirement that all publicly-traded banks under $10 billion have a risk committee with at least one risk expert; the requirement for more information on consumer and home mortgage loans; new disclosure rules under Fair Lending and the Real Estate Settlement Procedures Act (RESPA); and new reporting requirements on whether the applicant for a small business loan is women-owned or minority-owned. And this is before regulators decide how to actually implement many of the bill's other provisions.

Small community banks typically designate one employee to serve as the compliance officer along with other duties while many employees monitor compliance within their daily activities. Under the new rules, this designated individual will need assistance to manage compliance. How many new employees are needed and what will they cost? How big must a bank be or what new sources of noninterest income must a bank generate to cover these added costs? Management must determine the true costs of providing all products and services as well as the dead-weight costs involved with compliance and other nonrevenue generating services. Sarah Wallace, who chairs the board of directors at First Federal Savings and Loan in Newark, Ohio, argued that her bank would "be making regulation compliance decisions instead of credit decisions" as a result of the Dodd-Frank bill.[7] In addition, the bank would lose an estimated 75% of its interchange fee income under the new regulations which would force the bank to impose fees elsewhere because they viewed these fees as offsetting the expense associated with providing electronic banking services. Without a better understanding of these costs, bank managers will not know how to bundle and price services. Operating costs could potentially overwhelm net interest income. At best, these higher costs will reduce the returns to stockholders.

Integrate Risk Management With Strategic Planning and Budgeting

Most banks conduct annual budgeting planning during the late summer and fall each year. Budgets are often prepared in line with the bank's long-term objectives but independent of the bank's current strategic initiatives. Strategic planning efforts should identify key objectives for the organization, alternative paths or strategic options to achieve the objectives, and then model or project potential outcomes under each path. The modeling involves forecasting changes in the bank's balance sheet and income statement and is thus intertwined with management's specific strategies, risk analysis and ultimately budgeting. This analytical modeling is effectively stress testing performance outcomes under different scenarios.[8] Banks that can integrate these activities and conduct regular stress tests will better understand the trade-offs of different decisions going forward.

Consider a bank that is facing a potential ratings downgrade due to asset quality, earnings and capital weaknesses. A decision tree like that in Exhibit 2.1 outlines different paths or strategic choices. Initially, management and the directors must decide whether they want to remain independent or sell the bank. Assuming they want to remain independent, they need to conduct a detailed risk assessment incorporating current financial information regarding asset quality, liquidity, capital structure and earnings. This assessment should provide estimates of bank value using metrics such as tangible book value, cash earnings and the core deposit franchise. Assuming that the bank is currently undercapitalized due largely to asset write-downs, the next critical decision is whether or not to raise external capital. If the decision is made to not immediately raise capital, the next decision is to address how to raise capital ratios by changing the balance sheet and building a fortress bank. This decision tree framework is the basis for stress testing performance over adverse economic conditions. It is essential that managers integrate this type of risk analysis with their traditional planning and budgeting efforts.

Exhibit 2.1 Strategic Decision Tree:
Bank Faces a Potential Ratings Downgrade

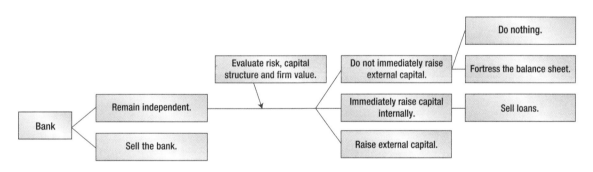

In this type of analysis, management will map out a plan of actions that incorporates strategic objectives. The actions may include selling assets (securities) and paying off wholesale liabilities to shrink the bank; reducing loan concentrations by loan sales and new lending focus; and creating a strategy for moving problem loans through the collection process and repositioning the bank's liquidity facilities with the Fed and FHLB. Given the anticipated rate environment and balance sheet adjustments, management can assess the impact on earnings and modify the budget accordingly. In this example with a smaller bank, management should reduce operating expenses to offset loan charge-offs and potential realized losses on security sales. The essential point is that given the complexity of managing a bank in today's environment, risk management and strategic planning should be integrated with budgeting.

Conduct Own-Institution Stress Tests

In March 2009, the U.S. government conducted stress tests on 19 of the largest financial institutions to assess the adequacy of their capital. In mid-2010, European authorities conducted similar stress tests on over 100 large institutions. The U.S. stress tests revealed that 10 of the 19 firms needed to raise an additional $75 billion in common equity. Fortunately, most of these firms were able to sell common stock in the public markets and effectively recapitalize themselves.

The stress tests were conducted under different macroeconomic scenarios. One of the scenarios assumed a sharp downturn with sustained high unemployment and negative then slow positive GDP growth. Government officials then modeled loan losses, asset write-downs, revenue losses and the adverse impact on earnings to assess whether the institutions remained adequately capitalized.

Comprehensive Capital Analysis and Review (CCAR)

Federal regulators now require the largest institutions to undergo formal periodic stress tests designed by the regulators but also conduct similar stress tests internally on an ongoing basis. Regulatory-mandated stress tests are coming for community banks. This is both reasonable and beneficial. It is reasonable because regulators and investors need to know whether individual banks can survive adverse economic conditions. Many community banks have concentrated loan portfolios and limited access to external capital. Brokered deposits and other wholesale funding are viewed more negatively than core deposits. Stress tests will better reveal whether the bank can adequately meet unanticipated cash outflows and how much capital is required to adequately buffer against adverse events. The tests will thus better link capital planning to the various risks that banks assume. The beneficial outcome is that managers will better understand the nature and magnitude of risks assumed. The tests will quantify the importance of having a diversified loan portfolio and diversified funding base. So, start stress-testing your bank.

Enter into Partnerships for Critical Services

Competition and the current regulatory and legislative environment mandate a critical review of the products and services offered and how they are delivered. There is some minimum size which a bank must attain to offer certain products by itself. Otherwise, it cannot spread the cost of capital investment across enough transactions to get the unit price low enough to attract customers and cover the bank's investment. For example, with many bank customers moving to Internet banking and mobile banking, community banks need to partner with vendors to provide these services as the technology is rapidly changing and the initial investment to offer these services alone is too great. The alternative is losing tech savvy customers forever. Community banks should consider establishing broader relationships with their bankers bank, correspondent banks and state bank trade associations. Alternatively, they should consider forming partnerships via reverse holding companies, in which a group of banks own a vendor who provides services to each owner.

Work Closely with Regulators

Community bankers recognize that the supervisory process is important in maintaining the safety and soundness of banks. When banks experience problems, regulators generally respond by identifying *matters requiring attention* (MRAs) in the regulator report of examination that follows safety and soundness exams. Any bank getting an MRA in a report of examination must address it appropriately as soon as possible and well before the next exam.[9] When regulators identify serious problems they will put the bank under an enforcement action. Politicians and analysts often criticize regulators for not anticipating the problems and reacting with a lag to impose sanctions. Bankers, in turn, frequently argue that the sanctions are too strong.

It is important that a bank have a good relationship with its regulators. This does not mean that the individuals examining a bank are best friends with a bank's managers. It does mean that both groups should communicate regularly and openly. Regulators expect a bank's board of directors and senior management to provide information promptly and that the information is sufficiently comprehensive to allow regulators to appropriately assess risk. Bankers, in turn, expect regulators to be consistent in their interpretation of regulations. How can management make decisions if the rules are constantly changing?

Thus, bankers should work closely with their institution's regulators. Why not inform the regulators when making important changes in the bank's organizational structure or operating structure? In fact, why not run the changes by regulators prior to implementing them to ensure that there are not surprises? Discuss any concerns or problems as soon as possible.

Positive Aspects of the Future Banking Environment

While community banks will be under increased pressures due to regulatory and legislative changes, there are many beneficial aspects to the future banking environment. First, the U.S. economy will eventually expand sufficiently to generate increased loan demand and stimulate improved asset quality and earnings. Problem loans will continue to decline, new business and consumer loan demand will rise and businesses and individuals will again believe in a growing economy and opportunities. Second, the number of competitors will decline over time. There are many factors contributing to a sharp reduction in the number of banks.[10] Foremost is the increased regulatory scrutiny that banks face. The rules are changing and many bankers, especially those representing the smallest institutions, do not know what the rules are and what the associated costs will ultimately be. Rising compliance and other costs make banking even less attractive to new investors. The difficulties in managing a small organization in the new regulatory environment have taken much of the joy in running a bank to where some bankers say, "Banking isn't fun anymore." Not surprisingly, they are looking to exit the industry if they can get a reasonable price when they sell. Furthermore, as Exhibit 2.2 demonstrates, regulators are no longer liberally approving new charters. From 2009 to 2012, just 45 new institutions were chartered, 31, 11, 3 and 0, respectively, per year—which is well below the annual average of 144 from 1990

Exhibit 2.2

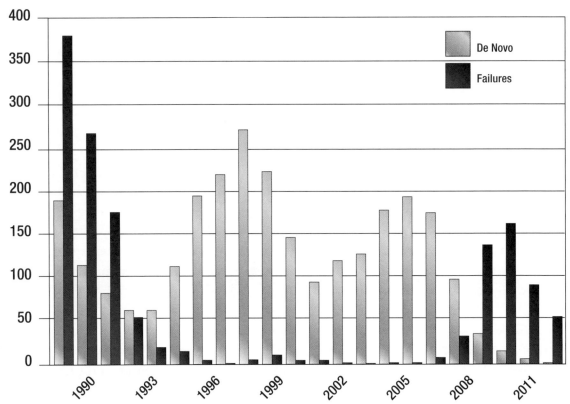

Number of Bank Failures and DeNovo Bank Charters in the United States 1990-2012

Data to construct the chart are from the FDIC's Statistics on Banking.

to 2008. Combined with the 440 bank failures from 2009 to 2012, the number of independent institutions fell from a peak of 22,459 in 1992 to just over 7,000 at year-end 2012. The three new banks in 2011 were actually takeovers of failed banks. Through September 2013, no banks were chartered during the year. Thus, there have been no new charters since 2010.

Finally, the lack of succession planning at many banks along with many bank owners and boards of directors eager to exit the industry, will likely produce an active merger and acquisition environment.

Given that TBTF banks have an implicit government guarantee and the preceding pressures on community banks, the U.S. will likely see more larger-sized institutions. In all likelihood, the largest banking organizations—Bank of America, JPMorgan Chase, Citigroup, Wells Fargo, Goldman Sachs and Morgan Stanley—who already dominate mortgage lending, derivatives and other product markets, will be more focused on meeting the credit and related banking needs of the world's largest corporations. They have less interest in small dollar loans and are generally loathe to operate full banking offices in small regional and rural communities such that community banks should do well offering these products in these markets.

On the asset side of the balance sheet, community banks must work to retain their niche in small business lending. Many small businesses have recently been effectively scorned by their previous bank when they requested loans. They represent a strong source of future business and will look with favor at community banks that offer consistent, high quality service. The future is, in fact, bright if community banks are willing to rethink their strategies and implement them accordingly. Being a fortress bank will allow each institution to better withstand future difficulties.

Strategic Checklist

- Understand your customer demographics.

- Research how many customers actively use multiple bank products and services, that is, know how much of a customer's overall banking business is conducted with your institution.

- Deliver banking services to customers in multiple channels (forms), including branch, kiosk, video-conferencing via ATMs, online and mobile banking.

- Develop strategies to retain younger individuals as customers as they potentially leave the local community—for they shall inherit.

- Have a calling program that touches key borrowers frequently.

- Be able to successfully identify profitable customers and the source of profits.

- Target a Tier 1 Leverage Ratio of at least 8%.

- To the extent possible, avoid loan concentrations, loans outside the local trade area and minority positions in participations.

- Hold a meaningful amount of short-term, unpledged high quality securities to meet potential liquidity needs.

- Price deposits and loans to ensure a minimum net interest margin.

- Invest only in securities that you understand.

- Diversify the bank's revenues to focus on increased noninterest income.

- Develop meaningful contingency funding plans and test them periodically.

- Establish credit (borrowing) lines with the Federal Reserve, Federal Home Loan Banks and correspondent banks and test them periodically.

- Integrate strategic planning with budgeting and stress testing.

- Consider partnering with other banks or bankers banks to jointly acquire access to services or specific expertise.

- Communicate regularly with the bank's regulators, particularly when key risks change and when pursuing new strategic initiatives.

- Have engaged directors and effective corporate governance practices.

CHAPTER 3
Bank Regulation and Regulatory Reform

Commercial banks are among the most heavily regulated firms in the U.S. Any group of individuals wanting to start a bank must apply for a charter and be formally approved by regulators. Because managers expect to use customer deposits to fund the bank's loans and investments, a bank obtains deposit insurance from the FDIC. The FDIC, in turn, is concerned about the bank's safety and soundness and wants to protect the deposit insurance fund so it regularly examines the bank's operations to ensure that management has not taken excessive risk. Regulatory agencies also have the capacity to restrict the types of products and services that banks can offer and the types of businesses that bank holding companies, or financial holding companies, can acquire. In order to ensure fair treatment of bank customers, regulators also stipulate disclosure requirements for interest rates and the terms of certain loans and deposits and mandate nondiscriminatory lending policies. Managers must diligently monitor the bank's performance along all these dimensions and ensure that the bank meets regulatory requirements.

The obvious question is "Why would anyone want to start a bank given this broad range of regulations?" In 2008, then nonbank firms such as Goldman Sachs, American Express, CIT, MetLife and GMAC, voluntarily applied to become bank holding companies and were quickly approved. Why did these firms desire to become banking entities subject to complex regulations that they largely avoided previously? The answers to these questions indicate the value of FDIC insurance and the federal government's role in providing liquidity to troubled financial firms during the recent financial crisis. Specifically, the FDIC insures most bank deposits. This provides banks with a stable, low-cost source of funds. The nonbank firms, in turn, borrowed heavily from the Federal Reserve when they needed funds to replace other liabilities that were maturing during the heart of the financial crisis and the Fed was the only source of liquidity available at the time.

Community banks currently operate in uncharted waters regarding the regulatory environment. During the financial crisis, many banks failed, the FDIC increased the cost of deposit insurance, regulators put more banks under enforcement actions and Congress passed legislation that mandated a wide range of new rules and regulations. While the pace of failures has slowed, the 389 bank failures in 2009–2011 effectively depleted the deposit insurance fund. In order to replenish the insurance fund, the FDIC imposed a one-time, special insurance assessment on all banks and then required healthy banks to prepay 13 quarters of deposit insurance premiums. It subsequently raised the amount of future premiums. These premium payments directly lower bank earnings by reducing the amount of earning assets. Furthermore, once regulators put a bank under an enforcement action and its CAMELS rating worsens, the bank is not only required to meet specific regulatory performance targets but must also pay sharply higher insurance premiums that make it more difficult to generate earnings. Fortunately, it appears that the worst problems are behind us. There were 51 failures in 2012 and just just 22 through September 2013, and the deposit insurance fund appears to be healthy.[1] Regulators are also now removing more enforcement actions than imposing new ones.

Finally, in July 2010, Congress passed the Dodd-Frank Wall Street Reform and Consumer Protection Act (Dodd-Frank Act) which authorized the creation of many new rules and regulations plus established a new Consumer Financial Protection Bureau (CFPB). The CFPB is responsible for establishing new consumer protection rules and enforcing existing laws. It will supervise most providers of consumer financial products including banks, consumer finance companies, mortgage originators, brokers and servicers, debt collection agencies, payday lenders and credit counselors, and has the authority to declare that specific practices are "unfair, deceptive and abusive." Banks with less than $10 billion in assets will continue to be examined by their primary regulators for compliance rather than the CFPB, but will be subject to any new rules stipulated. Still, the CFPB has back-up authority for all banks meaning that it can impose new rules on banks of all sizes.

The CFPB is an independent bureau housed within the Federal Reserve. One concern is that the CFPB will standardize many financial products. Standardization potentially forces customers to choose providers primarily on the basis of price and community banks don't normally win the game of lowest price. Another concern is that the CFPB will produce regulations that increase uncertainty about banking practices and thus induce banks to not provide certain products and services. As demonstrated later, the CFPB has created rules regarding what a Qualified Residential Mortgage (QRM) is. Banks that make mortgages meeting the QRM standard will not be forced to keep at least 5% of the loan in portfolio and can more readily avoid legal liability for not verifying the borrower's ability to repay the loan. Still, uncertainty exists about how new mortgage rules will be applied to nonprime borrowers such that some lenders are withdrawing from this market.

Structure of Bank Regulation

When trying to start a new (de novo) bank, the team of founding members can apply for a charter from the federal government or the state government or territory where the bank will be headquartered. All banks now have FDIC insurance. The Office of the Comptroller of the Currency (OCC) is the chartering agency at the federal level while the state banking department in each of the 50 states is the chartering agent at the state level. Banking authorities in U.S. territories, such as Puerto Rico, American Samoa, Guam and the Virgin Islands, can also issue charters. OCC chartered banks will have the word "national" in their title and are members of the Federal Reserve System. All other banks can decide whether to be members of the Federal Reserve System.[2] The Federal Reserve is the primary federal regulator for state-chartered banks that choose to be Fed members. The FDIC is the primary federal regulator for state nonmember banks. Importantly, only the chartering agency can formally close a bank, but the decision is made jointly with the FDIC.

The opportunity for a bank to choose its chartering agency and lead regulator is labeled the *dual banking system*. Importantly, after receiving its initial charter, a bank can switch charters and thus change from the OCC to state regulator or vice versa. As you might expect, this switch option creates competition among regulators.

The central banking agency in the U.S. is referred to as the Federal Reserve Bank (Fed) or Federal Reserve System. The Fed is an independent agency of the federal government with a Board of Governors that sets monetary policy and supervises bank holding companies and state member commercial banks. The chairman, Ben Bernanke during the financial crisis, is appointed by the President of the U.S. and heads the Federal Open Market Committee (FOMC), which pursues policies that effectively determine target levels for certain short-term interest rates relative to actual and expected inflation. More recently, FOMC policy has also targeted unemployment.[3] Generally, the Fed attempts to control the supply of banking system reserves and thus credit availability.

The Fed also provides liquidity to firms through its many borrowing facilities. National banks must be members of the Federal Reserve System in contrast with state-chartered banks that have the option of joining. All bank holding companies are regulated by the Federal Reserve such that any state-chartered bank that is part of a holding company is already subject to Fed supervision. Importantly, the Fed is financially independent given that it generates substantial revenue from its holdings of government and mortgage-backed securities and pays much less in operating costs and interest. During the financial crisis the Fed extended extraordinary amounts of credit to a wide range of firms through many different liquidity programs. It truly represented the lender of last resort that allowed many TBTF firms and others to continue operations and avoid bankruptcy.

Examinations and Enforcement Actions

The fundamental responsibility of every regulator is to regularly monitor bank performance to protect the deposit insurance fund and ensure safe and sound practices. In order to do this, regulators have a staff of examiners who conduct on-site examinations of a bank's profitability and risk profile as well as evaluate whether management is complying with all banking laws. After completing the examination, regulators file a report of examination which is used to formally communicate the key findings to senior management and the board of directors. To signal a high priority finding, regulators will include a list of *matters requiring attention* (MRAs) that the bank must address to prevent a serious problem from arising. Some of these MRAs require an immediate response to correct a specific regulatory concern and are thus labeled *matters requiring immediate attention* (MRIAs).

If a regulator determines that a bank is operating in an unsafe and/or unsound manner or that officers and directors are not following rules and regulations, it will issue an *enforcement action*. Exhibit 3.1 summarizes different types of enforcement actions. Some actions are punitive in nature because they are meant to punish specific behaviors. Several punitive actions are listed at the bottom including *civil money penalties* (CMPs), restitution and removals. CMPs are fines for bad behavior. For example, in December 2012, the OCC imposed a $500 million CMP against HSBC Bank for violating the Bank Secrecy Act and failing to comply with an earlier cease and desist order. Regulators can also force repayment for ill-gotten gains (restitution) and remove key officers and directors from the banking industry.

Other enforcement actions are remedial in nature. As such, they are designed to identify problems and provide a path for the bank to remove the enforcement action in the future. Informal supervisory actions are nonpublic with the objective that management and a bank's board of directors privately recognize problems and agree to steps to resolve them. Informal actions of increasing severity include a supervisory letter, board resolution and *memorandum of understanding* (MOU) as noted in Exhibit 3.1. Formal supervisory actions, in contrast, are public and legally require the bank to comply with the specific actions provided. In certain instances, the regulator may actually file an action in federal court to enforce specific provisions of the agreement.

Regulators base their decisions regarding the type of enforcement action on the reports of examination. In addition to the subject bank's financial condition, regulators assess the institution's response to previously identified actions and criticisms, its compliance record and the level of confidence in management's and the board's ability and willingness to correct the problems. Regulators may be satisfied with an MOU if they are confident in management's willingness and ability to effect change. If not, they will likely use a consent order. If there is a history of noncompliance, insider abuse and/or general resistance by management and the board to respond to perceived problems, regulators will use a cease-and-desist order rather than a consent order. Formal supervisory actions are publicized on the regulatory agency's website and thus are available to any interested party, including the media.

Written agreements, consent orders and cease-and-desist orders use formal, legal language to identify specific management and operating problems and stipulate required responses. The primary difference between a consent order and cease-and-desist order is that regulators impose the latter when management and the board resist the order directives. Banks under these orders must typically develop a capital plan to replenish depleted stockholders equity, improve liquidity, lower the amount of problem assets and increase earnings among other stipulations. Of course, it is often difficult, if not impossible, to raise capital externally during a financial crisis such that some banks under consent orders eventually fail. The media often publicize such orders so that affected banks then have to respond to public criticism and uncertainty that potentially further damages the bank's reputation. It is not uncommon that when a formal order is announced, some customers become concerned about the bank's viability and withdraw their uninsured deposits thereby potentially creating a run on the bank.

Exhibit 3.1 Types of Enforcement Actions and Implications

Type	Implication / Response Requirement
Informal Supervisory Actions	
Supervisory Letter	Applies when institution has a small number of supervisory issues; objective is to provide specific guidance to help resolve problems and limit further deterioration in performance
Board Resolution	Applies when institution has more supervisory issues, but problems are not pervasive; institution's board of directors must agree with provisions suggested to help resolve problems and adopt such a resolution formalized in board minutes; used when a bank's overall condition is sound
Memorandum of Understanding	Applies when institution (generally) is in less than satisfactory condition; negative performance trends exist and require specific management responses; written agreement which stipulates actions necessary to help resolve problems and must be signed by regulator and institution's management or board; failure to comply normally results in a formal enforcement action
Formal Supervisory Actions[4]	
Formal Written Agreement	Applies to institutions that are in less than satisfactory condition; firms often face substantive deterioration near-term if actions are not taken; provides specific actions necessary to address problems and operational issues; not enforceable in federal court
Prompt Corrective Action Directives	Applies to institutions with capital levels below Section 38 PCA guidelines with more stringent actions at lower capital levels; Section 39 allows a bank to file a safety and soundness plan that will correct any deficiencies found in operations—if the bank successfully meets plan terms, regulators may not require more formal orders
Consent Order	Applies to institutions in weak condition whose practices threaten the future viability of the organization; if the institution or any individuals have violated laws or unsound banking practices, the entity is required to cease the activities and take immediate action to remedy the problems and issues; generally issued when regulator is not confident that management will take the necessary corrective actions or when problems are sufficiently severe that lesser-actions cannot be justified; voluntarily executed by the bank and may be enforced in federal court
Cease-and-Desist Order	Applies to the same institutions as those under a consent order except that it has a formal notice of charges and typically is not voluntarily agreed to by the bank; enforced in federal court; regulators may impose temporary cease-and-desist orders in emergency situations
Civil Money Penalties	Pay a fine
Removal	Individuals or banking entities are prohibited from participating in banking activities unless approved specifically by regulators or the courts
Restitution	Individuals or banking entities must reimburse the bank or FDIC for unjust enrichment or for losses

Information is from "FDIC Enforcement Decisions and Orders" and "OCC Enforcement Action Types"

In 1991, Congress passed the FDIC Improvement Act (FDICIA) establishing minimum capital requirements for banks. If institutions operated with less capital than required, regulators were required to take "prompt corrective action—hence PCA" to close the presumably distressed firms. As capital ratios approached these minimums, regulators were expected to impose operating restrictions to limit risk taking and thereby protect the deposit insurance fund. If regulators determine that a bank is operating in an unsound and unsafe manner without a reasonable possibility of recovery, they will close the bank, which is then designated a *failed bank*. Formally, the chartering agency closes a bank with assistance from the FDIC as insurer. During the recent crisis, many banks that failed were first subject to formal supervisory actions.

Deposit Insurance

All newly chartered banks must join the FDIC and purchase deposit insurance. Today, a customer's deposits are insured up to $250,000 per account.[5] If a bank fails, the FDIC guarantees the deposit balance up to the insured amount. Customers who maintain balances that are fully insured do not have to worry about whether they will be fully paid if their bank were to fail. However, as insurance agent, the FDIC must focus on the safety and soundness of the insured institution. For state-chartered banks that are not members of the Fed, the FDIC serves as the primary federal regulator and typically conducts on-site examinations (in conjunction with the state banking department) of individual banks.

Still, the use of "insurance" is somewhat of a misnomer. Much like the Social Security system's reserves, there are no real reserves, or assets, backing insured deposits. Banks that pay into the fund similarly do not have a policy that links their contributions to expected receipts. The FDIC administers the Deposit Insurance Fund (DIF) and is required to maintain a reserve equal to at least 1.35% of the banking system's estimated insured deposits now measured as average consolidated total assets minus average tangible equity. Exhibit 3.2 indicates that the actual reserve ratio

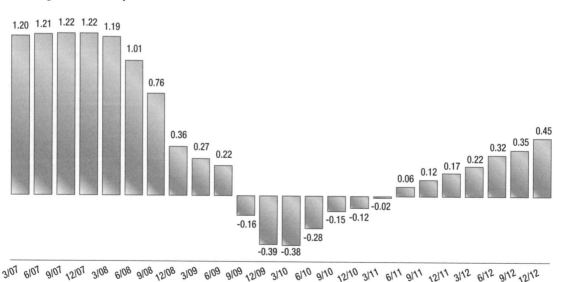

Exhibit 3.2 DIF Reserve Ratios
Percentage of Insured Deposits

Source: FDIC Quarterly Banking Profile, www.fdic.gov; DIF ratio equaled 0.63 in June 2013.

recently fell negative to −0.38% in March 2010, which demonstrated the necessity to replenish the fund during the crisis. Today, each bank pays a quarterly insurance premium based on its net assets (total assets minus equity capital).[6] The DIF is an accounting mechanism which tracks the value of cumulative assessments over time plus investment income net of operating expenses and provisions for losses from failed institutions. The fund can be negative because the FDIC reduces the DIF balance by the amount of expected payouts on failed institutions (provisions for losses). With the persistent problems faced by many banking organizations, the FDIC expected a large number of bank failures with extensive losses to the DIF in 2009–2010. When the DIF falls below the minimum, the FDIC is required to impose additional assessments on insured institutions to replenish the reserve. Given the sharp drop in DIF reserves, effective June 30, 2009, the FDIC imposed a special assessment of 0.05% of a bank's total assets minus equity capital to replenish the reserve. This special assessment was in addition to the normal deposit insurance paid by each bank.

Deposit insurance premiums used to be based on a bank's capital position and were set equal to a flat rate times insured deposits regardless of how much credit and interest rate risk a bank assumed. With FDICIA in 1991, the FDIC moved to a crude risk-based system in which required capital was based on the amount of risky assets and premium assessments increased with a bank's risk profile (measured by declines in a bank's capital position and overall risk rating).[7]

Higher FDIC insurance premiums and the special assessment fell disproportionately on community banks. For many banks, increased deposit insurance premiums reduced earnings by 25% to 50% during the second quarter of 2009. There are two important issues the FDIC and policymakers faced at this time tied to such DIF funding. The first is whether the special assessment and future assessments unfairly penalized community banks. Most analysts and market participants agree that the largest institutions (TBTF banks and shadow banks) contributed the most to the financial crisis. Yet, community banks bore a far greater relative burden of replenishing the insurance fund. The Dodd-Frank Act addressed this by moving to a net asset assessment base. Second, the system of replenishing the DIF is pro-cyclical. When times are good, the FDIC lowers insurance premiums because the DIF is flush and expected losses are small. When times are bad, it increases assessments which lowers bank earnings by even greater amounts and puts greater pressure on bank capital ratios. During good times, it would be beneficial to have higher assessments when banks are better able to absorb the premiums. During bad times, it would be beneficial to have lower insurance assessments so that banks could lend more in their communities. This issue has not yet been resolved.

FDIC-Insured Debt

In response to large bank liquidity issues, the FDIC established the Temporary Liquidity Guarantee Program (TLGP) in October 2008. One feature of the program allowed qualifying institutions to issue debt with maturities under three years with principal and interest payments guaranteed by the FDIC. This insured debt was functionally the same as insured deposits for which issuers paid low interest rates plus 0.75% of the amount issued.[8] The debt proceeds were held by the issuing entity to ensure that it had sufficient cash to cover promised interest and principal payments on existing debt. Importantly, the benefits of FDIC insurance were extended to some firms that previously did not qualify and had little or no history of paying FDIC insurance premiums. Consider the firms listed in Exhibit 3.3. While some of these firms operated small thrift institutions or industrial loan companies with insured deposits, they issued relatively large amounts of FDIC-insured debt under TLGP. This insured debt cost much less than noninsured debt and thus added greatly to these firms' profitability and financial stability. GE, Goldman Sachs, Morgan Stanley, American Express, Deere & Co. and MetLife are not traditional banks and did not contribute to the DIF in any meaningful way prior to the crisis—certainly not in comparison to other institutions and the dollar amount of federal government assistance they received. Yet, 97 of these and other individual institutions, bank holding companies and their noninsured affiliates issued $339 billion in FDIC-insured debt via the TLGP through mid-2009.

Exhibit 3.3 Issuers of Large Amounts of FDIC-Insured Debt*

Institution	FDIC-Insured Debt (billions $)	Institution	FDIC-Insured Debt (billions $)
Bank of America	$44.0	Regions	$3.5
GE Capital	40.5	SunTrust	3.3
JPMorgan	40.5	HSBC	2.7
Citigroup	34.6	Deere & Co	2.0
Morgan Stanley	23.8	KeyCorp	1.9
Goldman Sachs	19.5	Sovereign Bancorp	1.6
Wells Fargo	9.5	US Bancorp	1.6
GMAC Financial Services**	7.4	BNP Paribus	1.6
American Express	5.9	Bank of NY Mellon	0.6
State Street	4.0	Huntington Bancshares	0.6
PNC	3.9	MetLife	0.4

*Source: Dena Aubin and Pam Niimi, "FDIC-backed debt issuance totals for U.S. companies," Reuters, May 7, 2009.

Federal Government Liquidity Programs

During 2008–2009, the federal government introduced many new programs to provide liquidity to financial and nonfinancial firms. The TLGP was one of them. The creation of these liquidity facilities was a reaction to the freezing of the money and capital markets. At one point in late 2008 interest rates on short-term Treasury securities went negative meaning that investors paid the sellers to convert cash to federal government debt.

One of the most critical actions taken by the federal government during the heart of the crisis was to step in and provide liquidity to large firms to prevent bankruptcy. Initially, the Fed approved the conversion of nontraditional banks, such as Goldman Sachs, American Express and GMAC, to bank holding companies which gave the firms access to borrowings via the Fed's discount window. This action was critical given that money and capital markets operate on the basis of trust and faith that counterparties will perform. For many of these large firms, there was a crisis in the market for repurchase agreements (repos).[9] Specifically, repo lenders who were concerned about the quality of collateral backing their loans required institutions to increase the amount of collateral supporting the loans beyond the amount the firms had that was available to pledge. Many repo lenders thus called their loans. The Fed thus stepped in to provide replacement financing.[10]

One of the reasons that Treasury rates fell to such low levels is that firms were not confident that their trading partners would be solvent the next day. So, they converted holdings to Treasuries and balances held at other institutions and liquidity disappeared. In some cases, no party was willing to quote a price at which it would buy securities, such as federal agency debt, once viewed as low risk.

With the financial crisis sapping spending, businesses and individuals started de-leveraging their balance sheets primarily by paying down debts. Eventually, the government created the Term Auction Facility (TAF) for U.S. banks, the Term Securities Lending Facility and Primary Dealer Credit Facility for securities dealers and the Fed entered into foreign exchange and liquidity swap agreements with global financial institutions to make liquid funds available at relatively low cost to these groups. To further increase the availability of short-term funds to nonbank businesses and encourage securitization, the government introduced the Commercial Paper Funding Facility and Term Asset-Backed Securities Lending Facility. In total, the federal government flooded markets with liquidity and the Fed's balance sheet ballooned in size.

In 2011, Bloomberg analysts researched Federal Reserve emergency actions and concluded that the Fed committed $7.77 trillion in assistance via loans or guarantees as of March 2009.[11] On one day, December 5, 2008, the Fed loaned $1.2 trillion to troubled institutions. While the Fed charged interest and occasionally imposed fees, the all-in costs were well below what firms would have otherwise paid because in most cases market participants were unwilling to extend credit at virtually any rate. Bloomberg further estimated that beneficiaries of these loans and guarantees earned a combined $13 billion from August 2007 to April 2010 on the funds. Representatives of the Fed and Treasury argue that the creation of different liquidity programs and use of guarantees were necessary to prevent markets from collapsing and global economies from falling into deep recession. Clearly, the actions were successful is stopping the hemorrhaging.

Regulation of Community Banks

Safety and soundness regulation is designed to ensure that banks have acceptable risk management policies and practices. If successful, regulatory actions will maintain confidence in the financial system and protect the DIF. Members of a bank's board of directors along with senior management identify specific sources of risk, determine how to measure these risks, put in place a system to monitor risk-taking and establish procedures for adjusting risk exposures that are deemed to be excessive. A key element is having appropriate policies that outline acceptable practices and risk limits.

Bank regulators also have a formalized process for evaluating a community bank's performance and risk profile that is labeled the *uniform financial institution rating system* (UFIRS) that was introduced in 1979. With the addition of a component emphasizing interest rate and price risk, the formal ratings process now applied to banks is commonly labeled the *CAMELS rating system* and focuses on six risk components. Each letter in CAMELS refers to a specific performance factor:

C	Capital adequacy
A	Asset quality
M	Management quality
E	Earnings
L	Liquidity
S	Sensitivity to market risk

Regulators assign a rating or score for each factor ranging from 1 (strongest or lowest risk) to 5 (weakest or highest risk).[12] A bank's overall condition is determined by its composite CAMELS rating based on a weighting of the six factors using the same 1–5 scale. Any bank with a composite rating of 1 or 2 is deemed to exhibit relatively low risk. A bank that is rated a 3 overall is typically subject to an informal enforcement action requiring remedial actions. Banks rated 4 and 5 are exposed to significant risks and are thus typically subject to formal enforcement actions. Regulators view banks in these latter two categories as exhibiting "unsafe and unsound practices and conditions" or "extremely unsafe and unsound practices and conditions." Performance is both unsatisfactory and deficient and requires immediate assistance.

Banks are exposed to other significant risks in their normal operations, including potential compliance problems, legal issues and damaged reputations. Regulators are paying particular attention to compliance issues today focusing primarily on a wide range of specific consumer and other regulations to ensure that banks not engage in *unfair, deceptive or abusive acts and practices* (UDAAP).[13] The CFPB is encouraging consumers to file complaints regarding their perceptions of unfair treatment and will take action as it deems appropriate. It is not clear what acts the CFPB will deem as unfair, deceptive and abusive. These risks are commonly labeled operational risk, legal risk, reputation risk and compliance risk. Regulators conduct regular exams regarding banks' use of technology and whether they meet compliance regulations. Such exams also affect a bank's CAMELS ratings particularly through the management (M) component.

Problem Banks and Regulatory Enforcement Actions

The FDIC through its CAMELS rating system identifies problem banks as institutions that have a composite rating of either 4 or 5. These institutions have "financial, operational or managerial weaknesses that threaten their continued financial viability."[14] By their nature problem banks pose a significant risk to the DIF in the event of failure. The FDIC publishes quarterly a statement indicating the number of problem FDIC-insured institutions and the assets they control. Exhibit 3.5 shows recent trends in these totals. Note the sharp increase in the number of problem banks in 2008 to 2009 to a peak of 884 in 2010, or 11.5% of U.S. insured banks. Generally, banks that fail come from this list with most of these firms likely under informal or formal enforcement actions. The number of problem banks has fallen since 2010 as some banks fail and the U.S. economy improves allowing banks to improve their risk profiles.

Risk Controls

Community banks generally attempt to control risks by following effective risk management practices. First, they operate with relatively high levels of equity capital (low financial leverage). This allows them to invest more in loans which carry the highest promised yields but also the highest risk of default. With high capital, a bank can absorb a greater volume of loan losses before it depletes its capital. Second, to the extent possible, they diversify their loan portfolios across industries and customers. They limit how much they invest in any one sector and to individual borrowing entities. Third, they maintain high levels of funding from core, FDIC-insured deposits. These deposits are not as sensitive to changing interest rates and thus provide a stable source of funds to invest. Banks with high core deposits have usually experienced fewer large, unanticipated deposit outflows. Fourth, they buy high quality securities which can be readily sold in secondary markets if the bank needs funds and can be used to pledge as collateral against borrowings. Fifth, they charge reasonable fees for services and do not attempt to gouge customers.

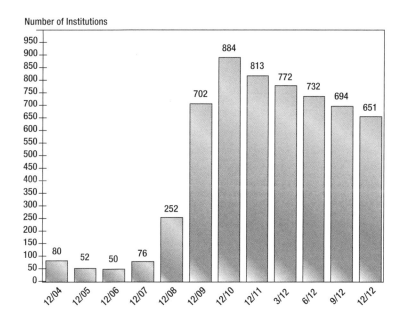

Exhibit 3.5 Number of Problem Banks, 2004–2012

Source: FDIC Quarterly Banking Profile. www.fdic.gov; there were 553 problem banks in June 2013.

Managers understand that they live in the same community as their employees and customers and frequently interact with them outside the workplace. Finally, employee turnover is low and compensation levels are reasonable. Many community banks have ESOPs and profit-sharing plans, but few offer incentive compensation packages which induce employees to take excessive risk. The net result for banks that follow such risk management practices is that management is rarely surprised by losses that arise in the normal course of business.

CHAPTER 3

Effective risk management requires that community banks understand the approach that regulators use to assess CAMELS ratings. Thus, for each of the risk categories subject to evaluation, they attempt to (1) identify risks, (2) measure risks, (3) monitor changes in risk and (4) control risks. This requires that every bank have an effective enterprise risk management approach to managing the institution.

Dual Banking System

The majority of community banks are chartered by the states and have the FDIC as their primary federal regulator. Exhibit 3.6 summarizes the number and average size of institutions chartered by the states and national regulatory groups. At year-end 2012, there were 7,083 distinct institutions of which 75% were state-chartered. Of the state-chartered institutions, 33% had less than $100 million in assets. In contrast, just 26% of the 1,780 institutions chartered by national or federal agencies had less than $100 million in assets. Thus, more of the smallest banks operated under a state charter. Not surprisingly, the average size of institutions measured by total assets is much lower for state-chartered banks at $842 million. The comparable figure for OCC-chartered commercial banks exceeds $7.5 billion. The largest banks have grown more than others since 2007 such that their combined market share continues to rise. They have benefited competitively versus other banks from the financial crisis.

Exhibit 3.6 Number and Average Size of Banks by Primary Regulator, December 2012

		Number		All Institutions
	All	Assets < $100 million	Assets > $100 million	Average Asset Size ($ millions)
State Charter				
All Institutions	5,303	1,737	3,566	$842.4
Commercial Banks	4,863	1,637	3,226	$848.7
Savings Institutions	440	101	349	$773.1
National Charter				
Commercial Banks	1,233	317	916	$7,513.2
Federal Charter				
Savings Institutions	547	150	397	$1,315.4
Totals	7,083	2,205	4,878	$2,040.2

Source: Quarterly Banking Profile and State Banking Performance Summary, www.fdic.gov,.

A disproportionate number of banks in the U.S. are small banks which operate in limited geographic markets. While the banks and bankers are important drivers of local business activity, they carry little clout nationally. Many market participants believe that bank regulators and federal government administrators are using the financial crisis to shrink the number of independent banking organizations–at least by attrition if not intentionally. Wouldn't it be easier at the federal level to have agencies regulate just a handful of banks rather than the 7,000 currently operating throughout the U.S.?

Costs of a Single Bank Regulator

Throughout our history, whenever there is a financial crisis, some analysts recommend consolidating regulators. While this proposal has to date never been implemented, it is important to note that any move to a single bank regulator has the potential to adversely affect local economies. There is strong evidence that local economies grow in line with the strength and willingness of local financial institutions to lend within their trade area. Historically, state banking regulators have worked closely with the FDIC and Fed in their supervision of state-chartered banks. State regulators who live in the markets where the banks they regulate are located are typically familiar with local economic conditions and development plans. They are responsive to concerns of local participants including both customers who desire consumer protection and the banks who provide credit, deposit, trust and insurance services. In essence, the voices of community bankers are heard by state officials.

The OCC as national bank regulator would naturally be less focused on local or regional issues. It has a long history of working closely with the nation's largest banking organizations which, due to their complexity and size, are the most risky. Most of the TBTF banks are regulated by the OCC and subject the financial system to systemic risk. Because community banks do not exhibit systemic risk, the OCC is less concerned about their roles in the U.S. economy and potential financial difficulties. Having the OCC or a similar national group responsible for the supervision of all banks would inevitably lead to the fast consolidation of banks. As such, banking resources would be increasingly concentrated in fewer institutions now evidencing even greater risk. This is quite a contrast to recent legislative proposals to break up the TBTF banks.

Factors Associated with Recent Failures

The principal causal factor of community bank failures during the recent financial crisis appears to be loan concentrations in commercial real estate in areas that suffered significant declines in real estate values or commercial loans in areas with sharp disruptions in associated business activity. In particular, concentrations in construction, land and development loans present serious problems with the decline in real estate values because such loans do not generate cash flows to service debt until the properties are eventually sold. For example, a loan for a new residential development will typically be approved for the purchase of lots, the development of the lots and surrounding infrastructure to support residences, and ultimately the construction of homes. Debt service payment will come from home sales. This process works if real estate values are stable or rising and the loans are appropriately underwritten. However, what happens if housing values fall, families cannot sell existing properties and the demand for new homes collapses with the excess inventory of lots and vacant homes? Importantly, the developer will not generate cash from the project to service the debt. If the bank can sell the loans or underlying properties, it will typically take a large loss and as a result must have sufficient capital to remain in business.[15] Banks that write these loans down to their new, lower appraised values without a sale deplete their capital by recognizing the reduction in value. Absent sales, the only other choice is to slowly reduce values until banks can sell the underlying properties without any additional loss. If they have extensive exposures in this type of loan, virtually every bank will need to raise external capital to support any of these actions.

Three other traits dominated the actions of large regional banks and community banks that experienced serious problems during the recent financial crisis. In each case, they reflect core business strategies that went awry. The traits are (1) an excessive reliance on advances obtained from the Federal Home Loan Bank (FHLB), (2) the extensive use of brokered deposits, and (3) conducting substantial amounts of business outside the bank's normal trade area. FHLB advances and brokered deposits are not bad by themselves, but their ready availability allowed banks to fund poorly underwritten loans that ultimately created problems. Excessive reliance on these funding sources was associated with inappropriate accumulation of speculative assets.

Consider the case of a group that started a de novo (new charter) bank in Atlanta in 2006. What would its business plan look like given Atlanta's high growth rates for new homes and businesses during the early 2000s? Suppose the bank raised $30 million in start-up capital from investors. It uses the proceeds to open its doors for business and thus must have a main office and hire a group of core employees in addition to members of its board of directors. Given the personnel and office expenses, management needs to invest the funds as soon as possible. In a fast-growing market like Atlanta, many banks concentrated lending in new real estate developments involving commercial or residential construction. Without a branch system to collect core deposits from local individuals and businesses, the bank would buy *brokered deposits* by paying market rates on certificates of deposit (CDs) that were sold to national investors. While brokered deposits used to refer to CDs sold to third-party depositors via brokers, the term now refers to deposits for which the bank pays above-market interest rates. When possible, the bank would join the Federal Home Loan Bank (FHLB) system and use FHLB advances to finance qualifying real estate related loans. The strategy was to fund the bank near-term with these higher cost and less stable brokered deposits or via FHLB advances secured with real estate loans in order to grow (leverage) the bank. Managers focused on growth in order to spread their operating costs across a larger asset base and obtain a meaningful market share. The bank would charge loan fees and often accept a lower spread on the credit in order to book the business. The strategy was to later emphasize profitability after reaching appropriate market penetration and size goals. The availability of the financing often induced highly speculative lending.

The strategy worked well in its early stages as investors willingly purchased stock in the de novo bank and bankers readily made speculative loans to real estate developers. Everything worked as long as real estate prices rose, or at least remained stable, and the developers could sell the properties. What happens though when real estate values fall? Because the properties served as collateral for the loans, a decline in real estate values depleted the value of the underlying assets. Developers found it difficult to sell the properties so they couldn't generate sufficient funds to cover the debt service. Too many borrowers could not sell their properties and thus could not pay the obligated interest and principal payments on the loans. The banks, however, were still obligated to make the interest payments on the brokered deposits and FHLB advances. Regulators closed many of these banks as loan losses wiped out equity and the value of remaining assets fell well below the amounts owed.

This scenario frequently played out in the same manner when banks moved outside their primary trade areas. For example, it was not uncommon for a bank located in a regional or rural market with limited growth options to open a branch or loan production office in a nearby major metropolitan area. Banks in rural Missouri might start doing business in Kansas City or St. Louis. Bankers in Nebraska might make loans in Scottsdale, Arizona, or Miami, Florida, where the bank bought another bank or opened a loan production office because the bank owner had a second home in the area. Unless the bank's lenders were familiar with these metropolitan markets, the bank's soft knowledge about potential customers fell sharply such that the default risk increased for any new loans in the area. Extrapolate this series of events to any bank in middle America or the Northeast that opens a branch or acquires a bank in Phoenix, Arizona or Las Vegas, Nevada and it is clear why out-of-market banking is higher risk. The recognition of how these traits influenced bank risk led the FDIC to impose higher deposit insurance premiums for banks exhibiting these high risk factors.

Key Regulatory Issues

Community bankers commonly cite regulatory uncertainty and compliance costs as serious impediments to normal business practices. For example, a 2013 survey of 6,700 banks with $350 million in average assets by Continuity Control concluded that community bankers spent 8.3 million hours complying with regulations during the first quarter of 2013 at a cost of roughly $250 million. With the increased complexity of regulations and large number of rules still to be implemented, these costs will continue to rise.

The serious problems identified during the financial crisis naturally produced new legislation and regulations that will take years for bankers to both understand and incorporate in their business plans. Three areas stand out as presenting logistical problems: (1) Dodd-Frank Act rules and regulations, (2) the Consumer Financial Protection Bureau's rulings on qualified mortgages and a borrower's ability to repay, and (3) the Community Reinvestment Act (CRA) and Fair Lending.

Dodd-Frank Wall Street Reform and Consumer Protection Act

The U.S. Congress passed the Dodd-Frank Act (DFA) in 2010 in response to the financial crisis. As the title of the act indicates, the presumed intent of the legislation was to promote financial stability by reforming Wall Street practices and better protecting consumers. The text of the DFA encompasses 2,223 pages and mandates 398 rules, many with specific deadlines for implementation. As of September 2013, just 39% of the rules were finalized, another 35% of the rules were proposed after the mandated deadlines but not finalized, with the remainder yet to be proposed and finalized. It is easy to understand banker uncertainty if these rules are being delayed.

DFA has several key components with most directed at the largest financial institutions that presumably impose systemic risk to the financial system. Many of the proposed rules are targeted at banks of extreme size, $50 billion or more in assets. But many community bankers believe that whatever rules are ultimately approved will be eventually applied as best practices to all banks. A brief summary of key DFA rulemaking areas is:

- *Creation of the Financial Stability Oversight Council (FSOC).* Council will identify risks to financial stability, eliminate expectations of federal government bailouts, and identify systemically important financial institutions (SIFIs). SIFIs will presumably be subject to additional charges and regulatory oversight.

- *Consolidate regulatory oversight of institutions.* Creates the Consumer Financial Protection Bureau (CFPB), eliminates the OTS and requires SEC registration of hedge funds that manage more than $100 million of assets.

- *Credit risk retention.* Firms that securitize instruments must retain at least 5% of the risk, requires credit rating agencies to justify their ratings across similar issues and requires some disclosure of asset-specific data.

- *Derivatives regulations.* Limits federal assistance to certain swaps providers, requires major swap dealers and participants to register to a regulator (to be determined later) and requires federal banking regulators to set new minimum capital and margin requirements to ensure safe and sound swaps transactions.

- *Investor protection.* Empowers the SEC to produce appropriate fiduciary standards for broker-dealers.

- *Reform credit rating agencies.* Subjects credit rating agencies to potential liability, mandates minimum disclosures and attempts to reduce conflicts of interest in the rating process.

- *Prohibits proprietary trading.* Known as the Volcker Rule after the former Fed Chairman Paul Volcker, these provisions limit certain proprietary trading activities of banking entities, impose higher capital requirements and/or limits on "approved" proprietary trading activities and authorize banking entities to retain an equity investment of no more than 3% of the total ownership interest in a fund that engages in proprietary trading.

- *Incentive compensation.* Requires publicly-traded firms to allow shareholders to vote (nonbinding) on executive compensation, requires minimum disclosure of total executive compensation and authorizes clawbacks when it is appropriate for a firm to recoup prior compensation payments.

- *Capital Requirements.* Requires the FSOC to make specific recommendations to the Federal Reserve for higher capital requirements on bank holding companies with total consolidated assets of $50 billion or more.

Qualified Residential Mortgages and the Borrower's Ability to Pay

Qualified Mortgage (QM)

In January 2013, the CFPB formalized rules at to what mortgage lenders must do to ensure that a borrower can afford a loan. The rules will go into effect in January 2014. The essence of the rules is that a borrower must have a demonstrated "ability to repay" the loan. If lenders meet the criteria outlined in the rules, the loan is labeled a "qualified mortgage" and the lender is protected from most borrower lawsuits. Presumably, lenders have made a good faith effort to assess credit risk such that they should not be penalized for simply extending credit.

There are three basic types of QMs: (1) general QMs, (2) balloon-payment QMs originated by certain lenders, and (3) transitional QMs. For general QMs, ability to pay requirements stipulate that the loan maturity cannot exceed 30 years, pricing cannot require points and fees that exceed 3% of the principal, the borrower cannot have a debt-to-income ratio above 43%, the borrower must verify income (no "no-doc" loans) and they cannot be interest-only or negative amortization loans. Balloon-payment QMs must be originated by lenders with less than $2 billion in total assets operating in rural areas. Finally, transitional QMs are mortgages where the borrower's debt-to-income ratio exceeds 43%, but all other ability-to-pay criteria for a general QM are met along with the underwriting criteria of the applicable government-sposored enterprise (GSE), such as Fannie Mae, Freddie Mac, FHA, VA, USDA/FSA and Rural Housing Service.

Qualified Residential Mortgage (QRM)

Federal regulators are similarly determining the conditions under which lenders can sell loans without having to keep a portion of each loan in portfolio—the "skin-in-the-game" rule. The intent is to induce lenders to make less risky loans because they will be directly harmed along with investors in the securities if the underlying borrower defaults. Loans that meet the criteria to avoid skin-in-the-game requirements will be labeled qualified residential mortgages and lenders do not have to hold any portion of the loans in portfolio. For non-QRM securities, the securitizing firms will be forced to keep at least 5% of the credit risk associated with the underlying assets when they sell or transfer asset-backed securities. In general, it appears that QRM loans will have maximum loan-to-value ratios, will require minimum downpayments, will cap rate increases on adjustable-rate mortgages, and will require a lower debt-to-income ratio for the borrower.

While the definitions and criteria will reduce uncertainty regarding safe harbor loans, there are always unintended consequences. Many lenders argue that such rigid rules will restrict credit, on average. Two examples demonstrate potential problems. First, individuals from immigrant communities often pool resources to finance housing. How do you treat a family of four working adults who pool their incomes to buy a home in San Francisco? Is the combined debt and income of all four included in the calculation of borrower debt-to-income? Or do you evaluate only the individual with the best data when evaluating the loan request? If the rules are not clear, lenders may shy away from extending credit to such borrowers. Second, many community banks in rural markets make fully-amortizing mortgages using 30-year maturities, but the loans have a maturity of 5-7 years at which time the remaining principal is due. These are balloon mortgages. The maturity is kept short to help the bank manage interest rate risk associated with the potential loss of earnings if interest rates rise sharply after origination. They hold these loans in portfolio because they offer reasonable yields and the bank is servicing the local community. Without such balloon loans, few lenders would make longer-term fixed-rate mortgages in small markets with limited housing activity. At maturity, the bank will typically refinance the loan at the prevailing rate without charging new appraisal and origination fees. The issue is how to define a rural market when evaluating balloon loans.[16] Many community banks that view their institutions as relationship lenders who know (and have known) their customers for years are located in what the OMB does not recognize as a rural market. They will likely not make any mortgages without the QM safe harbor.

The fundamental issue is whether any lenders will extend credit outside of what meets the QM requirement, particularly in less-populated markets. Without mortgages, many community banks lose their principal earning assets. Most of the abuses in the mortgage markets occurred with the largest lenders—witness the lawsuits against Countrywide (now part of Bank of America). Yet the smallest banks suffer the most from many of the new rules.

Community Reinvestment Act and Fair Lending

Congress passed the Community Reinvestment Act (CRA) in 1977 to monitor whether regulated financial institutions were appropriately meeting the credit needs of their local communities, particularly the needs of low-income and moderate-income neighborhoods. The objective was to penalize discrimination in lending and provide "fair and equal access to credit" for all creditworthy borrowers. Regulators periodically examine insured institutions for compliance and assign a CRA rating. Lenders that do not meet the minimum standards of these regulatory reviews will suffer reputation damage and will face regulatory limits on branching, merger and acquisition opportunities, and the expansion of other products and services. CRA has expanded to include bank investments and services beyond lending. Consumer advocacy groups have a legal right to comment on banks that do not meet CRA standards and invariably pursue it.

Bank regulators also enforce a wide range of Fair Lending laws and regulations that encompass efforts to reduce discrimination. The CFPB, in particular, has demonstrated a strong interest in monitoring whether banks comply with these laws and regulations under threat of charging banks with Unfair, Deceptive or Abusive Acts and Practices (UDAAP). Every bank must have a compliance process in which employees meet the requirements of these regulations. This means that banks must have the appropriate documents with appropriate disclosures, such as loan closing documents and marketing media, and must have systems that calculate interest rates and fees appropriately. The regulatory intent is to try and ensure that customers have the relevant information in an easy to understand format that allows them to make informed decisions.

Specifically, the Equal Credit Opportunity Act (ECOA) prohibits discrimination on the basis of race, religion, national origin, sex, marital status, age and applicant income derived from public assistance. The Consumer Credit Protection Act makes loan and deposit terms more transparent and clear to borrowers and savers primarily by specifying certain disclosures, such as the annual percentage rate. The Fair Housing Act prohibits discrimination in all aspects of residential housing (purchases of dwellings, real estate loans, brokering or selling real estate, repairing real estate and renting).

What does unfair, deceptive and abusive mean in practice? We are waiting for the CFPB and courts to address this question. However, some practices have been deemed to meet the legal criteria and now must be eliminated or modified.

- *Credit cards*: In December 2008 banking regulators formally identified five practices as unfair including those pertaining to whether a customer is given a reasonable time to make a payment, are payments allocated to maximize lender interest, when card issuers can increase interest rates, two-cycle billing and the financing of fees and deposits on cards with low limits.

- *Overdrafts*: Banks cannot include the amount of credit that is available on overdraft protection plans when disclosing a customer's deposit balance; banks cannot charge deposit customers fees unless they provide an opportunity to opt-out of overdraft protection programs and disclose the amount of fees. They must also regularly report the amount of overdrafts paid by each customer.

- *Credit life and disability*: Banks cannot pursue deceptive tactics to sell products and services such as insurance by misleading customers about benefits, providing incorrect information about costs, or creating incentives for sales representatives to provide inaccurate information.

- *Mortgage lending*: Mortgage originators cannot steer borrowers to a residential mortgage loan in which the borrower doesn't have a reasonable ability to repay or which has predatory characteristics.

Federal courts have formally recognized three "proofs of lending discrimination" all based on the concept of *disparate impact*. Illegal disparate impact is established when a "lender explicitly considers prohibited factors (overt evidence) or by differences in treatment that are not fully explained by legitimate nondiscriminatory factors (comparative evidence.)"[17] Disparate treatment is also legally proved when a lender "treats a customer differently based on one of the prohibited bases" whether or not there is evidence of prejudice or intent to discriminate. This might be demonstrated by a loan rejection for a borrower in a protected class when a similar loan for a borrower in a nonprotected class was approved (comparative evidence). Lenders are required to document why they treat similar applicants differently. Finally, lenders must not have any policy or practice that "disproportionately excludes or burdens certain persons on a prohibited basis." In practice, this is determined to mean that if a policy prevents credit from being granted to a protected class of borrowers and is not justified by business necessity, the lender has demonstrated illegal disparate impact.

Such rules may be reasonable if they are applied reasonably. But how do you manage these risks? Lenders saw red flags raised when President Obama appointed Thomas Perez to be Secretary of Labor. In February 2012, in his capacity as Assistant Attorney General (Department of Justice), Perez made a deal with the city of St. Paul, Minnesota, to not intervene in a lawsuit against the city if the city agreed to withdraw its appeal of another case involving a disparate impact claim against the city. Two House Committees and the Senate Judiciary Committee concluded that Perez felt that the Supreme Court would find disparate impact to be unsupported by the Fair Housing Act.[18] The accusation is that this quid pro quo deal allowed Perez to manipulate legal outcomes to protect his interest in pursuing disparate impact claims.

Some analysts believe that CRA requirements played an important role in the recent financial crisis and generally increased credit risk by expanding the pool of borrowers to include some without the ability to pay.[19] While there are strong believers on both sides of the argument, lenders are particularly concerned that pursuit of fair lending violations will ultimately lead to less credit being available to borrowers. The claim is that race-neutral policies and practices for underwriting and credit scoring can still be legally viewed as discriminatory if a claimant can demonstrate statistically that a disadvantaged group was harmed. Even though there is no evidence of overt or comparative disparate impact, the statistical outcome that members of a certain protected group got rejected more than nondisadvantaged members might subject a bank to a violation. There is presumed discrimination whenever disparities exist regardless of any intent or the cause of the disparity.

The CFPB and federal regulators are focusing on examinations of whether banks are complying with fair lending laws. The CFPB is initially collecting data and soliciting complaints from customers. Banks that charge lower loan rates on loans to borrowers with high credit scores must now monitor whether classes of protected borrowers are paying higher rates, on average. As noted below, the CFPB is putting pressure on auto lenders and banks about including extended warranties and insurance in financing agreements under the presumption that such deals discriminate against African-Americans and Hispanics. The cost of validating whether the bank meets all regulations is high. The costs of defending formal charges are potentially quite high if the CFPB or DOJ sues. How do you manage this compliance risk and at what cost?

ARE ADD-ONS IN AUTO LENDING DISCRIMINATORY?

In early 2013, the CFPB and Department of Justice issued subpoenas to various automobile lenders in search of discrimination. The concern is that auto lenders were discriminating against African-Americans and Hispanics with low credit scores by requiring them to purchase add-on products at high markups in order to get financing. When an automobile dealer makes a loan to finance a vehicle, the dealer generates additional profit if the customer purchases add-on products such as an extended warranty, credit life insurance, and the like. In most cases, such products are optional and cannot be mandated as a condition of financing. Auto dealers, in turn, often have arrangements with banks to share in interest charges to a customer that exceed some threshold level. As expected, these interest rate markups are higher for borrowers with low credit scores and poor credit histories. The CFPB has indicated that it would like to eliminate interest rate markups in lieu of a direct fee agreement between dealers and banks. The CFPB also has the authority to fine auto lenders and restrict certain practices if it determines that the dealers are discriminating against classes of borrowers. How do you prove discrimination in this type of lending?

Summary

This chapter describes the general regulatory environment facing community banks. It documents the structure of regulation, the nature of regulatory enforcement actions and deposit insurance, recent causes of bank failures, the range and impact of federal government liquidity programs and key regulatory issues facing community banks in the near future. The primary concerns going forward are that the bulk of Dodd-Frank Act rules and regulations are not yet known. How and when these rules will be applied to community banks, how rulings on qualified mortgages and the borrower's ability-to-pay will affect the availability and risk of mortgage lending and how regulatory efforts to enforce CRA provisions and fair lending rules will affect credit need to be addressed to fully free up lending.

Understanding Community Bank Performance

CHAPTER 4
Basic Financial Statements and Key Risk Ratios

The financial crisis dramatically altered the risk profile and profitability of all banks. The Too-Big-to-Fail banks were the first to show deteriorating performance as the collapse in housing values, residential mortgages and related loan and security holdings led to asset write-downs and large losses. With securitization no longer in favor, many of the shadow banks simply disappeared. Large regional banks experienced declining profitability as business activity deteriorated along with business loans and commercial real estate loans, particularly construction and land development loans tied to falling housing values. While most community banks experienced solid profitability and little change in perceived balance sheet risk through 2008, performance in 2009–2011 dropped sharply. U.S. unemployment reached 10.2% nationally in October 2009 and over 15% in some troubled states. The U-6 unemployment rate, which adds the underemployed (part-time and discouraged workers) to those actively looking for work who cannot find it, reached almost 18%. Conditions stabilized and improved in 2012–2013 with unemployment hovering between 7% and 8%, but economic growth as measured by *gross domestic product* (GDP) was anemic compared with historical norms during a recovery. Consumers were cautious in their spending and generally focused on deleveraging or paying down debt.

As individuals watched their 401(k)s and home equity plummet in value and feared for job security, they cut spending and increased saving as they paid down their debts. The recession that started in December 2007 cut loan demand and worsened many borrowers' ability to repay outstanding debts. Personal bankruptcies skyrocketed and real estate values fell sharply. Not surprisingly, many community banks reported sharp increases in loan charge-offs and problem loans, particularly institutions that focused on construction lending. In response, they increased loss provisions, which often led to losses and declining capital levels. It was a very difficult period with management focused on improving asset quality, ensuring liquidity and maintaining capital levels. By mid-2011, markets were starting to stabilize. The decline in real estate values slowed with some locales showing appreciation, with housing values rising through 2013. Many economic indicators signaled that unemployment would remain relatively high for several years and GDP growth would be modest at best. Ben Bernanke, Federal Reserve Bank Chairman, strongly signaled that the Federal Reserve would keep short-term interest rates relatively low at least to 2015 because inflation was modest and unemployment was too high. Banks with commercial real estate exposure continued to write-down problem loans as they searched for additional capital.

CHAPTER 4

The objective of this chapter is to demonstrate how to read and interpret community bank financial information. It introduces financial statements and key risks in running a bank. Chapter 5 then introduces key performance ratios as a more formal way to assess a bank's basic strategies, fundamental risk exposures and core profitability. After completing the two chapters, the reader should better understand the types of risk that community banks take, how banks generate earnings, what causes earnings to fluctuate and the rationale behind core strategies to improve performance. The final section contrasts recent community bank performance with that of large, regional banks and TBTF institutions. It documents that TBTF banks have increased market share at the expense of other institutions, which reflects the difference in business models and the benefits of the implied government guarantee for the nation's largest banks.

Financial Statements for Community Banks

As highly regulated firms, banks report quarterly financial information to their regulators which is readily available to the public. At the end of March, June, September and December each year, banks report balance sheet and income statement information that is published by the FDIC via its web site (www.fdic.gov) under the title Uniform Bank Performance Report (UBPR).[1] The UBPR lists the general types of loans and securities that banks own, the amounts of funding from deposit customers versus other borrowings, how much equity a bank operates with, and both current and historical revenues, expenses and profits. It thus reveals basic strategies that banks follow. Furthermore, it uses these figures to construct financial ratios to assist in interpreting the data. Because it compares a bank's financial ratios with average ratios for peer institutions over time, the UBPR essentially represents a scorecard indicating how well a bank is performing. The appendix provides summary UBPR information for a sample bank compared with peer banks having assets between $300 million and $1 billion.[2] For each ratio, bank-specific data appear in the first column, the average value for peer banks nationally in the same size category appears in the second column and the third column indicates the percentage of peer banks with a lower ratio versus the bank in question.

The Balance Sheet

A bank's balance sheet indicates what a bank owns (assets), what it owes (liabilities) and what is left over for the owners (equity) at a specific point in time. Basic accounting requires that the amount of assets equals the sum of liabilities and equity. It does not indicate the value of or exposure to off-balance sheet activities, such as loans that are committed but not funded, and the value of a bank's derivatives positions. Most community banks have loan commitments as a normal part of funding business borrowing, but have little or no exposure to derivatives. Consider the data for First Community Bank (FCB), headquartered in Lexington, South Carolina, provided in Exhibit 4.1. The data are generally referred to as book values because they indicate values reported on the "books" of the bank on a specific date.

Exhibit 4.1 Balance Sheet Data for First Community Bank
December 31, 2012 (Figures in Millions)

Assets	Amount	Percent of Total	Liabilities + Equity	Amount	Percent of Total
Noninterest Cash	$ 11.5	2%	Core deposits	$456.7	76%
Interest bearing balances & federal funds sold	7.1	1			
Investment securities	203.0	34	Noncore liabilities	79.6	13
Loans (net)	337.2	56	Total liabilities	$ 536.3	
Other assets	44.6	7	Stockholders equity	67.1	11
Total	$ 603.4	100%	Total	$ 603.4	100%

At year-end 2012, FCB reported $603 million in assets with $536 million in liabilities and $67 million in book value of stockholders equity. Investment securities and loans made up 91% of the bank's assets which were financed 76% by core deposits, 13% by noncore liabilities and 11% by equity. These figures are representative of those for community banks of this asset size throughout the United States.

Assets

Investment securities consist primarily of fixed income securities issued by government entities or corporations. They are categorized by issuer type in the UBPR:

- *U.S. Treasury and agency securities* are either issued or guaranteed by the federal government and its agencies.

- *Mortgage backed securities* (MBSs) are securities that are backed by principal and interest payments on a specific pool of mortgages that serve as collateral, including government-guaranteed securities, or are corporation obligations.

- *Municipal securities* are issued by states, local governments and their political subdivisions representing borrowing for purposes such as water treatment facilities and schools.

- *Other securities* are securities issued by corporations, foreign entities and holdings of participation certificates in private pools of residential mortgages and any other asset-backed securities.

Community banks generally concentrate their investments in Treasury and agency securities, mortgage-backed securities and municipals. One of the appeals of municipal securities is that interest received is exempt from federal income taxes and is also often exempt from state income taxes where relevant.

The primary appeal of investment securities is their high degree of liquidity, low risk of default, predictability of income and value for pledging purposes. While these characteristics are more fully described when discussing bank risk, note that banks typically realize little, if any, loss from default of securities as issuers generally repay the full amount of principal borrowed. Most banks purposefully buy securities that carry low risk of default. Of course, there are times when some investment securities default so nongovernment guaranteed instruments do carry the risk that the investing bank will not receive the entire promised return of principal.

FCB has invested 56% of its assets in *loans*. In fact, loans typically represent the dominant asset among community banks as they are often the principal driver of the relationship between a bank and its business customers. They are again categorized by the type of borrower in the UBPR reflecting the use of proceeds:

- *Real estate loans* are loans secured by real estate.

- *Commercial loans* are loans to businesses and obligations (other than securities) of state and local governments.

- *Individual loans* are made to individuals for purposes other than the purchase of real estate.

- *Agriculture loans* represent loans to farmers and businesses for the purpose of financing agricultural production.

- *Other loans* includes all other types of loans.

Community banks hold all types of loans with the allocation reflecting the nature of business and consumer activity in their trade area and the specific markets they serve as well as their overall credit expertise and general business strategy. Most banks report significant amounts of real estate loans because they accept real estate as collateral, even when the use of proceeds might be for operating and general business purposes. Banks in rural markets will often make large amounts of agriculture loans because their customer base includes farmers, ranchers or businesses engaged in agriculture. Typically, loans to individuals and other loans comprise small portions of community bank portfolios, in part because credit card lending is not important for many of these banks.

Most loans represent a negotiated credit agreement between a borrower and the bank. A loan officer works closely with a borrower to understand the purpose of the loan, how much credit the borrower needs and its timing, the expected source of cash flow to repay the loan, the risks that might affect the borrower's ability to repay the loan and when the borrower is expected to repay the loan. For their services and the greater risk, banks charge higher rates compared to what they can earn from investment securities and often charge fees for loan origination. The primary appeal of loans is that they represent a key component of a customer's bank relationship and promise higher above-average expected returns when viewed as part of a total customer relationship.

Importantly, the aggregate loan amount is reported net of a bank's *allowance for loan and lease losses* (ALLL). The ALLL is also referred to as the loan loss reserve. The allowance is essentially a bookkeeping entry which represents funds allocated in anticipation of loan charge-offs. Because most loans exhibit real risk of default, banks are required to report a provision for loan losses as an expense item in anticipation of future loan losses.[3] The allowance equals the cumulative amount of provisions for loan losses minus the amount of actual losses charged-off plus recoveries of loan losses over time. First Community Bank's loan portfolio activity since 2008 reflects the impact of the financial crisis on the economy and loan demand. In particular, FCB's net loans totaled $328.3 million in 2008, increased by a net $11 million in 2009 and then fell to $323.3 million in 2011. With the economic recovery, net loans then increased by almost $14 million in 2012 which was still below its peak in 2009.

Noninterest cash and due from banks represents currency and coin held in the bank's vault plus noninterest-bearing deposit balances held at other institutions. While banks hold cash to meet the currency needs of local customers, it is held primarily to meet regulatory requirements and to assist in the processing of checks and other transactions. To assist in processing items, banks also hold some cash-equivalent assets as interest bearing balances at other banks and as federal funds sold. Federal funds sold are effectively unsecured (not collateralized) short-term loans typically to other financial institutions. Finally, other assets include the value of bank premises and fixed assets, other real estate owned and other items. These two categories represent a small portion of community bank assets. FCB thus earns interest on 91% of its assets with the other 9% nonearning.

Liabilities

As the label suggests, **core deposits** are the most basic and valuable source of funding for banks. Think of an apple's core representing the source of strength for the fruit. Core deposits are stable sources of funds that do not typically flow into and out of the bank when interest rates change. In economic terms, they exhibit low interest elasticity. The components differ based on whether the holder can write checks or make payments (transfer funds) electronically for purchases and the size of balances held.

- *Demand deposits* are transactions accounts which pay no interest to the holder;

- *NOW & ATS accounts* represent interest-bearing transactions accounts other than money market deposit accounts;

- *Money market deposit accounts* (MMDAs) pay interest but the account holder is allowed to write no more than three checks or make three telephone transfers per month;

- *Savings accounts* including passbook savings and overdraft protection accounts;

- *Time deposits at or below the insurance limit* are deposits with set maturities where the holder has up to $250,000 in the account.

Core deposits are the other principal driver of a bank's relationship with its customers. Many individuals initially select a bank by identifying one that has an office or branch convenient to work or home or by using one which employs people they know. Gen Y customers are more inclined to choose their initial bank based on whether it offers a wide range of online and mobile banking services and related technology. They are looking for convenience. They will open a checking account that they use to deposit their paycheck and make payments. Over time, they may save part of their income by investing in an MMDA, savings account or small-time deposit; but they want the convenience of moving funds between accounts electronically. The importance of the $250,000 amount for the time deposits is that the FDIC insures deposits up to $250,000 per account.[4] Prior to the financial crisis, the insured amount was $100,000. Any deposit holder who keeps balances under $250,000 does not have to worry because the FDIC will make good on the deposit in the event the bank fails. Interest rates on these accounts and interest-checking accounts are typically low relative to other rates due to the explicit FDIC guarantee. When an individual wants to borrow to take out a student loan, purchase a car or buy a home, he will initially contact the bank where he has his transactions account.

Importantly, an individual's choice of bank may reflect other factors. As mentioned previously, younger customers and business managers often look for convenience in the form of available electronic banking services, such as mobile banking, online bill paying and the availability of *automatic teller machines* (ATMs) across different states and countries. Some business customers may want quick access to deposit services via remote capture and cash management services. Older individuals may, in turn, want friendly faces in the branch they frequent regularly. As the U.S. population ages, banks are rethinking how to best organize and structure branches. Why does a bank need brick-and-mortar offices? Should branches be mobile in kiosk form? In all cases, core deposits are highly valuable because they represent stable, predictable balances that remain at the bank for long periods. They are relatively low-cost sources of funds because of the low rates paid.

Noncore liabilities include all other forms of bank debt. For community banks, these consist primarily of uninsured deposits exceeding $250,000, which are typically in the form of *certificates of deposit* (CDs), plus federal funds purchased and FHLB advances. Funding in this form is labeled "noncore" because the party that makes the loan to the bank is presumed to be highly interest sensitive. As such, the party may withdraw its funds as soon as possible when interest rates change. *Brokered deposits* are one type of liability that regulators label as noncore because the bank obtains the deposit via a third party and this group typically charges a fee. As such, the deposit holder does not directly place the deposit with the bank, but instead goes through another institution. Regulators thus view a bank to be buying funds by paying a market rate when using a third-party broker. Noncore liabilities are also referred to as hot money and *volatile* or *wholesale liabilities*:

- *Uninsured time deposits in excess of $250,000* typically have set maturities but the critical feature is that the funds do not have the backing of the FDIC in the event of bank failure.

- *Federal funds purchased* are short-term (typically one day) borrowings of deposit balances held at the Federal Reserve or other depository institutions. Banks lend and borrow these "Fed funds" to invest excess reserves or meet clearing balance requirements.[5]

- *Federal Home Loan Bank (FHLB) borrowings* or advances are secured borrowings from the regional FHLBs; most have set maturities but may be fixed rate or variable rate; in all cases the borrowing bank posts collateral to the FHLB.

- *Other borrowings* is a catch-all category including all other liabilities, but it is typically small at community banks.

Noncore liabilities are viewed as interest rate sensitive and less stable compared with core deposits and thus are deemed to be riskier by regulators. Evidence suggests that holders of uninsured deposits are more likely to withdraw their funds when a bank experiences problems. Similarly, institutions that lend fed funds can pull (eliminate) these lines without notice. FHLBs can increase collateral requirements for the borrowing bank which might force it to pledge additional loans and securities as collateral and thus reduce the amount of assets it might sell in the event it needed cash. Generally, investors in these liabilities will reduce their balances or move them if another institution offers a higher rate or if the issuing bank is perceived to be in financial trouble. As discussed later, the types and amounts of funding from these noncore sources affect a bank's liquidity and overall risk. In most cases, the interest rates that banks pay on these noncore liabilities exceed those on core deposits of similar maturities.

Stockholders Equity

Stockholders equity refers to a bank's capital. It essentially represents the sum of the initial contribution of owners' capital invested, the cumulative amount of earnings not paid out to stockholders as cash dividends (retained earnings), and the amount of capital raised externally via offerings of common stock and preferred stock. The important feature of equity capital is that the bank does not have to make dividend payments to owners. The greater is the amount of financing via capital, the lower are the bank's obligated interest payments on debt. Along with the allowance for loan losses, capital helps absorb losses and reduces the likelihood of failure. A bank is technically insolvent if the value of liabilities exceeds the value of assets. Remember the requirement that assets equal liabilities plus equity. If the value of liabilities exceeds the value of assets, equity capital is negative. This situation typically arises when a bank has significant losses associated with loan charge-offs and other asset write-downs. Higher amounts of capital help absorb losses and thus protect the bank from failure.

INSIGHT:

Consider a bank that is financed 100% by common stock held by a single investor. The bank will generate a return to the investor by paying a dividend and by increasing the value of the stock over time. The bank has no insured or uninsured deposits or other liabilities and thus pays no interest expense. Absent fraud or other legal problems, the bank cannot fail.

Some bank regulators and policymakers believe that banks should be forced to operate with much higher levels of common stock (equity), which thereby reduces overall risk in the banking system. If this were to happen, all else held constant, banks would be less risky in general. However, as demonstrated in the next chapter, the expected return on equity would be sharply lower thereby encouraging owners to (1) withdraw from the industry, (2) take greater risk off balance sheet, and (3) consolidate ownership via mergers and acquisitions. We would have a less dynamic economy as less lending would take place and financial assets would be even more concentrated at the largest institutions.

Would you want this?

FCB's balance sheet is typical for a community bank. The majority of assets is in loans with the principal funding from core deposits. Its equity contributes 11% of total financing. Remember that banks are financial institutions which exhibit high financial leverage relative to nonfinancial firms. In a simplistic sense, FCB can experience a reduction in asset values up to 11% before it is technically insolvent - absent other influences. Alternatively, its assets divided by equity equals 10×, which is well below comparable ratios for TBTF institutions, Large Regional banks and the shadow banks.

The Income Statement

A bank's income statement compares revenues with expenses and taxes. Because most of a bank's assets and liabilities either earn or pay interest (hence the label *financial intermediary*), interest income and interest expense are the largest components. The difference in these figures is net interest income (interest income − interest expense), which represents the driver of community bank earnings. Banks do generate fee income and other noninterest revenues as well as pay overhead expenses. Consider FCB's 2012 income statement summarized in Exhibit 4.2. The data represent all revenues and expenses related to activities throughout the year in contrast with balance sheet data (see Exhibit 4.1), which reflect values as of a set date. Two important factors affect how to interpret the data. First, a portion of a bank's interest income is exempt from federal (and sometimes state) income taxes. For example, most state and local government bonds (labeled *municipals*) pay interest that is exempt from federal income taxes. Similarly, some loan interest is not taxed. Because FCB owns a large amount of municipals and some tax-advantaged loans, a portion of interest income is actually not taxed such that the reported $4.8 million is the tax-equivalent, or pretax, value of interest income. Second, some of a bank's expenses, such as provisions for loan losses, are noncash expenses. Thus, cash flows realized from operations may differ sharply from reported net income.

For 2012, FCB reports $23.3 million in interest income and $4.8 million in interest expense which provides $18.5 million in net interest income. FCB's net operating revenue equals the sum of net interest income and noninterest income, or $26.5 million, with $8 million in non-interest income. Provisions for loan losses equals $0.5 million with noninterest expense equal to $19 million. As demonstrated later, the amount of provisions for loan losses is determined relative to the perceived quality of bank loans and essentially represents a forecast of future loan charge-offs. Noninterest expense, in turn, consists largely of personnel and overhead costs. In 2012, FCB also sold securities for a $0.2 million loss. With taxes of $2.2 million, FCB reported $4.6 million in net income.[6]

Exhibit 4.2 2012 Income Statement for First Community Bank
(Figures in Millions of Dollars)

Interest income	
Loans (te)	$ 18.3
Investment securities (te)	4.8
Due from banks, fed funds & other	0.2
Total (te)	23.3
Interest expense	
Core deposits	− 3.2
Noncore liabilities	− 1.6
Total	− 4.8
Net interest income	18.5
Provisions for loan losses	− 0.5
Noninterest income	8.0
Noninterest expense	− 19.0
Pre-tax operating income	7.0
Realized gains/losses on securities	− 0.2
Taxes (te)	− 2.2
Net income	$ 4.6

Net operating revenue = $26.5

Pre-provision operating income = $7.5

*te refers to tax-equivalent values that are grossed-up to reflect a
pre-tax value of the income components; provisions for loan losses is an noncash expense.

Analysts focus on three core elements of the income statement to evaluate aggregate performance: net interest income (interest income − interest expense), provisions for loan losses and net *overhead expense or burden* (noninterest expense − noninterest income). They generally pay little attention to realized gains/losses on securities unless they are large. Banks report a gain or loss when they sell securities based on whether the sale price exceeds (producing a gain) or falls below (producing a loss) the initial purchase price. Gains or losses are viewed as extraordinary one-time events and not core components of earnings. Typically, community banks report small amounts of gains or losses as they do not actively trade investment securities. The income statement can thus be reduced to that in Exhibit 4.3.

Exhibit 4.3 First Community Bank's Components of Net Income for 2012
(Figures in Millions of Dollars)

	Net interest income	$18.5
−	Provisions for loan losses	−0.5
−	Net overhead expense	−11.0
+	Realized gains on securities	−0.2
−	Taxes	−2.2
	Net income	$4.6

Net interest income is the driver of community bank profitability. Note that all other summary items in Exhibit 4.3 are negative, particularly net overhead expense (burden), which indicates that noninterest expense exceeds noninterest income by $11 million. In short, FCB would not be profitable if net interest income was not large enough to cover the sum of each of these expense items.

Hence one of the challenges to be a strong community bank is to systematically generate a large net interest income. Interest income and interest expense are determined by the volume and mix of assets and liabilities, respectively, and the associated interest rates charged and paid. For example, management could increase interest income, at least temporarily, by increasing loans and reducing holdings of securities because promised loan rates are higher than rates on securities. Of course, loans are generally riskier and the important question is whether the bank is being adequately compensated for the higher risk. If not, high provisions for loan losses will eventually lower earnings substantially over time.

The largest expense at community banks is typically noninterest (overhead) expense. It has three components: personnel expense, occupancy expense and other expense. Personnel expense consists primarily of salaries and benefits paid employees. Totals for each component will vary based on how many branches a bank has and how many different lines of business (insurance, leasing, brokerage, etc.) it operates. Occupancy expense includes the cost of fixed assets, such as the bank's building and equipment, and net rental expense if appropriate. Finally, other expense includes items such as FDIC deposit insurance premiums and amortization of goodwill. The greatest source of noninterest income at community banks is typically service charges on deposit accounts. Loan fees are included as interest income on loans. Exhibit 4.4 documents the components of noninterest income at all FDIC-insured institutions in 2012. Note that service charges contribut-

Exhibit 4.4
Composition of Noninterest Income at FDIC-Insured Banks, December 2012

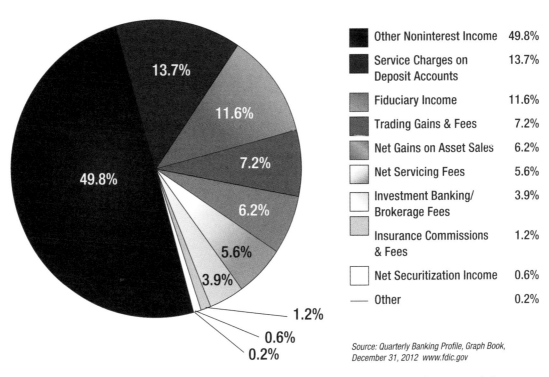

Other Noninterest Income	49.8%
Service Charges on Deposit Accounts	13.7%
Fiduciary Income	11.6%
Trading Gains & Fees	7.2%
Net Gains on Asset Sales	6.2%
Net Servicing Fees	5.6%
Investment Banking/Brokerage Fees	3.9%
Insurance Commissions & Fees	1.2%
Net Securitization Income	0.6%
Other	0.2%

Source: Quarterly Banking Profile, Graph Book, December 31, 2012 www.fdic.gov

ed 13.7% of the total. Fiduciary income (from trust operations) contributed 11.6% while servicing fees contributed 5.6%. Some community banks are active in these arenas. However, unlike their larger counterparts, community banks do not generally offer investment banking services or brokerage and insurance operations and do not run trading desks or take equity positions in businesses and other investments (no proprietary trading). Thus, community banks' noninterest income contributes less to operating income both in dollar terms and relative to overall earnings.

One measure of a bank's effectiveness in managing the non-interest side of operations is to compare noninterest expense with noninterest income via net overhead expense. The greater is this figure, the greater is the burden imposed on management to generate more net interest income. Thus a second challenge to grow earnings at community banks is to reduce this burden. Many community banks are focused on growing noninterest income which is difficult to do given the limited noncredit services that they offer. In the short-run, they have instead tried to cut operating expenses.

Finally, in today's environment, it is important to pay attention to reported provisions for loan losses. Banks are required to make *provisions for loan losses* (PLL) in anticipation of future loan charge-offs. Given recent asset quality problems, provisions increased dramatically beginning in 2008 as demonstrated in Exhibit 4.5. The amount reported as provisions reflects an assessment of the quality of bank assets (primarily loans) adjusted for the amount of actual loan charge-offs and loan recoveries. As part of ongoing operations, banks regularly classify loans on their books in terms of whether they are paying as expected or evidence slow payment or nonpayment of principal and interest. When a bank formally recognizes that a loan will not be repaid, it charges-off (writes the value down to zero on its books) the remaining principal amount owed. Note that in 2008–2009 banks typically set PLL above net charge-offs indicating a likely worsening of credit quality going forward. From mid-2010 to 2012, however, net charge-offs exceeded PLLs suggesting that the worst was over. The analysis of credit risk is discussed in Chapter 8.

Provisions for loan losses is a noncash expense, but any allocation reduces net income and ultimately the amount of stockholders equity. Given uncertainty about what actual losses will be in the future, some analysts focus on pre-provision operating income, which equals $7.5 million for FCB in 2012.

Exhibit 4.5 Quarterly Net Charge-offs vs. Loan Loss Provisions 2008–2012

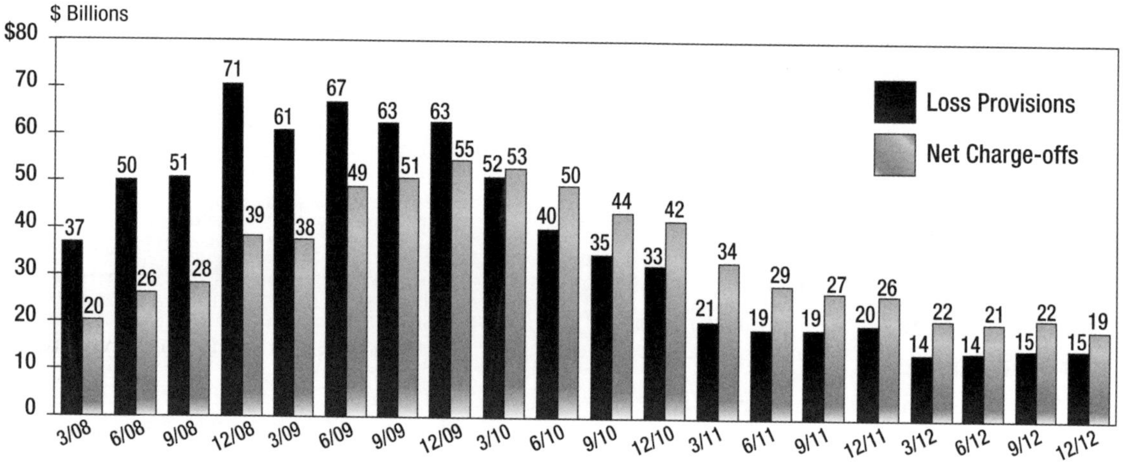

Source: Quarterly Banking Profile, Second Quarter 2011 and Fourth Quarter 2012 www.fdic.gov; net charge-offs fell to $14 billion in June 2013 with loss provisions at $9 billion.

Off-Balance Sheet Activities

In their normal business activity, many banks engage in off-balance sheet activities that are not necessarily high risk. For example, a bank that offers a borrower a loan commitment (think of a line of credit) stands willing to finance a future purchase or debt repayment up to a pre-determined, fixed amount. The borrower has discretion as to when and how much to "take down" against the line and thus has control over the transaction once the terms are negotiated and the loan is booked. The bank will charge a fee for making credit available and will charge interest only when the customer borrows against the commitment. In contrast, some off-balance sheet activities, such as the use of futures, forwards and swaps for speculative purposes, may be high risk depending on the complexity of the contracts and how they are used.

TOO BIG TO FAIL: THE FINANCIAL CRISIS

During the financial crisis, many TBTF institutions, particularly Citigroup and AIG, assumed extraordinary amounts of risk via off-balance sheet transactions. Citigroup was one of the largest creators of *structured investment vehicles* (SIVs). An SIV is an off-balance sheet entity created to hold investment securities, loans or derivatives which are financed by short-term commercial paper and longer-term liabilities plus a small amount of equity. The SIV was expected to profit from the difference between the rates charged on the assets and the lower rates paid on the liabilities. Using SIVs allowed Citigroup to originate many loans, thereby generating loan origination fees, move the loans off-balance sheet so the bank wasn't forced to hold capital in support of the lending, and earn management fees on the SIVs' activities. Unfortunately, when many of the loans (subprime mortgages and other high risk instruments) defaulted, the groups that invested in the SIVs' commercial paper refused to renew their investment. In response, Citigroup had to initially make loans to the SIVs to replace the maturing commercial paper. When an SIV was unable to reissue the commercial paper and other debt, Citigroup then moved the assets back onto its balance sheet thereby absorbing large losses.

AIG's Achilles heel was *credit default swaps* (CDSs). Without going into extensive detail, think of a credit default swap as an insurance policy written against a credit event, such as the default of Lehman Brothers' bonds. AIG sold the CDSs or equivalently issued the insurance policy. The buyer of a CDS paid AIG a quarterly premium for the insurance. In the event that Lehman Brothers defaulted on its bonds, AIG would pay the CDS buyer the difference between the value of the bonds at initiation of the trade and the value at default. AIG wrote large volumes of these CDS insurance policies. As the values of the underlying assets (Lehman bonds) plummeted, AIG had to post additional collateral that it did not have against its CDS positions. Instead of allowing AIG to go bankrupt when market participants made their collateral demands, the U.S. Treasury stepped in and paid AIG's counterparties. AIG was officially declared TBTF. Do you think AIG's management realized how much risk there was in this business if subprime mortgages and related debt instruments decline in value? Were there any real constraints on how much insurance AIG could write? The answers to both questions are no! AIG's management demonstrated poor risk management while government regulatory oversight of AIG's derivatives business was virtually non-existent.

Most community banks do not use CDSs, futures, options, swaps and other off-balance sheet instruments. When they do use them, they are part of explicit hedging programs intended to reduce risk. Community banks did not create SIVs and do not conduct off-balance sheet activities with the intent of generating large amounts of fee income. While they often make loan commitments, they are dealing with customers who are regular borrowers with the bank and they know these customers personally. If they use futures and options, it is typically associated with hedging activities to assist farmers and agriculture businesses.

Fundamental Risks in Community Banking

The Federal Reserve uses a framework that identifies six general risk factors in banking: credit, market, operational, liquidity, legal and reputational risks. As demonstrated in Chapter 3, regulators assign CAMELS ratings when evaluating a bank's safety and soundness. The process is structured in the sense that examiners review each bank's activities to assess whether management has (1) identified the key components of each type of risk, (2) assessed the magnitude of risk and direction in which it is changing, (3) a system in place to regularly monitor the different risks and (4) policies and procedures in place to control these risks. The term, *enterprise risk management*, refers to the formal process of identifying, measuring, monitoring and controlling risks in line with meeting target profitability for the bank. Among other factors, regulators look to a bank's capital to help determine how well it is positioned to withstand potential losses from assuming the risks.

The term CAMELS, introduced in Chapter 3, is an acronym that identifies six types of risk faced by banks. When addressing a bank's safety and soundness, regulators assign a rating to each component from 1 (lowest risk) to 5 (highest risk) and a composite rating again from 1 to 5. The associated components are:

C = Capital
A = Asset Quality
M = Management Quality
E = Earnings
L = Liquidity
S = Sensitivity to Market Risk

Banks face additional types of risk including operational risk, technology risk, reputation risk and legal risk but regulators address them by conducting examinations focused on potential risks and problems associated with these factors. The following discussion focuses on asset quality, sensitivity to market risk, liquidity and other risks. Earnings performance is examined in Chapter 5.

Asset Quality (A)

Banks hold financial assets in the form of loans and securities. The fundamental question is whether borrowers will make timely principal and interest payments on these instruments. When assessing a bank's asset quality, management and regulators essentially focus on how much credit (default) risk the bank has in its loan and securities portfolios. Credit risk refers to the possibility that a borrower or counterparty to a contract will not make the obligated interest and principal payments as agreed, that is, will default on the obligations. In the case where a borrower doesn't perform as planned, the bank may take a loss. For community banks, loans exhibit the greatest credit risk. While some securities exhibit real credit risk, particularly municipal bonds, and some off-balance sheet activities have credit risk with counterparty promises, most defaults occur in the loan portfolio. Managers attempt to manage this risk by carefully evaluating the nature of each loan request, the proposed use of proceeds, the borrower's character and financial condition, the potential sources and timing of cash flow for repayment and the potential for unforeseen circumstances to adversely affect performance. When appropriate, they require that a borrower post collateral and provide a personal guarantee. In order to manage credit risk for the entire portfolio of loans, managers try to control loan concentrations in a single industry, to a single borrower and in general categories, such as commercial real estate. They also try to limit the rate of loan growth. Each bank also establishes a credit culture under which the process for approving loan requests, managing the credit relationship and working with problem borrowers meets sound banking practices. The credit culture determines management's risk tolerance and how a bank measures, monitors and controls credit exposures.

Senior management and the board of directors regularly assess a bank's credit risk by examining the current levels and trends in a series of ratios. The first type of ratios focuses on historical loan loss experience. *Gross loan losses* equal the dollar amount of loans formally charged off as uncollectible. *Loan recoveries*, in turn, represent the amount of loans that were previously charged off but collected during the current period. Finally, net loan losses equal gross loan losses minus recoveries. The second type of ratios provides information about expected future losses. *Noncurrent loans* are those that are either past due or in nonaccrual status. *Past-due loans* accrue interest, but promised interest and principal payments have not been made as scheduled. The longer that a loan is past due, the greater is the likelihood that the borrower will default. Nonaccrual loans are those that are currently not accruing interest. If interest has not been paid for at least 90 days, a loan is generally put on a cash basis, which means that a bank cannot recognize interest revenue until it actually receives an interest payment. *Other real estate owned* (OREO) refers to real estate property that is owned by the bank but is not used in normal business operations. It is typically real property taken as collateral against defaulted loans and is thus a nonearning asset.

Regulators have recently paid special attention to *troubled debt restructurings* (TDRs). A TDR is a loan in which the lender grants a concession that it would normally not consider to a borrower in financial difficulty. The concession may be a reduction in the interest rate, the forgiveness of principal and interest owed or a lengthening of final maturity. The purpose is to help the borrower work out of the loan rather than have the lender initiate default or foreclosure proceedings. Some of these troubled loans represent nonearning assets because the bank does not receive interest income from them. In fact, it is more burdensome because the bank must pay carrying costs (taxes, homeowner dues, etc.) to retain control before they eventually liquidate the loan or underlying collateral. Obviously, a high level of noncurrent loans, OREO and restructured loans is an indicator that future loan losses may be high.

Finally, the third type of ratios signals how well a bank has prepared for future losses. Under accounting and regulatory standards, banks set aside *reserves (allowances) for future loan losses* (ALLL).[7] This accounting procedure essentially requires that a bank report provisions for loan losses as a deduction from revenue as part of the income statement. This noncash expense item is used to increase the loss reserve in anticipation of future charge-offs. Actual loan losses reduce the loss reserve while loan recoveries increase it. Management determines the amount of provisions for loan losses in conjunction with setting the size of the loss reserve at the end of the reporting period. Because noncurrent loans are an indicator of future losses, the final loss reserve typically varies directly with the amount of gross loan charge-offs and noncurrent loans.[8]

Exhibit 4.6 provides the aggregate loan loss reserve (ALLL) accounting for FCB in 2012. Note that $600,000 in net charge-offs exceeds $500,000 in provisions such that the size of the allowance decreases by $100,000. The decrease is a signal that FCB's management believes that the bank is facing lower credit risk going forward. FCB's provisions for loan losses reached a peak in 2009 at just over $3 million with net charge-offs of $2.8 million that year, but fell each year after along with net charge-offs.

Exhibit 4.6
Analysis of the Loan Loss Reserve for First Community Bank in 2012 (millions)

Loan loss reserve: December 31, 2011	$ 4.7
Gross loan losses	− 0.7
Loan recoveries	+ 0.1
Net loan losses	− 0.6
Provisions for loan losses	+ 0.5
Loan loss reserve: December 31, 2012	$ 4.6

Data on pages 7 and 8 of a bank's UBPR provide information regarding key credit risk ratios. Panel A of Exhibit 4.7 summarizes 2012 data for First Community Bank regarding aggregate loan losses and related asset quality information. Similar data by loan type are also available. Relative to peers, FCB experienced lower gross loan losses, lower recoveries and lower net charge-offs. Peers are banks nationally with total assets between $300 million and $1 billion.[9] Absent other information, these ratios signal relatively low credit risk for FCB versus peers. Panel B provides data on trends in noncurrent loans at FCB for 2010–2012 and related ratios for FCB relative to peers in 2012. FCB's noncurrent loans totaled $1.8 million in 2008, jumped to $6.3 million in 2010 reflecting the severity of the financial crisis, and subsequently fell back to $2.6 million in 2012. Noncurrent loans and restructured loans were lower than peers in 2012 reflecting better credit quality when combined with the lower net charge-offs. In contrast, OREO was above peers indicating that FCB appears to move problem assets through the pipeline faster than peers. Importantly, a bank cannot collect on a defaulted loan until it takes possession of the collateral (OREO) and sells it. The last ratios indicate FCB's exposure to commercial real estate loans and particularly to construction and land development loans. Chapter 8 demonstrates that construction and land development loans have been the most problematic for community banks across the nation, on average.

The final group of ratios also signals that FCB's asset quality is likely better than peers. Specifically, provisions for loan losses and the ALLL were lower in 2012 relative to loans versus peers because FCB held fewer problem assets. This is consistent with the ALLL being a higher fraction of net losses and noncurrent loans. FCB appears to recognize problem loans sooner by charging them off and appears to have lowered reserves in line with a smaller and hopefully cleaner loan portfolio. If a bank makes smaller than warranted provisions given high levels on noncurrent loans, it generally signals that the bank has been under-reserving for future losses and thereby overstating profits.

Exhibit 4.7 Credit Risk Measures for First Community Bank
(Data for December 31, 2012 unless otherwise noted.)

Panel A: Historical Loss Experience

	2012 Data		
Ratio	Value for FCB	Peers	Pct
Gross loss to average total loans	0.22	0.62	29
Recoveries to average total loans	0.05	0.09	43
Net loss to average total loans	0.17	0.51	32

Panel B: Expected Future Losses ($000)

	2012	2011	2010
Loans 90 days and over past due	55	25	373
Total nonaccrual loans	4,714	5,402	5,890
Total noncurrent loans	4,769	5,427	6,263
Loans 30–89 days past due	2,588	3,209	2,308

	2012 Data		
Ratio	Value for FCB	Peers	Pct
Noncurrent loans to total loans	1.40	2.04	45
Loans 90+ days past due to total loans	0.02	0.07	55
Noncurrent loans to ALLL	103.20	114.54	52
Noncurrent loans to (ALLL + equity)	7.11	12.64	40
Current plus noncurrent restructured debt to total loans	0.71	1.49	40
Other real estate owned to total assets	0.91	0.70	69
Construction & development loans to total capital	34.14	41.02	48
Total commercial real estate loans to total capital	314.59	274.11	63

Panel C: Preparation for Future Losses

Ratio	Value for FCB	Peers	Pct
Loss provision to avg. assets	0.08	0.30	22
ALLL (loan loss reserve) to total loans	1.35	1.73	31
ALLL to net losses	8.05X	7.38X	69
ALLL to noncurrent loans*	0.96X	0.85X	48

*Calculated as [1/(noncurrent loans to ALLL)]

Some analysts calculate a *Texas Ratio* as an indicator of whether a bank is in financial distress. During the 1980s, Gerard Cassidy and colleagues at RBC Capital Markets introduced the Texas Ratio, noting that when a bank's ratio exceeded 100%, the bank demonstrated a high probability of failure. Tangible common equity equals stockholders equity minus intangibles (primarily goodwill) with ALLL equal to the current period's allowance for loan losses.

$$\text{Texas ratio} = \frac{\text{Nonperforming loans} + \text{OREO}}{\text{Tangible common equity} + \text{ALLL}}$$

From 2008-2011, FCB's Texas Ratio increased from 5% to 16% before falling to 9% at year-end 2012.

Sensitivity to Market Risk (S)

Most community banks focus on revenues, expenses and earnings when constructing their budgets and evaluating performance. As noted in the income statement for FCB, the primary source of profit at community banks is net interest income. *Market risk* refers to the possibility that a bank's net interest income will decline unexpectedly.[10] Because net interest income equals interest income minus interest expense, a drop typically reflects one or more of the following:

- Shift in asset mix away from loans and into lower yielding securities
- Shift in liability mix away from lower cost core deposits into purchased liabilities, such as brokered deposits
- Rising noncurrent and restructured loans and other real estate owned
- Increase in nonearning assets
- Decrease in demand deposits which pay no interest, and
- Changes in interest rates that affect the repricing of loans and securities different from the repricing of interest-bearing liabilities

Each of these factors will affect the amount of interest earned versus the amount of interest paid to fund operations. We thus focus on the impact that changing interest rates have on earnings which is labeled *interest rate risk*.

Bank CFOs spend considerable time modeling changes in the balance sheet and the impact of changing interest rates on both interest income and interest expense. When assets and liabilities reprice at different times and by different amounts, net interest income will change.

Consider the following simplified example where a bank owns a $4 million loan with a 1-year maturity and the loan is financed via a 3-month CD. The loan carries a fixed-rate of 5% with interest paid at maturity and the CD pays a 1% fixed-rate. The initial spread between the two rates is 4%. What is the bank's interest rate risk?

Asset	Liability
Commercial loan @ 5% 1-year maturity $4 million	Certificate of deposit @ 1% 3-month maturity $4 million

Initial interest rate spread = 4%

Suppose that all interest rates rise immediately after the items are booked. What will happen to the bank's net interest income on this transaction? In three months, the bank will have to replace its maturing CD while the loan rate is unchanged for a year. If it chooses to issue another 3-month CD, it will have to pay a rate above 1%. In this case, the interest rate spread between the loan yield and CD rate will fall below 4%. One measure of interest rate risk is the mismatch between the repricing of a bank's earning assets and the repricing of its interest-bearing liabilities. An increase in rates in this example lowers the spread and lowers net interest income. If rates decreased instead, the bank could issue a new 3-month CD at a rate below 1% such that the rate spread would increase. Thus, interest rate changes can either hurt or benefit the bank depending on the structure of the balance sheet.

The analysis of interest rate risk is more complex than this example because bank customers have many options in managing their bank relationships. For example, if rates fall, the commercial loan customer might choose to refinance the loan elsewhere and the bank loses the earning asset. The deposit customer may, in turn, choose to redeem the deposit prior to maturity when rates rise and move the funds to another institution. Interest rate risk analysis takes into account these options and other factors.

Data from the UBPR are not particularly useful in evaluating a bank's interest rate risk. Banks subsequently use detailed models, introduced in Chapter 10, to assess the institution's risk exposure. The UBPR (page 9) does provide aggregate measures which signal potential problems associated with a bank owning large amounts of long-term assets that are not balanced against long-term liabilities. Given a typical bank's balance sheet, most liabilities mature within one to three years. The exception is some portion of checking accounts which are held for transactions purposes. In 2012, FCB reported that it held 10.4% of its assets in loans and securities with contractual maturities over 15 years. The comparable figure for peers was 7.4% indicating a much greater exposure (70th percentile rank) to longer maturity assets. Because long-term assets typically carry fixed rates, a high ratio implies that rising rates will potentially produce losses as interest expense will rise relative to interest income. Another way of viewing these holdings is that rising rates will lower the market values (prices) of the assets if FCB attempts to sell them. FCB similarly reports nonmaturity deposits (largely checking accounts) equal to 128.8% of long-term assets while the comparable figure for peers was 143%. FCB appears to have little net exposure as nonmaturity deposits which are largely core deposits with low interest elasticity exceed the bank's holdings of long-term assets.

CHAPTER 4

Liquidity Risk (L)

Liquidity risk refers to potential losses that may arise from a bank's inability to meet payment obligations in a timely and cost-effective manner. The most serious problems typically arise when deposits leave the bank unexpectedly, which may occur during the normal course of business when a depositor transfers a large amount of funds without giving advance notice or fails to renew a deposit as anticipated. Liquidity problems arise generally when firms cannot replace borrowings as they mature. For example, during September 2008, large investment banks faced liquidity crises when they were not able to roll-over short-term repurchase agreements used to finance operations. Several firms requested permission to immediately convert to bank holding companies in order to access discount window borrowing from the Federal Reserve. The description of Bear Stearns' liquidity crisis in 2008 demonstrates the problem. (see below, "The Collapse of Bear Stearns") A bank may also find itself short of clearing balances if a loan customer unexpectedly draws down a previously unfunded loan commitment.

THE COLLAPSE OF BEAR STEARNS

On March 16, 2008, JPMorgan Chase agreed to buy Bear Stearns in a stock-for-stock transaction that initially valued Bear Stearns at $2 per share. At the time, Bear Stearns was the fifth largest investment bank in the U.S with over 14,000 employees globally. Just one year earlier, Bear's stock price exceeded $170 per share. The purchase was assisted by the Federal Reserve, which two days earlier committed to lend Bear $25 billion collateralized by Bear's assets because lenders in the repo (repurchase agreement) market refused to roll-over their loans. This loan was ultimately not granted because the Federal Reserve Bank of New York, instead, provided $30 billion in financing for JPMorgan's purchase and agreed to cover $29 billion in losses from Bear's assets.

Bear Stearns was the victim of a severe liquidity crisis. In early March, rumors were circulating that the firm was facing a liquidity crisis. Lenders were increasing collateral requirements if they were even willing to advance funds. Christopher Cox, SEC Chairman, noted that Bear's liquid assets fell from $18 billion on March 10 to just $2 billion on March 13. On March 11, Alan Schwartz, CEO of Bear Stearns, stated that Bear's "balance sheet, liquidity and capital remain strong."* At the time of its closing, Bear's debt carried investment grade ratings. In November 2007, S&P lowered Bear's credit rating to A from AA—still investment grade—when the firm announced its first loss in over 80 years.

* Kate Kelly, Greg Ip and Robin Seidel, "Fed Races to Rescue Bear Stearns in Bid to Steady Financial System Storied Firm," WSJ, March 15, 2008.

Community banks meet their liquidity needs, in part, by holding cash and short-term investment securities classified as available-for-sale that are not pledged as collateral. Consider FCB's holdings of $18.6 million in noninterest bearing cash, interest bearing bank balances and federal funds sold as reported in Exhibit 4.1. These cash assets consist of coins and currency held in the vault and deposit balances held at the Federal Reserve Bank or another commercial bank. Coins and currency do not earn interest, so banks keep just enough in stock to meet customer demands. The primary form of cash equivalent assets is balances held at other institutions. These balances are used to help clear checks or electronic transfers drawn against the accounts of its customers and to pay for services provided by the institution. Only recently did the Fed start paying interest on bank deposits held with it, but it pays low rates. Thus, banks generally hold as little cash as possible.

Short-term securities are attractive because they exhibit little price risk; that is, the market values are relatively stable even when interest rates change. The disadvantage is that they carry low rates. Furthermore, at the time it purchases securities a bank must designate the securities as *available-for-sale* (AFS) or *held-to-maturity* (HTM) depending on its objectives. In general, a bank cannot sell an HTM security without adverse accounting and operating issues. Because it doesn't expect to sell the security prior to maturity, it records the value of the security at amortized cost on its balance sheet and changes in interest rates do not affect reported income or stockholders equity. A bank that wants to retain the option to sell a security prior to maturity classifies it as AFS, but must record the value of the security at its current market value at each reporting period. Thus, when interest rates fall it reports a higher value and corresponding increase in equity; but when interest rates rise it reports a lower value and decrease in equity. The essential point is that only AFS securities are liquid. Furthermore, banks are required to pledge securities as collateral against liabilities, such as public deposits and borrowing from the FHLB or Federal Reserve. Because they are pledged, these securities are typically held by a third party trustee and cannot be sold without the trustee formally releasing them.

In summary, short-term securities improve a bank's liquidity because the bank can readily sell the securities to meet cash outflow requirements. Pledging requirements, in turn, hamper liquidity because when a bank pledges a security as collateral against a liability, it cannot sell the security thus rendering it illiquid. HTM securities cannot be sold unless one of several 'safe harbor' conditions is met.

Community banks also meet liquidity needs by borrowing deposit balances from other banks or the Federal Reserve. To maintain this opportunity, they typically arrange federal funds and repo lines with other institutions. *Federal funds purchased* are unsecured borrowing of deposit balances while repos are borrowing of the same form except the bank pledges securities as collateral. The institutions who commit to make this credit available are labeled *correspondent banks*. The value derives from the fact that such funds are readily available at a reasonable rate as long as the borrowing bank is not perceived to be in trouble.

Suppose that one of FCB's deposit customers has $10,000 in a checking account and decides to withdraw the full amount. By the end of the day, FCB will have to hold enough on deposit at the

Fed to cover the $10,000 drawn on the bank as its balance will be reduced when the check clears. It does so by carefully managing its daily cash position which involves comparing cash inflows with cash outflows during the day and positioning the balance sheet to access additional cash when needed. The primary sources of cash in the near-term are *federal funds sold* — loans to other financial institutions that mature daily — and potential borrowings from other institutions in the form of federal funds purchased or repos. As a secondary source, FCB might sell an unpledged short-term security. A liquidity crisis would arise if FCB could not borrow these clearing balances or if it didn't have assets that it could sell quickly at minimal loss. Banks have strong incentives to hold short-term securities that are not pledged as collateral which they can sell in a crisis.

In response to the recent financial crisis, regulators have focused attention on how much funding a bank gets from noncore liabilities, particularly brokered deposits and Federal Home Loan Bank (FHLB) advances. When banks borrow from a FHLB, they must post specific collateral for each advance. If a bank fails, the FHLBs claim on the collateral is superior to the FDIC's claim on the bank's assets because of the specific collateral agreement. Thus, the FDIC's loss from the failed bank increases with the amount of funding in this form. In addition, many of the institutions that failed in 2008–2012 were relatively young banks that relied heavily on brokered deposits to finance growth. Regulators then linked the probability of failure with the amount of brokered deposits. Since the crisis, regulators strongly encouraged banks to reduce their reliance on noncore liabilities.

Bankers often evaluate liquidity risk by looking at static (balance sheet) liquidity ratios and by having a contingency funding plan. The latter compares expected cash inflows with cash outflows under different 'stress scenarios' over different time intervals and identifies sources of cash in the event that unexpected cash outflows might materialize. Chapter 6 describes the basic features of a contingency funding plan.

The UBPR (pages 10 & 10A) provides summary information about different ratios that signal how much liquidity a bank has within its investment securities. It also provides ratios which signal potential illiquidity caused by the bank excessively relying on noncore liabilities. Exhibit 4.9 presents key ratios for FCB versus peer banks in 2012. A short-term instrument has a maturity of one year or less while a long-term instrument has a maturity greater than one year. To help interpret the ratios, note that noncore funding (liabilities) consists primarily of federal funds purchased and repos, brokered deposits and FHLB advances. The net *noncore funding dependency* (NCFD) ratio is defined as:

$$\text{NCFD} = \frac{\text{Noncore liabilities - Short-term investments}}{\text{Long-term assets}}$$

and indicates the extent to which a bank has more short-term liquid assets or more noncore liabilities. When NCFD is positive, the bank is potentially exposed to a liquidity problem if wholesale borrowings disappear. When NCFD is negative, the bank holds more liquid assets than its wholesale borrowings and is very liquid.

The top block of ratios indicates that FCB holds fewer short-term securities relative to peers but also relies less on short-term noncore funding, particularly brokered deposits. Its core deposits exceed 75% of assets but fall below peer amounts. With three out of four assets financed with core deposits, FCB has a stable funding base. The bottom block of ratios indicates that FCB holds fewer loans versus peers recognizing that loans are generally the least liquid asset class. FCB classifies all its securities as AFS so that it can sell every unpledged security it owns at its discretion. Because it pledges just 15% of its securities as collateral, it has the capacity to sell 85% of its holdings which is far more than peers. Finally, the net noncore funding dependence ratio indicates that FCB has a net borrowing exposure which is negligible as the value is close to zero. In general, FCB's liquidity risk appears to be low.

However, it is important to recognize that these static ratios do not adequately capture true liquidity risk. Remember that Bear Stearns and Lehman Brothers held large cash balances at the time they were closed. Both faced liquidity runs when customers withdrew their balances and refused to do business with the firms. As balances fled the firm's accounts, they were unable to sell assets or borrow to replace the lost deposits. Hence, Bear Stearns collapsed into JPMorgan's arms while Lehman failed.

Exhibit 4.9 Liquidity Ratios for First Community Bank
(Percentages, December 31, 2012)

Ratio	FCB	Peers	Percent
Short-term (ST) investments to total assets	5.46	7.85	42
Core deposits to total assets	75.69	77.49	35
Short-term (ST) noncore funding to total assets	5.42	6.73	45
Brokered deposits to deposits	0.00	2.26	41
ST investments to ST noncore funds	100.82	177.51	46
Net loans to deposits	70.58	73.95	40
AFS securities to total assets	33.57	19.91	82
HTM securities to total assets	0.00	0.68	60
Pledged securities to total securities	14.93	42.50	17
Pledged loans to total loans	12.83	25.92	34
Net noncore funding dependence*	7.76	3.49	62

*Deposits of $250,000 or less are designated as core.

Management (M)

When assessing management, regulators consider the performance of senior management and the bank's board of directors in providing oversight for implementing effective risk management policies and practices. A bank's board should have established appropriate risk policies and systematic procedures to identify, measure, monitor and control the various risks. Important responsibilities relate to having meaningful internal policies and controls, timely and accurate reporting of financial information, adequate audits, and the like. It should further ensure that all actions and activities are in compliance with regulations and laws. Of course, the board of directors is responsible for selecting and monitoring the bank's CEO. In essence the management rating is a composite rating linked to how well management plans for and responds to different risks.

Maintaining Adequate Capital to Ensure Solvency (C)

During the recent financial crisis, 140 banks failed in 2009, 157 failed in 2010, 92 failed in 2011 and 51 failed in 2012. Failed banks ultimately saw their capital wiped out because asset values fell below the value of liabilities. When a bank fails, the FDIC attempts to find a buyer for the failed firm's remaining assets and deposits, but must pay insured depositors the full amounts of their claims. Failures produce losses for the FDIC insurance fund. A bank is technically insolvent when the value of its liabilities exceeds the value of its assets. Every bank faces the risk (capital risk) that it might find itself in this position unless, of course, it is considered to be Too Big To Fail.

Regulators expect every bank to operate with an adequate amount of capital which is determined by the types and magnitude of risks assumed in its day-to-day operations as well as management's ability to identify, measure, manage and control the risks. The greater are the risks and weaker are risk management practices, the greater is the amount of capital required. Remember that banks do not have to pay dividends on equity. Higher amounts of equity reduce the amount of financial leverage—and thus lower required interest payments on debt—and raise the amount of assets that must default or losses the bank can realize before the bank is insolvent. Forcing a bank to operate with greater amounts of capital reduces risk but also lowers opportunities to generate profits. High capital increases the likelihood of solvency.

Formally, regulators specify minimum amounts of capital relative to a bank's total assets and risk-weighted assets. There are three formal capital ratios used to assess capital adequacy:

Tier 1 leverage ratio:	Tier 1 capital / Average total assets
Tier 1 risk-based capital ratio:	Tier 1 capital / Risk-weighted assets
Total risk-based capital ratio:	Total capital / Risk-weighted assets

While Chapter 7 addresses capital regulations and planning, key definitions appear below[11]:

- *Tier 1 capital.* Common stock, undivided profits, paid-in surplus and noncumulative perpetual preferred stock minus the sum of intangible assets, identified losses and a portion of deferred tax assets

- *Tier 2 capital.* A portion of the loan loss allowance, cumulative perpetual preferred stock, mandatory convertible debt, term subordinated debt and intermediate-term debt

- *Total capital.* Tier 1 capital plus Tier 2 capital

- *Risk-weighted assets (RWA)*. Assets are placed into categories based on perceived risk with weights assigned to each group from 0% (lowest risk), 20%, 50%, and 100% (highest risk); RWA equals the sum of the dollar amount of assets in each category multiplied by the associated weight

- *Tangible equity.* Tier 1 capital plus cumulative perpetual preferred stock minus intangibles; tangible equity ratio equals tangible equity divided by average total assets

For example, consider a bank with $10 million in cash, $30 million in investments, $65 million in loans, and $5 million in other assets for $100 million in total assets. If these assets are assigned risk weights of 0%, 20%, 100%, and 100%, respectively, RWA equals $76 million as follows:

RWA = 0 ($10) + .20 ($30) + 1 ($65) + 1 ($5) = $76 million

This sample bank will have to operate with its Tier 1 capital and Total capital equal to some minimum percentage of average total assets and risk-weighted assets according to the three ratios introduced earlier. Specifically, regulators classify banks into one of five capital categories based on the values of the three capital ratios according to the measures listed in Exhibit 4.10.

Exhibit 4.10 Capital Categories under Prompt Corrective Action as Part of the FDIC Improvement Act

Category	Total Risk-Based Ratio	Tier 1 Risk-Based Ratio	Tier 1 Leverage Ratio
Well capitalized	> 10%	> 6%	> 5%
Adequately capitalized	> 8%	> 4%	> 4%
Undercapitalized	> 6%	> 3%	> 3%
Significantly undercapitalized*	< 6%	< 3%	< 3%
Critically undercapitalized**	< 6%	< 3%	< 3%

* Tangible equity ratio must be > 2%.
** Tangible equity ratio is < 2%

Each bank must maintain sufficient capital that exceeds each of the target thresholds in Exhibit 4.10 to reach the different capital categories. Thus, to be well capitalized, a bank must maintain at least a 10% Total risk-based ratio, at least a 6% Tier 1 risk-based ratio and at least a 5% Tier 1 leverage ratio. Importantly, banks that are well-capitalized and adequately capitalized have the greatest freedom from regulation and pay the lowest FDIC deposit insurance premiums. Banks that are in the bottom three categories are subject to severe restrictions in how they conduct their business and pay the highest premiums. A primary focus of bank management today is how to increase capital to ensure solvency and allow the pursuit of all normal business strategies.

Sample Bank Example

Assume that management wants its bank to be well-capitalized for regulatory purposes. According to the data in Exhibit 4.10, the sample bank with $76 million in RWA and an assumed $100 million in average assets will have to have a minimum $5 million in Tier 1 capital and $7.6 million in Tier 1 plus Tier 2 capital to meet the minimum capital requirements; (5% of $100 million or 6% of $76 million for Tier 1 and 10% of $76 million) to be well capitalized.[12] Note that a shift in asset holdings may change a bank's RWA and thus its minimum capital requirements. For example, suppose that the sample bank has $5 million in loans mature and invests the proceeds in securities with a 20% risk weight. In doing so, the bank will decrease RWAs by $4 million and thus its required capital because loans carry a higher risk weight. The essential point behind risk-weighting a bank's assets is that a bank with riskier assets will have higher RWA and thus will need to hold a greater amount of capital.

The UBPR provides summary data regarding a bank's capital components, risk-based assets and regulatory capital ratios on pages 11 and 11A. At year-end 2012, FCB reported a Tier 1 risk-based capital ratio of 16.9% (peers = 14.4%), Total risk-based capital ratio of 18.1% (peers = 15.6%) and a Tier 1 leverage ratio of 10.3% (peers = 9.7%). These ratios easily place FCB in the well-capitalized category and all ratios allow FCB's regulatory capital to rank between the 70th and 80th percentile.

STRESS TESTS FOR COMMUNITY BANKS

Banks with capital ratios below requirements to be adequately capitalized are subject to prompt corrective action (PCA) under the Federal Deposit Insurance Corporation Improvement Act (FDICIA) of 1991. However, PCA provisions have been largely ignored during the recent financial crisis. Virtually every material loss review of a failed institution concludes that regulators should have acted sooner.

One regulatory response is a renewed effort to have banks stress test their performance under different economic scenarios. In early 2009, regulators required the 19 TBTF banks to undergo formal stress tests in which regulators conducted a forward-looking assessment of each firm's financial condition under adverse economic conditions.** The intent was to determine whether each firm had sufficient capital to absorb potential losses. The conclusion was that 9 firms were sufficiently well-capitalized, while the 10 others needed to raise a combined $74.7 billion in external capital. Under the most adverse scenario, all firms would have lost an estimated $599 billion largely from residential mortgages and credit card loans. Regulators required additional stress tests for these firms in May 2010 after which they approved many of the firms to pay dividends on common stock. These large institutions are now required to undergo at least an annual *comprehensive capital analysis and review* (CCAR) involving similar stress tests. Since 2011, most large firms have passed subsequent stress tests and many started paying higher dividends and repurchasing stock with regulatory approval.

Given the failure of PCA, regulators will eventually require that all banks conduct stress tests as part of their normal strategic planning and risk assessment. The implication is that the formal regulatory capital ratios are mere guidelines. Regulators will expect banks to have sufficient capital to absorb losses in adverse situations using forward-looking capital ratios. While it is important to have sufficient capital today, it is equally important to have sufficient capital to absorb future losses.

*The analysis was labeled the Supervisory Capital Assessment Program (SCAP). When the results were revealed, the financial markets reacted positively in the belief that participants now had a better handle on how bad the problems might be.

Operational Risk

Banks are expected to identify the risk of loss "resulting from inadequate or failed internal processes, people, and systems, or from external events."[13] In a practical sense, operational risk refers to potential losses from errors, disruptions, fraud or abusive and deceptive practices from having inadequate IT systems, breaches in internal controls, transactions processing and related activities that may interrupt the normal course of doing business with customers. The best way to measure these risks is to regularly evaluate the frequency of adverse events and associated costs from resolving the problems. The best approach to managing operational risk is to have strong policies that have been well-communicated to employees and have controls in place to manage processes and reduce exposures. It is furthermore critical that a bank have detailed internal audit procedures to monitor processes and controls. Regulators have identified these risks as areas of emphasis particularly related to UDAAP and know-your-customer risks.

With rapidly changing technology, banks constantly face cyber attacks from thieves and terrorists, among others. The term *cybersecurity* refers to efforts to protect information from being stolen or compromised in some manner. An example is the *distributed denial-of-service* (DDoS) attack in which hackers flood a computer system with requests and information to try and shut the system down. In May 2013, a group of criminals from around the globe stole $45 million in a few hours by hacking into the databases of prepaid debit cards at large banks in several countries. They fraudulently added funds to individual accounts, removed limits on the amounts that could be withdrawn and obtained account access codes. At a designated time, field operatives simultaneously withdrew funds from the banks' ATMs in many different cities. Why rob a bank with a gun and mask when it's easier and safer to "turn digits into cash?"[14] Banks must invest in secure systems and constantly upgrade their technology to avoid these types of losses.

Legal and Reputational Risk

Legal risk refers to potential loss that might arise from a bank entering into unenforceable contracts and from lawsuits and adverse judgments. *Reputational risk* refers to potential loss of business from negative publicity. Both risks may adversely affect how a bank conducts its operations because they can alter normal business practices. They may also involve large litigation costs and the loss of revenue from departing customers.

It is difficult to measure these exposures. However, to mitigate these risks banks should have an effective risk management committee which employs a chief compliance officer. These individuals are responsible for ensuring awareness of and compliance with key regulations, such as Anti-Money Laundering, the Bank Secrecy Act, the U.S. Patriot Act, the Community Reinvestment Act and related legislation and regulatory requirements related to consumer compliance. When problems arise, employees should be well-versed in how to respond externally to customers and the media to protect the bank's reputation. Finally, senior management must ensure that the bank has the appropriate internal controls and must periodically test these controls to validate the bank's preparedness.

Summary

It is important to understand how a bank generates profits. It is also important to know how to accurately assess a bank's risk profile. While every bank is different, most community banks rely on net interest income to drive overall profitability. The spread between interest earned and interest paid must be sufficiently large to cover operating costs in excess of noninterest income, provisions for loan losses and taxes. If these expenses are unusually high, as is common at banks reporting large provisions because they have significant volumes of problem loans, a bank will report a loss. Any subsequent loss, in turn, depletes stockholders equity unless the bank raises external capital. This chapter introduces a bank's basic balance sheet and income statement. It then identifies the key components of a bank's risk profile in the context of CAMELS. This acronym refers to a bank's capital adequacy (C), asset quality (A), effectiveness of management (M), earnings (E), liquidity (L), and sensitivity to market risk. It also introduces operational, legal and reputation risk. To help demonstrate how to interpret data, the chapter incorporates historical UBPR data for First Community Bank, a midsize bank headquartered in Lexington, South Carolina. It specifically introduces balance sheet and income statement data for 2012 and key risk ratios for 2012 and preceding years.

The next chapter examines how to interpret key profitability ratios and metrics commonly associated with shareholder value. It is important that bank managers and directors develop an ability to critically evaluate reported profit and risk ratios and these valuation metrics. They should also develop an early warning system of key risk ratios so that they can anticipate problems before they become extreme. Valuation metrics will, in turn, signal whether the bank is creating value over time.

Appendix

FDIC Certificate # 34047 OCC Charter # 0 Public Report	FRB District/ID_RSSD 5 / 2328137 County: LEXINGTON				FIRST COMMUNITY BANK ; LEXINGTON Summary Ratios--Page 1				
	12/31/2012			12/31/2011			12/31/2010		
Earnings and Profitability	BANK	PG 3	PCT	BANK	PG 3	PCT	BANK	PG 3	PCT
Percent of Average Assets:									
Interest Income (TE)	3.90	4.23	27	4.22	4.50	29	4.52	4.78	30
- Interest Expense	0.80	0.66	69	1.12	0.90	73	1.47	1.22	72
Net Interest Income (TE)	3.10	3.56	19	3.10	3.60	18	3.06	3.56	19
+ Noninterest Income	1.34	0.78	85	0.98	0.71	73	0.74	0.72	57
- Noninterest Expense	3.18	2.93	67	2.99	2.93	55	2.86	2.94	48
- Provision: Loan & Lease Losses	0.08	0.30	22	0.23	0.53	32	0.31	0.80	26
Pretax Operating Income (TE)	1.17	1.16	46	0.86	0.89	41	0.62	0.59	40
+ Realized Gains/Losses Sec	-0.03	0.07	3	0.05	0.05	64	-0.12	0.05	4
Pretax Net Operating Income (TE)	1.15	1.25	41	0.91	0.95	40	0.50	0.65	35
Net Operating Income	0.77	0.92	38	0.63	0.67	39	0.37	0.44	36
Adjusted Net Operating Income	0.76	0.90	38	0.59	0.68	36	0.38	0.56	34
Net Inc Attrib to Min Ints	0.00	0.00	98	0.00	0.00	98	0.00	0.00	98
Net Income Adjusted Sub S	0.77	0.83	41	0.63	0.60	41	0.37	0.38	36
Net Income	0.77	0.92	38	0.63	0.67	39	0.37	0.44	36
Margin Analysis:									
Avg Earning Assets to Avg Assets	92.02	93.26	32	91.12	93.16	22	91.09	93.08	24
Avg Int-Bearing Funds to Avg Assets	85.27	78.22	80	86.30	79.79	83	84.59	81.05	67
Int Inc (TE) to Avg Earn Assets	4.23	4.55	29	4.63	4.85	35	4.97	5.15	36
Int Expense to Avg Earn Assets	0.87	0.71	71	1.23	0.96	76	1.61	1.31	74
Net Int Inc-TE to Avg Earn Assets	3.37	3.83	20	3.40	3.88	20	3.36	3.84	22
Loan & Lease Analysis:									
Net Loss to Average Total LN&LS	0.17	0.51	32	0.50	0.80	46	0.54	1.01	42
Earnings Coverage of Net Losses (X)	12.57	11.79	69	4.04	7.50	51	3.07	5.56	52
LN&LS Allowance to LN&LS Not HFS	1.39	1.77	31	1.45	1.93	30	1.49	1.97	33
LN&LS Allowance to Net Losses (X)	8.05	7.41	69	2.88	4.85	48	2.70	3.72	55
LN&LS Allowance to Total LN&LS	1.35	1.74	30	1.43	1.90	30	1.49	1.94	34
Total LN&LS-90+ Days Past Due	0.02	0.07	55	0.01	0.08	47	0.11	0.11	66
-Nonaccrual	1.38	1.91	47	1.65	2.64	43	1.79	3.06	42
-Total	1.40	2.06	45	1.65	2.79	40	1.90	3.24	41
Liquidity									
Net Non Core Fund Dep New $250M	7.76	3.45	62	12.39	5.83	69	13.56	9.12	64
Net Loans & Leases to Assets	55.88	62.30	30	54.44	62.82	25	54.33	65.77	17
Capitalization									
Tier One Leverage Capital	10.34	9.67	69	9.27	9.40	49	8.48	9.02	37
Cash Dividends to Net Income	6.91	32.27	33	0.00	28.25	37	0.00	26.27	42
Retained Earnings to Avg Total Equity	6.69	4.49	67	6.55	2.74	72	4.18	0.71	55
Rest+Nonac+RE Acq to Eqcap+ALLL	13.48	23.10	40	25.15	31.13	54	27.82	35.71	54
Growth Rates									
Total Assets	1.60	5.13	34	-0.73	4.09	26	-1.05	1.78	34
Tier One Capital	11.22	6.44	80	8.11	5.82	65	5.13	3.67	50
Net Loans & Leases	4.27	3.64	55	-0.52	-0.56	52	-4.21	-1.99	40
Short Term Investments	147.59	33.76	86	-57.99	36.82	9	107.57	58.11	76

This UBPR information is from the FDIC's web site, www.fdic.gov, under the Analysts tab. It includes summary performance ratios related to earnings, net interest margin, loans, liquidity and capitalization. The first column describes a specific ratio or data item. The three blocks of ratios are annual data for the years 2010, 2011 and 2012. For each year, the first column titled 'Bank' provides the ratio for First Community Bank (FCB). The second column titled 'PG 3' presents the same ratio representing the average value for all bank's in FCB's peer group. Peer group 3 refers to all insured commercial banks having assets between $300 million and $1 billion. The third column titled 'PCT' provides the percentile rank for FCB's ratio. As such, the bank's ROA (Net Income as a Percent of Average Assets) of 0.77% in 2012 is less than the peer group 3 average of 0.92% such that FCB's ROA was higher than 38% of the 1,200 banks in the peer group.

CHAPTER 5
Earnings and Shareholder Value Analysis

Toward the end of every calendar year, most banks attempt to develop a budget and refine their strategic plan for the upcoming year. In recent years, the focus has often been on defensive strategies to navigate through the difficult economic times and uncertain regulatory environment. In short, many banks have focused on risk management efforts to increase capital and liquidity while improving asset quality. While important, growing earnings has received far less attention.

However, to thrive in the increasingly competitive environment banks must again focus on growing earnings and shareholder value. When asked how well your bank is performing, most directors and managers mention trends in the dollar amount of net income along with aggregate profit ratios. They cite terms such as return on equity (ROE) and return on assets (ROA) along with comparisons to peer institutions. There is great comfort in noting that profitability exceeds peers even when the dollar amount of earnings is low. Very few directors and managers discuss shareholder value and key measures that track changes in this value. Of course, banks that want to grow and/or acquire other firms must continually increase shareholder value. Similarly, bank owners and managers who want to position their institution for sale should focus on value creation which will determine what a buyer might pay.

This chapter initially examines standard measures of profitability and shareholder value. It then examines traditional measures that represent drivers of shareholder value. It thus lays a foundation for developing strategies to enhance profitability and increase shareholder value over time. A bank's board of directors is responsible for setting the strategic direction of the institution and ensuring that management has sound policies and procedures in place to achieve key objectives. Senior management is responsible for implementing the strategies.

Profitability Analysis Using Financial Ratios

Most analysts attempt to evaluate a bank's profitability by constructing ratios that indicate the source and magnitude of revenue, expense and net income over time and relative to a peer group of banks. Because of differences in organizational structure, business strategy, size, and the types of markets served, a bank's management should identify a specific group of peer institutions that operate in the same geographic markets, follow the same basic business strategies, and offer the same types of products and services. It is also important to control for size due to differences in operating efficiencies. The ratios selected for comparison purposes should reflect the measures that the bank's board of directors has determined will best guide strategies going forward. Thus, most managers will decompose revenue and expense ratios into factors related to the mix and volume of earning assets, interest-bearing liabilities and noninterest-bearing deposits.

The following analysis again focuses on performance ratios for First Community Bank (FCB) which was introduced in Chapter 4. Exhibit 5.1 presents aggregate profitability ratios for FCB compared with the same ratios for national peer institutions in the same size category using 2012 data. Data in the final column indicate the percentage of banks with a lower figure compared with peers. For a more comprehensive understanding of performance, an analyst should examine these ratio comparisons over a longer period of time to determine important trends and longer-term values. This effort should lead to further areas of research to better understand a bank's performance drivers.

Exhibit 5.1 Key Profitability Ratios for First Community Bank, (December 31, 2012)

Ratio	Value for FCB	Peers	Percent
Return on equity (ROE)	7.19%	8.72%	37
Return on assets (ROA)	0.77%	0.92%	38
Total assets / Equity (EM)	9.3×	9.5×	67
Interest income (te) / Total assets	3.90%	4.23%	26
Yield on earning assets (te)	4.23%	4.55%	29
Yield on loans (te)	5.54%	5.65%	46
Yield on investments (te)	2.41%	2.71%	38
Interest expense / Total assets	0.80%	0.66%	69
Rate paid on interest-bearing deposits	0.68%	0.76%	41
Rate paid on all interest-bearing funds*	0.94%	0.85%	59
Net interest margin (NIM) (te)	3.37%	3.83%	20
Net loans / Total assets	54.70%	62.58%	27
Real estate loans / Total loans	92.31%	76.60%	92
1–4 Residential loans / Total loans	31.33%	25.17%	68
Owner-occ. nonfarm, nonresidential / Total loans	22.68%	16.58%	76
Other nonfarm, nonresidential / Total loans	30.04%	16.06%	89
Commercial & independent loans / Total loans	6.06%	13.63%	15
Municipal securities / Total securities	15.95%	23.77%	37
CMO & REMIC MBSs / Total securities	43.56%	11.28%	91
U.S. Treas. & Agency securities / Total securities	27.84%	23.60%	61
Core deposits / Total assets	75.90%	76.85%	39
Demand deposits / Total assets**	3.84%	9.18%	19

Ratio	Value for FCB	Peers	Percent
Earning assets / Total assets	90.14%	91.99%	23
Interest-bearing funds / Total assets	85.27%	78.23%	80
Noninterest income / Total assets	1.34%	0.78%	85
Noninterest expense / Total assets	3.18%	2.93%	67
Net noninterest expense / Total assets	1.84%	2.15%	
Personnel expense / Total assets	1.83%	1.56%	75
Avg. personnel expense per employee ($000)	$69.93	$68.36	59
Assets per employee ($ millions)	$3.79	$4.71	33
Occupancy expense / Total assets	0.42%	0.36%	68
Efficiency (Noninterest expense/Operating income)	71.68%	66.81%	67
Provision for loan losses / Total assets	0.08%	0.30%	22
Realized gains/losses on securities / Total assets	–0.03%	0.07%	3
Pre-tax net operating income (te) / Total assets	1.17%	1.17%	46
Net operating income / Total assets	0.77%	0.92%	38

*Reflects the cost of a large amount of FHLB advances.
** Reported demand deposits are relatively low because FCB sweeps "excess deposits" into savings

Aggregate Profitability Ratios

When reporting summary profit ratios, most bank managers initially cite the bank's ROE and ROA. These ratios compare a bank's net income to average stockholders equity and average total assets, respectively, and thus represent aggregate profitability:[1]

ROE = Net income / Average stockholders equity

ROA = Net income / Average total assets

Define a bank's *equity multiplier* (EM) as average total assets divided by average stockholders equity. A bank with $100 million in assets and $10 million in stockholders equity will thus have an EM = ($100/$10) = 10×. Another bank with $100 million in assets but just $5 million in equity will have an EM = ($100/$5) = 20×. As such, an EM measures financial leverage or the amount of assets financed by equity and debt. The greater the EM, the greater the financial leverage because proportionately more assets are financed with debt and less with stockholders equity.

In general,

ROE = ROA × EM

or

ROE = (Net income/Avg. total assets) × (Avg. total assets/Avg. stockholders equity)

In 2012, FCB's ROE equaled 7.19% while its ROA was 0.77%, both of which were below national peers ranking the bank in the 37th and 38th percentiles, respectively.[2] FCB was thus a below-average performance bank in terms of these aggregate profit ratios. In terms of EM, FCB's assets were 9.3× greater than equity, or slightly below the 9.5× factor for peers indicating that FCB operates with lower relative amounts of debt (greater equity) than peers. It is thus slightly less risky because it has proportionately more equity. At the same time, FCB generated an ROA that was 0.15% (15 basis points) below peers' ROA. The cumulative impact was to lower ROE well below peers.

It is important to decompose ROA to determine why aggregate net income differs from peers. The next block of ratios indicates that FCB generated less in interest income versus peers. First, it earned lower average yields on loans and securities. Second, the net loan to asset ratio indicates that FBC invested proportionately less in loans and more in securities versus peers with loan yields, on average, much higher than security yields. Finally, FCB held fewer earning assets and thus more nonearning assets. These different rate, mix and volume effects lowered interest income. In turn, FCB's interest expense was 14 basis points more (0.80% vs. 0.66%) relative to assets. This was caused by paying higher rates on other liabilities, by holding fewer noninterest bearing demand deposits and by paying interest on a much higher fraction of its total funding (85.3% vs. 78.2%). Again, these rate, mix and volume effects worked against FCB by raising interest expense. The combined impact was to push net interest income 46 basis points lower than peers as measured by the net interest margin (3.37% vs. 3.83%).

Related ratios signal a different business strategy for FCB than the average peer institution. For one, FCB is more heavily exposed to real estate loans and less invested in commercial and industrial loans. Of the real estate loans, FCB holds more one-to four-family family residential mortgages, nonfarm owner-occupied real estate, and other nonfarm real estate. The lower loan yield is a result of this lower risk loan mix. Similarly, while FCB holds more securities than peers relative to assets, its holdings are concentrated in U.S. Treasury and agency securities and relatively low-risk *collateralized mortgage obligations* (CMOs). Hence, the bank earns a lower average yield on its total securities portfolio.

The lower NIM, however, is partially offset by substantially greater noninterest income. FCB operates Palmetto South Mortgage, an active mortgage division, and First Community Financial Consultants, a fee-based financial planning and investment advisory division. In 2012, FCB reported noninterest income that was 0.56% higher than peers as a percentage of assets. Even with deposit service charges dropping from $2.7 million in 2008 to $1.6 million in 2012, total noninterest income rose from $4.5 million to $8 million over the same period. One of FCB's greatest strengths is its diversified revenue stream. With pressure on NIM in recent years, FCB has been able to rely on fees from noninterest sources to grow earnings.

In 2012, FCB reported noninterest expense that was 0.25% higher relative to assets when compared with peers. The higher noninterest expense can be attributed to higher personnel and occupancy expenses. Personnel expense includes wages, salaries, and employee benefits while occupancy expense includes charges associated with fixed assets and overhead costs. FCB's personnel expense exceeded peers because it pays commissions to certain employees in its mortgage and advisory divisions. Because it has two fee-generating divisions where compensation is tied to sales, FCB focuses on its net noninterest expense (noninterest expense - noninterest income) to total assets to assess performance. As noted in Exhibit 5.1, this net figure was 31 basis points below peers suggesting better overall performance.

Some analysts examine the *efficiency ratio,* which compares noninterest expense with the sum of noninterest income and net interest income (*labeled net operating income*):

$$\text{Efficiency ratio} = \frac{\text{Noninterest expense}}{\text{Net interest income} + \text{Noninterest income}}$$

This ratio indicates how much a bank pays in total noninterest expense to produce $1 of revenue. A lower figure is generally viewed as better because it signals a lower unit cost to generate revenue. FCB's efficiency ratio was 71.7% in 2012 or almost 5% more than that for peers suggesting that it was less efficient. One criticism of the efficiency ratio is that it doesn't consider the potential returns on investing. For example, the traditional method to evaluate new investments is a net present value approach whereby the initial investment is compared with the present value of the stream of future net cash flows generated from the investment. The efficiency ratio captures none of this and may direct attention to short-run performance rather than true returns over time. Consider the investment in mobile banking. It will likely immediately increase noninterest expense and thereby raise the efficiency ratio suggesting a lack of effective spending. In reality, failure to invest in mobile banking may eventually drive profitable customers to other venues such that long-term performance is seriously damaged.

The last block of ratios further indicates that FCB reported lower provisions for loan losses (0.08% vs 0.30%) in 2012 relative to assets consistent with its better asset quality (lower credit risk) as discussed in Chapter 4. During the financial crisis, this ratio peaked at 0.49% for FCB in 2009 when the comparative peer figure also peaked at 1.12%. While lower provisions helps increase ROA, the benefit to FCB going forward will be small as the bank will likely not reduce its provisions below zero. In terms of securities gains or losses, FCB sold securities as a net (small) loss which lowered ROA slightly. Finally, the last two ratios suggest that FCB is paying proportionately more in taxes than peers. This is consistent with the bank holding fewer tax-sheltered municipal bonds.

Impact of Organizational Structure on Profit Ratios

It is important to note that a bank's organizational structure and business strategy play a large role in determining aggregate profitability measures. Consider the data for an S Corp bank that has fewer than 100 stockholders and thus does not pay corporate income tax at the federal level. Instead, the bank passes income through to its stockholders who pay income taxes on the amounts transferred at their personal tax rate. Without a federal corporate tax obligation, an S Corp bank will report a higher ROA that uses after-tax net income, holding everything else constant. It is thus inappropriate to compare the performance of S Corp banks with otherwise comparable C

Corp banks. Similarly, in good times a bank that is loan driven and focuses on commercial and industrial (C&I) or consumer lending should report higher pre-provision earnings in the short run especially compared with a bank facing limited loan demand that is deposit driven. Pre-tax and pre-provision loan yields are much higher than security yields such that net income is typically much higher during good economic times. Of course, during times of credit crises, loan driven banks will report higher charge-offs, higher nonperforming loans, and thus higher provisions for loan losses which leads to lower ROE and ROA. The essential point is that a bank's business strategy and clientele will also drive relative profitability.

Consider Exhibits 5.2 and 5.3, which present industry averages for ROE and ROA from 2004 to mid-2013. During the early 2000's, industry average ROE fell modestly from over 15% to 11.5% only to drop sharply from 2007 to 2009 when it actually went negative. It has subsequently increased due largely to the recovery in earnings at the largest banking organizations. Exhibit 5.3 documents the same pattern for ROA falling from 1.4% to 1.2% only to fall negative during the crisis. By 2012, the industry average returned to 1%. As described previously, S Corp banks reported sharply higher ROAs than C Corp banks or mutuals with assets below $1 billion because they don't pay income taxes at the federal level. Exhibit 5.4 documents a difference of 0.85% at mid-2013.

Exhibit 5.2 FDIC-Insured Banks: Quarterly Return on Equity (ROE), Annualized, 2004 -2013

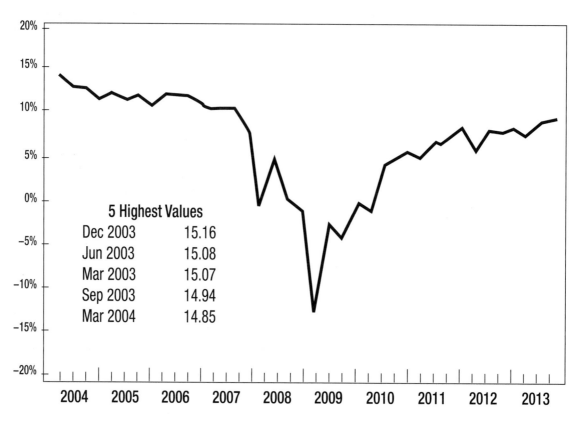

Quarterly Banking Profile, FDIC at www.fdic.gov

COMMUNITY BANKING | FROM CRISIS TO PROSPERITY

Exhibit 5.3 FDIC-Insured Institutions: Quarterly Return on Assets (ROA), Annualized, 2004 - 2013

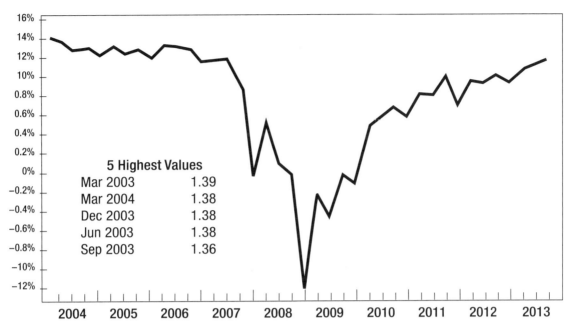

Quarterly Banking Profile, FDIC at www.fdic.gov

Exhibit 5.4 FDIC-Insured Institutions:
Quarterly Return on Assets of Subchapter S Corporations vs. Other Banks, Annualized, 2003–2013

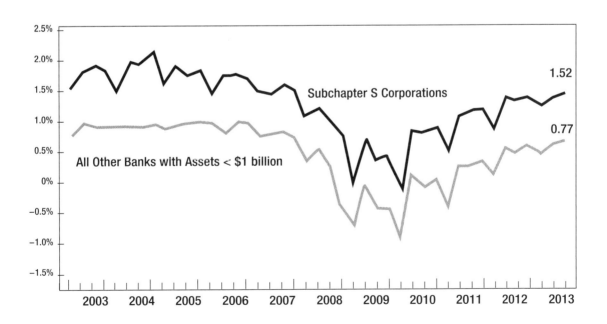

Strategic Performance Objectives

Managers of banks that have publicly-traded stock recognize that the price of a share of the bank's common stock reveals the market's ongoing perception of the bank's current and expected performance. Of course, the information content in the quoted price depends on how widely held the stock is among different investors, how frequently the stock is traded and how much confidence investors have in management. For example, if an ownership group has controlling interest in the bank or if a bank's stock is thinly traded without much liquidity, the stock price is much less informative. Still, the stock price is an indicator of performance.

How Do Investors in Banks Realize Value?

Assume that you buy 100 shares of common stock in your local community bank at $10 per share. Ignoring the commission, you pay $1,000. Your objective is to generate a true financial return and not simply support a local business. How do you expect to earn a return on your investment? The answer is that value creation potentially comes in three different forms. First, the bank may pay cash dividends or stock dividends. In this case, you will periodically receive cash based on the amount of the dividend payment per share or you will receive additional shares. Second, the price of the stock may increase above $10 such that you have the opportunity to sell your shares for more than $1,000. Finally, the bank may be sold. If the buyer pays more for your shares than your $1,000 investment, you have effectively generated a return from share price appreciation driven by the buyer's willingness to pay a premium.

The ultimate questions are thus what factors lead to an increased ability to pay dividends and/or drive the market stock price higher? What factors increase the potential market value to an acquirer? While the questions are straightforward, the answers are complex. Banks are heavily regulated. Their business strategies and operating performance must thus conform to what regulators view as sound banking practices. In addition, analysts regularly track bank performance ratios to assess value. As such, bank managers must be aware of analysts' critiques and expectations and general market conditions and adjust their strategies accordingly.

There are three basic drivers of shareholder value creation for a community bank from the view of stockholders:

- Cash earnings per share
- Tangible book value of equity
- Core deposit funding.

Banks that attempt to maximize these metrics will realize increases in shareholder value if they successfully increase these performance measures over time. This is true regardless of whether or not the bank has publicly-traded stock. Managers should attempt to maximize these value drivers while they simultaneously ensure that the bank's other stakeholders—customers, employees and the community at large—are treated favorably. In addition to these financial metrics, managers should also focus on customer satisfaction and retention, employee satisfaction and retention, and the pecuniary and nonpecuniary contributions of the bank and its employees to the local community. Such a balanced emphasis benefits the community and stockholders.

Cash Earnings Per Share

In normal times when analysts have confidence in a bank's asset quality and the associated profit measures, they value a bank on the basis of how much a bank earns relative to the number of shares of common stock outstanding.[4] The typical measure is *earnings per share* (EPS) defined as net income divided by the number of common shares outstanding. It is better, however, to ignore noncash items, such as provisions for loan losses, depreciation and amortization because operating cash flow is a better determinant of long-term value. One-time gains and losses, such as those associated with the sale of a subsidiary or the gain or loss on securities transactions, should be viewed as having a temporary rather than permanent effect on earnings:

$$\text{Cash earnings per share} = \frac{\text{Operating Cash Flow}}{\text{Number of shares of common stock outstanding}}$$

where operating cash flow equals net income adjusted for non-cash and one-time items.[5] The value of the bank is then determined as some multiple of the cash EPS figure. Note that management can effectively increase this measure either by increasing operating cash flow or by reducing the number of shares outstanding. In good times, many banks have implemented stock buyback programs intended to reduce the number of shares outstanding and thus put upward pressure on cash EPS and the bank's stock price. Generally, EPS changes over time with changes in net interest income, noninterest income and noninterest expense. Managers attempting to increase EPS thus typically focus on growing net interest income, fee-based services, and managing noninterest expense to maximize long-term returns.

The link between cash EPS and value creation comes initially via dividend payments. A bank that is growing earnings is increasing capital through retaining earnings. This enables management to actively grow loans and pursue new investments. Managers and the board also have the capacity to pay dividends and increase dividend payments over time. Both of these, in turn, increase a bank's stock price by signaling to investors that they will receive a periodic return on investment and not have to wait until they sell their shares.

Common measures that reflect value creation from dividends (ultimately earnings) are:
- Dividends per share ($)
- Growth rate in dividends (%)
- Dividend yield (%)
- Dividend payout ratio (%)
- Stock dividends or stock splits

Suppose that the bank that sold you $1,000 of stock at $10 per share paid $0.40 per share in dividends the first year you owned the stock. Your realized dividend yield was 4% ($0.40/$10). If it increased the dividend to $0.45 the next year, your dividend yield would increase to 4.5%.[6] The growth rate in dividends would be 12.5% for the second year. In general, markets cite dividend yields as the annualized cash dividend divided by the current share price. Thus, if the share price rose to $11 in the second year when the bank paid $0.45 per share, the quoted dividend yield would be 4.09%. This yield reflects what a new investor in the stock might earn if the dividend remains at the most recent level. For most community banks, stock prices will rise as dividends and dividend yields increase, everything else held constant.

Investors also consider a bank's dividend payout ratio. This figure measures the proportion of net income that the bank pays out in cash dividends. A bank with a low dividend payout ratio is generally presumed to have a greater capacity to increase dividend payments in the future if net income remains strong. A stock dividend

$$\text{Dividend payout ratio} = \frac{\text{Cash dividends paid}}{\text{Net income}}$$

arises when a bank pays a dividend in the form of additional shares of common stock rather than cash. In the original example, if the bank gave you one shares of stock for each 100 shares you owned, you would receive a 1% stock dividend, or 0.01 shares for each share owned. Of course, the bank is simply increasing the number of outstanding shares of stock, which should lower the price of each share. A stock split is functionally the same as a stock dividend because the bank simply creates more shares from existing shares held by investors. For example, a 4-for-1 stock split would mean that an investor owning 100 shares now owns 400 shares. Again, the total dollar value of shares outstanding does not change from the pre-split value.[7]

The link between EPS and value creation is also driven by share price appreciation. Specifically, there is a positive relationship over time between EPS growth and share price appreciation. This derives from an expected increase in stockholders equity in dollar terms, an expected increase in the bank's ability to pay cash dividends, and the recognition that a stockholder has an increasingly valuable claim against a perpetual stream of bank cash flows. In one sense, a stock's price equals the present value of expected future cash flows provided by the bank which should rise with earnings over time.

Common measures that signal potential share price appreciation include:

- EPS and EPS growth
- Stock price (P) to earnings multiple (P/EPS = P/E multiple)
- Tangible book value per share (TBVS)
- Stock price to tangible book value per share (P/TBVS)
- Market depth and trading liquidity

The potential impact of these factors can be demonstrated via examples using the bank stock information presented earlier. Suppose that the bank which sold the investor 100 shares for $10 per share reported cash EPS of $1 for the year. Given the economic and regulatory environment, bank stocks were trading at a multiple of 10× earnings (P = $10 for each $1 of EPS). This means that the common stock of the bank would be trading around $10 per share (10 × $1). As such, changes in both the price to earnings multiple (P/E = 10×) and EPS affect the market value of the stock. If the $1 of bank EPS grows by 12.5% next period to $1.125 and the price to earnings multiple stays at 10×, the banks share price will rise to $11.25 (10 × 1.125). Thus the level and growth in EPS impact market value along with the P/E multiple.

Stock market analysts and consultants are especially enamored of peer group comparisons. Whenever they assign a valuation to a bank, they almost always cite it relative to peers. Hence, they often support P/E multiples that are "in line with peers' multiples." In the previous case, an analyst might justify the 10× P/E multiple because it reflects the trading value for an group of peers with publicly-traded stock. This obviously ignores factors unique to a specific institution. It also ignores problems with identifying the best (or correct) group of peer institutions.

Changes in a bank's book value of equity affect market values in a similar manner. The next value driver is a bank's tangible book value of equity per share (TBVS), which is formally defined in the next section. View this conceptually as the liquidation value of common stock to a bank investor upon bankruptcy. Market participants value banks as some multiple of book value much like the P/E multiple where the value changes with economic conditions and the regulatory environment. Suppose that the above bank had an initial TBVS of $8. At $10 per share, it was valued at a multiple of 1.25 × TBVS.[8] Suppose further that TBVS grows by $0.125 reflecting the growth in EPS where the bank pays no dividend. If the book value multiple remains at 1.25×, the stock price will rise to $10.16. With strong earnings growth, book value multiples typically increase so the actual jump in share price would likely be greater. To get the same $11.25 stock price under the price to EPS framework, the tangible book value multiple would have to increase to 1.37× ($11.125/$8.125).

These valuation metrics work best for banks with publicly-traded stock where the depth of trading is deep. Banks with privately-held stock should continuously track these metrics, but quoted share prices will typically not reflect such changes in value. The reason is that liquidity in the stock is low. Liquidity is often discussed in terms of market depth. Market depth and liquidity are deep when there is a consistent high volume of trades so that single large orders do not move the stock price. Banks with stocks traded in highly liquid markets can regularly get a good estimate of actual market value of stock. Without an active secondary market, quoted stock prices are stale. This is especially the case where one party or family has a controlling interest in a company. Quoted prices will not generally reflect the true underlying value of the bank because the owners make the rules in deciding when to sell. A buyer of new stock cannot affect the behavior of the majority owners in any meaningful way so the quoted price is not all that revealing.

CHAPTER 5

Takeout Value

The final way that investors realize value in owning bank stock is when the bank sells to a new ownership group. This takeout value is affected by many factors, but measures of TBVS and the value of core deposit funding receive considerable attention. In good times, buyers of banks often pay premiums of 30% to 50% over the current share price.

Tangible Book Value of Equity Per Share (TBVS)

Another valuation driver uses balance sheet values of all assets and liabilities in order to estimate the value of a share of stock if a bank were to liquidate in a bankruptcy. Formally, tangible book value of equity per share equals the amount of net tangible assets divided by the number of shares of common stock outstanding. Net tangible assets, in turn, equals the amount of assets reported on a bank's balance sheet (books) minus all intangible assets, minus all liabilities, and minus the par value of any outstanding preferred stock:

$$\text{Tangible book value of equity per share} = \frac{\text{Net tangible assets}}{\text{Number of shares of common stock outstanding}}$$

where

$$\text{Net Tangible Assets} = \text{Book value of total assets} - \text{intangible assets} - \text{liabilities} - \text{par value of preferred stock};$$

intangible assets include items such as goodwill and the value of trademarks and patents

Conceptually, this figure represents what a shareholder could expect to receive upon liquidation of the bank if the bank could sell all tangible assets at the values reported on the balance sheet and pay back all debts and preferred stock at the values reported. Buyers of banks will pay some multiple of this tangible book value of equity depending on market conditions at the time of the purchase. As demonstrated previously, the actual price paid will equal a market-determined multiple (reflecting prevailing economic and regulatory conditions) times this book value figure. This multiple is commonly cited in tracking the appeal of bank acquisitions to both buyers and sellers. When banking was booming, community bank sellers would often hold out to receive at least 2× book value (a higher multiple of TBVS). With the difficult economic environment and additional regulatory scrutiny about bank activities, the days of 2× book value are gone.

Core Deposit Funding

It is widely recognized that a primary source of value for a bank is its core deposit balances. Because these deposits are FDIC-insured, banks pay rates below what they would otherwise pay for uninsured deposits. Customers hold these balances for business purposes and liquidity and are not especially sensitive to the interest rate they earn. In economic terms, core deposits exhibit low interest elasticity. This means that when banks change the interest rate paid on the deposit, the dollar amount of balances does not change by a greater proportionate amount. Witness what has happened since the onset of the financial crisis. Since 2008, banks have generally lowered rates paid on interest checking, savings accounts, MMDAs, small-time deposits, and the like; and banks are flush with these deposits and the corresponding liquidity.

Bankers have coined the term *core deposit premium* to measure this value. Specifically, in a market transaction where one bank buys another bank or in a failed bank transaction, the core deposit premium equals the amount an acquiring bank pays in excess of the book value of the deposits for the selling bank. Acquiring banks are willing to pay a premium for core deposits (accept less than the book value of the deposit liabilities when they assume them in an acquisition) because (1) they can invest the proceeds at a profitable spread to the rate paid on the deposits, (2) they will have the opportunity to cross-sell nondeposit products and services to the acquired bank's customers, and (3) it may be a relatively low-cost approach to enter new geographic markets. This holds true even in a low interest rate environment.[9] Of course, there are significant risks in that some customers will not want to deal with the acquiring bank and thus some deposits will run off.

Bank analysts and managers recognize that core deposits represent a fundamental driver of a bank's value. Thus, they examine the amount and proportion of funding derived from low-cost core deposits. Note the emphasis on low cost. Core deposits generally include all transactions accounts, money market deposit accounts, savings accounts, and small (< $250,000 denomination) time deposits. These deposits are typically stable and do not leave the bank when interest rates change. The core deposit premium equals a percentage of these balances:

Core deposit premium = (%) × low-cost core deposits

It is important to recognize that not all balances are truly "core" because banks can buy these deposits by agreeing to pay high interest rates. In fact, one significant impact of the financial crisis of 2007–2011 was that it motivated banks to shift their funding from borrowed funds to core deposits. Not surprisingly, some banks pursued this strategy by paying rates on CDs and transactions accounts that were well above rates available on borrowed funds. Ally Bank (the former GMAC Bank) remains one of the most aggressive participants typically paying rates among the five highest rate payers in the United States on all types of transactions and savings accounts, money market deposit accounts, and CDs. No buyer of a bank would pay a premium for these balances as the bulk of them will leave when the bank stops paying high rates.

The previous discussion emphasizes the importance of multiples in determining takeout value when a bank sells. As mentioned, consultants and analysts typically justify the multiples used by citing acquisition values for comparable peer bank transactions. However, a bank acquisition also potentially affects value by increasing the potential dividends paid to the acquiring bank. For example, suppose that an acquiring bank can successfully reduce expenses (combined) after an acquisition without affecting the quality of customer service. The bank now has a capacity to pay higher dividends to its stockholders. Analysts attempt to measure this incremental value by estimating the present value of the incremental dividends that could be paid from the expense savings.

CHAPTER 5

Value Creation at First Community Corporation

First Community Bank is a subsidiary of a bank holding company, First Community Corporation (FCC). It operates 11 branches located in the central region of South Carolina and two divisions, First Community Financial Corporation and Palmetto South Mortgage. The divisions offer financial planning and investment advisory services and mortgage services, respectively. FCC's common stock trades on the NASDAQ Capital Market under the symbol FCCO. Exhibit 5.5 presents valuation data for FCC rather than FCB. The data are values for 2012 and year-end 2012 as noted.

FCC had an extraordinary year in terms of performance and operating structure. During 2012, it raised $15 million via a common stock offering and used the proceeds to repay $11.3 million in preferred stock it previously issued to the U.S. Treasury under the Troubled Asset Relief Program (TARP) – capital purchase program (CPP) and redeem $292,500 in warrants. It also repurchased $2.5 million in outstanding subordinated debt. FCC thereby sharply changed its capital structure to increase common stock outstanding and lower other forms of regulatory capital. After reducing its quarterly cash dividend from $0.08 to $0.04 for three years, the bank raised it to $0.05 per common share at the end of 2012. The valuation metrics in Exhibit 5.5 incorporate the increased number of shares outstanding and restructure of the balance sheet.

These measures reflect the unusual environment facing community banks. As discussed in Chapter 4, FCB exhibits above average asset quality, capital, and liquidity. Chapter 5, however, documents earnings that are below the average for national peers. Most of the valuation measures are consistent with common themes for community banks. First, cash EPS exceeds EPS due to the existence of numerous noncash expenses and some extraordinary items. FCC, in turn, reported a one-time loss on the extinguishment of its outstanding subordinated debt. Net income available for common stockholders is less than what FCB reported as net income because the bank paid a substantial dividend to preferred stockholders under the TARP-CPP.

At the end of 2012, FCC's common stock was trading at $8.39 per share. This was just 6.8× cash EPS but equaled 10.4× EPS. Book value and TBVS are close because FCC has few intangible assets. As such, the P/TBVS of 0.80 is close to the price to book value ratio. Note, however, that each of these is well below 1.0. This indicates that investors are not even willing to pay the full amount of book value if the bank were to liquidate. Clearly, the bank's stock is out of favor or investors do not believe that book values reflect true economic values. Is there a continued distrust of how banks value loans and securities on their books? Or is this an indication that bank earning power is modest going forward?

Exhibit 5.5 Valuation Measures for First Community Corporation. December 31, 2012

Drivers of Shareholder Value	2012
Net Income available for common shareholders (year)	$3,292,000
Earnings per share available for common shareholders	$0.79
Cash earnings per share*	$1.20
Book value per common share	$10.37
Tangible book value per common share	$10.23
Core deposits	
Cash dividends declared**	$0.16
Cash dividend payout ratio (TTM – common stock)	15.2%
Cash dividend yield (using year-end stock price)	1.91%
Common stock price per share (Dec. 31, 2012)	$8.39
Cash EPS growth (2011 to 2012)	–7.0%
Price to EPS	10.4×
Price to cash EPS	6.8×
Price to book value per share	0.79
Price to TBVS	0.80
Average shares traded daily: Q1 – 2013	1,503

*Measured as net income available for common shareholders plus depreciation and amortization of intangibles, plus net losses on the sale of securities and other assets, the fair value loss adjustment and the loss on the extinguishment of debt divided by the number of fully diluted common shares outstanding.

**FCC declared a quarterly common stock dividend of $0.05 per share payable in February 2013. By September 2013 the share price was $10.60.

Summary

In order to create value, it is important to first understand how to measure profitability and risk and stockholder value. This chapter introduces profitability measures based on a bank's financial ratios obtained from balance sheet and income statement data. It provides an explanation for key ratios and demonstrates how bank managers and analysts compare profit performance for a single institution over time and versus peer institutions. As with Chapter 4, it uses data for First Community Bank in South Carolina as an example.

It then explains how investors in bank stocks generate a return and the different measures used to assess whether management is increasing bank value over time. It defines and explains terms such as earnings per share, tangible book value of equity, and core deposit premium that are used as common metrics in community bank valuation analysis. Bank managers and directors should understand these metrics to identify strategies that will create value in the future. Subsequent chapters will offer specific strategies to increase value in community banking with the value creation reflected in a bank's ability to grow earnings, increase cash dividend payments, and increase common stock price over time.

Strategies for Improved Risk Management

CHAPTER 6
Funding the Bank

"Liquidity is confidence."
—Kevin Warsh, Board of Governors of the Federal Reserve System

One of the greatest lessons of the financial crisis is that the smooth functioning of financial markets and institutions is based on the confidence that market participants can transact business as anticipated at reasonable prices. Buyers and sellers can readily quantify risks and there is a high probability that both parties to a trade will perform as expected. Liquidity breaks down when uncertainty swamps confidence. When risks are not known or are difficult to quantify, investors become highly averse to entering transactions. The run on IndyMac, the failure of Lehman Brothers and the rush to become bank holding companies by Goldman Sachs, Morgan Stanley, American Express and others demonstrate the power of confidence, or the lack thereof.

The business of banking is about confidence. As financial intermediaries, banks accept deposits from customers and use the proceeds to make loans or investments. Many of these deposits are transactions accounts which customers can immediately withdraw without notice. Consider what would happen to a bank if all its transactions account holders demanded payment at the same time. The bank would be unable to sell all loans and investments immediately to meet the payment needs, so it would have to borrow elsewhere to obtain funds. But what if the groups that typically loaned the bank these funds (other financial institutions) didn't have confidence that the bank would repay the loans? In this scenario, the system would collapse. The bank could not borrow or sell enough loans and securities at acceptable prices without depleting the bank's capital. It would not be able to immediately pay its depositors. Customers who were not able to access their deposits would panic clamoring for their money. The 'news' would create a run on other banks with their customers simultaneously trying to withdraw their deposits. This bank and others would likely be closed.

From this scenario, it is easy to understand the importance of FDIC deposit insurance. With insurance, the government assures qualifying depositors that they will receive the full amount of their insured deposits even in the event of a bank failure. Insurance increases confidence and reduces the likelihood of bank runs. The scenario also demonstrates how important it is for bank managers to maintain an appropriate mix of assets and liabilities that best positions the bank to meet funding requirements. They must keep ample amounts of cash on hand and have immediate access to additional cash on short notice.

CHAPTER 6

This chapter documents how community banks typically fund their operations. Initially, it introduces two different business models with one focusing on deposits, the other focusing on loans. Each model has different implications for funding. It then demonstrates the value of core deposits and the costs and benefits of other funding sources. Given the importance of liquidity planning, the chapter introduces more detailed measures of liquidity risk and emphasizes the importance of cash flow analysis. The final sections summarize the role played by the different government liquidity programs introduced in 2008-2009 to stem the liquidity crisis and provide a framework for constructing a contingency funding plan, respectively.

Alternative Business Strategies and Implications for Funding

Community banks typically follow one of two general business models. The more traditional model focuses on building a strong, core deposit base and is thus labeled *deposit-driven banking*. The other model, popularized in good economic times, focuses on generating assets, typically loans, and is thus labeled *loan-driven banking*. As the names suggest, each model emphasizes value creation in different forms.

Deposit-driven banks build value primarily by growing a low-cost, stable funding base in the form of transactions accounts, MMDAs, savings accounts and small time deposits. Most of these deposits are FDIC-insured unless the balances exceed $250,000. Deposit-driven banks typically operate with larger branch and ATM networks, which attract deposits because customers can conduct business in more convenient locations. Of course, demographic trends suggest that branches will become less important over time as younger customers prefer to conduct more business electronically online and via mobile devices. Deposit-driven banks typically offer electronic services but continue to rely on funding from customers who prefer branches. They continually redefine what constitutes a branch by offering in-store (such as grocery store) branches and kiosks in shopping areas. The size of the loan portfolio is determined by the deposit base. Generally, deposit-driven banks make fewer loans as a fraction of assets and hold more securities. If loan demand increases in the near-term, they fund the growth via noncore liabilities, such as FHLB advances, but they rely proportionately less on such purchased funds. Because core deposits pay low interest rates, these banks can still produce relatively high net interest margins. Not surprisingly, many S Corp and closely-held banks are deposit driven because the owners (often families) rely primarily on the bank as their primary source of income and wealth.

Exhibit 6.1 presents a sample balance sheet for a deposit-driven bank. Note the relatively high funding from core deposits, the limited funding from noncore liabilities, high capital and large securities holdings relative to loans.

Exhibit 6.1 Basic Balance Sheet Data for a Deposit-Driven Bank

Assets	Percent of Total	Liabilities + Equity	Percent of Total
Cash	3	Core deposits	74
Investment securities	32	Noncore liabilities	14
Loans (net)	60		
Other assets	5	Stockholders equity	12
Total	100	Total	100

Loan-driven banks build value primarily via earning assets, such as mortgages, commercial loans and commercial real estate loans. In good times, loan growth is strong which forces management to borrow wholesale funds because core deposit growth is much lower. During good economic times when real estate values are stable or rising, such loans are relatively easy to obtain, banks can charge significant loan origination fees and price the loans at high mark-ups over prime or LIBOR. Loan-driven banks often operate out of a main office with few branches and thus rely more on brokered deposits, FHLB advances and other forms of wholesale funding. In good times they generate strong NIMs and do not experience significant problem loans and loan charge-offs. Of course, when the cycle turns and loans start to go bad, loan-driven banks must slow loan growth and they find it increasingly difficult to obtain wholesale funding. Even when wholesale funding is available, these banks must pay higher rates on this "hot money," which sharply lowers NIMs. During the recent financial crisis, problem loans and loan charge-offs skyrocketed such that many loan-driven banks were forced to shrink assets. Wholesale funding was more expensive and, in situations where a bank was placed under an enforcement action, was prohibited by regulation. Many of these fast growing loan-driven banks recently found their capital depleted. They have tried to raise capital when it is generally not available for community banks and when it is very expensive in the event it can be obtained.

Exhibit 6.2 presents a sample balance sheet for a loan-driven bank. Note the relatively high investment in loans and heavy reliance on wholesale (noncore) liabilities. Loan-driven banks often operate with lower capital as they emphasize growth.

Exhibit 6.2 Basic Balance Sheet Data for a Loan-Driven Bank

Assets	Percent of Total	Liabilities + Equity	Percent of Total
Cash	2	Core deposits	50
Investment securities	13	Noncore liabilities	42
Loans (net)	80		
Other assets	5	Stockholders equity	8
Total	100	Total	100

Which model is riskier for the underlying banks? Think about how banks fail. It's not because they take losses on core deposits. Failures generally arise from banks with asset quality problems that eventually face a liquidity crisis because they cannot borrow via uninsured liabilities. Is it good risk management that loan-driven banks have lower equity capital and thus higher equity multipliers (financial leverage)? What are the implications for the income statement?

- When times are good and loan problems are minimal, loan-driven banks generate large NIMs and ROAs as provisions for loan losses are modest.

- When asset quality problems appear, NIMs drop sharply with the jump in noncurrent loans such that NIMs are greater at deposit-driven banks.

Noninterest income is generally greater at loan-driven banks. Noninterest expense is likely greater at deposit-driven banks given their fixed asset investment in branches and a greater number of employees needed to service the branches and related retail delivery systems. Deposit-driven banks typically have less volatile earnings streams over time.

Core Deposits Drive Franchise Value

If core deposits reduce risk, why don't all banks aggressively solicit them? The answer is both simple and complex. The simple response is that all bank managers recognize the value of core deposits and do pursue them. Unfortunately, it takes time and considerable investment (noninterest expense) to successfully build a core deposit base. The proven way to obtain low-cost deposits is via branches, which entails buying property and building physical branches or negotiating contracts with retail outlets and malls to develop in-store branches and kiosks. This takes time, requires more human labor and marketing cost and has a lengthy build-out of value because the deposits grow slowly over time. The problem is demonstrated by the actions of new start up (de novo) banks. Individuals who start de novo banks must deploy their capital quickly to cover overhead and become profitable and thus initially focus on making loans. They operate out of a main office with plans to open branches over time. They often choose to book loans funded by wholesale deposits or FHLB advances until they build the branches and grow core deposits. It's no wonder that relatively young banks failed in large numbers during 2008–2012 given their emphasis on loan growth.[1]

The more complex response is that the value of core deposits varies with the economic cycle because they are more or less attractive depending on the level of interest rates and economic growth. Consider recent experience. When the Federal Reserve and central banks throughout the world keep short-term interest rates low, banks can borrow wholesale funds at rates comparable to those offered on core deposits. The short-run incentive is thus to increase financial leverage, which greatly increases profits as long as problem loans don't accelerate. From 2001 to the early part of 2007, the economic environment encouraged bankers and others (hedge funds, mutual funds, investment banks, etc.) to assume greater risks because the profits from relatively high net interest margins came easy. Core deposits were important, but relatively less so. Of course, the recent crises changed this thinking and behavior. While rates remain low, wholesale funding disappeared for many participants and bank regulators prohibited banks with poor CAMELS ratings from paying rates deemed to be above their local market rates. Regulatory enforcement actions, in turn, mandated that subject banks reduce their reliance on brokered deposits and other wholesale funding.

Core deposits and sound loans are the primary drivers of value in community banks today. Consider the account pricing at First Community Bank (FCB) in mid-2013, which appears in Exhibit 6.3. FCB offers "free" checking with no monthly or transactions fees and no minimum balance required to open the account or to avoid fees. Funds do not earn interest. This type of account is available to both individuals and businesses, but businesses are limited to 500 "free" debits, credits and deposited items. Overdraft fees do apply. FCB also offers interest checking accounts but the bank pays interest as long as the balance exceeds some dollar threshold. The higher the threshold is, the higher the rate paid. The premium interest checking account for individuals pays the highest rates, but has a $15 monthly maintenance fee and $0.40 ATM debit fee if a $2,500 minimum balance is not met. FCB also offers a sweep checking account where balances in excess of $25,000 are swept overnight into a savings account that pays 0.28%. While savings account rates are higher, checks and debit card transactions cannot be applied to this account. FCB also offers a program for qualifying customers 50 years or older, which offers "free" online banking and no fees as long as the customer keeps a minimum $500 in the account.[2]

FCB's CD rates increase with maturity, but are at low levels compared with historical norms. In 2013, the prime rate was 3.25% and the Federal Reserve's stated policy was to keep short-term interest rates low through at least 2015. If FCB made a one-year fixed rate loan to a commercial customer priced at prime (3.25%), it would expect to earn a 3.05% spread on a pre-provision basis over the rate paid on a 1-year CD assuming it match-funded the loan with a similar maturity CD. This spread must be sufficient to cover operating costs, provisions for loan losses and generate a reasonable return to stockholders. If FCB could finance the loan with a mix of interest checking, money market and savings accounts, the spread would be higher.

Exhibit 6.3 First Community Bank's Deposit Pricing, August 2013

"Free" Checking
No minimum to open account; no minimum balance required to avoid fees; Overdraft fees do apply
Businesses are limited to 500 "free" debits, credits and deposited items per month; otherwise an item charge applies
'Free' online banking and bill pay, free phone banking, free checks, a rebate on ATM charges from using another institution's ATM

Premium Interest Checking
$2,500 minimum balance to earn interest

	Annual Percentage Yield
Balance: $2,500 – $9,999	0.03
$10,000 – $24,999	0.05
$25,000 – $299,999	0.10
$300,000 & Above	0.15

Free online banking & bill pay, free phone banking, free checks, a rebate on ATM charges from using another institution's ATM

Exhibit 6.3 First Community Bank's Deposit Pricing, August 2013 (continued)

Savings

Minimum balance to earn interest $100

	Annual Percentage Yield
Balance: $100 – $2,499	0.05
$2,500 & Above	0.15

Certificates of Deposit

Maturity	Annual Percentage Yield
7 – 31 days	0.05
1 – 5 months	0.05
6 – 11 months	0.10
12 – 23 months	0.20
24 – 35 months	0.25
36 – 59 months	0.45
60 months	0.50

What Is a Core Deposit?

While the regulatory definition is straightforward, there is considerable disagreement as to what constitutes a true core deposit. For example, which of the following items represents core funding for a bank? The FDIC insures deposits up to $250,000 per account:

- $250,000 held by an individual in a 7-month CD special that pays 1.1%; the bank pays 0.30% on a traditional 6-month CD
- $500,000 held by a director of the bank in a 1-year CD that pays 0.60%, the current rate offered by the bank for this maturity
- $100,000 held by another financial institution in a 3-month CD that pays a market rate of 1%, but the funds are obtained through a third-party broker

According to bank regulators, the 7-month CD is a core deposit while the 1-year CD and 3-month CD are not. Why? Regulators essentially require that core deposits meet three criteria. The first is that the principal balance does not exceed $250,000 such that it is fully FDIC-insured. The second is that the balance not be obtained through a third party broker. The final criterion is that – in certain circumstances where the bank is viewed as high risk – the bank issuing the liability cannot pay an above market rate.

In the previous example, the $500,000 deposit exceeds the $250,000 threshold while the 3-month CD was obtained through a broker. Thus both are viewed as brokered deposits by regulators. In contrast, the 7-month CD has a $250,000 balance and, as long as the bank is not viewed as high risk, it can pay virtually any rate it chooses.

If, instead, you view these deposits from an economic rather than regulatory perspective, the answer is quite different. A true core deposit is a low cost, stable source of funds over the long-term. Low cost means that the issuing bank does not have to pay an above market rate. Stable means that the deposit holder exhibits *low interest elasticity*. This latter feature indicates that small changes or differences in interest rates do not induce the deposit holder to withdraw funds in search of higher yields elsewhere. The issuing bank is not buying the funds by paying high rates but, instead, obtains the funds by offering a range of services to the customer in which the deposit is just one type. The deposit customer has a relationship with the bank that extends beyond the price of a specific bank product. In this context, the fact that a director of the bank holds the $500,000 deposit likely signals that the funds do not represent hot money that will flee at maturity. It is truly core funding.

Similarly, many banks obtain some deposits through third-party brokers that have greater core deposit features than the CD special and traditional brokered deposits. Consider Promontory Interfinancial Network's Certificate of Deposit Accounts Registry Service (CDARS). In a typical reciprocal transaction, a customer with more than $250,000 to deposit can obtain FDIC insurance on amounts up to $50 million at one bank via CDARS. Any bank that is a member of the Promontory Network accepts the customer's deposit and distributes the funds to other members in amounts of $250,000 or less via the Bank of New York, Promontory's agent. In return, the bank receives the same amount of funds that it distributed from other banks in the network in increments of $250,000 or less. According to Promontory, the average reinvestment rate for these reciprocal deposits is just under 90% and the typical cost averages 40 basis points less than the cost of traditional brokered deposits.[3] The $50 million amount reflects the number of member banks in Promontory's Network. Most community banks believe that reciprocal CDARS are true core deposits because the originating deposit arises from a core customer and a large percentage of the balance is retained year-to-year. Technically, the bank trades the uninsured portion of the customer's deposit for insured deposits from other banks. The FDIC generally recognizes these features of reciprocal CDARS and now requires banks to report their funding in this form. The FDIC does not formally recognize CDARs as core deposits, largely because their existence depends on a network which could revoke a bank's membership.[4]

In order to measure whether an account is a true core deposit, management must understand who the depositor is and what the depositor's true motivation for opening the account is. In the above example, the holder of a CD special with an odd maturity, such as seven months, is normally a rate shopper. The bank offers the unusual maturity to attract new funds and not cannibalize existing traditional deposit accounts by inducing current customers to move their balances. At maturity, the CD special reverts to a traditional maturity (six months) and is priced at the bank's traditional rates. Here a bank is buying deposit funding by paying an above market rate. The likelihood that the rate shopper will withdraw the funds at maturity is high unless the bank can successfully cross sell other services or agrees to again pay an above market rate. The fact that one of the bank's directors holds the $500,000 deposit makes it a core deposit unless it is clear that the balance will be held temporarily. Finally, funds obtained via a third party broker are not core deposits because the holder does not generally have a relationship with the bank. The reason the bank obtains the funds is that it pays an attractive rate. Once the bank lowers its rate relative to other banks' rates, the funds will likely leave.

Funding Analysis

There is a disconnect between what counts as a core deposit for regulation purposes and which deposits will leave a bank when interest rates rise. Bank managers should carefully analyze the composition of their deposit base. Such a core deposit study will examine the time series history of all large balances held by various depositors and identify the following features:

- Identity of the deposit holder and relationship with the bank
  (loan customer, director, bank officer or relative, held in trust, etc.)
- Number and types of products and services the deposit holder has with the bank;
  more services suggests a stronger, core relationship
- Length of time the bank has kept the deposit including the frequency
  with which it has matured and been rolled-over
- Location of the deposit holder as those who live close to existing
  branches are more likely to be core customers. Those in remote
  locales are more likely to be transitory customers.
- Minimum, average and maximum amount of the deposit over time;
  whether the accounts have tiered pricing breaks
- Interest rate paid versus the market rate for like deposits
- Number of transactions per account; are they active
  accounts; does the account holder use direct deposit?
- Change in balances when interest rates increased by substantive amounts
- Amount of balances; anything fully-insured is more likely core.

Clearly, some loan customers and bank officers or directors maintain minimum balances that fund the bank for long periods of time. Depending on the results of this analysis, the bank can better estimate which customer deposits and amounts are truly sensitive to rate changes and which exhibit core deposit features. Regulators should consider this information when assessing the bank's overall liquidity.

Rate Boards

This discussion demonstrates how some firms effectively arbitrage the regulation of brokered deposits. One example is QwickRate, which represents a rate board or listing service. The FDIC classifies a rate board as a nonbrokered deposit listing service if it charges a subscription fee that is not based on the number of deposits placed or value of the deposits placed and does not participate in placing the bank's deposit with an investor. As such, rate boards simply collect and publicize information that banks and investors use to make funding and investing decisions. As long as the deposits are in amounts under $250,000, they are classified as core deposits for regulatory purposes.

Consider the data in Exhibit 6.4 from a hypothetical rate board. The rate board charges firms that advertise rates they are willing to pay (issuing banks) a subscription fee for the right to list rates. It also charges investors a subscription fee for the right to view the rates offered. Parties cannot post their rates or invest in the underlying deposits if they do not pay the subscription fee. Importantly, the fees are not based on how many deposits a bank offers or issues or on the deposit amounts. The advantage to the issuing bank is that it can offer rates that its current depositors are not aware of such that the posting will not cannibalize existing deposits. Investors indicate what maturity they are considering and the rate board lists the issuing banks and rates from high to low. The banks in Exhibit 6.4 are ranked by rates offered on 1-year deposits.

Exhibit 6.4 Sample Data Provided by a Rate Board, September 2013

Issuing Bank	Rates Offered (%) Maturity			
	182 Days	1 Year	2 Years	3 Years
City National Bank	0.420	1.010	1.255	1.470
State Bank	0.435	1.000	1.200	1.500
County Bank	0.400	0.991	1.160	1.480
Valley Bank	0.361	0.980	1.181	1.420

Many banks subscribe to rate boards because they can easily obtain nonbrokered (core) deposits according to regulatory definition. If they post a high rate, they can anticipate being flooded with requests from investors willing to open accounts. The process imposes a real burden on the bank's employees who must manually handle these typically e-mail requests. Interestingly, many of the investors are credit unions looking for high rates on fully-insured deposits. We thus have the curious situation that banks are being funded in this form largely by their nemesis, credit unions. The important point is that regulators designate funds obtained in this form as core deposits. Yet, investors are clearly rate driven and will move their balances if the issuing bank does not pay high rates when the deposits mature. In economic terms, these deposits are brokered and the issuing banks know it! The interest elasticity is quite high.

Deposit Service Charges

Service charges represent the primary source of noninterest income at most community banks.[5] Most of the fees are tied to transactions accounts, MMDAs and savings accounts in the form of monthly account maintenance fees and overdraft fees. Banks also charge for issuing new checks, instituting stop payments on checks, excessive balance inquiries and early withdrawals prior to maturity for small time deposits. Generally, account maintenance fees are imposed on accounts with small balances and help defray the cost of preparing statements and delivering information to the customer.

Overdrafts arise when a customer spends more (overdraws) than the balance he or she has in an account. It doesn't matter if the transaction is by check, debit card or ATM. For qualifying customers, banks will automatically cover the transaction by making the payment, but will charge a fee. The benefit is that the customer avoids a bad check fee from the merchant. The cost is that the customer pays the bank an overdraft fee usually on a per item basis. The customer's reputation is protected because the individual is not being put in an embarrassing position. Of course, the bank could simply refuse to pay the transaction amount and the customer would suffer accordingly. Bankers argue that most customers prefer to pay a fee and thus avoid the embarrassment of having purchases denied.

Criticisms of Overdraft Practices

In response to the recent financial crisis and recession, banks were criticized for overdraft practices that presumably preyed on vulnerable individuals. The bad practices included:

- Charging a large fee for overdrafts as small as $1
- Ranking a customer's transactions by amount and clearing transactions with the largest balances first to create more overdrafts
- Not limiting the number of overdrafts charged per day

In 2013, the average overdraft fee was $30 per item regardless of the overdraft amount.[6] Moebs notes that large banks charged an average $35 per overdraft while community banks and credit unions charged $25. In 2012-2013, overdraft revenue at all insured banks stopped declining largely because banks raised the per item fees in response to declining overdraft volume. Overdraft volume is likely to continue to decline as more customers use mobile banking to regularly check account balances and move funds between accounts when an overdraft might seem to occur.

Prepaid Cards

Many customers, such as those without traditional bank checking accounts, have increasingly used prepaid cards in lieu of having a bank relationship. Customers can purchase a card that is pre-loaded with a fixed dollar amount of credit toward future purchases anywhere that credit or debit cards are accepted. In 2013, consumers are expected to load over $200 billion onto prepaid cards![6] According to an ABA survey, over one-third of 310 commercial banks surveyed offered prepaid cards in 2012. There are many fees associated with most of these cards including fees to obtain and activate the card, monthly service fees charged for visiting with a service representative, etc. The Pew study identified 7 to 15 different types of fees. Unlike bank card services, prepaid cards are largely unregulated and carry significant risks. Still, the study noted that prepaid cards cost $22.15 per month, on average, which was less than the $28 per overdraft fee for a bank checking account customer who had one overdraft per month.

When Sheila Bair was FDIC Chairman, she argued that overdrafts were credit products for which banks as lenders should disclose *annual percentage rates* (APRs) so customers would know how much they were paying for the service.[7] Suppose, for example, that you overdraw your account by $100 and your bank charges $30 for the overdraft. If you repay the $100 in 30 days, your effective interest rate is around 365%. While this may deter some spending, most customers understand the overdraft charge and rationalize paying it rather than forgoing a purchase.

In November 2009, the Federal Reserve imposed a rule that prohibited banks from requiring customers to enroll in overdraft protection programs. Since July 2010, customers have had to "opt in" to overdraft plans for most debit and ATM transactions. Bank of America, JPMorgan Chase, U.S. Bancorp and Wells Fargo subsequently changed their policies to limit the number of overdrafts charged per day and no longer charge for overdrafts under some small amount, such as $5.

Wholesale Funding

Banks rely on wholesale funding when they have asset growth in excess of what can be funded by core deposits, to match fund an asset or when they want to quickly alter their interest rate risk position. Community banks generally choose from the following sources: federal funds and repurchase agreements, brokered deposits and FHLB advances. Public funds representing deposits of state and local governments and their political subdivisions are another source of wholesale funds. Wholesale funds have several common attributes. First, the issuing bank pays a market rate and occasionally pays fees to a third - party broker to obtain the funds. Second, the balances are not FDIC insured. Third, the issuing bank can generally access funds in this form as long as its financial condition is viewed as strong. However, once a bank's financial condition deteriorates, its cost of borrowing rises if it can get funding at all. Again, liquidity is confidence. Lenders will refuse to advance funds and may call outstanding loans when they are unsure that the issuing bank will meet its payment obligations. Even when a distressed bank has obtained funds in this form, the lender (often a FHLB) may impose higher collateral requirements against the borrowing. The obvious intent is to better protect the lender and, at least indirectly, reduce the borrowing amount.

With the large number of bank failures and the associated losses for the Deposit Insurance Fund (DIF) in 2008–2011, federal regulators pressured banks to restructure their funding by deemphasizing wholesale funds. Regulators often lower a bank's liquidity rating (L) under the CAMELS system if it relies 'excessively' on brokered deposits or FHLB advances. In particular, regulators monitor growth for CAMELS 1 and 2 rated banks while they require CAMELS 3, 4 and 5 rated banks to have plans to limit growth and stabilize or reduce their reliance on wholesale funds. As demonstrated in the previous chapter, regulators have increasingly focused on a bank's net noncore funding dependence, which compares noncore liabilities less short-term investments relative to long-term assets. Too high a ratio typically triggered a downgrade. The FDIC, in turn, imposes higher deposit insurance premiums for banks that are not well capitalized if the banks obtain too much funding from either brokered deposits or FHLB advances. The combination of lower CAMELS ratings and an adverse funding mix often increased a bank's deposit premiums by a multiple of four to six times.[8]

Different wholesale funding alternatives offer different benefits and costs to community banks and are used for different purposes. A brief description of each type follows.

- *Federal funds purchased and repurchase agreements.* Banks can borrow or lend deposit balances held at a regional Federal Reserve Bank or another financial institution. *Federal funds purchased* refers to the liability that arises when a bank borrows these balances while federal funds sold refers to the asset created on the lending side of the transaction. The maturity is negotiated ranging from overnight to several months. Importantly, the transaction is not collateralized. If the borrower defaults, the fed funds seller is another general creditor. Repurchase agreements (repos) are viewed as comparable to federal funds transactions except that repos are collateralized transactions. Formally, borrowing under a repo is labeled as a security sold under agreement to repurchase. To engage in this transaction, the borrower must pledge a security as collateral against the borrowing. The lender in a repo transaction (reverse repo) effectively makes a collateralized loan. The existence of collateral produces a repo rate below the comparable maturity federal funds rate. Community banks with excess funds typically sell federal funds to their bankers bank or other correspondent bank. Most banks negotiate federal funds lines (lines of credit) with larger institutions that they can tap when they have a temporary liquidity need. Unfortunately, these lines may be withdrawn when a bank's financial condition deteriorates. Note that the Federal Reserve uses the federal funds rate as its target rate for monetary policy. In 2013, the Fed's formal target rate was still 0% to 0.25%, signaling Chairman Bernanke's commitment to keep short-term interest rates low until the economy improves.

- *Brokered deposits.* Banks may obtain deposits purchased directly or indirectly through brokers who act as agents for the actual owners of the deposits. The use of a broker signals that the funds are hot money and likely to flee at the first sign of trouble. Two advantages to the borrowing banks are that these deposits do not require collateral and they can be obtained quickly. Regulators view brokered deposits negatively today because they were used extensively by newly chartered banks that eventually failed. Small banks that failed in 2008–2011 had roughly four times the amount of brokered deposits as the national average. In response, regulators have increased the burden on banks that use brokered deposits by lowering their CAMELS ratings and thus increasing their deposit insurance premiums. There are two related restrictive aspects to brokered deposits for institutions that are less than well capitalized. First, if an institution is undercapitalized, it may not accept any new brokered deposit or renew (roll over) an existing brokered deposit. Second, effective January 10, 2010, a bank that is not well capitalized cannot pay rates significantly above (more than 75 basis points) national rate caps as determined by the FDIC unless it can formally demonstrate that it operates in a high-rate market. Both rulings limit the subject banks in their financing alternatives and will likely lead to them shrinking assets.

- *Jumbo CDs.* Jumbo CDs are large denomination time deposits with a common denomination of $1 million. Jumbo CDs of $1 million or more are highly liquid because they are attractive to institutional investors and widely traded in secondary markets. Their interest cost may be above or below that for core deposits, such as retail time deposits and MMDAs, depending on the bank and source of funds. Because any deposit is insured up to $250,000, a portion of many jumbo CDs is not FDIC-insured. As such, any problems associated with the issuing bank will quickly be reflected by the secondary market rate rising on its outstanding jumbo CDs. While jumbo CDs are not formally designated as brokered deposits, in practice, regulators view any balances obtained from a single depositor in excess of $250,000 as noncore whether or not the funds arise through a third-party broker. Thus, the $500,000 CD held by a bank's director in the earlier example is noncore and viewed negatively unless management can convince regulators that it is truly stable. Neither brokered deposits nor jumbo CDs require a bank to post collateral.

- *FHLB Advances.* For almost 20 years, FHLBs have offered short-term and long-term funding for community banks in the form of advances. At times, advances carry interest rates below those on comparable maturity deposits and thus represent a low cost source of funds. If necessary, banks can use advances to balance portfolio interest rate risk by making a fixed-rate loan and match funding it with a comparable advance. Previously, community banks could not access long-term funding in any form. FHLB advances have leveled the playing field with large institutions with long-term funding sources. Still, because many failed banks relied extensively on FHLB advances, the FDIC potentially penalizes usage by increasing the direct cost of advances by increasing deposit insurance premiums if a bank is perceived to rely too much on such advances. Still, banks are allowed to have greater proportionate funding via FHLB advanced versus brokered CDs, yet the CDs do not require collateral and thus are less restrictive to the bank (or to the FDIC at a bank's failure).

- There are two substantive issues with advances. First, FHLBs require collateral such that a bank cannot borrow without pledging residential mortgages, commercial mortgages, commercial loans, etc. against the debt. In difficult times, the FHLBs lend less against collateral by advancing just a fraction (60% to 80%) of the book value. While the haircuts protect the FHLBs, they sharply lower a bank's borrowing capacity. Second, all advances carry yield maintenance prepayment penalties such that a bank trying to pay off an advance prior to maturity must pay a fee equal to the FHLB's lost income from its advance. For example, suppose that a bank match funds a $2 million, 5-year fixed-rate bullet loan yielding 5.5% with a $2 million 5-year fixed rate advance paying 2.5% with the loan principal and advance principal due at maturity. If interest rates fall within the five years, the loan customer may prepay the loan and the bank would need to repay the advance to balance its interest rate risk. By rule, it will have to pay the FHLB a prepayment penalty equal to the income the FHLB loses by not having a loan to the bank at 2.5%. To protect itself, the bank should charge its loan customer an equivalent prepayment penalty.[9] The use of advances has risks associated with collateral and prepayment restrictions. So why are there lower limits on the use of brokered CDs at problem banks?

- FHLB advances come in many forms including a line of credit, short-term and long-term (up to 15 years) fixed-rate borrowings with a fixed principal amount and with amortizing principal balances, short-term and long-term adjustable rate advances and even advances with conversion and call or put option features. Adjustable rates can be linked to Treasury rates, the prime rate or LIBOR at the bank's discretion. Advances with options are complex instruments which provide either the bank or the FHLB an option to exit or convert the advance from a fixed to adjustable rate.

Government Liquidity Programs

The federal government responded aggressively to the lack of liquidity during the financial crisis by opening access to the Federal Reserve's discount window and introducing a wide range of programs that targeted specific markets and types of borrowers. In essence the Federal Reserve and also Treasury made funds available to institutions in perceived need. The end product is a dramatic increase in the size of the Federal Reserve's balance sheet, Treasury funding through Congressional authorization and additional FDIC guarantees. A wide range of programs have provided liquidity to support the markets for commercial paper, money market mutual funds, residential and commercial mortgages, asset-backed securities, and others, as well as specific institutions, such as the TBTF firms. Some community banks are active users of seasonal loans under discount window borrowing.

- *Discount Window Borrowing from the Federal Reserve.* The discount window was established to provide liquidity when banks had an emergency, such as when Katrina hit; for predictable seasonal needs, such as for banks serving agriculture customers; and for short-term liquidity purposes. Borrowing banks must post collateral, but the Fed is lenient in what qualifies. Community banks are regular users of the seasonal borrowing privilege. In this case, banks with customers that generate predictable loan needs and deposit inflows, such as those who lend to farmers and in tourist areas, effectively pre-qualify for short-term liquidity funds to help finance loan demand. These discount window borrowings are typically repaid when loans are repaid.

- *Term Auction Facility (TAF).* In December 2007, the Fed introduced the TAF, which allowed all banks to participate in a bi-weekly auction to access funds with maturities ranging from 28 to 84 days. The Fed would announce how many billions of dollars would be available and then allow banks to bid on the amounts they wanted. Funds were allocated to those banks willing to pay the highest rates. Many large institutions were regular users during the early stages of the financial crisis, borrowing in the billions of dollars per institution, but eventually withdrew as other funding became available. Most community banks did not use the facility even when the borrowing rate was just 0.25% and they could invest in like maturity assets at a positive spread. TAF was terminated in late 2009.

- *Temporary Liquidity Guarantee Program (TLGP).* In October 2008, the FDIC created the TLGP as a means to provide additional liquidity for insured institutions. It did so in several ways. First, it fully guaranteed all noninterest bearing transactions deposits under a *transactions account guarantee program* (TAGP). Initially, banks had to pay 10 basis points for this insurance through 2009 with the rate subsequently raised to 15 – 25 basis points depending on a bank's CAMELS rating. As anticipated, the guarantee stabilized bank funding in this form and actually served to attract additional deposits. Community banks were active beneficiaries of this program until the TAGP benefits were terminated in 2012. Second, it authorized qualifying institutions with debt maturing in the near-term to issue FDIC-guaranteed debt which carried low, subsidized rates. Banks issuing this debt paid fees ranging from 50 to 100 basis points. The primary beneficiaries were the TBTF firms and other large financial institutions.

Liquidity Planning

In light of the financial crisis, most community banks are focused on liquidity planning. In part, regulators recognize that many of the large institutions that effectively failed, such as Bear Stearns, Lehman Brothers and Wachovia, lacked liquidity because counterparties refused to roll-over trades and the institutions knew they wouldn't have sufficient cash on hand to meet payment obligations. Community banks are trying to position their balance sheets to avoid deposit runs and have access to sufficient cash in a crisis.

Liquidity planning entails positioning a bank's assets to generate sufficient cash inflows to meet cash outflows and structuring liabilities and potential borrowing sources to access cash as necessary. Community banks structure their loans and investments to produce interest and principal payments that produce steady cash receipts. They also identify a minimum amount of liquid assets that can be readily sold at predictable prices in the event of a large cash need. Liquid assets include the following:

- Cash and balances held at other institutions
- Federal funds sold and reverse repos that mature near-term
- High-quality, short-term securities classified as available for sale that are not pledged as collateral
- Portions of loans that are government guaranteed

Banks must hold enough deposits at the Fed and other institutions to meet clearing requirements and cover required reserves. As a first line of protection, many community banks hold fed funds sold that effectively mature daily and thus add to clearing balances if not rolled over. The negative is that these balances earn just the fed funds rate which has been under 0.25% for the past few years. They also recognize that Treasury bills and short-term agency, municipal and corporate securities can also be readily sold if they are not pledged. Again, the negative is that these instruments carry low yields. In essence, a bank is giving up earnings for liquidity protection. Finally, some banks make SBA loans of which 90% is government guaranteed. If necessary, the guaranteed portion is readily saleable. Of course, any security is viewed as liquid if its current price exceeds its purchase price. In this situation, management can sell the security at a gain and report a profit as well as access cash. Management must recognize, however, that a security trades at a higher price because its coupon yield (interest income) exceeds that currently available in the market for a bond trading at par.[10] It is forgoing higher future interest income for an immediate gain.

In response to the financial crisis, regulators often require that banks beef up their liquidity analysis and those facing financial difficulties hold more liquid assets. Some banks under enforcement actions have had to meet the following minimum balance sheet liquidity requirements:

Minimum Liquidity Ratios

$$\frac{\text{Cash + Equivalents}}{\text{Deposits + ST borrowings}} \geq 2\% \quad [4\% \text{ if troubled}]$$

$$\frac{\text{Cash + Equivalents + Liquid Securities}}{\text{Deposits + ST borrowings}} \geq 10\%$$

$$\frac{\text{Cash + Equivalents + Liquid securities + Available borrowings}}{\text{Deposits + ST borrowings}} \geq 20\%$$

Given that short-term interest rates have been low for several years, by holding large amounts of liquid securities banks are forgoing significant returns to be more liquid. The cost is high.

Contingency Funding Planning

The past few years have demonstrated that a bank's access to liquidity can change quickly in light of global and national events or firm-specific problems. In the event of a liquidity crisis, every bank should have in place a formal contingency funding plan to serve as a guide for how to resolve potential problems. The plan is essentially a blueprint of policies and procedures to access cash.[11] It addresses which individuals are responsible for specific actions and data monitoring, the administrative structure in making decisions and specific action plans that should be implemented when funding needs arise. It also provides the specific metrics to measure liquidity needs and available funding sources over different time horizons.

As demonstrated previously, traditional liquidity analysis focuses on balance sheet ratios. Community banks maintain liquid assets that can be converted to cash quickly. They should have a diversified funding base broadly dependent on core deposits. Greater capital, in turn, reduces the risk of deposit runs and allows the bank to borrow wholesale funds at lower rates.

In contrast, contingency funding planning focuses on cash flows, specifically a comparison of potential cash outflows with expected and potential cash inflows over precise time intervals. It is essentially a "What if?" scenario analysis in which management models the impact of events that may adversely affect cash flows. For example, banks face liquidity risks associated with unanticipated large deposit withdrawals, asset quality problems, reduced borrowing capacity, reduced mortgage prepayments, and bad publicity.

A *contingency funding plan* (CFP) is a written document. While it can take many forms, it should contain the following[12]:

- Identify different liability funding sources and their attributes
- Identify funding available from the securities portfolio
- Identify funding available from the sale of loans or loan participations
- Determine potential crisis events that might arise and trigger both short-term and long-term funding needs
- List the names, titles and contact information for individuals responsible for different aspects of managing liquidity during a crisis
- Document the methodology and specific assumptions to conduct a "What if?" analysis, that is, to stress test the bank's access to cash over different scenarios and thereby estimate potential funding needs over different time intervals
- Provide a summary of specific funding sources addressing how the bank will meet potential liquidity needs over different time intervals

The CFP should provide, as an appendix, a wholesale funding report that lists the various sources of wholesale funds, the bank's policy limit for each source, how much in funding is available, what the current usage is, and what the terms of any borrowing are. This cash flow analysis represents a more meaningful measure of a bank's true liquidity.

Components of a Sample CFP

Liability Funding Sources	Policy Limit (Percent of Assets)
• Retail deposit base	NA
• QwickRate (Internet) deposits	10
• Federal funds purchased & repos	20
• CDARS	15
• Total brokered deposits (includes CDARS)	25
• FHLB advances	25
• Discount window at Federal Reserve Bank	15

For each source, the CFP will indicate how much is available, what amount is currently used, and the terms. For example, with federal funds purchased and repos, the CFP might indicate that the bank has arranged fed fund lines with two different banks (City National Bank and Frontier Bank) in the amount of $10 million at each institution. At present, there are no outstanding balances, but over the past year the bank has borrowed $5 million three times at each institution. The bank tests each facility every six months. With FHLB advances the CFP might state that the bank has a $15 million facility with the FHLB of Topeka currently outstanding collateralized by 1-4 residential mortgages. The bank has sufficient collateral to support an additional $20 million in borrowing. The bank generally uses fixed-rate nonamortizing advances and plans to maintain at least $15 million in borrowing capacity at all times. Furthermore, the bank should address the following areas of concern.

- *Securities portfolio.* The bank should hold unpledged securities with maturities of five years or less at least equal to 10% of assets. These securities will be sold, preferably at a gain, if it is the best option in terms of cost and profitability.

- *Sales of loans and participations.* The bank holds the SBA guaranteed portion of loans, but does not anticipate selling loans to meet liquidity needs in normal circumstances.

- *Crisis events.* Crisis events can arise from many sources including both external events and internal causes and may persist over both short-term and long-term horizons. Short-term scenarios will likely be associated with (1) weather-related issues (tornados and flooding), (2) acts of war, (3) a deposit run on an institution in the local trade area, and (4) public relations issues. These events may lead to the withdrawal of a significant amount of deposits and/or the elimination of wholesale funding sources. Long-term scenarios will likely be associated with serious global, national and local financial crises and may potentially lead to failure of the bank as holders of the bank's liabilities demand immediate payment. It will normally be part of an industry wide crisis at which time all funding sources may potentially disappear. The bank currently funds 10% of its assets via brokered deposits obtained through RJM Brokerage. This funding would likely be called in this scenario. Longer-term liquidity problems may also be triggered by the bank reporting any of the following:

    - Nonperforming assets > 8% of total assets
    - Net loan charge-offs > 5% loans
    - Capital ratios fall below well capitalized (regulatory) standards
    - Large deposit withdrawal > 10% deposits

- The bank will attempt to use funding from federal funds and repos, discount window borrowings, FHLB advances and QwickRate deposits to meet short-term crisis needs. If necessary, it will sell unpledged securities. In the event of a long-term crisis, the bank will likely not be able to access any brokered deposits or fed funds lines. As such, the bank will use the rate board QwickRate, FHLB advances and the Fed's discount window. In all likelihood, it will be necessary to liquidate unpledged securities and SBA guaranteed loans.

- *Stress tests.* The bank will conduct stress tests across four scenarios with increased stress on liquidity. The first scenario incorporates normal and expected cash flows over the next three months and twelve months. The next two are bank specific and incorporate funding an additional 10% of assets (Mild Scenario) over the next three months and 20% of assets (Severe Scenario) over the next twelve months, respectively. The final scenario involves a Systemic Disruption in which the bank must identify new funding equal to 30% of assets over the next three months. The bank has never experienced a loss of deposits in excess of 10%, so these scenarios are relatively conservative.

- Exhibit 6.5 provides a general framework for reporting stress test results. The top panel summarizes uses of cash (cash outflows) by balance sheet item for each of the next three months. Thus the bank expects to add to fed funds sold and repos from $3 million to $9 million each month. It similarly expects to add modestly to loans at just $5 million over the three months while it simultaneously experiences a deposit run off. The largest deposit outflows come from time deposits, savings and MMDAs. The bank also faces an expected $20 million run-off in FHLB advances with other borrowing declining by another $45 million.

- The bottom panel, labeled sources of cash, summarizes cash inflows associated with maturing (or sold) assets and new liability borrowing. Savings, MMDAs and retail time deposits contribute $18.6 million and $20.9 million in new funding, respectively. The bank also anticipates borrowing $10 million from wholesale time deposits (jumbo CDs) and $20 million in other borrowings.

- The result is an estimated net cash outflow in each month amounting to almost $50 million in January and declining thereafter. The importance of these figures is that they represent crisis funding required at the margin. Specifically, the bank must have access to an additional $50 million in new funding in January to prevent a severe liquidity event. Returning to the CFP, the bank will likely go to the Federal Reserve's discount window, QwickRate deposits and brokered deposits as they are available.

Exhibit 6.5: Analysis of Cash Flows: Bank Specific Severe (millions)

Uses of Cash	January	February	March
Fed funds sold & repos	$9.0	$3.0	$5.0
Investment securities	-	-	-
Loans (gross)	1.0	2.0	2.0
Less allowance	0.3	0.5	0.5
Noninterest bearing deposits	1.5	0.6	0.6
Interest bearing checking	5.0	2.0	1.6
Savings & MMDAs	11.3	4.6	2.7
Time deposits, retail	12.5	5.1	3.3
Time deposits, wholesale	4.8	12.2	1.4
FHLB advances	15.0		5.0
Other borrowings	35.0	10.0	—
Potential Outflows – Total	$95.4	$45.0	$17.1
Sources of Cash			
Investment securities	$10.0	$3.0	$5.0
Loans (gross)	1.0	0.8	1.0
Noninterest bearing deposits	0.4	0.4	0.2
Interest bearing checking	1.7	1.5	1.0
Savings & MMDAs	7.7	6.0	4.9
Time deposits, retail	5.3	6.6	4.5
Time deposits, wholesale	-	10.0	-
Other borrowings	20.0	-	-
Potential Inflows, total	$46.1	$28.3	$16.6
Net Cash Flow Surplus or (Deficit)	($49.3)	($16.7)	($ 0.5)

CHAPTER 6

Summary

Every community bank should regularly evaluate its funding mix and potential sources of funds in the event of a crisis. Management should develop policies and procedures to measure liquidity risk, monitor changes in risk and manage the risk in normal conditions and in the event of a liquidity crisis. Ideally, the bank will increase its core deposit base over time and rely on wholesale funding for interest rate risk management purposes and to fund incremental asset growth. Management and the board of directors should ensure that the bank's written contingency funding plan is realistic and correctly ties in with the bank's asset and liability management practices.

Appendix
Wholesale Funding Report

In order to manage and monitor wholesale funding, managers should track the amounts available, actual usage at a point in time and the specific terms of different liabilities used to buy funds. Such funds may ultimately be used to meet net cash flow deficits under the stress scenarios described earlier. Exhibit 6A.1 demonstrates the type of information that should be regularly monitored. Note that management in conjunction with the board of directors specifies policy limits for each source of funds and for total wholesale borrowing as a fraction of assets. The report compares how much the bank has borrowed versus the amount available and discloses the terms of borrowing. A key element is what amount of credit is available and not used. In this example, the bank has additional wholesale borrowing capacity of $52 million. This assumes that the bank has sufficient collateral to post against additional borrowing and that the lenders do not pull their lines in the event of a crisis.

Exhibit 6A.1 Wholesale Funding Report

Date: September 30, 2013
Assets: $100 million
Policy Limit: Total wholesale funds no more than 40% of total assets

Source of Funds	Amount Available	Amount Borrowed	Rates/Terms
(Policy Limit: Percent of Assets)			
Fed funds purchased (15%)	$5 million (Big Bank)	$5 million	0% – 0.25%
	$3 million (AmFirst)	—	
	$3 million (Bankers Bank)	—	
Repurchase agreements (15%)	$6 million (AmFirst)	$2 million	0.15%
Fed discount window (20%)	$20 million	—	
QwickRate internet (15%)	$15 million	$7 million	year, 1.26%
CDARS (15%)	$15 million	$10 million	reciprocal
Brokered CDs (20%)	$20 million	$5 million	6-month, 0.80%
		$5 million	1year, 1.30%
FHLB advances (25%)	$25 million (Topeka)	$11 million	2 year, 2.1% (fixed-rate)

CHAPTER 7
Capital Protects and Provides Opportunities

When you don't need it, you can get all you want.
Unfortunately, when you need it, it is costly if you can get it at all.

In bad economic times, capital is king. Firms that are flush with capital are the survivors. They are not worried about failure. They have the capacity to expand their businesses either through internal growth or acquisitions. They can make strategic investments when prices are relatively low and potential returns are greater. They are not focused on getting through problems but rather on growth opportunities. So why don't all firms simply operate with large amounts of capital? Unfortunately, capital can be expensive and high levels may lower profitability in the short run. In good economic times, many firms try to increase their financial leverage (increase assets relative to capital) because it magnifies overall earnings when the firm makes a profit. But too little capital carries risks. Hence the dilemma – how much capital is appropriate?

Since the onset of the financial crisis, bank regulators have focused considerable attention on the amount of capital (C in CAMELS) each bank has. Upon completing their periodic exams, regulators often required institutions facing asset quality problems and unfavorable funding mixes (high amounts of brokered deposits and FHLB advances) to increase their capital ratios. During crisis times, bankers recognize that FDIC stands for 'Forever Demanding Increased Capital.' The problem is that in a crisis when facing potential loan losses and higher cost funding, banks do not have a capacity to increase capital. New investors do not want to invest in a bank and watch management charge off additional loans. They are generally wary that a problem bank might fail so they prefer to wait to invest until better times appear and the capital will be funding new growth opportunities. Management often asks existing owners to invest more, but the amounts available are typically small. At the opposite extreme is the environment in good times when investors are eager to contribute new capital to finance growth.

This chapter examines the role that capital plays in community banks. It documents what constitutes capital, how banks raise capital when it's available, and the costs and benefits of different forms of capital. It describes bank regulatory capital requirements and demonstrates the need for rigorous capital planning and stress testing. Bank owners, directors and managers must fully understand a bank's capital position to implement the appropriate business plans and increase long-term value to owners.

Capital Protects Against Failure

What does it mean to be "flush with capital"? Think of how a firm finances its operations. It can obtain funds either from owners or it can borrow. Each type of financing has costs and benefits. Owners invest their own equity, which is labeled capital. They make decisions regarding how to operate the firm and expect to generate a profit which should increase the value of the firm over time. Owners expect to get a return on their investment in the form of cash dividends and/or price appreciation of the company's stock. Importantly, the payment of dividends is discretionary and stock prices may both rise and fall thus entailing risk to owners.

There are numerous benefits to capital financing versus debt financing. First, capital investments provide some degree of management control because stockholders vote on directors and certain governance issues. Second, capital financing reduces cash payment obligations because stock dividends are not mandatory. Finally, capital provides protection against failure (bankruptcy). Note that a firm is insolvent when it has more debts (liabilities) than assets and a bankruptcy court rules that the firm cannot pay its debts. A firm that is 100% owner-financed cannot fail because it has no debts. At the same time, there are two significant costs to capital financing. First, the cost of raising capital is high relative to debt as owners expect a higher rate of return given the greater risks that ownership entails. Remember also that interest on debt is tax deductible while dividends are not which lowers the after-tax cost of debt relative to equity for the bank. Second, it is more difficult to generate large profits as measured by ROE without using debt (financial leverage). All equity-financed firms are safer, but less profitable, on average. The key benefit from using debt is the lower financing cost and multiplier effect on profitability.[1] The primary costs are that debt financing increases the volatility of earnings and that interest and principal payments on debt must be paid or the firm is in default potentially leading to failure.

Capital serves as a buffer against losses. The greater is the amount of capital financing, the less likely it is that a bank will fail holding everything else (such as asset quality) constant. When banks are viewed as high risk, regulators increase the amount of capital required to operate because they want to protect against failure. Of course, as banks find that their assets fall in value and earnings power declines, it is increasingly difficult and costly to access new capital.

What Counts as Bank Capital?

Capital represents owners' claims in a business. In accounting terms, it equals total assets minus liabilities and is referred to as stockholders equity. From the investors' perspective, the initial investment is common stock in the firm. Over time, the firm will add equity internally by making a profit that it retains rather than pay out as cash dividends. As the bank grows, management may also choose to obtain external capital by selling new shares of stock or via other capital raising means. This equity capital represents ownership. As appropriate, the firm will pay dividends to stockholders but is not obligated to do so.

Bank Capital versus Accounting Capital. It is important to note that bank capital differs from accounting capital because bank regulators count certain balance sheet items as capital for regulatory purposes. For example, bank regulators count some forms of debt as capital to meet regulatory requirements because these types of debt instruments help protect the deposit insurance fund. Similarly, banks regularly set aside reserves for loan losses. Bank regulators count a portion of this allowance for loan and lease losses as capital because the allowance is increased by expensing provisions for loan losses which reduces reported earnings. Losses are charged against this reserve and do not adversely affect earnings until the reserve is deficient. Different components of regulatory capital are described in the section on meeting regulatory capital requirements.

The following discussion regarding a newly chartered bank demonstrates the source of initial bank capital and alternatives to increasing capital over time.

Newly Chartered (de novo) Bank

Consider a group of investors who want to open (charter) a new bank. The motivation is that large banks have recently acquired many of the best community banks in the area and the investors believe a new community bank can better serve small businesses and individual customers. Because the bank will rely on FDIC-insured deposits to help fund operations, it will need to get FDIC approval once it applies for and receives its charter. This particular bank has applied for a charter from the state and expects to become a member of the Federal Reserve System.

The organizing group, in discussion with state regulators, has decided to initially raise $25 million in start-up capital. It has identified individuals who will serve as *chief executive officer* (CEO), *chief financial officer* (CFO) and *chief credit officer*. Each officer has previously worked for another bank and wants to be part of the new start-up. Six of the organizers representing businesses and nonprofit organizations in the community will potentially serve on the board of directors, if approved. Members of the organizing group will contribute $15 million and expect to raise the other $10 million by issuing common stock with a $10 par value from local business operators and individuals. Thus, the bank will sell another 1 million shares. The organizing group has 10 members investing an average $1.5 million each and plans to sell shares throughout the local community with a minimum investment of $10,000. The organizers want to operate the bank as a C Corporation and thus sell the stock to as many potential customers as possible. The group's business plan is to focus on business customers emphasizing superior service.[2] Of course, every start-up mentions these parameters so that management must be able to differentiate what will make the bank better than its competitors to support its plan. The original plan targets a total asset size of $250 million in 7-10 years.

Depending on the economic and regulatory environment, it takes five months to over one year to obtain regulatory approval. Chartering agencies approved zero de novo banks in the past 4 years. During this period of getting approval and opening its doors for business while the bank is "in organization," the bank is burning through its initial $25 million investment. In this example, the *de novo bank* (DNB) is approved in early 2013 as described. Initially, DNB will hire a few employees and purchase an office building so that the balance sheet will initially look like that in Exhibit 7.1. Because it is not yet open for business, DNB will pay salaries and other operating expenses without any revenues until it has customers. The common stock represents ownership in the firm (2.5 million shares at $10 per share) such that the bank's initial capital is $25 million.[3]

Exhibit 7.1 Balance Sheet for a De Novo Bank in Organization (millions)

Assets		Liabilities + Equity	
Cash	$1		
Short-term investments	22		
Fixed assets	2	Common stock	$25
Total assets	$25	Shareholders' equity	$25

By the end of the year, DNB has opened its main office for business and has attracted $15 million in demand deposits, MMDAs and small-time deposits. It has only modestly started lending funds so it added to its investment portfolio. Because it operated less than 12 months with high noninterest expense, the bank lost $1.2 million for the tax year. Exhibit 7.2 reflects its year-end balance sheet. Note that the retained earnings account represents the cumulative profits (losses here) for the firm since formation. Stockholders equity has fallen by the amount of the loss to $23.8 million.

Exhibit 7.2 Balance Sheet for De Novo Bank, December 31, 2013 (millions)

Assets		Liabilities + Equity	
Cash and due	$2	Core deposits	$15
Investments	26.8	Common stock	25
Loans (net)	8	Retained earnings	–1.2
Fixed assets	2	Stockholders' equity	23.8
Total	$38.8	Total	$38.8

The example demonstrates two key components of bank capital; common stock and retained earnings.[5] There are other regulatory capital components depending on how a bank finances its operations. As mentioned previously, bank regulators count other types of funding as capital to meet regulatory requirements. Some banks, particularly larger institutions, sell long-term subordinated debt and preferred stock to investors. *Long-term subordinated debt* is a type of bond sold to private investors that is unsecured and at issue had an original weighted average maturity of at least five years. It is viewed as capital because the claims of the debt holders are subordinated (lower priority) to the claims of depositors and other debt holders. The fact that a bank borrows in this form helps protect the *FDIC insurance fund* (DIF) because more assets can go into default before the DIF is at risk. *Preferred stock* is a type of equity security that is similar to debt because it pays a periodic dividend and holders have no voting rights. The investors generally have claims that are senior to common stockholders (preferred stock owners have priority in payment) but junior to debt holders. As such, preferred stockholders receive dividends before common stockholders and are paid first in any liquidation of the issuing firm. Some shares are convertible into common stock and many are perpetual meaning that the issuer can redeem them but there is not a set redemption date. For bank regulatory purposes, it is important whether the shares are cumulative or noncumulative. If an issuer misses a promised dividend payment, the dividends accrue (accumulate for future disbursement) with cumulative shares while they do not accrue with noncumulative shares. Noncumulative shares put less of a burden on the issuer because dividends may never be paid.

The final two components of bank capital relate to a bank's lending and investing activities and the associated accounting. Chapter 4 introduced the concept of a bank's *allowance for loan losses* (loan loss reserve) when accounting for the possibility of loan losses. The allowance is a contra-asset that is reported as a reduction in gross loans on a bank's balance sheet. It is established in recognition that some loans will default over time. Management recognizes this possibility and builds up the allowance by reporting an expense (provisions for loan losses) each quarter. When a bank charges off a loan as uncollectible, it reduces the allowance by the amount of the charge-off. Conceptually, the allowance serves as a buffer in the sense that earnings are not directly reduced when a bank charges off a loan. If the size of the allowance is determined appropriately, it is sufficient to cover periodic charge-offs and retained earnings grow by the full amount of profits not paid out as dividends. Regulators include the allowance for loan losses as a form of capital up to some maximum.[6]

Another component reflects the change in value of a bank's investment security holdings. Under accounting rules, when a bank buys a security it must designate it as either *held-to-maturity* (HTM), *available-for-sale* (AFS) or held in a trading account reflecting management's intentions regarding why it purchased the security. As the names suggest, management intends to hold HTM securities until they mature such that earnings will arise from interest received and the bank will not realize a gain or loss (absent default) because it will hold the security until it matures. In contrast, management reserves the right to sell AFS securities prior to maturity. As such, earnings may arise both from interest received and price appreciation if the bank sells the securities at a gain while the bank will report a securities loss if the securities are sold at less than the purchase price or amortized value. Finally, banks may buy securities for trading purposes in which they hold them temporarily expecting to sell at prices higher than what they pay. Community banks don't operate trading accounts and thus do not have trading securities. While market values of all securities change over time and as market interest rates change, HTM securities are reported on the balance sheet at amortized cost and value changes are ignored. In contrast, AFS securities are reported at market values such that the balance sheet values increase when market rates fall and fall when market rates rise. The corresponding offset to the changes in values of these securities (as assets) is reflected in the stockholders equity portion of the balance sheet as *net unrealized gains or losses on AFS securities*. This portion of stockholders equity is generally not a component of bank capital for regulatory purposes unless it relates to a bank's holdings of equity securities.[7] Under Basel III rules, banks can 'opt in' or 'opt out' of including net unrealized gains or losses in Tier 1 capital. Community banks will likely opt out.

Exhibit 7.3 reflects DNB's balance sheet at the end of 2020 under the assumption that the bank issues $3 million in both long-term subordinated debt and noncumulative, perpetual preferred stock. By this time, DNB has $300 million in assets.

Exhibit 7.3 Balance Sheet for De Novo Bank, December 31, 2020 (millions)

Assets		Liabilities + Equity	
Cash and due	$10	Core deposits	$160
Investments	56	Time deposits > $100,000	64
Loans (gross)	218	FHLB advances	41
Allowance for losses	4	Liabilities	$265
Net loans	214	Subordinated debt	$ 3
Fixed assets	20	Preferred stock	3
		Common stock	25
		Retained earnings	2
		Net unrealized gain on AFS	2
		Stockholders equity	$ 32
Total	$300	Total	$300

According to bank regulation, DNB would count $36.2 million in bank capital as demonstrated:

common stock + retained earnings + subordinated debt + preferred stock
+ allowable portion of allowance for loan losses = 25 + 2 + 3 + 3 + 1.2 = 34.2

The $1.2 million represents the maximum allowable portion of the allowance for loan losses under current regulation.

This example demonstrates the different items that constitute bank capital for regulatory purposes. Most community banks don't issue subordinated debt or preferred stock so the principal components of their capital are common stock, retained earnings and a portion of the allowance for loan losses. It is extremely difficult to raise new external capital in the current environment. As demonstrated later, regulators want banks to issue new common stock while many investors would rather have preferred stock that pays a high dividend and is potentially convertible into common stock.

Regulatory Capital Requirements

Bank regulators specify minimum amounts of capital that banks must operate with or be subject to serious sanctions. The formal standards for community banks are based largely on perceived credit risk but regulators routinely increase the minimum requirements when they determine that a bank has assumed high levels of risk not reflected in the formal standards. Today you will hear bankers complain that they are required to hold 12% capital when the regulatory minimum is 6%. What does this mean?

The formal standards are based on risk weights and the composition of a bank's balance sheet assets as well as selected off-balance sheet exposures. Generally, loans are viewed as the riskiest assets on-balance sheet while unfunded loan commitments, letters of credit and net exposures from derivatives positions reflect off-balance sheet risk. Each bank is required to hold an amount of capital equal to some minimum percentage of risk-weighted assets. The steps to determine required capital include:

1. Classify assets into one of four risk categories as determined by regulation; each risk category is subject to a different risk weight with higher weights applied to riskier assets.
2. Convert off-balance sheet exposures into credit-equivalent amounts of on-balance sheet risk assets.
3. Multiply the dollar amount of assets in each risk category by the associated risk weight and add the amounts for each category, which equals risk-weighted assets.
4. Multiply the amount of risk-weighted assets by the minimum percentage regulatory requirement.

Exhibit 7.4 provides a summary of selected bank assets across the four risk categories with risk weights of 0, 0.20, 0.50 and 1, respectively. As expected, the lowest risk assets (0 risk weight) are government guaranteed loans and securities and cash. The weights increase as perceived credit risk associated with the instruments increases. Thus, loans that are conditionally guaranteed by the federal government (0.20 risk weight) are riskier than loans unconditionally guaranteed (0 risk weight). Similarly, municipal bonds backed only by revenues generated from the project financed (revenue bonds) are riskier than municipal bonds backed by the full faith, credit and taxing authority of the issuer (general obligation bonds). The highest risk assets are comprised primarily of loans and fixed assets.

Exhibit 7.4 Risk Categories and Risk Weights for Bank Assets

0% Risk Category
Vault cash
U.S. government securities
Loans and securities unconditionally guaranteed by the U.S. government

20% Risk Category
Balances due from other depository institutions
Loans and securities conditionally guaranteed by the U.S. government
   (VA and FHA mortgages, student loans, etc.)
Loans collateralized by securities issued by federal government-sponsored
   enterprises (GNMA, FNMA and FHLMC pass-through securities)
General obligation municipal securities

50% Risk Category
Loans secured by first liens on 1-4 family residential properties
Privately issued mortgage backed securities (if they represent ownership or the
   mortgages are prudently underwritten and not past due or in nonaccrual)
Municipal revenue securities

100% Risk Category
Other loans and securities issued by private obligors
Premises and other fixed assets
Other real estate owned

Assuming that DNB in Exhibit 7.3 holds $10 million in vault cash, $10 million in U.S Treasuries, $23 million each in municipal general obligation and revenue bonds, all loans are private obligor assets and the bank has no off-balance sheet exposures, it would have $254.1 million in risk-weighted assets (RWA):

$$\text{DNB's RWA} = (0)\$20 + (0.2)\$23 + (0.5)\$23 + (1)\$238 = \$254.1 \text{ million.}$$

Under the FDIC Improvement Act (FDICIA) which was effective at the end of 1991, banks are subject to three capital ratios as noted in Exhibit 7.5; a leverage ratio and two risk-based ratios. The rules further distinguish between significantly undercapitalized banks (tangible equity of 2% or more) and critically undercapitalized banks (tangible equity under 2%). Banks in this latter category are on the verge of failure.

Regulators assign each bank to one of five categories based on whether each of the bank's three capital ratios exceeds the regulatory minimum for that category. To be in a specific capital category, each of a bank's three capital ratios must meet or exceed the minimum target. Definitions of these ratios appear in Chapter 4.

Exhibit 7.5 Minimum Regulatory Capital Ratios Across Capital Categories Under FDICIA

Capital Category	Minimum Regulatory Ratios		
	Total Risk-based	Tier 1 Risk-based	Tier 1 Leverage
Well capitalized	10%	6%	5%
Adequately capitalized	8	4	4*
Undercapitalized	6	3	3**
Significantly undercapitalized	< 6%	< 3%	< 3%
Critically undercapitalized	< 6%	< 3%	< 3% and tangible equity ratio < 2%

* 3% for CAMELS 1 - rated banks with low growth
** Under 3% for CAMELS 1 - rated banks with low growth

As noted previously, regulators count many balance sheet items as capital. The "best" capital, however, is common equity which imposes the least burden on bank management because there are no mandatory dividend payments.[8] Noncumulative perpetual preferred stock also counts as Tier 1 capital but most community banks do not issue this type of capital. Tier 2 capital consists of balance sheet items such as a portion of the allowance for loan losses and long-term subordinated debt, both of which protect the FDIC insurance fund in the event of a bank failure. If DNB's total assets averaged $300 million in 2020, with Tier 1 capital of $30 million and Tier 2 capital of $4.2 million, its capital ratios would have equaled 13.46%, 11.81% and 10%, respectively, thereby easily meeting the minimum regulatory requirements to be well-capitalized.

Recent Focus on Tangible Common Equity

With the financial crisis, bank regulators and many bank analysts increased their focus on a bank's *tangible common equity* (TCE) relative to tangible assets. The apparent rationale is that considerable uncertainty about the quality and value of bank assets (loans and securities) and bank earnings power makes it difficult to understand how safe and sound a bank is. The commonly cited TCE ratio is listed below. The numerator represents what the owners would receive if the firm was liquidated. It essentially equals tangible assets minus liabilities and preferred stock. Tangible assets, in turn, equal total assets minus intangible assets such as mortgage servicing rights, goodwill, and deferred tax credits.[9] Upon liquidation of a firm, these intangible assets have no value. Using the balance sheet data for DNB in Exhibit 7.4, TCE equals $29 million assuming that all assets are tangible. This $29 million is essentially the liquidation value of DNB. Note that TCE includes unrealized gains or losses on securities while it excludes preferred stock which is treated like subordinated debt.

$$\text{TCE Ratio} = \frac{\text{Tangible common equity}}{\text{Tangible assets}}$$

As a liquidation value, TCE indicates the amount of losses that a bank can take before stockholders equity is wiped out. In early 2009, Treasury conducted and publicized the results of detailed stress tests for 19 U.S. banks with more than $100 billion in assets. A key component of the stress tests was to determine whether the 19 banks had sufficient capital to absorb potential losses that might result from a severe economic downturn. Prior to the tests, one analyst forecast the TCE ratios for a subset of these banks which appear in Exhibit 7.6.[10]

Exhibit 7.6 Tangible Common Equity Ratios for Some of the Treasury Stress-Tested Banks

Bank	2007 TCE Ratio	2008 TCE Ratio	Forward-looking TCE Ratio**
Goldman Sachs	5.08%	6.19%	7.55%
Morgan Stanley	2.50%	4.33%	7.52%
JPMorgan Chase	4.05%	3.31%	2.70%
U.S. Bancorp	3.94%	2.62%	1.74%
Wells Fargo	2.94%	2.25%	1.73%
Bank of America*	2.99%	1.97%	1.30%
Citigroup	2.27%	1.19%	0.63%

* Data do not include Merrill Lynch data.
** Estimates extrapolate the percentage change from 2007 to 2008 for the 2009 value.

Historically, banks have operated with TCE ratios of 6% or more suggesting that only Goldman Sachs and Morgan Stanley, investment banks that converted to bank holding companies during the financial crisis, had TCE ratios that were likely sound in 2009. At the other extreme, had Citigroup seen a decline in asset values of just 0.63%, it would have wiped out its equity. Such a low ratio indicates high risk—at least to common and preferred stockholders—if the federal government hadn't designated the bank as Too Big to Fail.

The focus on TBTF institutions, their solvency issues and how to regulate systemic risk has re-introduced a discussion regarding contingent capital. *Contingent capital* refers to subordinated debt and preferred stock that potentially converts into common stock when a bank encounters financial distress. With such claims, the holders would be forced to convert their investment which currently pays coupon interest or a cash dividend into common stock, which is not mandated to pay a dividend. Such contingent capital better protects the issuing bank in a crisis because it lowers required cash payments and it protects the FDIC's deposit insurance fund. While not a common feature of bank capital today, it may be used in the future to reduce the costs associated with financial crises.

Capital Ratios at Community Banks versus Larger Banks

Community banks generally operate with much higher capital ratios than larger banking organizations. The common explanation is that they are less diversified such that credit risk is greater, they are not large enough to realize the advantages of economies of scale and scope (lower unit production costs), and they do not have the same earnings power. Each of these factors suggests that community banks are higher risk and thus should have more capital. Offsetting this is the strong link between ownership and management at many community banks. As owners, managers may better manage risk in line with expected long-term returns. They understand their products and customers better in their local communities and can subsequently adjust the bank's aggregate risk exposure more quickly. For closely-held banks and most S Corp banks, the owner/managers have more of their own "skin in the game" so they may monitor bank expenses and risks better.

Exhibit 7.7 provides average bank capital ratios for different-size banks and for FCB, which was introduced in Chapter 4. As demonstrated in Exhibit 7.5, banks must have a minimum 10%, 6% and 5%, values for the Tier 1 risk-based capital ratio (Tier 1 RBC), Total RBC ratio and Tier 1 Leverage ratio, respectively, to be well capitalized. The average bank in all size categories is well-capitalized as is FCB. The first three regulatory bank capital ratios exhibit a pattern consistent with conventional wisdom. Specifically, the smallest banks have the highest ratios and all ratios decrease with bank size. Thus, larger banks exhibit the highest financial leverage and hold the least amount of capital relative to total and risk-weighted assets. The final column reports the average amount of intangible assets per dollar of stockholders equity, which provides some indirect information regarding TCE. Note the high ratio of intangibles at banks over $3 billion in assets. TCE ratios are likely lower, on average, such that these largest banks are riskier.

First Community Bank's capital ratios suggest that it operates with less financial leverage and greater capital than the average bank in all other size categories. It has a greater buffer against future losses and can grow assets proportionately more and still remain within regulatory capital guidelines. It can take advantage of opportunities to expand its branch operation, invest in new subsidiaries, or even acquire other institutions. Capital creates opportunities.

Exhibit 7.7 Capital Ratios for Different-Size Banks, December 31, 2012

Institution	Tier 1 RBC	Total RBC	Tier 1 Leverage	Intangible Assets Bank Equity
Average Bank in PG15 (Assets < $50 million)	15.94%	17.14%	11.75%	0.07%
Average Bank in PG4 ($100 million < Assets < $300 million)	14.88	16.08	9.80	1.21

Exhibit 7.7 Capital Ratios for Different-Size Banks, December 31, 2012 (continued)

Institution	Tier 1 RBC	Total RBC	Tier 1 Leverage	Intangible Assets Bank Equity Average Bank in
PG3 ($300 million < Assets < $1 billion)	14.41	15.62	9.67	3.06
Average Bank in PG1 (Assets > $3 billion)	13.99	15.46	9.76	15.49
First Community Bank (Average Assets of $607 million)	16.87	18.12	10.34	1.09

Basel III and Community Banks

In July 2013, bank regulators approved new rules regarding regulatory capital requirements that are consistent with Basel III standards. Certain rules primarily related to risk weights apply to smaller, noncomplex banks that must comply with the requirements by January 1, 2015. Key provisions include the following, which will increase required capital compared with previous capital standards.

Minimum capital ratios: every bank must operate with the following minimum capital ratios:

- Common equity Tier 1 capital (CET1) ratio of 4.5%
- Tier 1 capital to risk-weighted assets of 6%
- Total capital to risk-weighted assets of 8%
- Leverage ratio (Tier 1 capital to adjusted average assets) of 4%

CET1 equals common stock, surplus and retained earnings less regulatory deductions. To avoid limits on capital distributions (dividends and share buybacks), a bank must have a *capital conservation buffer* of at least 2.5% of risk-weighted assets which will be phased in by 2019.

With these requirements, Exhibit 7.8 provides the new minimum capital requirements under Basel III effective January 2015. To meet the capital conservation buffer, add 2.5% to the adequately and well capitalized figures listed in Exhibit 7.8. The rules change what qualifies as capital depending on bank size and complexity.

Exhibit 7.8 Minimum Regulatory Capital Ratios Across Capital, Effective January 2015

Categories Under Basel III

Capital Category	Minimum Regulatory Ratios			
	Total Risk-based	Tier 1 Risk-based	CET1	Tier 1 Leverage
Well capitalized	10%	8%	6.5%	5%
Adequately capitalized	8	6	4.5	4
Undercapitalized	< 8	< 6	< 4.5	< 4
Significantly undercapitalized	< 6	< 4	< 3	< 3
Critically undercapitalized	Tangible equity / Total assets ratio < or = 2%			

- *Residential mortgages:* risk weights for 1-4 family residential mortgages remain at 50% for prudently under-written loans that are not past due, restructured or on nonaccrual. A 100% risk weight applies to other residential mortgages.

- *Commercial real estate* (CRE): risk weights are 150% for high volatility CRE loans and 100% for most other CRE loans.

- *Mortgage Servicing Rights:* risk weights are 250% with amounts limited.

- *Past-Due Exposures:* risk weights are 150%.

The new higher capital requirements will be phased-in over time, but demonstrate that regulators are enforcing higher capital requirements on all banks. This action is consistent with a belief that banks have generally operated with too much financial leverage. Of course, when banks must operate with higher proportions of common equity, it is more difficult to generate and maintain a high return on equity.

Capital Planning

Bank capital has many purposes: (1) it represents ownership – a key element of our economic system; (2) it protects the FDIC's deposit insurance fund; (3) it provides access to the financial markets at minimal cost; and (4) it constrains growth. In general, it imposes a market discipline on bank managers because it limits risk taking.

Capital is also expensive. Owners of banks expect returns that compensate them for the various risks associated with banking. During boom periods when loan growth and the quality of loans is strong, raising external capital by issuing new preferred or common stock is relatively easy as investors are more eager to acquire these claims. Bank stock prices reflect confidence in earnings power and risk controls such that new stock offerings do not dilute existing shareholders by much if at all.[14] Of course, the opposite occurs during economic downturns. Loan growth slows, banks are forced to charge-off more loans and recognize more nonperforming loans and earnings suffer. If losses are substantial, a bank may find that its capital base has deteriorated sharply. In this event, raising capital is quite expensive if such capital is even available. To make stock issues attractive, preferred stock may carry high dividend yields and be convertible into common stock at attractive prices. Common stock offerings, in turn, must be priced at a discount to book value and are extremely dilutive. Buyers of distressed banks can often invest relatively small amounts compared with the previous market capitalization of a bank and obtain effective control of the bank.[15]

How Much Capital Does a Bank Need?

The financial crisis increased regulatory and investor concerns regarding how much capital financial institutions should have to successfully meet their obligations without taking excessive risks. The formal recognition that many large institutions in the U.S. are too big to fail has changed the view of the role of capital and the minimal amount that should be required. Consider the types of institutions other than banks that the U.S. Treasury recently kept from failure under TARP. Exhibit 7.9 lists selected nonbank firms and the amount of federal government assistance each had outstanding at the end of 2009. Including banks, Treasury had committed almost $400 billion to 759 recipients. An additional 58 firms received and repaid the government over $143 billion. While most of this aid came in the form of preferred stock and some loans, the government owned almost 100% of Fannie Mae and Freddie Mac's common stock as well as more than 80% of AIG, 67% of GM, 34% of Citigroup, and 16% of Chrysler at the end of 2009. Except for Fannie Mae and Freddie Mac, all of these firms have subsequently repaid the government for this investment.

Exhibit 7.9

Selected Nonbank Firms Receiving Financial Assistance from the U.S. Treasury in 2008–2009, December 31, 2009 (billions)

Firm	Business	Amount of Assistance
AIG	Insurance	$ 69.8
Fannie Mae	Mortgage Finance	59.9
Freddie Mac	Mortgage Finance	50.7
General Motors	Automobiles	50.4
GMAC	Automobiles & Mortgage	16.3
Chrysler	Automobiles	12.5
The Hartford	Insurance	3.4
TCW Group	Investment Fund	3.3
Invesco	Investment Fund	3.3
Wellington Management	Investment Fund	3.3
Blackrock	Investment Fund	3.3
AllianceBernstein	Investment Fund	3.3
Angelo, Gordon & Co	Investment Fund	3.3
RLJ Western Asset Management	Investment Fund	3.3
Marathon Asset Management	Investment Fund	3.3
Discover Financial Services	Financial Services	1.2
American Home Mortgage Servicing	Mortgage Servicer	1.2
Litton Loan Servicing	Mortgage Servicer	1.1

Source: Eye on the Bailout, http://bailout.propublica.org/main/list/index ; authors are Paul Kiel and Dan Nguyen. The data are continually updated.

The concept of TBTF raises extraordinary questions. First, if the government guarantees that a firm will not default, what role does common equity in the firm play? Should such firms be treated like regulated utilities where allowable pricing is set to generate a predictable return on equity? How much common equity capital should the firms have in their capital structure? Should regulators set maximum compensation to senior managers and determine the makeup of the board of directors? How much should these firms pay the government for the guarantee? Upon the advent of serious financial problems, how does the government respond? Should management and directors be removed? Should common and preferred stockholders be wiped out in the event of a "nominal failure"?

TBTF also affects resource allocation. Because of the government guarantee, TBTF firms—all are included as systemically important financial institutions (SIFIs)—can borrow at below market rates. They are growing faster and capturing more resources than they otherwise would in truly competitive markets. Will they eventually drive nonguaranteed, less complex and smaller firms out of business? Will economic growth be hampered because TBTF firms don't cater to small business and individuals, particularly those located outside of major metropolitan areas? Virtually everyone recognizes the unfairness of TBTF firms. So why do we continue to subsidize them?

Orderly Liquidation Under the Dodd-Frank Act

The Dodd-Frank Act attempts to address some of these issues with its orderly liquidation provisions. The Act establishes a Financial Stability Oversight Council consisting of state and federal regulators with the group charged with "identifying systemically important financial firms for prudential regulation." These firms and bank holding companies with more than $50 billion in assets will be subject to enhanced capital regulation and risk management practices, and will also be subject to formal resolution plans in the event they fall into serious distress. In light of the previous discussion, these firms will be required to undergo annual stress tests to assess whether they are operating with sufficient capital.

The resolution will presumably involve the orderly liquidation of the firm outside the bankruptcy process with the FDIC as receiver. Initially, the firm must be designated as posing a significant risk to the financial stability of the U.S. In this event, the Fed and FDIC can recommend to Treasury that it appoint the FDIC as receiver of the firm if two-thirds of the members of the Fed's Board of Governors and two-thirds of the FDIC's board of directors vote in favor. The Treasury Secretary, in consultation with the President, may then appoint the FDIC as receiver. Orderly liquidation then involves the following:

- FDIC assumes management control of firm assets.
- Convertible debt instruments are converted into equity.
- Senior management is removed.
- Members of the board of directors are removed.
- Unsecured creditors take losses according to the priority of claims under the Act.
- Stockholders take losses according to the priority of claims under the Act.

The intent is that creditors and shareholders bear losses and both managers and directors who are presumably responsible for the excessive risk taking also bear losses. The obvious question is whether regulators and the Fed and FDIC board members will actually take the necessary actions. Remember that these same regulators made the arbitrary decisions as to whether Bear Stearns, Lehman Brothers, AIG, Washington Mutual, and others were saved or allowed to fail. If these regulators are "too connected" to the managers of the large firms as has been suggested during the financial crisis so that most firms were TBTF, why has that now changed? And the President must approve naming the FDIC as receiver. I can see the dilemma - 'Under my watch?'

Clearly, capital requirements are going to increase for banks. In late 2009, the Group of 20 global finance ministers agreed to new, higher capital requirements that would eventually require all large, systemically risky firms to raise additional external capital. But if a key catalyst behind the recent financial crisis was the lack of liquidity and a run on banks, simply raising capital ratios will not stop a financial collapse.[16] Effective regulation in this arena must limit risk taking by these institutions. Paul Volcker, former chairman of the Federal Reserve System, has proposed that the government should effectively reimpose Glass-Steagall–type restrictions on the activities allowed large institutions. In 2013, Senators Brown and Vitter introduced legislation that would increase the largest banks' minimum leverage ratio to 15%. Such a rule would ultimately force these firms to break-up as investors would demand it. The essence of these rules is the belief that insured commercial banks should focus on lending while banks that focus on securities underwriting, asset management, brokerage and proprietary trading should not be funded with insured deposits. Of course, efforts to raise capital requirements and limit risk taking will likely lower expected risk-adjusted returns for investors in bank stocks, which raises the cost of issuing common stock. A bank with a 15% leverage ratio will have real difficulty generating the types of returns that investors in large publicly-traded banks demand.[17]

Minimum regulatory capital requirements often place bank managers at odds with bank regulators. A common criticism from bankers during the financial crisis was that official minimum regulatory capital ratios were ignored. Regulators would advise banks under any form of enforcement action that the minimum Tier 1 leverage ratio was 8% and the minimum total risk-based ratio was 12%. Regulators, in turn, raised target capital ratios because they perceived higher risks at subject banks. The impacts adversely affected credit availability. If management must increase capital and external capital is not available, especially at low cost, the common strategies are to shrink the bank, thereby reducing total assets and paying down liabilities and/or shifting the asset mix toward lower-risk items such as government-guaranteed securities and away from loans. The economy suffers accordingly.

CHAPTER 7

Capital Planning for Community Banks

Given the importance of capital in determining firm survival and growth opportunities, bank managers continually evaluate whether the institution has sufficient capital to support current and planned activities. Capital planning is an integral part of strategic planning and general decision making. Managers must routinely address:

- What are the bank's risk exposures (credit, liquidity, market, operational, etc.)?
- What amount of capital is necessary to support the bank's business strategy in line with its assumed risks?
- What is the optimal mix of capital in terms of common equity, preferred stock, subordinated debt and the allowance for loan losses?
- If capital is issued at the bank holding company, where does the holding company obtain the cash to meet its payment obligations?
- What amount of capital can be reasonably generated internally in the form of retained earnings (net income not paid out as cash dividends)?
- What is the bank's effective cost of capital and subsequent required return on investment?

Answers to these questions are essential for managers to budget and operate the institution successfully.

Stress Testing Requirements

At present, community banks are not formally required to conduct annual stress tests to assess whether their capital is sufficient to cover anticipated losses. But this requirement is coming. A careful reading of consent orders for banks subject to regulatory enforcement actions indicates that the subject banks must raise additional capital. The amount, in turn, likely reflects anticipated performance over future years given the bank's current risk profile. All banks, whether or not they are under an enforcement action, will soon be conducting stress tests as part of their normal strategic planning, budgeting, and risk management analysis. These efforts should be part of an institution's comprehensive enterprise risk management program.

Think of forecasting an institution's financial statements one to five years in the future under a range of economic scenarios. In today's world, banks with high exposure in construction lending need to project their earnings and capital position assuming potential declines in real estate values and subsequent write-downs and charge-offs of loans. If the banks do not have sufficient capital to absorb such losses, they will need to hold higher capital regardless of whether they are currently well-capitalized because they meet the minimum regulatory capital ratios. This framework represents the new regulatory world.

Sources of External Capital

Under normal circumstances, community banks have been able to access external capital in one of four ways: issuing subordinated debt, issuing common stock, issuing preferred stock and issuing trust preferred stock. Most community banks do not view subordinated debt as an alternative because there is little demand for this security from investors. During 2008–2009, the market for *trust preferred stock* (TRuPS) effectively closed for community banks due to the large number of bank failures and the choice by some surviving banks that had issued trust preferred stock to not pay dividends. Moreover, the Dodd-Frank Act changed the treatment of TRuPS as capital, especially for larger institutions.

Community banks that issue *subordinated debt* realize some advantages. The instruments are effectively bonds that typically carry a maturity of 7-10 years with call protection through five years. Investors may also get stock warrants. The primary advantage is that interest payments are tax-deductible. As mentioned previously, subordinated debt counts as Tier 2 capital such that issues raise a bank's total risk-based capital ratio but not the Tier 1 leverage or risk-based ratio.

Trust Preferred Stock

During the early 1980s, many banks issued TRuPS in order to finance growth. They were particularly attractive given the low cost and long maturity up to 30 years. For regulatory purposes, TRuPS counted at Tier 1 capital - the same as common stock. For tax purposes, the dividends paid on TRuPS are effectively tax deductible. Issuing TRuPS involves the following steps:

- Bank holding company creates a special purpose entity (SPE) as a business trust.
- The trust issues nonvoting cumulative preferred stock to investors and uses the proceeds to buy subordinated notes issued by the bank holding company. The preferred stock has a fixed maturity and makes periodic dividend payments. The subordinated debentures issued by the bank holding company carry the same terms as the preferred stock.
- The bank holding company then uses its cash inflows to buy common stock issued by its subsidiary bank.

Upon consolidation, the bank holding company counts the outstanding preferred stock as Tier 1 capital. The bank holding company's interest payments to the trust on the subordinated debt are tax deductible. The trust, in turn, uses the interest receipts to pay dividends on its outstanding preferred stock. Most TRuPS have few covenants that restrict the bank holding company. While they lasted, TRuPS were an extremely low cost form of Tier 1 capital.

The use of TRuPS expanded as banks discovered the benefits of tax-deductible interest on new Tier 1 capital. It was common for investment banks to arrange private placements sold to directors, institutional investors and other banks. In order to market TRuPS from a single institution, the offering generally needed to exceed $15 million. However, banks that wanted smaller amounts could participate in a pooled TRuPS offering. With pooled TRuPS several bank holding companies issue preferred stock to a trust. Investors then acquire debt instruments that are collateralized by the pool of preferred stock obligations with the same net benefits to TRuPS issuing firms.

Importantly, TRuPS put pressure on the subsidiary bank(s) to generate sufficient cash flow to service the holding company debt. This cash flow typically comes from dividend payments the banks make to the holding company which owns the stock in the bank. What happens when a bank falls into distress? If it has no earnings, poor asset quality and too little capital, it cannot make dividend payments. Without sufficient cash receipts, the holding company cannot make its dividend payments on the subordinated debt. With reduced (or no) interest receipts the trust cannot make the dividend payments on the preferred stock it sold to investors. This is the situation currently facing some community banks. Today, investors show little interest in TRuPS given the number of bank holding companies that have stopped making payments on their subordinated debt. During 2009, several banks failed due largely to losses on their investments in other bank-issued TRuPS.

DFA makes TRuPS less attractive for all but the smallest issuing banks. Specifically, bank holding companies with less than $500 million in assets can still count TRuPS as Tier 1 capital. Under the new Basel III capital rules, TRuPs issued before May 2009 are grandfathered in as Tier 1 capital for smaller firms. Larger institutions can still issue TRuPS, but new issues are treated as Tier 2 capital and not Tier 1 capital, so they do not affect the Tier 1 leverage and risk-based capital ratios. For large institutions old issues of outstanding TRuPS will be phased out as Tier 1 capital over time. Tier 1 capital will be concentrated in common equity.

Common Stock Offerings

Many community banks have tried to raise Tier 1 capital in response to the financial crisis. Given the lack of demand outside the local community, current owners and managers typically look first to the institution's board of directors. It is extremely difficult to sell stock to institutional and other investors if management and the board do not demonstrate an interest and ability to buy shares individually. "Passing the hat around the board table" is a critical signal to the investing community that management believes the institution to be viable and the stock to be a good long-term investment.

After determining how much can be raised from insiders, management often examines how much is available from "friends and family." To the extent that they have the resources, these individuals may become stockholders because they know the management team well and trust their commitments regarding future viability and performance. Unfortunately, many once wealthy individuals have lost significant portions of their wealth given the decline in real estate and global stock and bond markets. Capital in this form is thus difficult to come by today.

The last alternative considered is whether to sell stock to institutional investors or other third parties. If the bank is in strong financial condition and in attractive product and geographic markets, it can successfully raise capital. Given the relative unattractiveness of community bank stock in a downturn, they must often sell the stock at less than book value and thus substantially dilute existing owners. The capital is expensive. If the bank is in a weak financial condition, current owners may ultimately give up control of the company. Of course, investors in distressed assets—in this case, common stock of troubled community banks—pay low prices such that they may get controlling interest.

Summary

Banks must have adequate capital to operate and compete effectively. Banks with large amounts of capital and high regulatory capital ratios have strategic advantages, especially in difficult economic environments. They can better price loans and deposits. They can better expand via branching or acquisition. The can operate proactively rather than defensively to build market share and franchise value. They will be acquirers rather than sellers.

The choice of how much capital to operate with and its form is critical to successful bank management. Higher amounts of equity capital lower financial leverage and put downward pressure on generating a high return on equity. But it ensures viability and the ability to plan to generate higher long-term profitability. Going forward, community banks will be required to conduct regular stress tests related to assessing the bank's risk profile in the future and whether the bank has sufficient capital to absorb losses in adverse economic conditions. Regardless of whether the bank meets current regulatory capital minimums, it may be necessary to raise additional capital to avoid regulatory sanctions and compete proactively in the future.

CHAPTER 8
Lending: We Eat Our Own Cooking

Lending is the lifeblood of community banking. Loans are the dominant asset and serve as the primary product that ties a business customer to the bank. If the analysis of the borrower's credit worthiness is done appropriately and the bank avoids unnecessary concentrations, loans generate the highest risk-adjusted returns and contribute greatly to operating income. In turn, a community's vitality and growth often reflects the ability and willingness of community banks to lend.

Loans also exhibit the greatest risk for community banks. Most bank failures are due to nonperforming loans that produce losses that wipe out capital or lead to a liquidity event. Because community banks lend locally to businesses, individuals, governmental units and nonprofit organizations, their loan composition reflects the limited geographic markets they serve. A bank in rural Iowa will make more agricultural loans than a bank in the heart of Minneapolis, which will make more commercial real estate loans and more direct business (C&I) loans. Because of their loan concentrations, community banks face extraordinary *execution risk* that their business model and plans may go awry if economic conditions worsen. It did not matter if local banks did no energy lending in West Texas and Houston during the 1980's oil bust because the welfare of businesses and individuals in their local communities depended on energy prices. The same holds true during the recent financial crisis. A community bank located in San Diego, Las Vegas, Miami, Phoenix or Detroit suffers as local housing values collapse and commercial real estate crumbles largely because it is located in a depressed market.

This chapter examines some of the unique attributes of community bank lending activities. It is not a tutorial on how to conduct credit analysis or implement an effective lending program, but rather a critique of factors influencing credit decisions and their outcomes. It will demonstrate the importance of the fundamentals such as "know your borrower," "don't keep all your eggs in one basket" and "cash flow is key." It will also explain why community banks hold large amounts of loans that are tied to local real estate values and why they experienced significant loan losses during the recent financial crisis. Importantly, it will help explain what information in a typical board report is important and help identify red flags indicating potential problems.

Credit Risk

Credit risk is the risk of loss due to a borrower not making interest and/or principal payments as promised. Loan officers make loans anticipating that the borrower will fully repay the debt, but recognize that economic conditions and the borrower's financial condition may change thereby rendering the loan uncollectible as promised. Every loan should be priced to reflect this risk and the bank should have policies in place to identify, measure, and control the amount of credit risk assumed within the bank's entire loan portfolio.

Senior management, under the guidance of the board of directors, establishes a bank's *loan policy*. A loan policy is a written document that states (1) the bank's lending philosophy including its mission and objectives, (2) specific credit approval guidelines, (3) the credit underwriting (analysis) process with specific loan authorities and responsibilities and (4) formal operating procedures to manage the portfolio and monitor performance after loans are made. Embedded in the policy are detailed guidelines regarding[1]:

Loan Administration
- Areas of credit expertise of lending personnel
- Target loan portfolio mix; maximum exposures for specific types of loans, i.e., acceptable concentrations of credit
- Target geographic markets for each type of loan
- What constitutes an acceptable loan; minimum creditworthiness requirements for each type of loan; how to prevent legal and regulatory problems with environmental liability
- Procedures to ensure 'Fair Lending'
- Maximum amount of a loan to any single borrower
- Specific documentation (type of financial statements, required collateral and when personal guarantees are required) and procedures for loan approval
- Which officers and committees have loan approval authority and the amount of a loan that they can individually approve (role of individual lenders, lending department managers and committees, the senior loan committee of bank officers and the board lending committee)
- Guidelines on loan participations (purchases) and loans to insiders
- Board responsibility in approving loans
- How exceptions to policy should be treated

Loan Review and Loan Grading
- Framework for credit analysis (type of ratio and cash flow analysis required and necessary documentation and specific guidelines for appraisals, loan-to-value requirements, when loans can be unsecured)
- Role of effective loan review and loan grading
- Criteria for risk ratings and loan migration analysis
- Loan pricing guidelines
- Independent internal loan review process and responsibilities

Loan Performance

- Procedures for monitoring loan portfolio performance
- General methodology and procedures for establishing the size of the allowance for loan losses
- How loans should be collected and how workouts are handled
- Procedures for handling *other real estate owned* (OREO)

Having a good loan policy does not eliminate loan losses. It simply provides a framework to better manage credit risk before loans are made, monitor loan portfolio performance after the loans are made and help the bank maintain an adequate loan loss reserve. A key component of regular board meetings is for management to present a report of loan portfolio performance, approved new and renewed loans and exceptions to policy. Policies, in turn, are only as good as management's implementation.

Credit Culture

Successful banks have a *credit culture* that determines the types and magnitudes of credit risk assumed in normal operations. Three general types of credit cultures may be labeled values driven, profit driven or market-share driven. Banks exhibiting the best recent performance are *values driven* focusing on strong risk management systems and controls, bank soundness and safety. Loan underwriting is conservative with an emphasis on making high quality loans. Values-driven banks generally have fewer loan losses but do not report large increases in annual loan volume and profits during boom times. Other banks are either *profit driven*, focusing primarily on current loan revenues, or *market-share driven*, focusing on capturing an ever-increasing share of loans among local competitors. As the labels suggest, loan underwriting is less conservative as management is attracted to higher-risk borrowers with greater profit potential. Market-share driven banks are typically younger and/or new to a trade area. The strategy is to first capture loan customers and the associated loans and subsequently build-out the branch and office franchise to fund operations. Initial funding comes primarily from wholesale sources such as brokered deposits, FHLB advances and core deposits that pay rates that are relatively high compared with rates offered by local market peers. Profits are low until the rate of loan growth slows substantially. More mature profit-driven banks do not necessarily exhibit the same high loan growth, but consistently report above-average noncurrent loans and loan losses. Profits are strong during good times and drop sharply during bad times.

Credit culture is closely tied to a bank's general business strategy. Firms that focus on building and maintaining a fortress balance sheet are values driven. The key performance attributes are strong core deposit funding with limited financial leverage (strong equity capital base), modest loan to asset ratios and large amounts of liquid, unpledged securities. Loan growth is secondary to long-term profitability. Owners and managers of these banks place a premium on sleeping well. Firms that focus on profits generally operate with higher financial leverage and higher loan-to-asset ratios. Loan opportunities drive the size of the balance sheet as managers will finance loan growth with large amounts of wholesale liabilities (FHLB advances, brokered deposits, etc.) as needed. During boom times, NIMs are higher, fee income is higher and profits are greater. Finally, banks that focus on market share are often "flippers." Management's long-term strategy is to grow the franchise in high-growth markets with the ultimate objective to sell (flip) the bank to a large organization that wants to expand in the target bank's geographic markets. Managers and owners expect the big payout not to come from periodic profits and dividends, but from stock price appreciation at sale.[2] Owners and managers of these two latter types of banks place a premium on eating well.

Loan defaults are a normal part of lending even for values-driven banks. Lenders believe that all loans are good when they are made, but economic conditions change as do personal employment and lifestyle situations for individual borrowers. A loan officer cannot fully anticipate all of these adverse outcomes so some level of loan losses is normal. Default losses are much higher than normal (versus peer institutions) when loan officers, managers and the board do not have or enforce a strong loan policy. Still, adverse economic conditions can severely damage performance given the limited diversification at many community banks.

Recent Loan Problems

Many factors contribute to potentially high levels of credit risk at community banks. Loan officers attempt to evaluate a borrower's capacity and willingness to repay a loan before granting credit. Prior to the recent financial crisis, too many bankers and bank directors put their institutions at higher risk in the following ways.

Excessive Loan Concentrations

Banks can extend too much credit to a single borrower and within a certain sector or line of business that produces a poorly diversified portfolio. With **"too many eggs in one basket,"** any deterioration in a single borrower's financial condition can lead to default as can economic deterioration within an industry (think of falling values in housing, commercial real estate, agriculture or energy) which puts pressure on businesses, governments and individuals. The fact that community banks operate in limited geographic markets exacerbates concentration risk. Consider a $100 million community bank located in rural Iowa. Agriculture-based business dominates the local trade area such that the performance of loans to farm and ranch operations, farm owners and laborers and local commercial businesses will depend on commodity and livestock prices and the efficiency of farm operations. In boom times, problem loans will be small such that the bank's loan portfolio will perform well. In contrast, during downturns in commodity and land prices, problem loans will increase such that the bank will be exposed to significant loan losses. Iowans remember this well as the collapse of farm prices during the 1980s devastated many local farmers and hurt bank performance. Thus, concentration risk is not entirely avoidable if a bank chooses to serve its local community.

Regulators limit how much a bank can lend to a single borrower at 15% to 25% of bank unimpaired capital plus surplus depending on whether the loan is secured or not.[3] They also routinely establish guidelines when economic conditions suggest that certain exposures might be excessive. For example, in January 2006 federal bank regulators proposed guidelines on *commercial real estate* (CRE) lending to emphasize their increased regulatory scrutiny of CRE loans. The guidelines established thresholds for determining when a bank had a CRE concentration that merits "heightened risk management practices." These same institutions were advised to have capital in excess of the stated regulatory minimums. The regulators set two thresholds:

CRE Threshold 1   Loans for construction, land development and other land represent 100% or more of the institution's total risk-based capital

CRE Threshold 2   Loans secured by multifamily and nonfarm nonresidential properties and loans for construction, land development, and other land represent 300% or more of the institution's total risk-based capital

To date, when regulators examine banks with CRE loans that exceed these thresholds, they expect detailed documentation of exposures, board approval of the overall CRE lending strategy and detailed exposures, documentation of loans exceeding loan-to-value guidelines, and regular reports "on changes in CRE market conditions and the institution's CRE lending activity that identify the size, significance, and risks related to CRE concentrations."[4] As economic conditions deteriorated, these guidelines became "bright lines" which regulators then used as specific targets for CRE banks' loan concentrations. If, for example, a bank's construction and land development loans (which generate no cash flow until the projects are finished and sold) equaled 130% of total risk-based capital, management was often told via an enforcement action to get the ratio under 100%. Thus, the bank could no longer make loans of this type to new borrowers even when existing borrowers might pay down their outstanding principal.

Loans at community banks are often secured by real estate. In part, this reflects larger banks shifting their attention and loan mix more toward large business borrowers and retail customers. It also reflects the types of collateral that are readily available and relatively (historically) easy to value in most communities. Consider a retail business in a shopping mall. Lenders may ask the business borrower to pledge the property as collateral because it does not change over time, as do inventory and accounts receivable. The property also has a more predictable and measureable value. In this sense, the loan is classified as a real estate loan even if the proceeds are used for operating purposes and the borrower uses operating cash flow to meet debt service requirements. The lender does not typically expect the loan to be repaid by liquidating the real estate collateral.

While bank managers are responsible for implementing lending policies, board members are responsible for policies and ensuring that performance is successfully monitored. Managers must communicate clearly what the bank's loan mix and performance is on a regular basis. Directors must clearly acknowledge when exceptions to policy are allowed and why.

CHAPTER 8

Other Types of Concentration Risk

Banks also potentially assume concentration risk in terms of the collateral that supports a loan and the physical location (geography) of borrowers. Think back to pre-crisis market conditions in high-growth coastal communities. Consider a bank with a high concentration of construction and land development loans. The loans are to developers who use a portion of the loan proceeds (interest reserve) to cover required interest payments until the underlying collateral—typically homes or buildings under construction and raw land—is sold. Until the time of sale, the financed real estate produces no cash flow. In hindsight, it is obvious that such loan concentrations create problems in fast-growing markets during boom times. Everyone was profitable. Many developers had multiple credit facilities with different lenders to fund multiple projects. The source of cash flow to service their debt came from selling lots and/or the home or building they built. When sales slowed or stopped and real estate values declined, borrowers (developers) didn't generate cash receipts to service debts. Banks holding too many of these loans and too much of this collateral were forced to charge-off the loans or sell them at a loss, both of which depleted capital.

Community banks make direct loans in limited geographic markets. While some banks attempt to diversify this risk by selling and buying loan participations with other lenders or bankers banks, many simply accept a loan portfolio that is highly sensitive to local economic conditions. Successful credit risk management limits these exposures by controlling loan growth, limited loan concentrations, understanding the true exposures of borrowers (fully aware of all contingent liabilities), and having access to ample liquidity and operating with above average capital.

Out-of-Market Lending

Community banks operate best when they deal with local customers. The bank's managers and owners understand the dynamics of the local economy and they know many of the principals when making loans because they live in the same area. Loan officers recognize the value in knowing the physical location of properties and being able to drive by the businesses and homes they are financing. Small businesses typically benefit from this local knowledge because as borrowers they prefer to deal with the same individual lender who understands their specific firm needs. They often have a performance history with the bank that demonstrates the business owner's philosophy and character in operating the business. Such is often the case with community bankers in agriculture markets who understand the various cycles in commodity and land prices and have observed how local farmers and agribusinesses have navigated previous downturns. While community banks cannot typically match the loan pricing offered by large, regional banks or the TBTF institutions, many small businesses are willing to pay a premium for the greater certainty of having a long-term relationship with their lender.[5] Importantly, credit decisions at community banks are made locally.

Banks often get in trouble when they move operations out-of-market. The reasons appear obvious today, but were largely ignored over the last decade by some institutions. Consider the many banks in low-growth regions of the country that either opened branches or acquired institutions in high-growth regions. It was not uncommon for banks in Nebraska and Minnesota to enter the banking business in Phoenix, Arizona or Las Vegas, Nevada. Banks in Georgia, North Carolina and South Carolina opened operations in Sarasota, Naples and Orlando, Florida. Oftentimes owner/managers chose the location based on where they had second homes. Out-of-market, by definition, signals that owners and managers are less familiar with local market conditions. While they may hire lenders who are familiar with local market conditions, there is less control over business activities by senior managers, the board and owners who generally live near headquarters in the original locale. They have taken on considerable credit risk if they do not know the key borrowers and fully comprehend the local business climate in the markets they enter.

Similar problems emerged with many of the loan participations that community banks booked. Loan participations are loans in which more than one lender extends credit to the borrower. A single bank typically originates the credit and sells (participates) pieces to other lenders. Each distinct lender is expected to conduct a detailed analysis of the borrower's credit risk, but many lenders don't conduct full due diligence. This may be because they trust the originating bank's credit standards and practices or because they do not want to commit the time and resources to fully understand the risks. Either way, it's a poor management practice to buy a participation without doing adequate due diligence. Not surprisingly, many of the problem loans that community banks held during the credit crisis are associated with these out-of-market credits generated via their own offices or via loan participations.

Poor Underwriting Standards

An integral part of a bank's loan policy is the establishment of underwriting standards. The standards specify the process that should be followed before a loan is approved including the type and quality of data analysis required and subjective elements that should be considered. Most loan officers conduct a detailed credit analysis of the borrower's character, capacity to borrow, capability in running a business, cash flow generation ability and initial capital invested, the associated collateral values and prevailing economic conditions and the loan terms relative to the borrower's financial condition.[6] For individuals, the analysis focuses on the borrower's employment history, sources and amounts of income, debt service requirements and net worth. For businesses, the analysis typically focuses on free cash flow that is generated by normal operations. In most instances, banks require some form of collateral as a secondary source of repayment especially when the borrower's cash flow may be viewed as risky and potentially insufficient to cover debt service. *Loan underwriting* is the label for this process.

The financial crisis revealed how lax bank underwriting standards were and how common practices exacerbated credit risk and the eventual losses from problem loans. Consider the following criticisms:

- *Loan concentrations exceeded reasonable thresholds.* Many banks focused on construction and development loans and loans for raw land (See CRE Threshold 1) and had portfolios well in excess of 100% of total capital. These loans generate no cash flow until the properties are built or developed and sold. Given the global decline in real estate values and the sharp drop in new home sales, many borrowers, particularly real estate developers without other sources of cash flow, defaulted on the loans. This problem reflects the fact that many lenders focused on collateral values and not cash flow. The financial crisis made it clear that real estate values fall and transactions volume can disappear. Without sales, borrowers cannot service debt. The value of collateral falls and borrowers have limited or no liquidity to service debt.

- *Banks provided 100% financing.* Banks generally enforce minimum loan-to-value (LTV) ratios when extending credit because it requires that a borrower have some "skin in the game." For example, an 80% minimum LTV ratio stipulates that the borrower initially put at least 20% equity into the project. The equity investment *reduces moral hazard* or the situation in which a borrower is willing to take on risk because he or she will not suffer consequences in the event of default. A homeowner who borrows 100% of the purchase price of a home is more willing to walk away from the mortgage when the value of the home falls below the outstanding loan amount. When a lender requires a 20% downpayment, the borrower's interests are more aligned with the lender's interests. During the crisis, many banks made loans requiring no downpayment. Subsequent declines in housing and related real estate values generated large losses and made the decision easier for some borrowers to walk away from their debts.

- *Banks did not verify the borrower's income.* Many banks relaxed standards to make "stated income" (liar) loans in which the bank did not obtain actual financial information but instead relied on the borrower to state his or her income. Not surprisingly, it was subsequently determined that many borrowers overstated their income in order to qualify for the loan. Imagine a borrower who did not formally report her income being told that she needed to have an annual income of $110,000 to qualify for the home loan she was seeking. She has a strong incentive to "state" that her income was at least $110,000, especially if she knew the lender would not verify the figure.

- *Banks did not obtain the borrower's current employment history or current income.* Even when they obtained financial information, banks often relied on old data. Relying on last year's tax return, for example, may produce unreliable decisions if employment conditions, outstanding debt or business activities change dramatically from the past year. This especially holds when the income is obtained from sources other than salary, such as commissions, royalties and dividends.

- *Banks did not verify the borrower's contingent debt or liquidity.* Many real estate developers are involved in multiple projects, often times using different *limited liability corporations* (LLCs) or partnerships. When submitting financial statements, loan officers would evaluate the borrower's financial condition in light of loans the bank extended, but they did not verify the amount of contingent debt associated with other LLCs or partnerships. Thus, even if the bank-funded project is successful, the borrower's contingent debt might lead to bankruptcy. Similarly, lenders consider a borrower's holdings of liquid assets when determining borrowing capacity and ability to repay a loan. Unless the liquid assets are held at the lending institution and/or pledged as collateral, they can disappear without the bank understanding that the borrower's condition is deteriorating.

Proposed solutions to poor underwriting include instituting more strict concentration limits, enforcing minimum LTV ratios well below 100%, verifying a borrower's current income and/or cash flow and verifying the borrower's contingent debt and liquidity. For the latter, the lender needs to require that a borrower hold sufficient liquid assets at the lending institution and obtain more frequent financial statements.

Insider Loans

A key negative to focusing on relationships is that relationships can be abused. One area of potential abuse is a bank's loans to insiders. The Federal Reserve defines insiders as executives, directors and principal shareholders of banks. Because of possible abuse and acceptable concentration limits, the Fed limits insider loans to any one borrower at no more than 5% of a bank's capital and to all insiders combined to no more than 100% of capital. Under Regulation O, a bank can extend credit to an insider as long as the loan "is made on substantially the same terms…as those prevailing at the time for comparable transactions…with other persons" and "does not involve more than the normal risk of repayment." Whether it is cronyism or a failure to conduct the appropriate due diligence, there has historically been a strong correlation between the amount of insider lending at a bank and a bank's underperformance including bank failure.[7] When a bank fails, the FDIC Office of Inspector General conducts a material loss review of the failed institution's performance. For banks that failed from 2008–2010, a high percentage of the reviews concluded that bank directors failed in their oversight of the institution with insider loans playing a key role. The implication is that directors are not sufficiently rigorous in approving insider loans. Sheila Bair, Chairman of the FDIC during the early stages of the crisis, stated "I'm deeply skeptical of any kind of insider lending."[8]

Troubled Debt Restructuring

When a borrower gets in financial distress, banks may choose to work with the borrower and modify the terms of the loan rather than force the borrower into default. The objective behind restructuring a loan is that the borrower may eventually pay sufficient principal and interest to where the bank recoups more than what it would have via a foreclosure. With default the bank must jump through legal hoops that are costly and potentially allow collateral value and repayment prospects to deteriorate. A *troubled debt restructuring* (TDR) is a loan in which a bank grants a concession to a borrower that it would not otherwise grant if the borrower was not in financial distress. Importantly, the fact that the terms of a loan are modified does not make the loan a TDR. For example, when the bank and borrower agree to a change in collateral underlying the loan the terms change but the loan is not necessarily a TDR unless the change was made because the borrower was in trouble financially. Banks with high levels of TDRs operate with significant credit risk. By definition, the underlying loans are troubled financially—post initial approval—such that the risk of loss is higher as is the loss in the event of default.

Know Your Borrower

The previous discussion summarizes recent problems in credit risk analysis. Another roundly-criticized culprit is the credit granting process known as the *originate-to-distribute* (OTD) model. As the name suggests, lenders originate loans with the intent of selling them to third-party investors. The loan originator is presumably less sensitive to the true riskiness of the borrower because it will not keep the loan in portfolio. As such, he is willing to make loans to less creditworthy borrowers simply to get deals done. If the process involves a securitization, it allows the rating agencies to grade the underlying securities backed by the loans favorably to make them more attractive to investors. Originators charge fees with the individual brokers paid on commission such that everyone has a strong incentive to continue generating new loans regardless of the quality.

The OTD model is tied to securitization in which the originator of loans doesn't intend to hold the loans in portfolio. Instead, the originator plans to sell the loans, which are packaged into a pool of similar loans that are used as collateral for new securities that are sold to investors. An underwriter who creates the securities works with the rating agencies to structure the securities backed by the loans to ensure the greatest marketability and highest overall ratings. Importantly, neither the underwriter nor rating agency gets paid if the securitization isn't completed. The originator typically holds on to the servicing rights on the loans through which it collects loan payments from the underlying borrowers, handles borrower inquiries and pays any insurance premiums and property taxes. If a borrower is delinquent or defaults, the servicer supervises the discussions and foreclosure process. The loan originator charges a fee for these services, but effectively transfers credit risk to the owners of the securities.

Many market participants view the OTD process as a key causal factor of the financial crisis. Ben Bernanke, Chairman of the Federal Reserve, supported this view in a speech during the early stages of the crisis that addressed subprime lending.[9]

> *At the point of origination, underwriting standards became increasingly compromised…In this case (of subprime mortgages), as in others, the incentives faced by originators were an important source of the breakdown in underwriting. The revenues of the originators of subprime mortgages were often tied to loan volume rather than the quality of the underlying credits, which induced some originators to focus on the quantity rather than the quality of the loans* [10]

If compensated by new loan volume, loan originators have strong incentives to relax both underwriting standards and their enforcement.[11] It is relatively easy to generate loan volume by making it easier for borrowers to qualify for loans. This was readily achieved by lowering downpayment requirements, creating *Alt-A* (no or low documentation) *loans* that allowed borrowers to lie about their financial condition or by creating option ARMs.[12] An *option ARM* is a mortgage with a 15-year or 30-year maturity, which gives the borrower several options regarding how much the monthly payment will be during the early part (first two years) of the mortgage. During the crisis the typical options ranged from a predetermined minimum payment, or an interest-only payment, to a payment that fully amortized loan principal plus interest. To attract borrowers, the interest rate during an initial short period was a low "teaser" rate. While borrowers could choose a different option each month, many always chose the option requiring the smallest payment. To further exacerbate the problem, the low payment option typically did not cover the full amount of interest or principal due under normal amortization such that the amount owed increased monthly, a situation known as *negative amortization*.

Consider a 30-year mortgage with $460,000 in principal carrying an initial teaser rate of 1%.[13] The teaser rate expired after three months when the loan converted to an ARM priced at one-month LIBOR + 2.90%. The initial payment was calculated based on the 1% rate and was fixed for one year. The payment subsequently increased by 7.5% annually (the maximum allowed under the loan) for the next four years. The fully-amortizing rate after the teaser expiration was 7%. In this case, the borrower would make a below-market payment that did not cover the amount necessary to fully amortize the loan for almost five years.

Exhibit 8.1 summarizes the scheduled minimum monthly payments for this option ARM. It assumes that the teaser rate applies for three months after which the borrower pays LIBOR + 2.90% while the loan rate equals a fixed 7% for the life of the loan. The minimum payment increased after the first year by the allowable maximum through most of year 5 after which it was "recast" and almost doubled to $3,747.83. Imagine being the borrower facing this "payment shock" as labeled by insiders.[14] At the time the payment increased to $3,747.83, the outstanding principal would have increased to $523,792.33, or almost $64,000 more than the original principal.

Exhibit 8.1 Sample Option ARM Monthly Payments For Pay Option ARM*

Year	Monthly Payment
1	$1,479.54
2	$1,590.51
3	$1,709.80
4	$1,838.04
5 (1st 9 months)	$1,975.89
Last 3 months of year 5	$3,747.83
6-30	$3,747.83

*$460,000 principal; 30-year maturity; 1% teaser for 3 months then floating at 1-month LIBOR + 2.90%.

A borrower could qualify for this mortgage if the lender approved the borrower using an initial payment based on the teaser rate and ignored the fully amortizing payment. In this context, borrowers with option ARMs could qualify for much larger mortgages based on the low, initial teaser payment. Still, after the first monthly payment date in the first year, the outstanding principal on the loan increases (negative amortization) by $1,554.59. Because each subsequent payment of $1,380.48 during the first year does not cover the obligated principal and interest at 7%, the outstanding principal will increase to approximately $479,000 at the end of the year. The only way the borrower (and ultimately the lender) wins with this option ARM is if the value of the home increases above the principal amount outstanding. Option ARMs were a bet on ever increasing home values. Why would lenders make such loans?

The OTD model failed because loan originators often did not have any skin in the game. If they could successfully securitize the underlying loans (mortgages, credit card loans, auto paper, etc.), they would generate revenues from fees and not loan interest. If loans defaulted after some predetermined period, the ultimate holders of the loans would not have recourse against the originators because they have assumed the credit risk. Mortgage brokers are paid on the basis of loan volume so they benefit from any deal that gets done even if the borrower doesn't have the financial strength to legitimately qualify for the mortgage.

Benefits and Costs from Knowing Your Borrower

Considerable research documents that smaller firms exploit "soft information" better than larger firms. For example, Brickley, Linck and Smith demonstrate that locally owned banks in Texas grant more decision-making authority to local managers who can use any information gained to better refine their estimates of risk and return.[15] The principal benefit of soft information is that bank managers should be better able to manage risk and generate higher long-term profits.

Knowing your customers is the essence of relationship banking and soft information. The fact that most community banks keep the loans they make in house and earn profits from the net interest spread further encourages a more careful assessment of risk and return potential. In essence, community banks "eat their own cooking." Many borrowers, in turn, prefer to deal with loan officers who have worked with them previously and thus know their business or personal financial situation. They do not want to continually retrain the loan officer as to any seasonality or specific quirks in the business, which is necessary when a new credit analyst reviews data underlying the relationship. The beneficial outcomes include faster decision-making when approving or rejecting a loan, the opportunity for the borrower to discuss specific issues with the same loan officer rather than dial a 1-800 telephone number, which allows for quicker and more direct resolution of problems and better pricing for the lender. Banks charge for generating the soft information. Borrowers from community banks are generally more willing to pay for the conveniences afforded them.

There are two fundamental costs to generating soft information. The first is that bank employees need to commit considerable time and effort to maintaining relationships. This is not inexpensive, particularly in terms of officers' involvement in local communities. The second is that lenders can become too close to their customers in the sense that they become advocates rather than observers of the associated relationships. When a borrower gets in trouble, the loan officer may be more willing to allow the customer to "work-out the problems" even to the detriment of the bank. A lender may essentially become blind to the risks involved in the relationship. Evidence of this difficulty appears in the large volume of problem loans to directors at many failed banks. In practice, senior management attempts to mitigate this conflict by moving the management of problem loans to individuals who were not involved in originating the underlying loans.

Loan Portfolio Credit Risk Analysis

Bankers and bank regulators evaluate individual loans on a case-by-case basis in terms of a borrower's character, capacity, capital, cash flow coverage of debt service, collateral available and prevailing economic conditions. The objective is to assess the nature of and magnitude or risk to better determine how much a borrower needs, what the loan proceeds will finance, whether and when the borrower might be able to repay the loan, and what collateral is appropriate. Typically, lenders collect a wide range of information regarding factors that impact the above questions and conduct both a quantitative analysis and descriptive analysis of the borrower's ability and willingness to repay. Quantitative analyses may involve credit scoring through which lenders use information available in credit reports to assign a "score" that presumably captures the level of risk associated with the borrower's financial history and current financial condition, or it may be modeled otherwise.

Cash Flow is King

When assessing whether to make a loan, lenders recognize that cash flow is the fundamental source of debt repayment. Some loans, such as a mortgage on a personal residence, are repaid periodically from disposable income and then ultimately when the underlying asset sells. Some loans are repaid when the borrower obtains financing from another source, such as a mortgage being refinanced with proceeds obtained from a different bank. Most loans are repaid over time with the source of funds from periodic disposable income or cash flow from business operations.

Many community banks rely on cash flow analysis to determine whether a borrower can service debt. With individuals, it often reduces to comparing disposable income to required interest and principal payments. Disposable income is calculated after netting out mandatory payments on other obligations, such as rent, utilities, and the like, and other loan payments. With businesses, lenders compare a borrower's cash flow from normal activities with periodic debt service requirements. Cash flow does not equal earnings (net income), but rather represents the difference between operating cash receipts and operating cash payments.[16] Unusual items ranging from receipts from asset sales to one time payments for production equipment do not affect the comparison. If the estimated periodic cash flow covers mandatory interest and principal payments over the life of the loan, a borrower can be expected to repay the loan under normal conditions.

Loan Portfolio Analysis

Bankers, bank regulators and bank analysts routinely attempt to analyze an individual bank's credit trends in order to assess the institution's overall safety, soundness and future profitability. The financial crisis and subsequent recession placed greater emphasis on asset quality issues. Banks that ultimately failed typically reported significant nonperforming assets followed by high loan charge-offs that depleted capital. As regulators imposed enforcement actions, the directives often required these struggling banks to improve asset quality, improve access to liquidity, grow earnings and raise capital. As might be expected, once participants recognize that a bank has asset quality problems and needs additional capital, investors shy away from committing new capital without knowing how severe the problems are and whether the new equity will simply "fill the hole" representing the capital deficiency. Once a bank reaches this stage, it is extremely difficult to raise any capital. If capital is raised successfully, existing owners substantially dilute their ownership and often give up control of the bank.

Bankers and bank analysts focus on a bank's asset quality by examining key performance measures related primarily to the loan portfolio. The UBPR introduced earlier emphasizes *noncurrent loans* defined as loans and lease receivables that are either past due 90 days or more (*nonperforming loans*) or in nonaccrual. *Nonperforming assets* (NPAs), in turn, equals nonperforming loans plus restructured loans and other real estate owned.[17] *Nonaccrual loans* are those more than 90 days past due but not in process of collection. *Net charge-offs*, also referred to as net losses, equals loans charged-off (formally recognized as uncollectible) minus gross loan recoveries (collections of receivables previously charged-off), while *provisions for loan losses* (PLL) equals the allocation to the allowance for loan losses reported on the income statement as an expense. The *allowance for loan losses* (ALLL), also referred to as the *loan loss reserve*, equals the contra-asset account representing cumulative provisions for loan losses since inception minus cumulative net charge-offs and is netted against total loans on the balance sheet to produce net loans. Every three months, banks report PLL and net charge-offs with the difference either increasing or decreasing the ALLL.

Finally, many banks calculate a *Texas Ratio* to capture risk exposure because some analysts, investors and regulators consider it a key indicator of potential insolvency in the future. In particular, a Texas Ratio in excess of one is deemed to be an indicator of a serious solvency problem.[18] In a post mortem of recent bank failures, Thomas Siems (2012) analyzed Texas Ratios for banks in different states and demonstrated that the percentage of banks with Texas Ratios above 100% was highest in Georgia, Florida and California from 2007 to 2012. As Exhibit 8.2 shows, the percentage of banks with Texas Ratios above 100% leads bank failures.

$$\text{Texas Ratio} = \frac{\text{Nonperforming assets + Other real estate owned}}{\text{Tangible common equity + Allowance for loan losses}}$$

COMMUNITY BANKING | FROM CRISIS TO PROSPERITY

Exhibit 8.2 The Texas Ratio

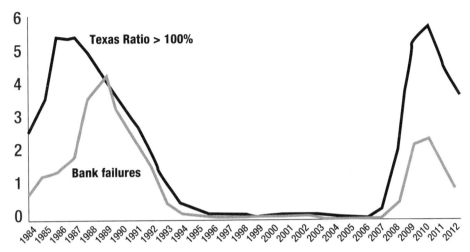

Sources: Reports of Conditions and Income, Federal Financial Institutions Examination Council, Federal Deposit Insurance Corp.; from Thomas Siems (2012).

Exhibit 8.3 Trends in Noncurrent Loans and Net Charge-offs, 2007–2013

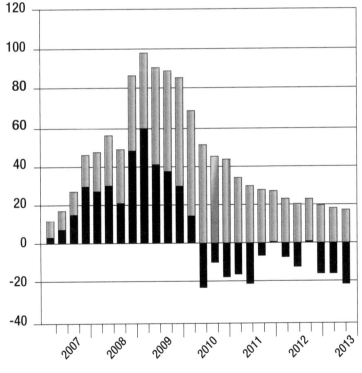

Data Source: Quarterly Banking Profile, www.fdic.gov.

Exhibit 8.3 reports quarterly data for net charge-offs and the change in noncurrent loans for all FDIC-insured banks from 2007 to mid-2013. Note the continuous increase in net charge-offs through 2009 and the corresponding greater changes in noncurrent loans at least through the first quarter of 2009. Because many noncurrent loans are eventually charged-off, an increase in noncurrent loans signals rising charge-offs at a later date. As expected, net charge-offs have fallen as the volume of noncurrent loans declined. Clearly, loan quality at insured banks has improved dramatically since 2010.

Exhibit 8.4 introduces several asset quality ratios that bank managers and analysts often emphasize when assessing aggregate credit risk. Obviously, values for these ratios will vary over time and should be compared with peer institutions to capture relative performance under similar economic conditions. It is difficult to compare ratios across banks because different institutions recognize loan losses at different stages and thus make provisions in different magnitudes relative to the same asset quality. In particular, there is considerable variation in when banks recognize that a loan in nonperforming. A bank that delays (is slow) recognizing nonperforming loans will generally report lower net loan losses over time. This, in turn, could lead to lower PLL and a smaller ALLL. The ratios listed in Exhibit 8.4 might then understate true credit risk.

Exhibit 8.4 Asset Quality Ratios

Ratio	Interpretation
Noncurrent loans / Gross loans	Higher: more loans potentially in default
Net loss / Average Total loans	Higher: more recognized loan charge-offs relative to loans; bank either recognizes uncollectible loans faster or has more uncollectible loans
PLL / Average total assets	Higher: more loans will likely be uncollectible
ALLL / Total loans	Higher: greater provisioning for loan losses over time net of charge-offs; bank either is more cautious in recognizing potential problems or anticipates greater amounts of net charge-offs
Noncurrent loans / (ALLL + Equity)	Higher: more loans potentially in default relative to equity capital
Texas Ratio	Greater than 100%: higher likelihood of future insolvency

Credit Risk Scoring

When extending credit, loan officers underwrite loans fully expecting the borrower to repay the loan. Otherwise, funding the loan would be irresponsible and potentially fraudulent. However, conditions change over time such that a borrower may not be able to repay the loan as originally promised even when the intention is to do so. Economic conditions may change and the borrower's financial condition may change due to shifts in demand for the underlying product or service, loss of employment, and the like. Consider the recent experience with the housing meltdown. Imagine that you run a commercial or retail business in Las Vegas or Phoenix. As the housing market plummeted and unemployment skyrocketed, demand for your products and services likely collapsed regardless of whether your activities were directly linked to housing. At the time a loan is originated, the lender assesses the riskiness of the borrower and structures the loan terms to best facilitate repayment so that the borrower has the ability and capacity to repay the loan and the bank is protected in the event of difficulties or loan default. The loan maturity, pricing and required collateral reflect this risk assessment. Lenders, in turn, aggregate their expectations of loan performance across the entire loan portfolio to better gauge aggregate losses.

Most banks use some form of a risk rating system, such as the credit risk scoring chart that appears in Exhibit 8.5, to categorize loans by estimated exposure. The first column lists key credit and financial characteristics of the borrower and loan request. The subsequent columns indicate

Exhibit 8.5 Credit Risk Scoring Chart

Credit/Financial Characteristics	Existing and New Loans					Loans in Liquidation		
	1. Excellent	2. Prime	3. Average	4. Acceptable	6. OLEM*	7. Substandard	8. Doubtful	9. Loss
Global Debt Coverage	>2.5X	>1.5X	>1.15X	>1.0X	Recent negative cash flow	1–2 years negative cash flow in non-accrual	2–3 years negative cash flow in non-accrual	Charge off
Business Income (Net) or Personal Income	History of strong, stable income	Relatively strong, stable income	Marginal but stable income	Marginal income	1 year of losses	2 or more years of losses; insufficient income to cover debt service	large, continuous losses	
Liquidity Current Ratio	High liquidity & unpledged assets	Good liquidty & unpledged assets	Average liquidity; unpledged assets	Limited liquidity	No liquidity; no unpledged assets	Negative net working capital	Assets in process of liquidation	
Financial Leverage Debt/Worth	0.5 to 1.0 no contingent debt	1.0 to 1.5 contingent debt < net worth	1.5 to 3.0 contingent debt = net worth	>3.0 contingent debt > net worth	Negative equity; current-year loss	Significant negative equity	Unable to service debt	
Capital/ Stockholders Equity/ Net Worth	Well capitalized	Strong capital	High leverage NW > $.5 million	Small, positive equity	Negative equity	Negative equity; losses will increase	Negative equity; new capital unavailable	
Collateral	Superior; easily liquidated LTV < 0.5	Good LTV < policy limit	Sufficient LTV within policy	Covers, but exceeds policy	Shortage	Insufficient; no other collateral	Potential for at least 50% loss	
Repayment History Credit Bureau Score	Excellent, no delinquency score > 800	Good; no collect. diff. score > 725	Some slow score > 650	Chronically slow score > 625	Serious delinquent. nonaccrual score < 625	Other repayment sources	Uncollectible loan without legal action	
Management	Long history, stable	Qualified but 5–10 years experience	No negative; <5 years experience	New/ unproven	Serious evident weaknesses	Loss confidence	No confidence	
Strength of Guarantors	Strong; liquid	Strong; limited liquidity	Average; just 1 guarantor	Unknown; no current financing	Little; some recov. Potential	Recovery doubtful	No strength or recovery potential	

OLEM refers to other loans especially mentioned.

loans by risk rating ranging from excellent (1-rated loans) representing the lowest risk credits to loans rated loss (9-rated loans) in which the bank recognizes that it will charge-off the outstanding loan balance. In this framework, loans rated 1 to 6 are performing, albeit some only marginally, while loans rated 7 to 9 are effectively in liquidation. Formally, loans rated 6 to 9 are labeled *classified loans*. Regulators view classified loans as those exhibiting higher than normal amounts of risk and thus more likely to produce a loss. When regulators examine banks, they pull a sample of loans and evaluate the associated riskiness and required documentation. If they disagree with management on a loan grade, they will typically require that management change the rating to a lower grade (such as from a 6 to a 7). This affects the amount of the ALLL as well as the potential treatment of the loan at maturity. For example, you would normally not renew a loan rated 7 or higher, while you may consider renewing loans rated as high as 6 if conditions warrant it.

The characteristics in the first column reflect metrics that help determine the credit risk inherent in a loan. For example, *global debt coverage* measures a borrower's annual net operating income divided by annual debt service including principal and interest. *Net operating income* (NOI) excludes noncash and extraordinary items and serves as a measure of operating cash flow. The term "global" indicates that many different revenues and expenses, and not just those associated with the specific property, individual or loan request, are considered. With a commercial mortgage, net operating income equals the net cash flow generated by the underlying property divided by the commercial mortgage payment. NOI may be converted to a global cash flow figure by summing the cash flows and debt service for the underlying property and property owner.[19] For an individual loan, the income and expenses used to produce net operating income are those associated with a specific borrower. Importantly, banks will set minimum coverage ratios with greater coverage signifying lower credit risk as noted in the exhibit.

The other credit and financial characteristics and associated descriptions within the risk categories demonstrate the types of information that affect perceived credit risk. Clearly, a loan in a lower risk category (1 to 3) has a lower likelihood of default than loans in higher risk categories. Similarly, management might reasonably expect that the loss the bank might realize in the event of default (LGD) would be smaller. Lenders should consider both the probability of default and potential loss exposure (LGD) when approving and pricing loans.

With high levels of nonperforming loans, many banks have incorporated *migration analysis* to help assess credit risk and determine the appropriate size of the ALLL. In its most basic form, banks examine the loss experience for a pool of loans over several years. The primary objective is to determine the rate of loss and extent of loss on specific categories of similarly-rated loans. Ideally, a bank would collect historical data over recent years on the number and amount of loans in each rating category from Exhibit 8.5. Management would track the frequency and magnitude of the amounts of loans moving from one rating category to another and ultimately the actual loss rate on loans in each category. This provides useful information on how much the bank might be able to collect and how long it might take to actually generate cash from a high risk loan.

Determining the Size of the Allowance for Loan Losses

During the financial crisis, a common headline related to bank performance might read "Net Loss for Suspect Bank Widens as Loan Loss Provisions Increase: Stock Price Falls Sharply." The article would proceed to document the increase in net charge-offs versus the prior quarter and one year previous, then indicate that the ALLL increased. It might also reference Suspect Bank's capital ratios to signal whether the bank was still well-capitalized or was now a problem institution. Even if a bank's stock is not publicly traded, the market's response to such information is typically negative. Not surprisingly, with asset quality issues the adequacy of the ALLL and ultimately the adequacy of a bank's capital is viewed in light of how management determines the size of the ALLL.

What constitutes an adequate ALLL is in the eye of the beholder. Not surprisingly, it often varies across the parties involved in establishing its value. Prior to the recent financial crisis, accounting standards had moved banks toward using recent loan loss experience in setting the ALLL. With few loan losses from 2000 to 2006, most banks were operating with low allowances because they were not permitted to increase PLL even when loan portfolios increased sharply in size. This changed with rising loan defaults following 2007. In today's world, bank regulators often view conditions as being more severe than internal bank management does and subsequently require loan downgrades (change the ratings from 1–4 to 5–8 in Exhibit 8.5). Accountants similarly want to protect the "objectiveness" of their analysis and take a negative view of future performance opportunities.[20] As such, a higher ALLL is often viewed as appropriate. Importantly, if management were to disagree with its accountants and the accounting firm subsequently gave a "qualified opinion" on the bank's financials, the bank will not likely be able to get *director and officer* (D&O) insurance. Management has limited choices as to how to respond.

Generally, the ALLL should be of a size that reflects expected losses across all loan types over some future time period. Banks, accountants and regulators are currently debating what the relevant future time horizon should be. Banks should analyze their loan portfolios by loan types and rating categories because loss rates and corresponding LGD vary across types. Ideally, management can examine factors such as historical magnitudes of nonperforming loans, the associated loan loss rates (frequencies) and LGD, which they can then relate to the current portfolio grouped according to the categories in a credit rating analysis like that provided in Exhibit 8.5. Management can then set the ALLL based on the loan grades and expected loss severity.[21] Many analysts have criticized banks for slow recognition of problem loans and potentially overstating profits by understanding provisions for loan losses and the ALLL. Exhibit 8.6 documents trends in noncurrent loans and the ALLL for all FDIC-insured banks from 2007 to mid-2013. Note the sharp increase in noncurrent loans with a smaller increase in loan loss reserves leading to the systematic drop in the reserve coverage ratio (ALLL divided by noncurrent loans). This decline suggests that the banking industry has recognized fewer potential losses relative to problem loans in recent years.

Exhibit 8.6 Reserve Coverage Ratio, 2007 – 2013 (billions)

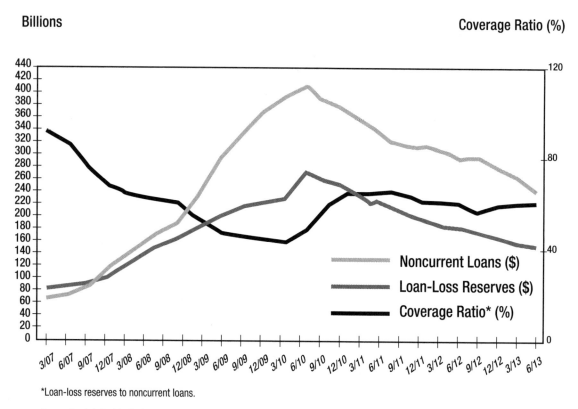

*Loan-loss reserves to noncurrent loans.

Source: Quarterly Banking Profile, www.fdic.gov

Reporting for Troubled Debt Restructurings

During the past few years, many banks have altered the terms of loans to increase the likelihood that a troubled borrower would be able to repay more of the promised principal and interest over time, thereby creating TDRs. Typically, the lender and borrower agree to a loan workout in which the original interest rate is reduced, the maturity date is extended or the principal owed is lowered.[21] These negotiations often arise because the borrower is facing foreclosure and the bank is faced with the option of going through the foreclosure process and taking possession of the collateral or renegotiating the loan terms. The banker's hope is that a restructuring will ultimately enable the borrower to repay more of the funds than what the bank might collect via foreclosure.

Under accounting rules, banks must report TDRs in their quarterly reports. The existence of TDRs affects the reporting of problem loans and subsequent loss reserve accounting. Specifically, while a TDR remains a TDR until the borrower repays it in full, a bank can stop reporting it in the calendar year after the TDR was originated if the borrower is meeting the modified loan terms and the loan yield is a market rate. Similarly, a bank can remove the TDR from its non-accrual loans once it is restructured. Thus, banks with TDRs may appear to have better asset quality and earnings power than other institutions without TDRs.

Loan Workouts

Most banks dedicate internal credit specialists to the loan workout function. With the recent financial crisis and subsequent recession, many banks have seen their nonperforming assets increase sharply such that workout specialists are quite busy. Loan workout refers to the process in which a lender and a borrower who is delinquent in making loan payments mutually agree to resolve the delinquency. Typically, the agreement involves modifying the terms of the original loan (hence a loan workout is often referred to as a loan modification) to where the borrower can meet the payment obligations. A TDR is a form of loan workout driven by legal and economic conditions. A loan modification is not normally a TDR.

When the loan terms are modified, the workout terms may involve any of the following:

- *Reduction in the periodic interest and principal payments*: a lender may reduce the amount of principal or possibly defer some portion to a balloon payment later in the future; it may also lower the effective interest rate paid.

- *Increase in loan maturity*: as maturity increases, an amortizing loan's periodic payments falls when the principal amount remains constant; if the principal amount is reduced and maturity increased, the periodic payment can fall sharply.

- *Change in the party that controls (owns) the underlying collateral*. A lender may have a claim on underlying collateral. A borrower may agree to give the lender the collateral in exchange for a release from liability. The lender may sell the collateral and use the proceeds to pay down the borrower's loan.

- *Change in the form of guarantee or guarantors*. As a condition of relaxing credit terms, a lender may agree to allow the borrower to add guarantors or pledge additional assets as collateral.

- *Modification of nonfinancial terms in the event of default*. A lender may agree to strengthen terms allowing it to pursue remedies in the event of default, such as adding new factors that trigger default and accelerate debt repayment, or waive the borrower's rights under default.

The negotiations presumably benefit both the lender and borrower. Logically, a lender would not foreclose on a delinquent borrower if the borrower could repay more by remaining in business with a modified loan. A loan modification accelerates collection because it occurs much faster than through litigation and helps collateral retain its value. Long-term it may also be lower cost and allow the lender to get a release from the borrower for any potential loss under a lender liability claim. A borrower, in turn, likely gets easier credit terms and avoids expenses associated with foreclosure litigation. Finally, a loan modification does not disrupt the borrower's business activity as much as foreclosure. The borrower remains in operation, doesn't face the impact of negative publicity and retains the opportunity to reclaim franchise value.

Other Forms of Loan Workouts

Other loan workout remedies are available. At one extreme, the lender can foreclose on the borrower. At the other extreme, the lender might suspend required loan payments (forbearance) until the borrower has the capacity to repay the loan. Because foreclosure is expensive, most lenders and borrowers pursue other options before initiating the foreclosure process. Some of the other solutions include:

Deed in Lieu of Foreclosure. Borrower conveys all interest in real property to the lender to satisfy a delinquent loan. The deed in lieu releases the borrower from almost all obligations associated with the loan. The benefit to a lender is that collection is accelerated. It is generally unattractive to lenders because many borrowers have a capacity to repay more of their obligations under defaulted loans. However, a lender is going to have to foreclose and pursue rights legally, which is expensive and may take considerable time that potentially allows the underlying property to deteriorate.

Pre-Foreclosure Sale. Sell the business or real estate prior to foreclosure and use the proceeds to pay off the loan. If the proceeds are insufficient to cover the outstanding principal, the transaction is referred to as a short sale.

Loan Assumption. New borrower steps in and assumes payment on the loan. Original borrower and new borrower enter into a side contract.

Forbearance. Reduce or suspend required debt service payments until the borrower's financial condition improves. Lender loses an earning asset and essentially "kicks the problem loan down the road."

Foreclosure. Lender obtains a court order that terminates a borrower's right to property. The lender can subsequently repossess the property that it then resells. Working through the foreclosure process takes considerable time given a borrower's rights and entails significant legal and opportunity costs as the lender foregoes an earning asset.

Loan workouts add value to the bank because they collect on outstanding obligations. They effectively convert nonearning assets into earning assets. Eventually, they reduce nonperforming assets and allow management to focus on core operations and growing the business.

Summary

Whether a bank is performing well or poorly in the current environment depends largely on its asset quality. Given the great recession and corresponding lapse in consumer spending, banks with heavy exposure in commercial real estate and other asset classes with problems are facing continued loan write-downs and charge-offs. These same banks find it difficult to raise external capital because investors do not have confidence that the problem assets are gone. Why invest if a bank is simply going to continue to charge off loans as uncollectible? This chapter examines factors that are associated with better credit risk management. It also examines efforts to work through existing problem loans.

CHAPTER 9
Managing the Investment Portfolio

Moody's Investor Services Inc., Standard and Poor's (S&P) Inc. and Fitch Inc. are well-known firms in the business of evaluating the credit quality of fixed-income securities issued by government entities and private corporations. Before they formally assign a rating, they evaluate the legal and financial condition of the issuer to assess the riskiness of the instruments to investors. Consider the data in Exhibit 9.1, which lists the general rating categories for Moody's and S&P. Moving from the top of the list to the bottom, the likelihood of default presumably declines. Thus, securities rated Aaa (Moody's) and AAA (S&P and Fitch) are deemed to be the highest credit quality and presumably embody the lowest risk of default.[1] In general terms, securities rated in the top four categories by both groups are labeled *investment grade* while those rated lower plus nonrated securities are labeled *junk*.

Historically, the federal government formally recognized the authority of these firms and a few others by granting each of them status as a Nationally Recognized Statistical Ratings Organization (NRSRO). This status was important because banks and other institutions, such as pension funds, were deemed to have met their fiduciary duty if they purchased investment grade securities. When conditions changed, these rating agencies were expected to raise or lower the ratings as appropriate. The implication was that these NRSROs provided reliable and credible ratings such that many investors around the world relied just on the ratings rather than performing their own due diligence. How wrong this proved to be!

During the financial crisis, many securities carrying the highest ratings defaulted soon after issue. In August 2008, the rating agencies lowered the ratings of preferred stock issued by Fannie Mae and Freddie Mac from AA to A (Aa to A) indicating greater credit risk even though the securities remained investment grade. They lowered the ratings another notch in September 2008 (to BBB and Baa) just before the federal government placed the firms into conservatorship and eliminated dividends on the preferred stock.[2] Not surprisingly, the securities quickly fell to junk status and plummeted in value. How would you like to own these preferred stock issues of Fannie and Freddie, well-known Government Sponsored Enterprises (GSEs) believed by many to carry a government guarantee, or an Aaa-rated mortgage-backed security only to see it fall in value by 70% after a few months? Of course, in order to mitigate their legal liability, the ratings firms cite their ratings as merely "opinions" and thus not subject to review for accuracy. How convenient.[3]

Exhibit 9.1 General Ratings Provided by Moody's and S&P

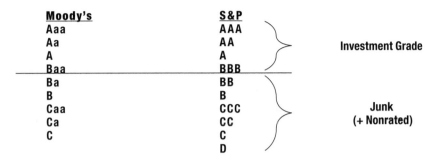

Dodd-Frank Act Response to Ratings

Section 939A of the Dodd-Frank Act (DFA) mandates that federal regulatory agencies modify regulations regarding standards of creditworthiness that were historically based on NRSRO ratings by removing any strict reliance on credit ratings. In June 2012, the bank regulators provided final rules and guidance that essentially removed references to credit ratings from the regulatory definition of *investment grade*. Effective January 2013, banks must independently determine that a security's default risk is low and that the "full and timely repayment of principal and interest is expected." Banks may use credit ratings to assist in this evaluation, but cannot rely exclusively on such ratings. Banks, like other investors, must now conduct their own due diligence when investing in bonds and short-term securities. They should maintain a credit file on each issuer and fully understand the sources and expected magnitudes of cash flows that support promised debt service payments. With the fiscal problems faced by the U.S. government and most states and local governments, there are no sure things anymore. Witness problems associated with Detroit filing for bankruptcy in August 2013 and the potential for principal losses on Detroit's outstanding general obligation municipals.

There are several obvious implications from requiring banks to do their own due diligence on bonds. First, it will increase the cost of investing in securities. Banks may hire or train experts to perform the detailed credit analysis or they may contract it out to a third party. Second, portfolio managers do not always have a meaningful period of time to conduct extensive due diligence before a new bond offering is sold. Consider the case with typical offerings of municipals. A bond broker contacts the bank's investment officer with the opportunity to buy an attractive in-state bond and indicates that the block will likely be sold out in one-to-two hours.[4] How does the officer perform a detailed credit analysis of the issue and issuer in such a short time? Many bank investment officers fear that they will be excluded from buying such attractive bonds. Finally, when buying bonds banks will likely purchase larger blocks to spread the higher cost of analysis across larger holdings of individual securities.

Characteristics of Investment Instruments

Banks invest heavily in fixed-income securities. A typical bank's investment portfolio consists primarily of short-term money market instruments, bonds and occasionally preferred stock. *Money market instruments* have maturities of one year or less and take the form of bills, commercial paper, CDs, repurchase agreements (repos) and municipal notes. *Bonds* represent debt instruments issued by governmental units and corporations and are traded through securities dealers. Different types of bonds are characterized by the issuing entity, which includes the U.S. Treasury, federal agencies such as Fannie Mae and Freddie Mac, corporations and state and local governmental units. *Preferred stock* exhibits characteristics of both bonds and common stock. It is a form of equity that pays a dividend to the holder that must be paid before any common stockholder is paid a dividend. It may be callable or convertible into common stock after a set deferment period. Holders have no voting rights but will be paid before common stockholders in the event of default by the issuer. All of these instruments are passive investments because the bank is a price taker who has no direct contact with the issuing entity. They generate interest or dividend income but also expose the bank to the potential loss of principal as demonstrated by Fannie and Freddie and periodic municipal defaults.

Why Buy Securities?

If loans and deposits drive a community bank's relationship with its customers, why do managers buy passive investment securities? When valuing a bank for acquisition purposes, buyers attach little value to the investment portfolio beyond its current market value because securities holdings bring no new relationships for the buyer to cross-sell other services. The obvious answer is that investment securities generate income and have a different risk profile than loans. In most cases, the instruments have less default risk and are more liquid versus loans. Of course, the precise rationale is more complicated.

Objectives of the Investment Portfolio

Banks buy investment securities to meet one or more of the following objectives:

- Preservation of capital
- Liquidity
- Pledging requirements
- Current income, yield and cash flow
- Interest rate risk management
- Diversification

The nature of the local markets served, the competitive environment, the structure of the bank's balance sheet and its organizational form all affect the portfolio size and composition and the extent to which each of the previous objectives is emphasized.

Preservation of Capital

Because banks take significant amounts of credit risk in their loan portfolios, they focus on preserving principal when buying investment securities. Regulators encourage this emphasis by requiring banks to buy investment grade securities or their equivalent. Banks thus concentrate their purchases on securities in the top four rating categories that are the equivalent of investment grade instruments. They also buy nonrated securities but justify that the credit risk is acceptable by conducting due diligence and maintaining the supporting credit file. Many banks got lazy over time by relying almost exclusively on the rating. If Moody's or S&P rated it A or higher, the bond presumably had relatively low risk. Banks could increase yield by moving from the highest-rated securities to the lowest investment grade securities (BBB or Baa), but often paid little regard to the risk of principal. The financial crisis demonstrated the folly of this approach. Banks holding preferred stock issued by Fannie and Freddie took huge write-downs when the government (by fiat) eliminated the stocks' dividends. Banks holding trust preferred stock issued by other financial institutions and private-label mortgage-backed securities experienced the same types of losses. The lesson is that some securities carry significant default risk regardless of rating. Banks must do detailed due diligence on the underlying issuers of all securities, even those rated investment grade given DFA provisions.

Liquidity

Periodically, banks experience unanticipated deposit outflows and must fund loans on demand. Investment securities assist in meeting these liquidity needs because they are assets that management can sell in the secondary market if they meet certain criteria. The most liquid securities have standard features, such as a well-known issuer with low default risk, a short maturity and no complex options. They typically trade at prices above or equal to par or amortized cost so the bank can sell them at a gain.[5] In response to the financial crisis, regulators now encourage banks to hold more liquid securities because history shows that accessing liquid funds by borrowing is not always possible. Banks that think they have credit lines with correspondent banks may find that the credit isn't available if the bank or its correspondent is viewed as being in distress.

Pledging Requirements

When banks make loans to businesses and individuals, they often require collateral as a secondary source of repayment if the borrower defaults. Think of a car loan in which the borrower pledges the car as collateral. If the customer defaults on the loan payments, the bank takes possession of the car. Banks, like their loan customers, must similarly hold collateral against some of their borrowings. Specifically, banks must pledge collateral to the Federal Reserve against borrowings from the discount window, to the Federal Home Loan Bank against advances, to the lender in a repo transaction and to public entities, such as states and local governments, against these units' public deposits held at the banks. Collectively, the collateral is held to meet pledging requirements. Each lender specifies the type of assets that qualify as collateral and the amount required. Most lenders accept readily identifiable and highly liquid securities as collateral at close to par or face value. They will require greater amounts of collateral when the securities exhibit significant default risk or trade in illiquid markets.[6] Banks buy securities to meet these collateral requirements and put them in escrow so that the lender is assured that they won't be sold without authorization. Such pledged securities are illiquid.

Yield, Current Income and Consistent Cash Flow

Managers obviously want to generate income from their securities purchases. Thus, the amount and timing of interest and dividends received play a role in influencing the choice of securities. Traditional bonds pay semi-annual interest. A 10-year maturity bond with $1 million in face value carrying a 5% coupon rate thus pays $25,000 in coupon interest (5%/2 × $1,000,000) every six months. Over 10 years, the issuer would make 20 interest payments of $25,000. Absent default, the $1 million in principal is paid at maturity in 10 years. Sometimes the focus on yield is misplaced. For example, a security's *yield to maturity* refers to the discount rate that equates the sum of the present values of promised cash flows from the security with the purchase price. It is an expected, or promised, yield because the cash flows are uncertain. It assumes that an investor reinvests any cash flow received at the calculated yield to maturity. It is thus a mathematical construct based on the underlying assumptions of whether and when the cash flows will arise and what the investor does with the cash flows until maturity. It is an opinion and not a fact. While some banks focus on yield, others are "yield hogs" who seek out securities offering the highest current income. For whatever reason, they often have a need for near-term revenue. Such banks focus on current yield measured as the annual cash flows from a security divided by its current price. This yield measure ignores present value and thus penalizes zero and low coupon instruments.

$$\text{Current Yield} = \frac{\text{Annual Cash Flow}}{\text{Price}}$$

Many banks look to the investment portfolio to generate steady, consistent cash flows that assist managers in planning. Each month they can accurately forecast cash receipts from maturing securities, coupon interest payments and dividends received, which allows them to better meet deposit outflows and new loan demand. For this reason, many banks follow a laddered-maturity

Exhibit 9.2 Laddered Maturity Bond Portfolio

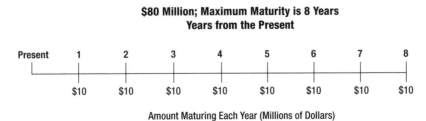

strategy when buying bonds. Examine the maturity schedule that appears in Exhibit 9.2 for a bank with an $80 million portfolio. Assuming that the bank doesn't want to own anything with a maturity beyond 8 years, it would structure the portfolio to have $10 million in bonds mature each year. Hence, the ladder is represented by equal maturities. Each year, the bank would receive interest and dividend income from the $80 million invested plus $10 million in principal. The annual investment decision is straightforward. Which 8-year maturity instrument should we buy to replace the $10 million in maturing securities? It is thus a passive investment strategy driven by a desire for constant cash inflows.

Interest rate Risk Management

The next chapter demonstrates that changing interest rates can create havoc for banks because loans are typically repriced at different times and by different amounts than deposits. Managers can readily buy and sell securities as needed to better balance the bank's exposure to changing interest rates. For example, if the bank is positioned to lose when rates increase, the bank may choose to sell long-term securities with fixed-rates and buy short-term securities. In this case, the bank would now hold assets that can be repriced sooner at higher rates if, in fact, rates do increase. Management has reduced its exposure to loss from rising rates. The appeal of securities in filling this role recognizes that there is no relationship between the bank and the issuer. The customer (issuer) doesn't know or care that the bank has sold its bond.

Diversification

Banks that compete in limited geographic and product markets have highly concentrated loan portfolios. Buying securities diversifies credit risk across borrowers. Some securities are issued by governmental units who pledge future tax receipts or revenues from projects against their debt. Some securities are collateralized by principal and interest payments on mortgages and may (or may not) carry a government guarantee of principal. Others are issued by private firms with firm cash flows securing the promised payments. Banks often limit their investments to known issuers, such as federal agencies, local government units and private corporations for which they know senior management. Historically, many banks trusted and accepted the credit analysis of the NRSROs who dramatically overstated the credit quality of many issues during the financial crisis. These rating agencies are paid by the investment banks who manage the security offerings, which creates a serious conflict of interest because no one gets paid if an offering isn't completed. Hence, the incentive for the issuer, investment bank and rating agency is to structure a deal to get the highest rating yet ensure that the deal gets done.

Accounting for Securities Holdings

Under *generally accepted accounting principles* (GAAP), banks classify investment securities on their balance sheets based on management's intent behind the purchase. Depending on the intent, different accounting rules apply regarding the reporting of gains or losses and the appropriate value for the balance sheet. There are three basic categories: held for trading (HFT), held to maturity (HTM) and available for sale (AFS).

- *Held for Trading (HFT)* Some large banks buy securities with the intent to quickly resell them. They expect to profit on the trades by timing the market, essentially by buying at a low price and selling at a higher price. Because this is a normal component of their business, banks record the gains and losses as operating income during the period they arise. Importantly, both realized and unrealized gains and losses are included. Banks record HFT securities on the balance sheet at their market values as of the reporting date.

- *Held to Maturity (HTM)* As the name suggests, banks buy HTM securities with the intent of holding them until maturity. Because the investment objective is long-term, the bank expects to receive periodic interest and principal until the obligation is totally repaid at maturity. There will be no reported interim gains or losses unless the security defaults. Thus there is no income statement impact other than recording the periodic interest. Similarly, banks report the value of HTM instruments at amortized cost on the balance sheet. Changes in market values do not affect the reported amounts.

- *Available for Sale (AFS)* By default, securities not classified as HFT or HTM are labeled AFS. By placing bonds in this category, managers retain the right to sell the securities prior to maturity. The intent is to hold them until management deems it appropriate to sell them. The accounting is thus close to that for HFT securities. Specifically, banks record the securities at market value on the balance sheet. Because market values change over time, they record the corresponding unrealized gains or losses as a component of equity in the form of *other comprehensive income* (OCI). Thus, if a security's value falls (rises) after purchase, the unrealized loss (gain) will reduce (increase) reported stockholders equity. Effective in 2015, banks have a one-time option to either include or exclude these unrealized gains or losses in Tier 1 capital under Basel III.

The accounting classification has two dramatic effects on risk management practices. First, HTM securities cannot be sold prior to maturity unless the underlying instrument's credit risk has increased, tax laws change to reduce the tax-exempt status of interest on the security, or regulators change risk weights for capital purposes, among other reasons. If a bank were to sell an HTM security in the normal course of business, it may be required to reclassify all securities as AFS and restate historical financial information. For all practical purposes, HTM securities are illiquid. Second, because the change in market values of AFS securities is reported on the balance sheet every quarter, a bank may see its reported equity rise or fall due entirely to falling or rising interest rates. Even when management has no intention of realizing the underlying gains or losses, parties who review a bank's financial statements may mis-attribute changes in equity to changes in the bank's operating earnings. Both increase the perception of how risky a bank's activities are.

CHAPTER 9

Types of Securities Owned

Banks own a variety of investment securities. Most are issued or guaranteed by governmental units and generate taxable interest income. As such, they generally exhibit low default risk but may carry significant price risk, option risk and be relatively illiquid. Others, such as private-label mortgage backed securities and trust preferred securities, are issued by private corporations and do not carry government guarantees. During the financial crisis, banks have been forced to write-down the values of many of these corporate securities because there was no secondary market as few investors wanted to hold them and because some issuers deferred dividends or defaulted outright. The following discussion summarizes the key characteristics of different securities and explains the fundamental managerial issue when assessing each as an investment alternative.

Treasury Securities

The U.S. Treasury regularly issues bills, notes and bonds to finance the budget deficit and to generate operating revenues between tax collections. Treasury bills are short-term instruments with an original maturity of one year or less and are sold at weekly auctions. Treasury notes and bonds have original maturities from 1 to 10 years and greater than 10 years, respectively. Treasuries are attractive because they are backed by the federal government's credit and taxing authority and are highly liquid. They are not sold with call and put options with longer-term instruments labeled bullet bonds (or bullet loans) because they have set maturities and all principal is paid at maturity. These features, in turn, mean that they carry low interest rates relative to other securities. Many investors compare yields on non-Treasury securities to Treasury yields for securities with the same maturity or duration. Hence, Treasury yields often serve as a benchmark yield curve for yield analysis.

Agency Securities

Agency securities are issued by U.S. government agencies and GSEs. Securities issued by the Government National Mortgage Association (GNMA or Ginnie Mae) are backed by the U.S. government's credit and taxing authority, but carry higher yields than Treasuries due to risks other than default. The list of GSEs includes Fannie Mae, Freddie Mac, the FHLBs, Tennessee Valley Authority and Federal Farm Credit Bank Funding Corporation. Because these are quasi-public entities with only an implied government guarantee, the securities carry some credit risk so that yields are again higher than comparable Treasury yields. One advantage for taxable investors is that interest on FHLB, TVA and Farm Credit bonds is exempt from state income taxes.

Agency bonds can be either bullets or callables. Many banks are particularly attracted to callable agencies because they offer higher promised yields compared with agency bullets of the same maturity. However, many bankers do not fully understand the different types of call options and how to value the options. Why is this important? The answer is that they are potentially overpaying for the security and giving up interest income over time. If the yield curve is upsloping as it is during normal times and if rates remain constant or fall over time, the issuing agency will call its bond (return the investor's principal prior to maturity) and the bank will be left to reinvest the proceeds at less attractive rates.

Understand the Call Option Embedded in Callable Agencies

A callable bond allows the issuer of the security to repay the principal at its discretion after a call deferment period. The call feature in a bond is an option. The issuer of the bond buys the option because it controls when the bond is called, that is, when the option is exercised. The investor (bank), in turn, sells the option for which it should get paid because it has given the issuer the right to pay the principal back prior to maturity. Callables appear to be attractive investments because they offer higher promised yields under normal yield calculations. In fact, many securities dealers compare yields on callables with yields on similar maturity bullets issued by the same agency. Consider the data in Exhibit 9.3 that compares yields on five-year maturity agency callables with different call features and a five-year agency bullet bond.

The agency call structures are referred to as American (Continuous), Discrete (Bermudan) or One-Time (European) call options. The term call date refers to the specific date when an issuer can redeem the bond by buying the bond back from the bond holder. The time until the call date is labeled the call deferment period.

- *Continuous*: after the call date, the bond can be called at any time until maturity.
- *Discrete*: after the call date, the bond can be called at predetermined intervals, such as quarterly, semi-annually or annually after the call date.
- *One-Time*: the bond can be called only on the call date.

Exhibit 9.3 Promised Yields on Callable Agency Securities: All Bonds Have a 5-Year Maturity

Call Feature/Structure	Call Deferment Period		
	6 Months	1 Year	2 Years
Continuous	2.15%	2.09%	2.03%
Quarterly	2.10%	2.04%	1.92%
One-Time	2.05%	1.98%	1.90%

Note: 5-year bullet agency bond yield is 1.75%.

Logically, the call option has greater value to the issuer when the deferment period is short and when the agency can call the bond most frequently. In the case of 5-year callables, it should be expected to pay the highest promised yield when the call deferment period is just six months and the option can be exercised at any time after the call date. In Exhibit 9.3, this agency security carries a promised yield of 2.15% that is greater than the yield on any of the other callables. But what is the economic value of the option? A securities dealer might quote it as the spread between yields on the callable and bullet, hence 0.40% in the case of the continuously callable agency with a 6-month deferment period. It is just 15 basis points (0.15%) for the one-time callable agency, which cannot be called for two years.

Intuitively, does it make sense to compare the yield on a security that might be outstanding for just six months with a bullet security where the principal is repaid in five years? Such a comparison essentially ignores the likelihood of the bond being called given the shape of the yield curve plus the level and volatility of interest rates. While it is beyond the scope of this discussion, investors should use a framework, such as option-adjusted spread (OAS) analysis, to better estimate the option's economic value. OAS analysis has the added benefit of allowing an investor to compare the yields on callable agencies alternatively to the Treasury yield curve, agency bullet yield curve and the LIBOR swap curve.[7] As might be expected with the decline in interest rates following the financial crisis, issuers have called many bonds from banks because they could refinance their principal at lower interest rates. Banks thus did not receive the initially anticipated higher interest payments for long periods and were forced to reinvest in similar securities at lower rates. Exercise of the call option lowered their interest income which, in turn, lowered net interest income and margin. In hindsight, banks that bought callables would generally have earned higher yields from buying bullet bonds of the same maturity.

Municipal Securities

Municipal securities are issued by state and local governments and their political subdivisions, such as a water treatment authority. Today, they exist as both tax-exempt and taxable instruments. If banks purchase tax-exempt municipals, they do not pay federal income taxes on the interest income. In some states, municipal interest is also exempt from state income taxes. If banks purchase taxable municipals, they pay income taxes on all interest earned.[8]

By statute, states and local governments are required to have balanced operating budgets. In order to help match operating cash inflows with cash outflows, the governmental units issue short-term municipal notes carrying labels such as *tax, revenue* or *bond anticipation notes*. Long-term municipals are issued to finance projects that provide benefits for more than one year. Examples include building new schools or a water treatment facility. The bonds are generally categorized as either *general obligation bonds*, with principal and interest payments that are backed by the full faith, credit and taxing authority of the issuer, or *revenue bonds*, with payments that are backed by cash flows from the specific project financed. These bonds often contain call options with deferment periods from five to ten years. Some bonds are bullets and some are serial bonds in which the issuer pays back a portion of the principal each year. Historically, default rates on municipal bonds have been relatively low.

Build America Bonds

While taxable municipals were introduced in 1986, the American Recovery and Reinvestment Act of 2009 authorized Build America Bonds (BABs) that pay taxable interest. The original intent was to encourage states and local governments to finance construction projects that would create jobs. These governments were finding it difficult to issue tax-exempt debt because of limited demand by tax-exempt investors. In contrast to tax-exempt municipals, BABs appeal to nontaxed investors such as pension funds and low-tax firms such as life insurance companies. As an incentive, Treasury pays 35% of the interest expense as a subsidy to the issuing governmental unit. BABs are effectively substitutes for corporate bonds, but carry the credit risk of government issuers. Following their inception in April 2009, BABs represented roughly one-third of new municipal issues through 2010, but the program expired at the end of 2010. During this period states and local governments issued almost 2,500 BABs financing almost $200 billion in (largely) infrastructure projects.

Banks buy both tax-exempt and taxable municipals but only *bank qualified* (BQ) tax-exempt municipals offer attractive yields. In general, investors cannot deduct interest expense incurred (carrying cost) to acquire and hold tax-exempt municipals. However, banks are allowed to deduct 80% of their carrying cost associated with certain bank qualified municipals. For this deduction to apply, the issuer must be a qualified small issuer, the proceeds must be used for a specific public purpose and the offering must be formally designated as bank qualified. A small issuer is a governmental unit that issues no more than $10 million in tax-exempt bonds during a calendar year. The $10 million limit was temporarily raised to $30 million under the American Recovery and Reinvestment Act of 2009.

Comparative Tax-Exempt and Taxable Yields.
The loss of interest deductibility complicates the comparison of yields on tax-exempt versus taxable securities. By disallowing a deduction for interest paid, a bank effectively pays a tax on the interest earned regardless of whether it is formally tax-exempt under the federal income tax. The following yield comparison reduces the tax-exempt yield by a factor, listed below, reflecting lost interest deductibility.

The *tax-exempt adjustment* (TEA) equals the BQ cost of funds × 20% × federal corporate income tax rate where the BQ cost of funds equals the bank's interest expense for the year divided by its average total assets. Thus, if a bank pays $5 million in interest expense and reports $250 million in average assets for the year, its BQ cost of funds equals 2%. With a federal corporate income tax rate of 35%, the bank's TEA equals 0.14%, or 14 basis points.

$$\text{BQ Cost of Funds} = \frac{\$5 \text{ million}}{\$250 \text{ million}} = 0.02$$

$$\text{TEA} = 0.02 \times 0.20 \times 0.35 = 0.0014$$

Suppose that this bank wants to compare the 3% quoted yield on a bank qualified tax-exempt municipal with the 4.23% quoted yield on a fully-taxable BABs with comparable maturity and credit risk. On an after-tax basis, the tax-exempt yields 11 basis points more (2.86% versus 2.75%) while on a tax-equivalent (pre-tax) basis, the tax-exempt yields 17 basis points more:

After-tax Comparison

Tax-Exempt: 3% − 0.14% = 2.86%   BABs: 4.23%(1 − 0.35) = 2.75%

Pre-tax Comparison

Tax-Exempt: $\frac{3\% - 0.14\%}{(1 - 0.35)} = 4.40\%$ BABs: 4.23%

These calculations are simply illustrations. The actual yield comparison will depend on each bank's specific cost of funds and the relative pre-tax yields on tax-exempt municipals versus BABs.

Municipal Defaults

Many investors believe that municipals have low default risk because they are issued by governmental units. This is only partly correct. As noted previously, only general obligation bonds carry a government's full backing. Revenue bonds, in contrast, are secured only by project cash flows. In early 2012, Moody's released a report on municipal defaults for the years 1970 to 2011.[9] The report concluded that (1) there were only 71 defaults of Moody's-rated issues over the entire period with 73% occurring in healthcare and housing project finance; (2) defaults in 2010–2011 averaged roughly twice the number of defaults per year versus the preceding years; (3) 5-year cumulative default rates for municipal securities are well below default rates on corporate securities ranging from 0.03% for investment grade instruments to 5.4% for noninvestment grade instruments. Comparable figures for corporates are 1.0% and 21.3%, respectively; (4) five-year cumulative default rates for municipal revenue bonds are much higher than comparable default rates for general obligation bonds; and (5) recovery rates on defaulted municipals are higher (65%) than those for senior, unsecured corporates (49%). One implication is that municipals and corporates that carry the same rating, such as Aa, embody different magnitudes of credit risk. S&P reported just 47 defaults of its rated issues from 1986 to 2011.

Understand the credit risk and callability of municipal bonds and the bank's effective marginal tax rate. Following the financial crisis and subsequent economic recession, many states and local governments remain in dire financial condition. Without federal stimulus funds, many of these governments would have reported significant budget deficits in 2009 and 2010. With a stagnant economy throughout 2013, along with continued high spending and limited tax receipts, many of the same governmental units were forced to cut spending and raise taxes and still found deficits to be the norm. With the housing collapse, some municipal bonds that financed housing-related projects fell into default. Recent economic conditions have improved and even California expected to have a budget surplus in 2013 (due to large tax increases). The realistic situation, however, is that many municipal bonds now carry greater default risk compared with previous years. For example, many of the proposals to increase federal tax revenues will burden states and local governments if implemented. Banks as investors need to conduct significant due diligence regarding the credit quality of the different issuers. As Detroit's bankruptcy filing demonstrates along with concerns about unfunded pension liabilities in Chicago and California, some municipals carry substantial default risk. Data are sometimes difficult to come by and prospectuses are difficult to read, but a careful review will likely minimize surprises going forward.

In particular, the newness of BABs created problems in assessing their risk. While BABs were well-received by both issuers and investors, significant questions continue to arise about the application of the Treasury subsidy payment. Operationally, issuers make the interest payments to investors that are fully taxable and thus exceed the amounts that issuers would pay if the interest was tax-exempt. Treasury then pays the issuer 35% of the total interest paid. In March 2010, the state of Florida stopped issuing BABs because Treasury announced that it would withhold the subsidy payments if an issuer owed money to the U.S. government under some other obligation. In June 2010, Treasury announced that it was going to audit BABs issuers to ensure that they had not priced BABs incorrectly, thereby increasing the subsidy payment. In February 2013, rumors circulated that the federal subsidy to states may be cut given federal budgetary pressures. Clearly, issuers of BABs assumed the risk that the Treasury would not make the subsidy payment and they may eventually have to divert funds from other sources to meet their budgets.[10]

Banks must similarly evaluate the value of the call option embedded in many agency securities and municipals. It is not sufficient to simply compare promised yields on callable securities with yields on noncallables. Furthermore, given the paucity of earnings, many banks will find that their effective marginal income tax rate is zero or sufficiently low such that tax-exempt municipals are unattractive. In this case, BABs will certainly yield more.

Mortgage-Backed Securities

Banks invest heavily in mortgage backed securities (MBSs), which are instruments that represent a claim on the principal and interest payments from mortgage loans. MBSs are created when originators make mortgage loans, some entity such as Fannie or Freddie collects them and creates a pool of comparable loans, and through the process of securitization an investment bank issues MBSs backed by the underlying mortgages. The loans may be for residential property, hence the label *residential mortgage-backed securities* (RMBS) or for commercial property, creating *commercial mortgage-backed securities* (CMBS). In many cases, Fannie, Freddie or Ginnie Mae guarantees the payments in the event of a borrower's default. The appeal of MBSs is that they exhibit low default risk and provide consistent cash flow. Unfortunately, this is not true for all MBSs. Because there are many different types with different claims on the underlying cash flows, investors must scrutinize the underlying mortgage loans as well as the structure which determine which investors receive payments across different economic environments.

Most MBSs are issued by Fannie and Freddie, despite their being taken into conservatorship by the U.S. government. The housing market continues to struggle so Congress has not addressed any restructuring of these GSEs, who have recently started reporting profits after years of large losses. While MBSs are formally bonds, they differ from traditional fixed-income bonds because they pay investors the monthly periodic principal and interest payments received from the actual mortgage borrowers minus fees.

Consider a 30-year, 6% fixed-rate mortgage with a scheduled fixed monthly payment of $1,000 for 360 months. Exhibit 9.3 illustrates the portions of the fixed monthly payment attributed to principal and interest. With the full amount of the loan outstanding at origination, most of the early period payments consist of interest with small amounts of principal reduction. Over time, the amount of interest decreases while the principal amount increases as the loan is slowly paid down.

Exhibit 9.3: Relative Principal and Interest Payments on a 30-Year Fixed Rate Mortgage

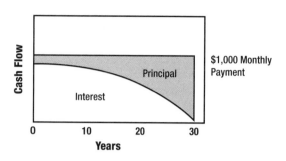

The most basic form of MBS is a *pass-through*. As the name suggests, an investor receives the actual principal and interest payments that are made and subsequently passed through (less fees) to investors.[11] When buying a MBS pass-through, each investor receives a pro rata share of the actual payments made equal to the percentage of the pool owned. Suppose that Freddie Mac creates a $1 million MBS pass-through based on 30-year fixed-rate mortgages with a 6% coupon. Normal amortization, with no prepayment of principal, would produce a monthly payment of $5,368.22. Four different investors buy $250,000 each. In the first month, the actual principal and interest payment is $5,600 (including $231.78 in principal prepayments) such that each investor receives $1,400. After three years, the MBS is prepaying at a higher rate such that the monthly payment is $16,800. In this case, each investor will receive $4,200 as its pro rata share. This continues until the entire pool of mortgage loans is paid off.

The first difference between MBSs and traditional bonds is that investors receive monthly cash flows consisting of both principal and interest, and not simply a semi-annual interest payment. The second difference is that the underlying mortgage loans contain an option whereby the borrower (property buyer) can prepay the mortgage prior to maturity. The borrower controls the option and chooses if and when to prepay the outstanding principal. When a borrower prepays a mortgage, investors receive the monthly promised interest and principal plus the prepaid amount. As such, an investor in MBSs does not know with certainty what the actual monthly cash flows will be. The final key difference is that an investor does not know with certainty the final maturity date when the last principal payment will be made. If any single mortgage borrower continues paying until maturity, an investor may have to wait 30 years for the final payment.

Prepayment Risk

Investors do not know with certainty when and what amounts of principal and interest they will receive on MBSs. Mortgage borrowers hold the option to prepay their loans. They will typically do so when they can refinance at lower rates or when they move from the home due to a change in jobs, family break-up or other reason. With prepayments, investors receive principal back earlier than originally scheduled. With smaller amounts of principal due on the mortgages, interest received also declines. In order to accurately value MBSs, investors much accurately estimate prepayments. Errors in forecasting prepayments and the corresponding uncertainty regarding the impact on value is the greatest risk in buying most MBSs.

Why do borrowers prepay their mortgages? The obvious reason is that falling interest rates may justify replacing an existing mortgage with a new one priced at a lower rate. Borrowers can reduce their monthly payments and if property values have increased, may potentially take cash from the refinancing. Other demographic factors also trigger prepayments. For residential mortgages, simple labor mobility where individuals move from one locale to another often tied to changing jobs requires selling one's home. Similarly, families break up which may cause the residents to move. Importantly, these latter factors are not driven by interest rates falling. Thus, some prepayments occur independent of the rate environment. This may actually benefit an investor who receives principal early and can reinvest the proceeds at higher rates.

The opposite side of prepayment risk is *extension risk,* which refers to the risk that mortgage rates may rise and slow prepayment speeds. In this case, investors will get principal back later than anticipated such that the average life and final maturity extend out farther from the present. Of course, with slower principal payments the amount of interest received rises. The essential point is that delaying or accelerating principal received may cause the price and yield on the MBSs to change dramatically.

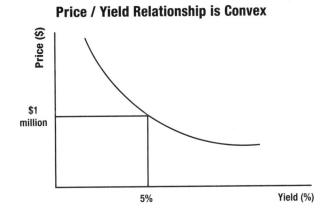

Exhibit 9.4 Price and Yield Relationship for an Option-Free Bullet Bond

Exhibit 9.4 provides a diagram that characterizes the relationship between yield to maturity and price for a 10-year, *option-free fixed-rate* bullet bond. The bond is not callable and there is no prepayment risk. The term "bullet" means that all principal is paid at maturity. When the bond is priced at $1 million par (face) value, it carries a 5% yield. As the rate increases above 5%, the bond's price falls below par. As the rate falls below 5%, the price rises. A bond trading at a price above face value is referred to as a *premium bond.* A bond trading below face value is called a *discount bond.*

Positive Convexity. Note that the shape of the price yield curve is nonlinear (not a straight line). In mathematical terms, the curve is "convex to the origin." The important implication is that this bond exhibits the attractive feature (labeled *positive convexity*) to an investor that when rates fall, price increases by an increasing amount, but that when rates rise, price falls by a decreasing amount.

Negative Convexity. Exhibit 9.5 provides a diagram that characterizes the relationship between yield to maturity and price for a 30-year, mortgage-backed pass-through. When the

Exhibit 9.5 Price and Yield Relationship for a Mortgage-Backed Pass-Through

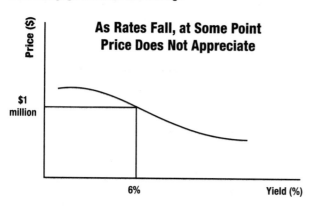

bond is priced at $1 million par value, it carries a 6% yield. As the rate increases above 6%, the bond's price falls below par much like that for the option-free bond. However, as the rate falls below 6%, the price initially increases then levels off. Unlike the option-free bond, an investor in this MBS does not realize the benefit of a substantial increase in price when rates fall because some mortgage borrowers prepay their mortgages. If the investor wanted to sell the bond, it would typically realize a gain, but the gain would be limited because the cash flows are coming back sooner than initially anticipated but must be reinvested at lower rates. With the pass-through, the limited potential gain is referred to as *premium resistance*. The pass-through thus exhibits the unattractive feature to an investor (labeled *negative convexity*) that when rates fall, any potential gain is limited.[12] As such, potential price increases with falling rates are not as large as potential price decreases with rising rates.

Potential price appreciation is limited with MBSs due to prepayment risk. As rates fall, more borrowers refinance their mortgages and investors get principal back on an accelerated basis. When evaluating MBSs, analysts appropriately focus on prepayment speeds. Two estimated prepayment rates are widely cited. A constant, or conditional, prepayment rate (CPR) equals the estimated proportion of outstanding principal for a pool of loans assumed to be prepaid prior to maturity during a specific period. A 10% CPR suggests that 10% of the outstanding mortgage loan principal will be prepaid annually. The greater is the CPR, the greater is the expected prepayment speed and the sooner the mortgage loans will be paid off. Prepayment speeds are also quoted in terms of PSA prepayment. This framework recognizes that new loans do not prepay at high speeds because borrowers do not generally refinance immediately after loan origination. PSA prepayment refers to a standard prepayment rate that increases by 0.2% monthly for the first 30 months a loan is outstanding. At the end of 30 months, the cumulative prepayment speed is 6% and is assumed to be constant thereafter. Analysts then quote prepayment speeds as some fraction of this PSA schedule. Thus, the estimated prepayment speed for a MBS might be quoted at 120 PSA, which means that after 30 months, the prepayment speed is equivalent to a CPR of 7.2% (1.2 × 6%). In month 5 after origination, 120 PSA would equate to a CPR of 1.2% (1.2 × 5 × 0.2%). Because of prepayment risk, most investors examine a MBSs' weighted average life as a measure of effective maturity.

Collateralized Mortgage Obligations. One way to help reduce the uncertainty surrounding prepayments is for investors to buy *collateralized mortgage obligations* (CMOs). CMOs are a type of MBS in which investors select a specific tranche, or class of bonds, which has claims on

Exhibit 9.6 Collateralized Mortgage Obligations

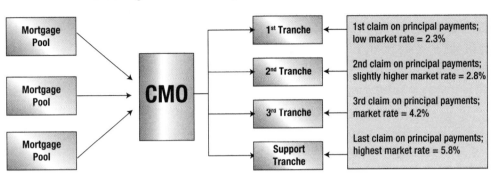

the underlying mortgage payments according to a specific set of rules. The tranches effectively separate mortgage cash flows into maturity groups by dedicating the underlying mortgage principal and interest payments to specific tranches so that the bonds are paid off in order of priority. Exhibit 9.6 demonstrates the structure of a CMO.

A CMO is a separate legal entity that pools mortgages. It then creates tranches, or classes of bonds, that have claims on the mortgage payments according to well-defined rules. Typically, investors in the first tranche securities have a claim on a high fraction of the initial amounts of principal payments on all the underlying mortgages plus applicable interest. The objective is to dedicate payments to these bonds first to ensure that the bonds have a relatively short maturity. Investors in the first tranche of a CMO do not know with certainty when the bonds will be repaid, but have a reasonable assurance that the maturity should not extend beyond two to three years even with 30-year mortgages serving as the underlying collateral. Investors in the second tranche know that their bonds will have the same prior claim on principal payments after the first tranche bonds are repaid. In this example, the maturity of the second tranche bonds might range from four to seven years. Investors in the third tranche have bonds with a longer expected maturity of 7 to 10 years while investors in the support tranche have the last claim on prepayments such that the bonds have an uncertain maturity. Given the greater prepayment risk as you move from the first tranche to the support tranche, the issuer can only sell these securities by offering successively higher yields.

Banks generally buy first tranche CMOs because of the lower risk. Obviously, they give up some return relative to other tranches, but even simple CMOs typically yield more than Treasury, agency and corporate securities with comparable maturities. Of course, creators have developed many complex types of CMOs, such as PAC CMOs and TAC CMOs.[13] Stay away from these unless you have a sophisticated understanding of MBS valuation models. Depending on the specific CMO, transactions costs (bid-ask spread) may be quite high because the securities can be difficult to sell in the near-term and thus are relatively illiquid.

Adjustable Rate Mortgages

Some banks like to buy adjustable-rate mortgage securities (ARMs) because they pay interest that changes based on movements in an index. In most cases, the amount of interest floats with Treasury rates or LIBOR and resets annually. Hybrid ARMs have the added feature that they pay a fixed rate for a preset period and then convert to a conventional ARM. These will be referenced as 3/1 or 5/1 structures indicating that the initial rate is fixed for three or five years, respectively, with the rate then floating annually thereafter. Many hybrid ARMs have caps on the rates that can be earned. For example, a 2/2/5 Cap indicates that an investor will receive a predetermined rate that can increase by no more than 2% at the first reset date. Subsequent increases in the rate on each reset date are also capped at 2% with the maximum rate increase allowed over the life of the instrument equal to 5%.

Investors must recognize that while ARMs allow for a periodic increase in yield, which is attractive in a rising rate environment, they have sold an option to the issuer. In the previous example, if rates (the index) rise more than 2% as of the first reset date, the bank does not receive more than a 2% yield increment. If rates rise by more than 5% over the life of the instrument, the amount of yield increment is capped at 5%. Obviously, rising rates reduce the volume and likelihood of principal prepayments. Investors may be stuck holding below market ARMs for long periods. Similarly, an investor who tries to sell a hybrid ARM will often find resistance in the market as other investors anticipate rising rates and discount the bond accordingly even before rates increase.

Trust Preferred Securities

Many bank holding companies used *trust preferred securities* (TruPS) to obtain low-cost Tier 1 capital as part of their financing. These firms created trusts that sold preferred stock to investors. The trusts used the proceeds to buy long-term subordinated debt (claims are subordinated to those of insured depositors) issued by the bank holding company. In this structure, a bank pays dividends to its parent holding company, which uses the proceeds to make interest payments on the subordinated debt. The trust uses the interest payments, in turn, to make the dividend payments on the preferred stock which is labeled a trust preferred security. For the bank holding company, the interest payments are tax deductible. The transactions were especially attractive because banks effectively issued low-cost debt that counted as the best (Tier 1) form of capital.

It is important to understand the structure of TruPS because regulators came to believe that they were abused by some institutions. In particular, many banks both raised capital via TruPS and used the proceeds and other funds to invest in TruPS. TruPS pay dividends either as floating rates tied to LIBOR (LIBOR + 2.5%) or at fixed rates. Regardless, the debt cost tied to issuing TruPS was well below the dividend yield.

The more serious problem, however, is that many banks that became problem institutions (CAMELS 4 or 5-rated institutions) sold TruPS as parts of pools put together by investment banks.

Many TruPS were packaged into *collateralized debt obligations* (CDOs) much like mortgages were packaged for CMOs. Like CMOs, CDOs are separated into tranches with investors in each tranche having a different claim on the dividends and principal payments of the TruPS securing the CDO. When these problem institutions got into difficulty, they suspended dividend payments on their TruPS or defaulted outright. More precisely:

- Problem banks could not make dividend payments to their parent holding companies because they were capital deficient (regulatory enforcement actions prohibited dividend payments).

- Bank holding companies did not have sufficient cash or cash inflows to make interest payments on their subordinated debt to the trusts that issued the TruPS.

- Without sufficient cash receipts, the trusts could not make their dividend payments on the TruPS; most trusts were allowed under provisions of the TruPS to defer dividend payments without any penalty for up to five years.

In this environment, the CDOs fell sharply in value and some defaulted. Banks that bought TruPS CDOs reported losses, in some cases leading to failure. Some banks bought the highest risk CDO tranches which defaulted well in advance of other tranches. For example, in July 2009, regulators closed six affiliated banks in Illinois that were deemed to be undercapitalized. Most of the problem assets were attributed to TruPS that were rated investment grade at the time of purchase. One of the banks was 141 years old at the time of failure and the president was the fifth generation family member to work at the bank.

Investigate the Credit Quality of TruPS

The rating agencies again misjudged the default risk with TruPS as they rated many TruPS CDO tranches investment grade. Over time, they realized the greater default likelihood of these securities and downgraded them accordingly. Of course, this was too late for the original buyers. Bank regulators, in turn, largely missed the investment concentrations of some banks in TruPS. Curiously, banks were not required to report their investments in TruPS separately. In fact, they were included in "other securities" which was a catch-all category.[14] This changed only in June 2009. As investors, bank portfolio managers may have felt comfortable buying TruPS issued by banks whose managers they knew. TruPS also paid high promised yields at a time when loan demand and interest rates were falling. Familiarity drove the decision rather than careful due diligence of the issuing bank's financial condition. Remember the adage, "Buyer beware."

Factors Affecting the Composition and Size of the Portfolio

A bank's risk profile and operating performance generally reflect the firm's ownership, organizational culture, geographic and product markets served and the overall economic environment. An S Corp bank or a closely held family-owned bank will likely be managed more conservatively emphasizing the preservation of capital, liquidity, and diversification of credit risk. Many of these are located in rural markets or small communities with limited growth. Typically, these banks will have lower loan-to-deposit ratios and larger investment portfolios. Their securities holdings will, in turn, be concentrated in lower risk instruments with more tax-sheltered municipals. Organizational culture similarly affects the structure of the balance sheet. When management emphasizes growth in order to capture market share, the bank grows the loan portfolio aggressively financed at the margin with wholesale funds. Not surprisingly, loans dominate so securities holdings are small and used primarily to meet pledging requirements. Banks in slow growth, rural locales typically find that loan demand is harder to come by. They are largely financed by core deposits and have larger and longer-maturity securities portfolios. Finally, when economic growth is strong, banks make more loans in order to meet the growing credit demands of good customers. In contrast, when the economy slows or falls into recession, loan demand collapses and banks build the investment portfolio.

Exhibit 9.7 Characteristics of Bank Securities Portfolios, 2005–2012*

A. C Corp Banks: $100 Million < Total Assets < $500 Million

Measure	2005	2006	2007	2008	2009	2010	2011	2012	Average
Securities (Book value) Total Assets	22.2	20.4	19.4	18.5	18.9	20.3	22.1	21.9	20.5
%AFS Securities	80.9	82.2	83.4	84.0	85.0	86.7	87.5	88.3	84.8
Tax-equivalent yield on securities	4.28	4.70	4.91	4.99	4.39	3.64	3.18	2.79	4.11
Pledged Securities Total Securities	38.3	39.0	39.2	40.2	38.1	34.4	32.2	33.7	36.9

B. S Corp Banks: $500 Million < Total Assets < $1,000 Million

Measure	2005	2006	2007	2008	2009	2010	2011	2012	Average
Securities (Book value) Total Assets	19.8	19.3	18.2	20.6	20.7	22.2	24.6	25.2	21.3
%AFS Securities	87.2	87.4	88.7	90.9	91.6	91.8	92.7	93.3	90.5
Tax-equivalent yield on securities	4.43	4.87	5.20	5.08	4.63	3.86	3.36	2.83	4.28
Pledged Securities Total Securities	50.4	52.3	52.8	48.1	45.5	41.9	38.8	37.6	45.9

* All figures are reported as a percentage. These figures are for 2,244 C Corp banks and 1,092 S Corp banks.

Exhibit 9.7 summarizes key characteristics of bank securities holdings for banks with $100 million to $500 million in assets at year-end 2012. Panel A provides information for C Corp banks while Panel B provides the same information for S Corp banks. For banks of this size, the basic implications are:

1. Since the onset of the financial crisis, both C and S Corp banks have increased the relative size of their investment portfolios as a fraction of total assets. At year-end 2012, S Corp banks held over one-fourth of their assets in securities.

2. S Corp banks classify more securities as AFS with the fraction of AFS securities increasing for all banks over time.

3. Tax-equivalent yields are higher, on average, for S Corp banks suggesting that the mix is different from that at C Corp banks. This suggests that S Corp banks assume greater risk in the investment portfolios. S Corp banks may hold longer-maturity securities or more nonrated or lower-rated securities. Not surprisingly, yields have been falling sharply with the low interest rate environment since 2008.

4. The fraction of securities pledged as collateral has fallen over time as banks built up the size of their securities portfolios. S Corp banks pledged substantially more of their holdings as collateral in all periods. This may reflect that S Corp banks are funded more heavily by public deposits from their local communities.

Composition of Securities Holdings

Exhibit 9.8 documents the proportion of securities classified as Treasuries, agencies, MBSs, CMOs, municipals and other for year-end 2008 versus 2012 for the same group of C Corp and S Corp banks. Several facts stand out. First, banks do not own Treasuries in any great magnitude. Of course, yields are low and the Fed appears to be buying the bulk of these over time. Second, these banks concentrate their holdings in agencies, MBSs and municipals. Third, both C Corp and S Corp banks appear to have substituted MBSs, CMOs, and municipals for agencies over time. This result is not unexpected as many banks owned callable agencies that issuers called when interest rates fell. Rather than replace them with other agency bonds at relatively low rates, these banks shifted their portfolios toward higher yielding securities. The shift out of agencies was greatest at S Corp banks. Fourth, banks increased their holdings of other securities, which includes corporates, foreign and other securities. This result is likely driven by the search for yield. Finally, S Corp banks hold more municipals than C Corp banks with the difference rising sharply in 2012.

Exhibit 9.8 The Composition of C Corp and S Corp Bank Portfolios: 2008 versus 2012

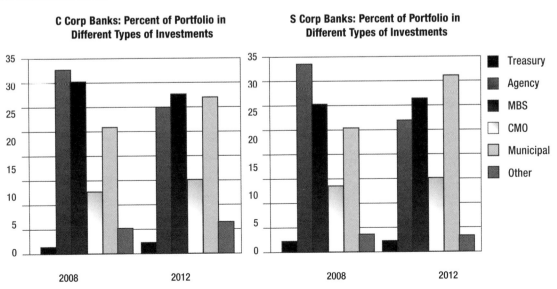

CHAPTER 9

Portfolio Strategies

Bank managers should apply simple rules when managing the securities portfolio. This basic blocking and tackling requires a systematic approach to deciding which securities best meet the bank's investment objectives and how decisions are made. Remember that the securities portfolio should be viewed in line with the bank's funding and loan portfolio. Securities are an important part of risk management decisions with changes made to meet credit, liquidity and interest rate risk objectives.

A bank investment portfolio manager should ask four basic questions before buying a security. If the answer to each question is not YES, the bank should not buy or own the security.[15]

Is an Investment Suitable for Your Bank's Portfolio?

To answer this question, we need to know the answers to the following questions:

1. Does the purchase meet one or more of the bank's objectives of the investment portfolio?
2. Can you understand the security's underlying cash flows and can you model changes in the cash flows under different interest rate and economic environments?
3. Does the security trade in an active secondary market so that you can get reasonable estimates of its current market value?
4. Can you use the security to meet pledging requirements so that you can borrow against it if necessary?

A suitable investment thus meets one or more objectives and has meaningful cash flows that meet the bank's liquidity needs and interest rate risk management targets. If necessary, the bank can get reasonable price quotes by market participants and is not at the mercy of the broker who initially sold the bank the bond. Finally, the ability to pledge a security improves the bank's liquidity profile.

Once you determine the types of suitable investments, you should take the following steps in pursuing portfolio decisions.

Steps in Making Strategic Investment Decisions

- *Assess the economic and interest rate environment:* Examine the current market environment to assess what the Fed is doing, changes in the levels of short-term and long-term interest rates, shifts in the yield curve, changes in key macroeconomic data, such as employment, inflation expectations, housing and durable goods activity, and the likely forecast over the next 90 days and one year.

- *Assess anticipated liquidity needs and the bank's current interest rate risk profile:* Where are there mismatches in expected cash inflows versus outflows? Is the bank positioned to benefit or lose from rising rates; and from falling rates? Can the bank readily meet pledging requirements and what fraction of the portfolio is unpledged? Manage the bank to meet specific risk objectives and not in response to an interest rate forecast.

- *Assess current securities holdings:* Examine the portfolio composition, yields across sectors, duration and average life of holdings and the consistency of cash flows. Examine the proportion of the portfolio that is fixed-rate versus floating. Discuss where there might be value (potential increases in return over time). Managers should review the portfolio's performance to determine whether any bonds have deteriorated in credit quality and how exercise of embedded options (called bonds, prepayments of MBSs) has affected returns. Ensure that the portfolio is in compliance with policy. Compare performance with peer institutions.

- *Project future cash flows:* Chart expected principal and interest payments by sector and cumulatively to ensure that no gaps appear. Examine anticipated cash outflows and the structure of liabilities to identify potential needs. Identify how the exercise of options may alter expected cash flows.

- *Examine potential strategies to reduce risks or enhance returns:* Evaluate potential sales and purchases of securities to assess the overall impact on credit risk, liquidity risk and interest rate risk. Evaluate the potential return impacts. The key is to fully understand what you own, why you own it and what the risks are in what you are buying.

Meeting Specific Objectives

Managing the investment portfolio is part of managing a bank's entire balance sheet. Because the bank can readily sell securities or buy new ones, it can be used at the margin to adjust a bank's risk exposure.

- *Objective is to increase asset sensitivity:* Suppose the bank is exposed to loss from rising rates. Management can help meet this objective by shortening the maturity, duration and average life of the securities portfolio. This can be accomplished by buying short-term instruments, floating rate securities, such as hybrid ARMs and certain CMOs, and shortening the average life of MBS pass-throughs. The primary cost is that the bank will likely give up yield and current income because the yield curve is upsloping.

- *Objective is to decrease asset sensitivity:* Suppose the bank is exposed to loss from falling rates. Management can help meet this objective by lengthening the maturity, duration and average life of the securities portfolio. This can be accomplished by buying longer-term instruments and fixed rate securities. Banks might focus on bullet bonds without options and zero coupon securities. If they have an appetite for tax-sheltered income, they might buy longer-term municipals. They should stay away from callable bonds with short call deferment periods. They should also buy MBSs that limit prepayment risk. With an upsloping yield curve the bank will initially gain yield and current income. The primary cost is that the bank will be exposed to greater price risk or loss if interest rates rise above expectations.

- *Objective is to increase liquidity:* Suppose that regulators have focused on the bank's high net noncore funding dependency and low level of liquid assets. Management can sell longer-term, high price sensitivity securities and concentrate purchases in shorter-term instruments that generate high cash flow. Some banks hold large amounts in federal funds sold and repos, commercial paper or in deposits with maturities under one year at other financial institutions. Depending on relative yields, the bank can buy other money market instruments, or Treasuries and agencies with short durations.

The Laddered and Barbell Portfolio Strategies

Some banks follow the laddered maturity strategy introduced previously. This strategy requires that management initially determine a maximum acceptable maturity for any security holding, such as 10 years. When making maturity choices, managers then target a set percentage of the overall portfolio to mature each year, such as 10%. If the bank buys bullet bonds, it will have 10% of the principal mature each year such that the expected cash flows are consistent annually. It may buy nonbullets as well, but then must make sure that 10% of expected cash flows from principal payments arise annually. A portfolio structured in this manner provides consistent liquidity and is very easy to manage. Each year, the principal investment decision is which securities to buy with the maximum acceptable maturity. Using the above example, managers would buy appropriate securities that mature in 10 years so that the ladder continues to exist with 10% of the portfolio maturing each year. Cash inflows from MBSs should be included in the overall analysis.

Barbell Strategy

Banks that follow a barbell strategy appreciate the liquidity and conservative nature of the laddered maturity strategy, but believe they can increase overall return by tweaking the maturity mix of the portfolio. The figure in Exhibit 9.9 demonstrates the maturity choice. Management again determines a maximum acceptable maturity for any single security, such as 10 years. However, rather than having an equal fraction of the portfolio (10%) mature each year, it concentrates holdings at near-term maturities one to three years out and at longer-term maturities, such as 7 to 10 years out. The shape of the portfolio allocations looks something like a barbell, hence the strategy's name,

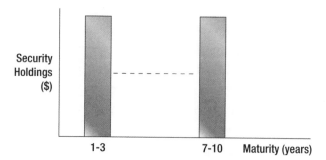

Exhibit 9.9 Portfolio Holdings By Maturity Under the Barbell Strategy

whereby the bank buys equivalent amounts of 1-3 year and 7-10 year maturity instruments. The objective is to take advantage of an upsloping yield curve, which is the marketplace norm.

In this example, the bank would buy securities with maturities of 10 years and 3 years. With an upsloping yield curve, the 10-year rate will be higher than the three-year rate for like risk securities. The basic intent is to hold the 1-3 year securities to meet liquidity needs. These securities will have shorter durations and exhibit less price volatility. The longer-term securities will have longer durations but if management can accurately estimate liquidity needs, the bank will not have to sell these instruments unexpectedly. In comparison with the laddered maturity strategy, the barbell approach meets liquidity needs but should produce higher annual coupon interest and potentially higher overall income by generating security gains. This last result arises from selling the long-term securities well in advance of maturity.

In order to meet the targeted barbell maturity structure, the bank would sell the original 10-year security three to four years after purchase when it has less than seven years until it matures. At the time of sale, the security will have a gain or loss depending on whether it trades at a premium or discount. The expectation is that no one can accurately forecast future interest rates. If the yield curve is upsloping and rates do not change, on average, the market rate on a six or seven year security will be below the market rate on the original 10-year security previously purchased. Absent a reasonable increase in rate levels, the security will be priced at a premium. Adding the gain (premium price less face value) to the periodic coupon interest increases the security's and portfolio's overall return. After two years, the bank will likewise sell the original three-year security or it may hold it until it matures. Returns on these shorter-maturity instruments will be swamped by returns on the longer-term securities.

Summary

A bank's investment portfolio is a critical component of the balance sheet and requires serious attention from management and the board of directors. First and foremost, it should be viewed as preserving the safety and soundness of the institution. Only in the case where a bank takes little or no credit risk, is it reasonable to take significant amounts of credit risk in the securities portfolio. Second, regulators will eventually require banks to rely more on securities to meet liquidity needs. The financial crisis demonstrated that sources of wholesale (borrowed) liquidity can readily disappear and that banks might then face a serious liquidity crisis if they did not have adequate unpledged assets to sell. Third, there are many complex investment securities being sold by securities dealers. Banks should stay away from these unless they can adequately understand the risks and sources of return. It pays to be cautious and suspicious of brokers offering the "Deal of the Day." Finally, banks must balance investment decisions with management's and the board's overall view of the bank's risk profile. Security decisions must be made in awareness of the bank's credit risk, liquidity risk and interest rate risk position and targeted at moving risk and return in the desired direction.

CHAPTER 10
Asset and Liability Management

Community banks generate the biggest portion of earnings from *net interest income*, which equals *interest income minus interest expense.* Loans and securities contribute the most to interest income while deposits and purchased liabilities produce most of the interest expense. For most community banks, noninterest income doesn't come close to covering noninterest expense. Thus, to grow earnings over time community banks must growth their net interest income while searching for fee income.

A bank's net interest income varies over time with the:
- Mix of assets and liabilities
- Amount of earning assets versus nonearning assets
- Amount of interest-bearing liabilities versus "free funds"
- Relationship between yields on earning assets and the rates paid on interest-bearing liabilities
- Changes in the level of interest rates
- Changes in the slope of the yield curve

Changes in net interest income, in turn, reflect how much interest rate risk the bank has taken in its operations.

Asset and liability management (ALM) refers to the process of actively managing a bank's balance sheet and off-balance sheet activities to meet profitability and risk objectives. ALM decisions typically arise from a bank's Risk Committee (or Asset and Liability Management Committee—ALCO), which is chaired by the chief financial officer (CFO). Given the importance of a bank's *net interest margin* (NIM) or *spread*, ALM decisions are a focal point of bank management.

Remember the significance of a bank's CAMELS rating where each of the letters refers to a category of risk or profitability. As demonstrated in Chapter 8, a key driver of performance is a bank's asset quality—the A in CAMELS. The management (M) rating similarly reflects a comprehensive assessment of corporate governance and how well senior management manages risk within the policies established by the bank's board of directors. All of the other components of CAMELS are the direct responsibility of ALM and the bank's Risk Committee. To help address asset quality issues, a bank's senior credit officer typically sits on the Risk Committee as does the bank's President/CEO. The committee's primary focus is to understand how the bank generates earnings, how much risk is assumed in individual and aggregate activities and operations and to identify strategies that enable the bank to meet or exceed earnings objectives within acceptable risk limits.

The following analysis examines the *sensitivity of market risk* (S) in detail as it applies to community banks. Factors affecting the other components are discussed in previous chapters. In practice, a bank's ALCO or risk committee will address the bank's credit risk profile, liquidity risk profile, sensitivity to market risk profile and capital position at every meeting, generally monthly. It will also address potential issues arising from technology risk, reputation risk and legal risk as well. As part of the ALM process, management should continually ask the following questions and seek appropriate responses.

- Is the bank measuring and managing the metrics and results that are truly important?
- What practices and activities create risk in the bank?
- What are the bank's current "bets" and how much risk is the bank taking in each area?
- Does the bank have appropriate policies in place with meaningful risk limits?
- Given the economic and interest rate outlook, is the bank currently positioned to best meet its objectives? If not, what changes should management make?
- What strategies should the bank pursue to best increase shareholder value? Are we pursuing them?

Interest Rate Risk at Community Banks

The S component of CAMELS refers to a bank's sensitivity to market risk. *Market risk* refers to the potential variation in earnings or the economic (market) value of stockholders equity associated with unanticipated changes in interest rates and market prices. Depending on the complexity of a bank's operations, market risk may arise from changes in foreign exchange rates, equity prices, commodity prices and interest rates. For most community banks, changes in interest rates will have the greatest impact on earnings and stockholders equity. This occurs because community banks typically conduct business in one currency—the U.S. dollar—and are not traders. As such, they do not make markets in securities or commodities, operate trading accounts or take equity positions in businesses and other assets.[1] Thus, while changes in prices of many products and services affect the operations of bank customers they do not directly affect the earnings of community banks. In contrast, changes in security prices and market interest rates can have a dramatic impact on bank earnings and value.

Interest rate risk (IRR) refers to the variation in earnings and economic value of a bank's stockholders equity associated with a change in interest rates. IRR arises for two basic reasons. First, bank assets and liabilities do not reprice at the same time and in the same direction. When interest rates change, the yields on some assets will change but the magnitudes and direction of the changes will often differ from how the interest costs of liabilities change. Consider the case when the Federal

Reserve changes its target for the federal funds rate. For example, suppose that the Fed increases the target fed funds rate from 0.25% to 0.50%. Most banks will immediately increase their prime rate by the same 0.25% such that the prime rate increases from 3.25% to 3.50%. However, these same banks will not normally immediately raise deposit rates by 0.25%. The bank's spread and net interest income will thus increase.[2] The spread normally falls for the same reason when the Fed decreases the target fed funds rate. Second, the market value (price) of a security is determined primarily by the market rate on the security and the amount and timing of the security's expected cash flows. When interest rates change, the prices of assets and liabilities change by different amounts.[3] Both sets of factors potentially produce a change in earnings and market value of stockholders equity. Bank managers must address these risks at the time they make portfolio decisions in order to control the potential for loss and meet earnings and value objectives.

Consider a simple transaction in which a bank makes a $100,000 loan that carries a fixed-rate of 5% and matures in one year. All principal will be paid at the end of the year along with the expected interest of $5,000. The bank finances the loan by issuing (selling) a $100,000 CD with a three-month maturity to an individual customer of the bank. The CD pays 2% (annualized) for the three months such that the bank expects to pay $500 in interest on the CD.[4] The following T-account summarizes the transaction:

1-Year Loan Financed by a 3-Month Deposit

Asset	Liability
Loan: 1-year $100,000 at 5%	CD: 3 months $100,000 at 2%

What interest rate risk is embedded in this transaction? Consider the concept of repricing and its relationship with interest income and interest expense. Absent loan default, the bank will report $5,000 in interest income for the year. During the first three months it will pay $500 in interest expense. If rates stay constant and the bank issues three additional three-month CDs as each successive one matures, the bank will expect to pay $2,000 total in interest and thus report $3,000 in net interest income for the year on the combined transactions. What is not known, however, is how much the bank will actually pay in interest expense for the remainder of the year after the initial three-month CD matures. This uncertainty associated with the different timing of when the loan and CD will reprice is a key component of interest rate risk. The bank has to pay the deposit principal to the CD holder after three months. It could choose to issue a CD that matures in nine more months so that the second CD now matures at the same time as the loan. When entering into the initial transaction, management should address what rate it might expect to pay on a nine-month CD at the end of the next three months. Alternatively, management might anticipate simply rolling the three-month CD over at each maturity date. It must now address what it expects the three-month CD rate to equal at the end of the next three, six and nine months, respectively. One facet of a bank's framework for analyzing interest rate risk will be to estimate the impact on net interest income of rising rates versus falling rates. In this sample transaction, one might reasonably expect the bank's net interest income to fall with an increase in rates because the bank's interest income on the loan is fixed at $5,000 while interest expense on the CD will increase with higher rates. Conversely, the bank's net interest income should rise with a decrease in rates because interest expense will now be lower.

Consider the impact of interest rate changes on prices. Both the loan and CD carry fixed rates. As rates on comparable loans and CDs change, the prices of the loan and CD will change. In particular, if the loan rate rises, the bank would be able to sell the 5% loan to another lender only if it lowered the price because a new, similar risk loan will carry a higher market rate. Similarly, if the rate on a comparable maturity CD rises, its price will also fall as a new depositor would not invest in the 2% CD if she could earn a higher yield on a similar maturity and risk newly-issued CD. The impact on the bank's stockholders equity depends on how much the respective prices of the loan and CD change. Generally, the prices will not change by the same amount because the instruments have different maturities (durations). In this example, the price of the CD will typically fall by a smaller amount due to its shorter maturity and duration. Using hypothetical figures, suppose the CD falls in price by $350 while the price of the loan falls by $1,000. The net effect is for the bank to lose $650 in equity value. If rates were to fall, equity value would increase because the loan would rise in value more than the CD increases in value. The final impact thus depends on whether the loan or CD is more price sensitive and whether interest rates rise or fall.

Types of Interest Rate Risk

There are four basic types of changes in interest rates that create interest rate risk. When assessing a bank's risks, management should identify its exposure to each type. Banks with straightforward operations and balance sheets do not face the same exposures as more complex institutions. Still, every bank should examine whether specific factors affect performance in a meaningful way and magnitude.

- *Repricing risk* arises because assets mature or reprice at different times than liabilities. It results from timing differences between when a bank receives cash inflows versus when it experiences cash outflows associated with changing interest rates. Cash inflows generally arise from interest and principal received on assets and the issuance of new liabilities. Cash outflows generally arise from interest and principal payments on liabilities and payments on asset purchases. When there is a net cash inflow or a floating rate loan resets, banks will invest the proceeds at prevailing rates. When there is a net cash outflow or rates on floating rate liabilities reset, banks will generally borrow at prevailing rates. The impact of repricing risk is reflected by how much net interest income, noninterest income, and net income vary when asset yields change differently than liability costs associated with the different cash flows.

- *Basis risk* exists when interest rate changes affect the repricing of a bank's assets differently from the repricing of its liabilities. The earlier comparison of the timing and magnitude of changes in the federal funds rate and prime rate versus changes in other bank deposit rates is an example of basis risk. Basis risk appears because different interest rates do not change by the same amount, at the same time and in the same direction.

- *Yield curve risk* results when interest rates on securities issued by the same borrower but with different maturities change by different amounts. For example, if rates on one-year and two-year maturity Treasuries rise by 50 basis points while rates on 10-year Treasuries rise by 90 basis points, the yield curve will have steepened. The issue is how much and in what direction the yield curve shift affects bank earnings and stockholders equity.

- *Option risk* arises then the timing or the amount of a security's cash flows can change as a result of a decision by a bank borrower or lender (depositor). Typically, a change in interest rates triggers the change in cash flow and the bank's interest income or interest expense may change. For example, fixed-rate mortgages embody option risk because borrowers may prepay their loans. If mortgage rates fall, some borrowers will refinance their mortgages and the bank will receive the outstanding principal earlier than what was originally anticipated. If the bank invests the proceeds in new mortgages, its interest income will be lower because mortgage rates are lower. Management must continually identify and measure the option risk faced by the bank both on-balance sheet and in off-balance sheet activities.

Embedded Options Greatly Influence a Bank's Interest Rate Risk

Many of the assets and liabilities on a bank's balance sheet contain embedded options. The most obvious examples are a loan customer's option to refinance a loan or a depositor's option to withdraw funds prior to maturity of the deposit. In addition, banks can enter into explicit contracts with options, such as buying a cap on an interest rate, that are recorded off-balance sheet. Every option can potentially alter a bank's interest rate risk. It is thus critically important that managers understand the nature of these options and how they may increase or decrease risk.

Every option has a buyer and a seller. The buyer, or owner of the option, has the right to exercise the option at his discretion. The seller of the option receives payment for granting the option to the buyer. Options may be contracts that are formally traded on exchanges or over-the-counter with a specific counterparty, or they may be embedded within the contractual terms of a balance sheet instrument. With options, principal payments are triggered when interest rates change. Thus, actual payments may arise sooner or later than what is normally expected. The embedded options that commonly appear in community bank assets and liabilities include:

1. Borrowers can prepay (refinance) loans.
2. Issuers of callable bonds can call the bonds (prepay principal) prior to final maturity.
3. Depositors can withdraw funds prior to final maturity.
4. FHLB advances may be called by the FHLB (principal payment demanded) prior to final maturity; some advances allow a bank borrower to pay off the advance early.
5. Loans and deposits may have caps or floors on rates that become binding when interest rates change.

When Interest Rates Fall

Borrowers may now find it attractive to refinance their loans. Issuers of callable securities that banks own may prepay the principal thereby forcing the bank to forego future coupon interest received. Customers with floating rate loans that have a floor may have to pay a higher rate than that determined by the contractual floating rate. Customers with floors on their deposits may receive higher rates than that determined by market conditions. In each case, the decline in interest rates triggers a different cash flow versus what would have arisen without the option.

- *Mortgage loan with a prepay option.* Borrower has a 15-year mortgage at 5.5%. When the market rate on similar mortgages falls below 5.5%, the borrower may refinance if the interest savings exceed the costs of prepaying the existing loan and obtaining a new loan.

- *Bond with a call option.* State of Texas issues a municipal bond with a 20-year maturity that is callable after five years. Bank buys $2 million of the bond offering yielding 4% in tax-sheltered income. If after five years the market rate on the bond falls below 4%, the state of Texas may pay the bank $2 million because it can refinance its outstanding debt at a lower rate.

- *Floor rate on a loan or deposit.* Bank makes a two-year loan priced at prime + 2% with a floor of 5%. The prime rate is currently 3.25% so the floating rate is 5.25%. Suppose that the prime rate falls to 2.75%. Because the floating rate of 4.75% is now below the floor, the loan customer pays the floor rate of 5%. Similarly, assume that a bank agrees to pay a customer three-month LIBOR plus 1% on a deposit with a 2% floor. LIBOR is currently 0.5% so the floating rate is 1.5%. Because the floating rate is below the floor rate of 2%, the customer receives 2%.

When Interest Rates Rise

Institutions or customers who lend to banks may now find it attractive to demand payment for their deposits or advances. Customers with floating rate loans that have a cap may pay a lower rate than that determined by the contractual floating rate. Customers with caps on their deposits may receive lower rates than that determined by market conditions. In each case, the rise in interest rates triggers a different cash flow versus what would have arisen without the option.

- *FHLB advances with call options.* Some FHLB advances can be called prior to maturity by the FHLB. Because rates have risen, the FHLB can demand a repayment of principal (the amount borrowed by the bank), which it will then lend to other firms at a higher rate.

- *Deposits with fixed rates.* Depositors earning fixed rates on their time deposits may withdraw their funds prior to maturity, pay the penalty for early withdrawal, and redeposit the funds in a higher yielding account.

- *Cap rate on a loan or deposit.* Bank makes a two-year loan priced at prime + 2% with a cap of 6.5%. With the prime rate currently at 3.25% the floating rate is 5.25%. If the prime rate rises above 4.5%, the bank will receive just 6.5% due to the cap even though the floating rate formula calls for a higher rate. Similarly, assume that a bank agrees to pay a customer LIBOR plus 1% on a deposit with a cap of 3%. With LIBOR at 0.5% the bank pays 1.5% on the deposit. If LIBOR were to rise above 2%, the bank would pay just 3% even though the floating rate formula would call for a higher rate.

Community banks typically have off-balance sheet activities that also carry embedded options. The most common is loan commitments or lines of credit in which a bank agrees to make a fixed amount of credit available to a borrower who can draw against the loan at his discretion. Banks may also use derivatives, such as interest rate caps and floors or interest rate swaps, which carry explicit options. The final section of this chapter examines the nature of derivatives and how community banks use them.

- *Loan commitment*: Bank agrees to make $400,000 available to a business customer for a working capital loan. The loan is priced at prime + 1.5% and the borrower determines both the timing and amount of the draw down as long as the amount borrowed does not exceed $400,000. The bank charges a 0.25% fee, payable quarterly, against the $400,000 amount for making the credit available with the fee paid regardless of usage. When credit conditions tighten, borrowers often borrow more against their lines. Thus, if the prime rate rises, customers will exercise their rights to borrow against their lines in greater volume.

The essential point is that interest rate changes potentially affect both net interest income and the market value of stockholders equity. This is the basic tenet of interest rate risk analysis. How can management effectively identify the various contributors to interest rate risk and thereby measure, manage and control the risks?

2010 Regulatory Guidance on Interest Rate Risk

In January 2010, the various bank regulatory agencies proposed specific guidance for how banks should manage their interest rate risk exposures. There are fascinating parallels between the timing of this guidance and regulatory guidance provided for concentrations in *commercial real state* (CRE) lending in 2006, which predated the financial crisis. In 2010, the primary concerns of the regulators were:

- Low prevailing interest rates
- Low inflation and modest inflation expectations
- Consensus expectations that interest rates would rise (upward sloping yield curves)
- Banks were flush with low cost demand deposits, time deposits and MMDAs, and
- Some banks were buying longer maturity (duration) securities because long-term rates exceeded short-term rates.

The advisory, which was updated in January 2012 and again in October 2013, emphasized the importance of effective corporate governance in managing interest rate risk.[5] Banks are expected to have effective policies and procedures, a greater ability to model interest rate risk robustly across different interest rate environments including those assuming extreme (+ or − 4%) rate moves, and adequate internal controls related to specific risk exposures. Each regulatory agency will assess whether an individual bank's process for measuring and managing interest rate risk is adequate given the institution's complexity and risk profile. Even noncomplex banks are expected to move to more comprehensive models that allow for stress testing the impact of economic and strategic factors on bank risk. Noncomplex banks are presumably those with relatively static balance sheets and few embedded options. If interest rate risk is deemed to be outside policy or excessive, management must take steps to reduce the risk, raise capital or pursue both strategies.

The 2012 and 2013 advisory updates emphasized the importance of validating the effectiveness of third party vendor IRR models, reemphasized that banks should model the impact of rate changes on both earnings and economic value of capital and should incorporate earnings simulations, affirmed the necessity to consider risk associated with nonparallel shifts in the yield curve, basis risk and option risk, and described examples of effective model-backtesting. Again, regulatory expectations regarding these matters increase with the complexity of the bank and its risk profile.

Importantly, the guidance emphasizes that the board of directors has responsibility along with management and the bank's ALCO to fully understand risk policy limits, the different approaches to measuring interest rate risk and the underlying assumptions of the models. Gone are the days of casual familiarity with procedures. It is thus important that at least one independent member of the board of directors develop expertise in interest rate risk analytics along with members of senior management.

Asset and Liability Management Committee Agenda

The ALCO agenda normally covers a wide range of topics related to various banking risks and overall profitability. A key emphasis is on how the bank measures and manages interest rate risk. A typical agenda will follow the outline provided. The committee will also examine the bank's capital position and strategic initiatives.

The objective of the ALCO is to help identify the bank's risks and strategically position the bank the generate earnings within acceptable risk limits. Committee members should focus on whether the bank is doing the right things given what's important in light of the current and expected economic and regulatory environment. For example, in 2010 regulators emphasized funding issues. In this environment, the ALCO would pay special attention to the structure of bank liabilities and their true sensitivity to changing interest rates, whether deposits were truly core or highly rate sensitive, whether deposits were obtained from known or out-of-market customers and whether the bank's contingency funding plan accurately captured potential cash inflows and outflows. ALCO member should also routinely evaluate the bank's risk limits to ensure that they are meaningful and the bank is in compliance. The committee should note when the bank operates outside risk limits and why as these exceptions often signal future problems. Still, the committee should always spend considerable time and effort analyzing and discussing strategic opportunities. The objective is to increase stockholder value over time.

A. Call Meeting to Order and Approve Minutes of the Last Meeting
B. Examine the Current Economic Environment and the Bank's Profitability versus Risk Profile
   1. Profitability Analysis
      a. Net interest income (NIM)
      b. Noninterest income and expense
      c. Key ratios, trend and peer comparison
   2. Balance Sheet Analysis
      a. Composition of assets (current and projected)
      b. Composition of liabilities (current and projected)
      c. Stockholders equity and capital (current and projected)
      d. Key ratios, trend and peer comparison
   3. Asset Quality
      a. Nonperforming assets (NPAs), classified loans and OREO
      b. Net charge-offs
      c. Allowance for loan losses (ALLL)
      d. Key ratios, trend and peer comparisons
   4. Interest Rate Risk Analysis
      a. GAP and income sensitivity analysis
      b. Duration and Economic Value of Equity (EVE) analysis
      c. Policy risk limits and compliance (exceptions)
   5. Liquidity and Funding
      a. Deposit and loan maturities
      b. Deposit and loan pricing
      c. Deposit and loan growth (projections)
      d. Contingency funding plan update
      e. Policy risk limits and compliance (exceptions)
   6. Investment Portfolio
      a. Composition of securities
      b. Security yields (returns), projected cash flows and maturities (average life)
      c. Duration analysis
      d. New purchases and sales of securities
      e. Policy risk limits and compliance (exceptions)
C. Analysis of Strategic Opportunities
D. Other Business
E. Adjourn

CHAPTER 10

GAP Analysis

Small community banks with noncomplex operations often begin the evaluation of IRR via static GAP analysis. However, the 2010 guidance specifically states that "computer technology is available which allows less sophisticated institutions to perform comprehensive simulations." Thus, all banks are now expected to conduct more detailed IRR assessments. There are two basic responsibilities of IRR analysis. The first is to determine how the bank has positioned itself noted at "What is the bank's IRR bet?" The second is to determine how much risk the bank has assumed, or "How big is the bank's IRR bet?"

The GAP concept compares *rate sensitive assets* (RSAs) with *rate sensitive liabilities* (RSLs) to approximate whether the bank is exposed to loss from rising or falling interest rates. The target measure is a bank's net interest income or *net interest margin* (NIM).

GAP = RSAs − RSLs

Consider the data from the simple transaction introduced earlier in which the bank made a one-year $100,000 loan initially financed by a three-month CD. Both items carried a fixed interest rate. If the time interval selected is 3 months, the GAP associated with the transaction is −$100,000 because the CD is a RSL. As demonstrated later, the negative sign suggests

GAP = 0 − $100,000 = − $100,000

that the bank will lose (net interest income will fall) when interest rates rise and will gain (net interest income will rise) when interest rates fall. The rationale is straightforward. If a bank has more RSLs and rates increase, it will reprice more liabilities versus assets at higher rates such that interest expense will rise more than interest income rises. Hence, net interest income will fall. In the sample transaction, if rates increase over the first three months, the bank would roll-over the CD at a higher rate while the loan rate is unchanged. The spread and net interest income would thus decrease. If instead rates fall, a bank with more RSLs will reprice more liabilities than assets at lower rates such that interest expense will fall more than interest income falls such that net interest income will rise. In the sample transaction the bank would roll-over the CD at a lower rate in this instance while the loan rate is unchanged thereby increasing the spread and net interest income.

What is a Bank's Interest Rate Bet According to GAP?

In the simple GAP framework, the sign of GAP indicates whether a bank is positioned to gain or lose when rates change. This presumably characterizes a bank's IRR "bet" at a point in time. The analysis assumes a parallel shift in the yield curve and GAP is assumed not to change when interest rates change. Neither of these conditions holds in practice. Still, the GAP exercise is useful for providing a framework to assess basic IRR.

Negative GAP (RSAs – RSLs < 0):   Rising rates lower net interest income
Falling rates increase net interest income

Positive GAP (RSAs – RSLs > 0):   Rising rates increase net interest income
Falling rates lower net interest income

A bank with a negative GAP is said to be *liability sensitive* and is positioned to benefit when rates fall. A bank with a positive GAP is said to be *asset sensitive* and is positioned to profit when interest rates rise. A bank might theoretically achieve a zero GAP implying no change in net interest income when rates either rise or fall. But no bank is perfectly matched in this sense. Conceptually, the closer the GAP is to zero (either positive or negative), the lower is the bank's IRR.

Many simple models of IRR use the basic equation listed below to characterize the impact of interest rate changes on a bank's net interest income.

$$\Delta \text{Net interest income} = \text{GAP} \times \Delta \text{interest rates} \qquad (10\text{-}1)$$

While the sign of GAP indicates the directional bet on rates, the size of GAP also presumably provides information regarding how much IRR a bank has taken. For example, compare two banks—each with $100 million in assets—that compete in the same geographic and product markets. County Bank has a one-year GAP of –$10 million and is liability sensitive while City Bank has a one-year GAP of +$5 million and is asset sensitive:

County Bank		City Bank	
RSAs = $55	RSLs = $65	RSAs = $60	RSLs = $55
GAP = – $10		GAP = $5	

If rates increase, County Bank will see its net interest income fall while City Bank will see its net interest income rise. The opposite impact on net interest income occurs if rates fall. The two banks have different IRR bets. Which bank exhibits greater IRR? Suppose that each bank initially expects to report net interest income for the upcoming year of $4 million. If rates rise 1%, County Bank's net interest income will fall by $100,000 according to equation 10-1 while City Bank's net interest income will rise by $50,000. If rates fall 1%, the banks' net interest income will rise by $100,000 and fall by $50,000, respectively. Regardless of which direction rates move, County Bank will see a greater change in net interest income. In addition, for the same adverse change in rates, County Bank has a greater possible maximum loss. It has thus assumed greater risk.

CHAPTER 10

Steps in GAP Analysis

GAP analysis involves several steps and is quite simplistic given the complexity of most bank activities. Yet, is a useful concept when assessing a bank's aggregate risk for a specific interest rate environment. The steps in GAP analysis include:

1. Select an interest rate environment
2. Select a series of successive time intervals
3. Assign each asset and liability and selected off-balance sheet items to the different time intervals based on management's expectations of when the item will reprice given the assumed interest rate environment
4. Calculate GAP for each time interval (periodic GAP) and the cumulative GAPs across all time intervals
5. Forecast net interest income and net income

GAP is a balance sheet concept. In this framework, it is the principal amount that counts. An asset or liability is labeled as rate sensitive if management expects to reprice the item during the time interval *given the assumed interest rate environment.* Notice the italicized words. What is important is whether management expects to reprice an asset or liability and not what the underlying contract formally says. In addition, determining whether an asset or liability is rate sensitive depends on the assumed rate environment. If the item can be repriced, expected interest income and expense may potentially change.

What makes an asset or liability rate sensitive, in turn, depends on the specific characteristics of the instruments. In terms of step 3 above, an asset or liability is rate sensitive if it:

1. Matures within the time interval: at maturity of an asset, a bank can reinvest the proceeds; at maturity of a liability, a bank must pay off the holder and potentially reissue (re-borrow) another liability. Each is potentially rate sensitive because the underlying rate that the bank can earn (reinvest) or must pay (reissue) may change from the current rate thereby changing expected interest income and expense.
2. Is priced off of an index and the index is expected to change within the time interval: an asset priced at prime + 1% will change in yield (expected interest income will change) when the prime rate changes; a liability priced at LIBOR + 1% will change in cost (expected interest expense will change) when LIBOR changes.
3. Involves a partial principal payment during the time interval: any amortizing loan or debt requires periodic principal payments that can be repriced; even when a car loan carries a fixed interest rate, a bank can reinvest the principal portion of the monthly car payment at whatever rate prevails when the payment is received.
4. Carries an embedded option and the option is exercised within the time interval: a loan that is refinanced produces a principal prepayment that a bank must reinvest at prevailing rates; a deposit that is withdrawn prior to maturity will normally be replaced with a new deposit that pays a higher rate.

The process of conducting static GAP analysis produces a rate sensitivity report like that appearing in Exhibit 10.1 for Victory State Bank (VSB) with $300 million in total assets and $26 million in stockholders equity. The principal amounts of assets and liabilities that are allocated to the different time buckets used are based on the assumption that interest rates remain constant for one year at levels prevailing at the end of 2013.

The first column of data identifies amounts of assets and liabilities that are priced off of base rates (indexes) that can change at any time. As noted, VSB has $65 million more in assets than liabilities tied to base rates that can change at any time. These immediately repriceable amounts are allocated across the time intervals based on when management actually expects the base rates to change. Importantly, if interest rates are assumed to remain constant, the prime rate and other base rates will likely be unchanged so these items will not reprice as quickly as when rates do change.

Exhibit 10.1 Rate Sensitivity Analysis for Victory State Bank, December 31, 2013*

Interest Rates Assumed to Remain Constant (millions)

	Immediately Repriceable	1–90 Days	91–180 Days	181–365 Days	Over 1 Year	Nonrate Sensitive	Total
Assets							
Short-term securities		$3	$5	$3			$11
U.S. Treasury & agency securities		6	3	7	$12		28
Municipal securities				6	20		26
Federal funds sold and repos	$5						5
Commercial loans	47	11	18	9	23		61
Real estate loans	56	16	17	27	55		115
Consumer loans	14	4	2	7	17		30
Earning assets							$276
Cash and due from banks						$6	6
Other assets						18	18
Nonearning assets							$24
Total assets	$122	$45	$45	$59	$127	$24	$300
Liabilities and Equity							
Interest checking accounts	$16	$21		$10	$10		$41
Money market deposit accounts	$32	$10		4	18		32
CDs under $100,000	1	7	$7	21	31		66
CDs of $100,000 or more	8	11	13	28	24		76
Federal funds purchased and repos							
Savings accounts					15		15
Interest-bearing liabilities							$230
Demand deposits						$40	40
Other liabilities						4	4
Equity						26	26
Nonpaying liabilities and equity							$70
Total liabilities and equity	$57	$49	$20	$63	$98	$70	$300
Periodic GAP	$65	–$4	$25	–$4	$29		
Cumulative GAP		–$4	$21	17	$46		

* Ignores off-balance sheet items.

Assume, for the moment, that the data are allocated appropriately for a flat (no change) rate environment. We initially compare RSAs with RSLs within the same time buckets that are reported as periodic GAP figures. A positive GAP indicates that more assets than liabilities are expected to reprice within the time interval. A negative GAP indicates that more liabilities than assets are expected to reprice within the specific time interval. Periodic GAPs are most useful in identifying timing differences in repricing that potentially create risk. If the GAPs differ sharply from zero, there is a considerable mismatch between RSAs and RSLs for that period. If management wanted to reduce risk, it might examine the periodic GAPs to assess what structural changes in pricing or maturities might best accomplish the task.[6]

A bank's cumulative GAP provides more useful strategic information. The cumulative GAP figures represent the sum of the periodic GAPs from day 1 through the end of the period within each time bucket. Thus, the cumulative GAP of $21 million equals the sum of the −$4 million and $25 million periodic GAPs. Alternatively, it equals RSAs minus RSLs [($45+45) − ($49+$20)] for the period 1 to 180 days from the present or the sums of the various RSAs and RSLs through the last day in the period. Small banks that use GAP models typically focus on the one-year cumulative GAP, denoted as GAP1, as a measure of IRR. For VSB, GAP1 equals $17 million or 5.7% of assets. VSB is thus asset sensitive through one year. The application of equation 10-1 below demonstrates that VSB is positioned to profit if rates rise 1%. Of course, if rates were to fall, VSB's net interest income would fall.

$$\Delta \text{ Net interest income} = \text{GAP1} \times \Delta \text{ interest rates}$$
$$= \$17{,}000{,}000\ (0.01)$$
$$= \$170{,}000$$

Many banks have IRR policies that set allowable limits in accordance with a bank's one-year cumulative GAP. The concept is that a GAP close to zero signifies low risk. Note that if GAP equals zero in equation 10-1, the change in net interest income will equal zero regardless of the direction or size of the change in interest rates. Management sets allowable IRR by limiting the size of GAP relative to earning (or total) assets. A typical policy limit requires the one-year cumulative GAP to be within +15% or −15% of earning assets.[7]

$$-15\% < \frac{\text{1-year cumulative GAP}}{\text{Earning assets}} < +15\% \qquad (10\text{-}2)$$

Impact of Embedded Options and Basis Risk

There are many weaknesses with the GAP framework primarily because there are serious measurement errors and it ignores the time value of money. Virtually all banks have subsequently moved to models involving sensitivity analysis and simulation to best capture IRR. The benefits of these models are described below, but it is useful to first demonstrate some of the problems with GAP viewed by itself.

Embedded Options

Banks have many different types of options embedded in various balance sheet items. These options are exercised (alter the underlying instrument's cash flows) when interest rates change. GAP analysis holds interest rates constant in order to classify RSAs and RSLs. It then attempts to measure the impact of changing interest rates on net interest income by using a fixed GAP amount (see equation 10-1) when it is widely known that the true amounts of RSAs and RSLs change when rates change.

Consider the data for VSB in Exhibit 10.1 generated under the assumption of constant interest rates for which many of the floating rate loans that are immediately repriceable are assumed not to reprice. If interest rates instead increase, these loans will reprice within a year and will convert to RSAs within the GAP framework. Immediately repriceable liabilities will also reprice thereby increasing RSLs. Because there are almost twice the amount of immediately repriceable assets versus liabilities, the bank's GAP figures will likely be much more positive. For example, suppose that $20 million of the loans that are assumed to reprice after one year in Exhibit 10.1 are floating rate loans that actually reprice as rates move higher during the year. The bank's RSAs through one year would be $20 million higher, which would make the bank's one-year cumulative GAP even larger at $37 million absent any change in RSLs.[8] The essential point that the bank is actually more asset sensitive in a rising rate environment. Equation 10-1 is a poor approximation of reality because GAP changes when interest rates change.

Basis Risk

The GAP framework presumes a parallel shift in the yield curve in which all rates that can change, do change by the same amount, in the same direction and at the same time. This never happens. Not only do yields on loans change by different amounts than yields on securities, most banks consciously change deposit rates differently than asset yields. When the Fed increases the target fed funds rate, banks quickly change their prime rate but lag changes in deposit rates so the spread normally widens, at least temporarily. Similarly, when the Fed lowers the target fed funds rate, banks try to delay lowering their prime rate while they lower deposit rates as quickly as the market will allow.[9]

Earnings Sensitivity Analysis

The most commonly used model to assess IRR is some form of earnings sensitivity analysis. It is also commonly referred to as *rate shock analysis*. Using this framework, bank managers essentially forecast the components of a bank's balance sheet and income statement across different assumed interest rate scenarios. It is typically "dynamic" in the sense that the forecasts allow for changes in the mix of assets and liabilities, growth in deposits and loans and changes in customer behavior along with changes in the future path of interest rates. Ideally, it incorporates both on and off-balance sheet positions. The rate shock terminology reflects modeling where interest rates are changed by amounts such as +1%, +2%, –1% and –2%, and so on, and balance sheet and income statement values change accordingly.

The steps in conducting earning sensitivity analysis track the steps listed earlier for GAP analysis. The starting point is an assumed base case interest rate environment with a bank modeling the balance sheet and income statement for periods extending out two or more years. Given the assumed rate environment, management incorporates assumptions about embedded options and changes in business strategy to forecast the composition of assets and liabilities and overall growth of the balance sheet. Using the assumed interest rates, it then forecasts net interest income and net income. The income statement forecast incorporates specific assumptions regarding when and how much different RSAs and RSLs reprice.

Management then alters the assumed interest rate environment by "shocking" rates higher or lower.[10] As rates are assumed to vary, the corresponding assumed balance sheet varies because the underlying economy differs. The mix of deposits and liabilities and the growth in loans and deposits will be far different if rates are higher versus lower when compared with rates in the base case. Furthermore, some embedded options will be exercised when rates rise (early withdrawals of deposits and binding caps on loan rates), while others will be exercised when rates fall (prepayments on loans and bonds being called), which further changes the portfolio composition.

Even though earnings sensitivity analysis is more complex than GAP analysis, the summary output is relatively easy to interpret. A typical shock analysis compares forecasts across seven or nine interest rate scenarios with the base case as one scenario representing the point of reference for the other scenarios. Consider the data for VSB in Exhibit 10.2. The base case is an environment where rates remain constant for the next two years at the values prevailing at the end of 2013. This is a flat or no change rate scenario. The different columns of data indicate the estimated levels for interest income, interest expense, net interest income and the percentage change in net interest income across environments with higher and lower rates. Rate shocks are typically characterized in terms of a benchmark, or driver, interest rate for the model. Assume that the federal funds rate serves as the benchmark. In this case, the fed funds rate would have to be above 4% at the end of 2013 for rate shocks of –4% to be meaningful.[11]

Exhibit 10.2 Rate Shock Analysis and Earnings at Risk for Victory State Bank December 31, 2013 (Millions)
Interest Rates Assumed to Remain Constant: Rate Shocks are Instantaneous

Item	\	\	\	\	Interest Rate Environment	\	\	\	\
	−4%	−3%	−2%	−1%	Base Case	+1%	+2%	+3%	+4%
					Forecast for 2014				
Interest income	$12.3	$14.1	$15.2	$16.0	$16.7	$17.6	$18.7	$19.4	$20.2
Interest expense	3.2	4.3	4.9	5.5	5.9	6.2	6.8	7.4	8.1
Net interest income	8.9	9.8	10.3	10.5	10.8	11.4	11.9	12.0	12.1
% Change vs Base	−17.6	−9.3	−4.6	−2.8	—	+5.6	+10.2	+11.1	+12.0
					Forecast for 2015				
Interest income	12.1	14.0	15.6	16.6	17.5	18.4	19.3	19.9	20.4
Interest expense	3.3	4.1	5.2	5.8	6.2	6.7	7.3	8.2	9.7
Net interest income	8.8	9.9	10.4	10.8	11.3	11.7	12.0	11.7	10.7
% Change vs Base	−22.1	−12.4	−8.0	−4.4	—	+3.5	+6.2	+3.5	−5.3

For the data in Exhibit 10.2, assume that the federal funds rate equals 4.25% in the base case. Rate shocks of +1% and –1% indicate that the fed funds rate rises to 5.25% and falls to 3.25%, respectively. These assumed rate changes are instantaneous in which the fed funds rate is "shocked" so that it immediately rises or falls. Alternatively, you can model a gradual change in rates in which the change occurs systematically over the one and two year period. Assuming a gradual +1% rate shock through two years, the modeled shock would be represented by the fed funds rate increasing by 4.17 basis points per month over 24 months. All other rates change by varying amounts depending on the specific assumptions made.

The key results of the earnings sensitivity analysis are revealed by the data in bold print. In terms of the one year forecast for 2014, VSB's net interest income is forecast to be $10.8 million if interest rates remain constant at 2013 levels. If the fed funds rate increases, net interest income will rise by increasing amounts. For a +2% shock, net interest income will rise by an estimated 10.2%. If, instead, the fed funds rate falls, net interest income will fall by as much as 17.6% in a down 4% rate move. The bank is asset sensitive because it is positioned to lose (gain) in a falling (rising) rate environment. The data suggest that the model incorporates the impact of embedded options and lags in deposit versus loan pricing because the dollar changes in net interest income are not symmetric. Here, the proportionate increase in net interest income for a +1% rate change exceeds the proportionate decrease for a -1% rate change, which also holds for rate changes of ±2% and ±3%. Interest income falls greatly in a –4% rate environment presumably because prepayments accelerate sharply.

The forecast for 2015 reveals a similar asset sensitive position through a +3% shock, albeit with smaller upside benefits under rising rates and greater losses under falling rates. This seems logical because banks that sold options (loan prepayments, callable bonds, floors on deposit rates) will see more options exercised with a longer sustained drop in rates. Similarly, banks will eventually have to raise deposit rates comparably with higher loan rates in a rising environment so that the corresponding increase in interest expense will ultimately match the increase in interest income and thereby narrow the bank's spread. The drop in earnings with a +4% rate shock might reflect the impact of caps on loan rates.

Measuring the Magnitude of IRR Using Earnings Sensitivity Analysis

Rate shock analysis indicates whether a bank is positioned to benefit or lose when rates rise and/or fall. The estimated increases or decreases in net interest income signal the direction of the bank's interest rate "bet." When assessing the magnitude of risk assumed, bank managers are generally concerned about loss potential. As such, they will ask questions like "What is the most the bank can be expected to lose if rates rise or fall by 2%?" In this context, the board of directors will often set IRR policy to designate a maximum acceptable loss when interest rates change by a predetermined amount.

Sample IRR Policy Statement

A policy statement might state "an instantaneous change in rates of ±2% should not lower net interest income by more than 5% from the base case forecast."

The base case would, in turn, be designated as the flat rate (no change) environment. Such a policy allows the bank to generate as much upside potential as possible as long as the maximum loss is within acceptable limits.

As expected, the greater is the loss potential, the greater is the amount of risk assumed and thus the size of the bank's IRR bet. Importantly, when the estimated loss exceeds the maximum allowable loss under the bank's IRR policy, management must note the exception and should pursue strategies to reduce the risk. Such strategies may involve changing the mix of assets and liabilities, altering the pricing of loans and deposits between floating rate and fixed rate instruments, or using off-balance sheet instruments. With a risk reduction (hedging) objective, the intent would be to better match the effective repricing of assets and liabilities. A later section discusses some derivative applications that community banks may use.

Alternative Base Case Interest Rate Risk Analysis

Risk managers should shock their portfolios in many different ways encompassing a wide range of potential outcomes. The balance sheet may be static (unchanged from the present), but would normally incorporate growth and changes in mix. Interest rate shocks may be instantaneous or gradual and the yield curve may be allowed to change in slope. The most critical assumptions are:

- Are all balance sheet accounts with significant impacts modeled separately?
- What is the benchmark (driver) interest rate?
- What is the base case interest rate scenario?
- Are the different rate scenarios realistic?
- Is the model static or does it allow for growth in loans, securities, deposits and wholesale funding?
- When each type of embedded option is exercised, is the assumed cash flow impact realistic?
- What does the model assume regarding nonmaturity deposits (demand deposits)?
- What are assumed betas and decay rates and are they realistic?

Consider the case when the Treasury yield curve and LIBOR swap curve are sharply upsloping. The consensus view in the market is that interest rates will rise in the future. Using a base case of flat rates ignores the consensus view. As such, some banks start with a base case that uses implied forward rates for the assumed rate environment. As described in the chapter on investments, implied forward rates increase the farther out in time with an upward sloping yield curve. In this situation, the base case already incorporates the expectation that rates will rise because the benchmark rate increases over time. The estimated net interest income will equal that expected if the benchmark rate follows the path implied (expected) by prevailing yields. This makes the interpretation of data like that in Exhibit 10.2 more difficult. Specifically, an assumed +1% rate shock actually compares what net interest income is estimated to equal if future rates exceed expected rates versus what it might equal under a scenario where the yield curve is "correct." In other words, the rate environments should be interpreted as signaling outcomes when interest rates are either higher (+1%, +2%, etc.) or lower (–1%,–2%, etc.) than what is currently expected. Obviously, the base case will change whenever the yield curve and level of rates changes. Importantly, the ALCO should model rate changes that realistically represent likely outcomes given the prevailing economic environment. These results will drive strategic decisions.

Economic Value of Equity Sensitivity Analysis

Earnings sensitivity analysis focuses on shorter-term outcomes through one or two years. Economic Value of Equity (EVE) Sensitivity Analysis is an alternative model of IRR that emphasizes the impacts that changing interest rates have on market values, or prices, of assets and liabilities. In order to calculate market values, we must have reasonable estimates of expected cash flows on each asset and liability throughout its entire life and reasonable discount rates. Because the analysis discounts all future cash flows, including those occurring after one or two years, it effectively focuses on longer-term outcomes.

EVE analysis measures IRR in terms of how much a bank's EVE changes when interest rates change. Importantly, EVE is a residual, or plug figure, and represents a liquidation value for the bank. The number by itself is not all that meaningful because it ignores franchise value, brand value and the value of management. However, changes in EVE over time provide useful information about IRR.

Consider the data in Exhibit 10.3. The sample bank owns loans, securities and a variety of nonearning assets that are financed by core deposits, large CDs and stockholders equity. Given prevailing interest rates and economic conditions, management estimates that it could sell the assets for $100 million. At the same time, it would have to pay $80 million to buy back its liabilities. The bank's EVE is the difference between the market value of assets (MVA) and the market value of liabilities (MVL) such that it is a plug figure:

$$EVE = MVA-MVL$$

In this example, EVE equals $20 million. This figure does not represent the *market capitalization* of the bank, i.e., how much the stock market currently values the bank, but rather estimates how much would be left for stockholders if all items sold at today's prices and management used the proceeds from the assets to pay off the liabilities.[12]

Exhibit 10.3 Sample Bank Economic Value of Equity, December 31, 2013 (millions)

Market Value of Assets		Market Value of Liabilities +EVE	
Loans	$60	Core deposits	$70
Investments	30	Large CDs	10
Nonearning assets	10	Market Value of Liabilities	$80
		EVE	20
Market Value of Assets	$100	Total	$100

Link Between Duration and EVE

The critical issue is to determine how much EVE changes when interest rates change. EVE is thus the target measure for determining a bank's longer-term IRR. Changes in EVE are linked to how price sensitive each of the bank's assets and liabilities is to a change in interest rates. This sensitivity, in turn, is reflected in each item's duration.

The *modified duration of a fixed-income security* (DUR) is a measure of how much the price (P) of the security will change for a given change in the underlying interest rate on the security.[13] For securities without options (option-free securities), it is measured in units of time. Duration is best viewed as an elasticity measure with a straightforward interpretation. *The greater (lesser) is duration, the greater (lesser) is price sensitivity.*

Consider the following approximate relationship:

$$\frac{\Delta P}{P} = -\text{DUR} \times \Delta \text{rate} \qquad (10\text{-}3)$$

As noted in the chapter on bank investments, interest rates and prices move in the opposite direction for option-free securities. As such, when interest rates increase, the price of the security falls; when interest rates decrease, the price of the security rises. The negative sign in relation 10-3 captures this inverse relationship. Suppose that a bond currently priced at par ($100) carrying a market rate of 4% has an estimated modified duration of 3 years. According to (10-3), the bond's price will fall to approximately $98.5 ($100 − $1.5 = $98.5) if the rate on the bond immediately rises to 4.5%:

$$\Delta P = -3[0.0050]\$100 \quad \text{or} \quad \Delta P = -\$1.5$$

If another bond with a modified duration of six years is similarly priced at $100 with a 4% rate experiences a 50 basis point increase in rate, its price would fall by $3 per $100 or twice as much. This demonstrates that the greater (longer) is duration, the greater is price sensitivity.

The duration of a portfolio of securities, such as loans plus investments or core deposits plus large CDs, is the weighted sum of the durations of the individual instruments and has the same interpretation as the duration of a single instrument. The weights equal the market value of each item as a fraction of the *market value of all assets* (MVA) or *liabilities* (MVL), whichever applies. DUR is then linked to EVE through the relative price sensitivities of MVL and MVA.

Suppose that the sample bank in Exhibit 10.3 owns investment securities with a duration of four years and loans with a duration of two years while the duration of nonearning assets is zero. The duration of core deposits is 1.5 years while the duration of jumbo CDs is 1 year. The weighted durations of assets (DURMVA) and liabilities (DURMVL) are thus:

$$\text{DURMVA} = (60/100)\,2 + (30/100)\,4 + (10/100)\,0 = 2.4 \text{ years}$$
$$\text{DURMVL} = (70/80)\,1.5 + (10/80)\,1 = 1.15 \text{ years}$$

Because the portfolio of assets has an average duration that is more than twice that of the portfolio of liabilities, the bank's assets are much more price sensitive, on average.

We can use these duration values to estimate the impact of changing rates on EVE. Assume that the average earning asset yield is 7% while the average rate paid on liabilities is 3%. Consider the (unlikely) case where all interest rates increase by 1% immediately. On average, the market values of the bank's assets will fall as will the market values of the bank's liabilities. Because the asset duration is greater, the assets should fall more in value. Note that the decrease in MVL with higher rates simply indicates that the bank has locked deposit customers into below-market rates. If it wanted to buy the deposits back in a secondary market, it would have to pay less because they would trade at a discount. Approximating these changes:

$$\Delta MVA = -2.4 (\$100) (0.01) = -\$2.40$$
$$\Delta MVL = -1.15 (\$80) (0.01) = -\$0.92$$

Exhibit 10.4 Sample Bank Economic Value of Equity: December 31, 2013
After a +1% Instantaneous Rate Shock (millions)

Assets	Liabilities+EVE	
	Market Value of Liabilities	$79.08
	EVE (shocked)	18.52
Market Value of Assets $97.60	Total	$97.60

As demonstrated in Exhibit 10.4, the bank's MVA falls from $100 to $97.60 while its MVL falls from $80 to $79.08. Thus, the bank would see its EVE fall to $18.52 or by $1.48 (million).

The decline in EVE follows from the greater price sensitivity of assets. If a bank invests in longer duration fixed rate loans and investments, it generally assumes significant risk because its liabilities have shorter maturities and durations. If rates rise, the bank is unable to reprice its loans and investments while its liabilities will be repriced at higher rates when they mature. The greater drop in MVA versus MVL captures the present value of this differential repricing. If rates fall, the opposite occurs. MVA will increase more than MVL increases such that EVE increases. Here, a bank with longer duration loans and investments (option-free) will see their prices jump while the prices of liabilities will rise proportionately less. Thus EVE would rise.[14]

This leads to the following general relationships that characterize a bank's IRR "bet":[15]

- If a bank's average duration of assets exceeds its average duration of liabilities, its EVE will fall (rise) when interest rates rise (fall).
- If a bank's average duration of liabilities exceeds its average duration of assets, its EVE will rise (fall) when interest rates rise (fall)

Management can thus approximate its IRR bet by knowing the relative durations of assets and liabilities. The magnitude of IRR assumed will again be reflected in how much EVE changes when rates change, which is linked to the difference in effective durations of all bank assets versus all bank liabilities.

Modeling EVE Sensitivity

The steps for EVE Sensitivity Analysis are comparable to those for Earnings Sensitivity Analysis. The starting point is again an assumed base case interest rate environment, normally the flat rate (no change) case. There is no future time frame because all cash flows for all instruments are discounted to their present values to estimate market values. Given the assumed rate environment, management incorporates assumptions about lags in loan versus deposit pricing, the exercise of embedded options and changes in business strategy to forecast the composition of assets and liabilities and overall growth of the balance sheet. Different discount rates are used for each asset and liability reflecting current market conditions. In many cases, management will use estimated durations to assess price sensitivity of individual balance sheet items, so it will initially include these duration estimates along with the base case EVE estimate.[16] It will then shock rates and repeat the analysis with a new set of assumptions.

Exhibit 10.5 provides sample output for EVE Sensitivity Analysis assuming that rates rise and fall by as much as 4%. The base case is again flat rates. Note that market values rise when rates fall and fall when rates rise because some of the assets and liabilities carry fixed rates. The bottom three rows of data provide information regarding EVE. VSB's EVE in the base case is $30.5 million which exceeds its book value of stockholders equity ($26 million) by $4.5 million. As rates decrease, EVE falls by the ever increasing amounts as indicated by EVE at Risk. As rates rise, EVE rises except for a +4% shock to rates when EVE falls by $3.4 million.

Exhibit 10.5 Rate Shock Analysis and EVE at Risk for Victory State Bank, December 31, 2013
Interest Rates Assumed to Remain Constant; Rate Shocks Are Instantaneous; initial equity is $26 (Millions)

Item	Interest Rate Environment								
	−4%	−3%	−2%	−1%	Base Case	+1%	+2%	+3%	+4%
Market Values									
Assets	$338.5	$338.2	$337.9	$326.7	$323.0	$320.1	$314.3	$301.3	$294.8
Liabilities	317.0	311.5	308.7	296.6	292.5	288.8	280.6	270.2	267.7
EVE	21.5	26.7	29.2	30.1	30.5	31.3	33.7	31.1	27.1
EVE at Risk	10.4	3.8	1.3	0.4	—	—	—	—	3.4
Percent Change vs. Base	−34.1	−12.5	−4.3	−1.3	—	+2.6	+10.5	+2.0	−11.2
EVE at Risk vs. Initial Equity	−40.0	−14.6	−5.0	−1.5	—	—	—	—	−13.1

What do these results suggest regarding VSB's IRR? First, the bank is positioned to benefit if rates rise by as much as 3%. Any greater increase in rates will lower the market value of VSB's assets by more than it lowers the market value of liabilities. VSB is positioned to lose if rates decrease although the losses are quite small for rate declines up to 2%. Generally, the bank appears to be well hedged against losses as long as rates do not decline by more than 2%. In terms of durations, the bank's weighted asset and liability durations are roughly matched with small changes in rates. As rates rise 2%, the bank will benefit because the market value of liabilities falls much more (proportionately) than the market value of assets. Intuitively, more of the bank's assets may be short-term or carry floating rates versus its liabilities. This reverses for a rate move of +4%. Second, the magnitude of VSB's risk appears to be relatively modest. Most firms using EVE analysis will have a policy limit regarding acceptable risk by specifying a maximum acceptable loss in EVE for a predetermined rate move. For example, a policy might read "For a +2% or –2% instantaneous rate shock, the bank's EVE should not fall by more than 20% from the base case EVE in a flat interest rate environment." If this were VSB's policy, it would be well within its limits as only the –4% rate shock environment produces an estimated EVE loss of more than 20%. The last row of data show the EVE at Risk compared with a bank's initial stockholders equity. Clearly, a bank with large amounts of equity can absorb greater losses. If the potential drop in EVE is a small fraction of equity, the bank assumes little IRR.

Earnings Sensitivity Versus EVE Sensitivity

Banks should use both frameworks to analyze IRR because they measure risk from two different, but related perspectives. Earnings sensitivity emphasizes shorter-term effects on earnings. EVE sensitivity emphasizes longer-term effects on the value of stockholders equity. Generally, a bank that is liability sensitive such that it loses when interest rates rise, will have longer duration assets so its EVE falls when interest rates rise. In contrast, an asset sensitive bank will lose when rates fall while a bank with longer duration liabilities will similarly lose when rates fall.

Banks that have any assets and liabilities with embedded options should incorporate both models in their regular IRR analysis. They should similarly have policies that specify acceptable risk limits for a maximum acceptable loss in earnings and EVE versus the respective base case values. Under the 2010 IRR guidance, a bank's board and risk committee members should fully understand assumptions underlying the models. Management should regularly validate the models and test the accuracy of the models (conduct backtests) after substantive rate moves.

Managing the Bank's Interest Rate Risk Profile

Managers can alter a bank's IRR profile by taking actions on balance sheet or by using off-balance sheet derivatives. Strategically, management may position the bank to take advantage of rising interest rates or falling interest rates, as deemed appropriate, or may choose to hedge IRR as much as possible. The concept of hedging involves taking positions to reduce overall risk such that changes in rates and/or prices of assets and liabilities have little or no impact on earnings or EVE.

Consider a bank that focuses on earnings sensitivity analysis over a one year horizon by conducting rate shock analysis. It is easier to understand what actions might be appropriate by examining how individual transactions affect the rate sensitivity of all assets versus liabilities. For example, suppose that the bank is currently perfectly hedged in the sense that interest rate changes in any direction will not affect net interest income. Now management wants to position the bank to take advantage of anticipated increases in interest rates over the next year. What should it do?

Exhibit 10.6 summarizes several general opportunities in terms of what the bank's objective is regarding changing RSAs or RSLs on balance sheet. In this example, the bank wants to profit if rates rise, so it should either increase asset sensitivity (increase RSAs) or decrease liability sensitivity (decrease RSLs). This would call for actions that shorten asset maturities and price more loans on a floating rate basis. Alternatively, it might be achieved by lengthening fixed rate liability maturities.

Exhibit 10.6 Balance Sheet Transactions to Alter Rate Sensitivity of Assets & Liabilities

Risk Management Actions

Objective	Action
Reduce asset sensitivity	Buy longer-term securities. Lengthen the maturities of loans. Move from floating-rate loans to fixed-rate term loans.
Increase asset sensitivity	Buy short-term securities. Shorten loan maturities. Make more loans on a floating-rate basis.
Reduce liability sensitivity	Pay premiums to attract longer-term, fixed-rate deposit instruments. Issue long-term subordinated debt.
Increase liability sensitivity	Pay premiums to attract short-term deposit instruments. Borrow more via noncore purchased liabilities.

In each case, how might a bank use interest rate swaps, caps and floors?

Suppose, instead, that management wants to position the bank for an anticipated drop in interest rates. Strategically, it would attempt to reduce asset sensitivity while it increases liability sensitivity by the actions noted in Exhibit 10.6. Of course, the success of these transactions depends on whether—and how much—a bank must pay to alter its balance sheet sensitivity. If, for example, market participants, on average, believe that rates are going to rise sharply in the near future, short-term rates will be much lower than long-term rates and fixed rates on loans will be much higher than floating rates. Buying short-term securities has a significant opportunity cost near term as does making floating rate loans as the bank will give up interest income.[17] The opportunity cost is much lower when market expectations differ sharply from the bank entering the transactions. Importantly, banks can accomplish the same effective changes in overall IRR exposure by using off-balance sheet transactions.

Community Banks and Derivatives

Derivatives have gotten considerable press with the financial crisis. *Credit default swaps* (CDSs), in particular, have been heavily scrutinized because firms such as AIG lost large amounts trading them with losses borne by the U.S. taxpayer because the federal government bailed them out of their problems. AIG's use of CDSs was clearly excessive and damaging to the global financial system. The U.S. Congress has subsequently tried to pass legislation that redesigns how derivatives are traded and potentially places limits on their use.

Despite the many abuses of derivatives, some derivatives can be very beneficial when used appropriately. The key is to fully understand the nature of the instruments and inherent risks, how they are priced, how they can be used to reduce risk and the associated accounting and cash flow requirements. This section briefly describes interest rate swaps and their use by community banks in managing IRR. The essential point is that they can help mitigate risk and meet customer preferences if done correctly. Community banks should generally avoid CDSs and other complex derivatives that are traded over the counter.

Community banks and their customers often use derivatives in their normal operations. A derivative is an agreement between two parties who take opposite positions based on the value of some underlying asset or contract. The agreement (which can be traded as a financial instrument) varies in value as the value of the underlying asset changes such that it derives its value from the future value of the underlying. Consider a *pass-through mortgage-backed security* (MBS) that a bank might buy for its investment portfolio. This security has a claim on the actual principal and interest payments made on residential mortgage loans that were packaged into a pool and used to back or collateralize the pass-through. Banks like many of these instruments because they are issued by Fannie Mae or Freddie Mac with promised principal and interest payments guaranteed by Ginnie Mae.[18] Such MBSs are derivatives because they derive their value from the value of the mortgage payments made by homebuyers. Many farmers and ranchers similarly use financial futures and options to hedge risks associated with raising cattle and growing crops. They essentially take positions in derivative contracts that change in value in the opposite direction as the value of the assets that the rancher/farmer owns. Thus if the value of corn falls between planting and delivery, a farmer who has appropriately hedged might offset some or all of the loss in sale price with a gain from trading the derivative. The key point is that derivatives, by themselves, are not bad.

Characteristics of Basic Interest Rate Swaps

A basic interest rate swap is an agreement whereby two counterparties agree to exchange interest payments. Much like a bond, a swap has a maturity, a principal amount and periodic payments or receipts. One party agrees to make a series of periodic payments equal to a fixed rate times a notional principal amount while the other party agrees to make similarly-timed periodic payments equal to a floating rate times the same notional principal amount. The principal amount exists only as a reference number as it never changes hands. Hence the notional label. The swap then consists of exchanging the difference in the calculated payments at each payment date.

When entering into a swap contract, a bank must select a term (maturity), principal amount, floating rate index and the frequency of payment. Much like other instruments, the swaps are traded so a bank will have a counterparty such as one of the Federal Home Loan Banks or a large commercial/investment bank. Both the bank and the counterparty will pledge collateral against the swap in case the value declines over time. Swaps are based on many different floating rates, including three-month LIBOR, the prime rate and federal funds rate. Swaps representing fixed versus floating payments based on popular floating rates and with fixed principal amounts are very efficiently priced because the market is quite deep in terms of volume. Swaps, like futures and options, are off-balance sheet instruments. Banks are required to hold capital against these types of off-balance sheet positions and the associated cash flows do affect reported income and expense. There are also significant accounting issues involved when using swaps that are outside the scope of this analysis.[19]

Consider a three-year swap based on three-month LIBOR and a $5 million notional principal amount. Payments will be made every three months for three years so there are 12 potential payments or receipts. The current three-month LIBOR rate equals 1.5%. A call to the regional FHLB reveals the following bid and offer:

	Fixed Swap Rate
Fixed-rate Payer: Bank agrees to pay a fixed rate and receive LIBOR	2.05%
Floating rate Payer: Bank agrees to pay LIBOR and receive a fixed rate	2.00%

The following time line in Exhibit 10.7 indicates the known payments or receipts at the time the bank enters into the swap. The first row indicates the payment date represented by the number of months after entering into the swap today. The fixed-rate payer agrees to make a fixed payment of $25,625 every three months and will receive LIBOR times $5 million every three months. The floating rate payer agrees to receive a fixed payment of $25,000 every three months and will pay LIBOR times $5 million every three months. By convention, the LIBOR that prevails at the time the parties enter into the contract determines the floating rate payment/receipt at the first value date in three months. Assuming LIBOR initially equals 1.5%, this floating rate amount equals $18,750.

Exhibit 10.7 Timeline for Basic Interest Rate Swap

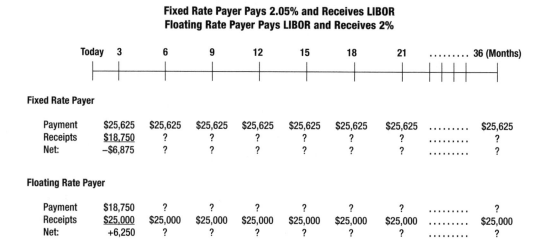

Note that the payments from both counterparties are netted. In this example, the FHLB as a swap dealer attempts to find a party that wants to be a fixed-rate payer for three years and match it with a party that wants to be a floating rate payer. At each value date, each party pays or receives the difference between the fixed rate and LIBOR times $5 million. By convention, the fixed-rate payer knows it will make a $6,875 payment in three months while the floating rate payer will receive a payment of $6,250. If the FHLB finds counterparties for both sides of the transaction, it earns $625 from the bid-ask spread.

What is not known on the swap is what LIBOR will equal for the 11 remaining value dates. The rate that will be used for the second period in six months is the actual value of LIBOR that prevails in three months. The rate used for the value date in nine months is prevailing LIBOR on the value date in six months, and so forth. Thus, at the time the parties enter into the swap, both parties might forecast LIBOR at three month intervals to get an estimate of the net payments or receipts over the life of the swap. In practice, participants use forward rates derived from the yield curve as estimates of expected LIBOR. Solving for the rate that produces a zero net present value of expected cash flows for both positions then adjusting to provide the dealer a spread determines the fixed rates that make a swap a "fair" trade.[21] The pricing mechanism indicates that any party who speculates using swaps is betting that the forward rates are either too high (Floating Rate Payer) or too low (Fixed Rate Payer).

Using Swaps to Reduce Risk

Convert a Floating Rate to a Fixed Rate

Some community banks use basic interest rate swaps to convert a floating rate asset or liability to a fixed rate or vice versa. Suppose that VSB is asset sensitive through three years and does not want to increase its risk exposure as measured by its earnings at risk. A high quality business customer wants to borrow $5 million at a floating rate because the CFO expects rates to remain low and there is a high probability that the firm will pay off the principal prior to maturity. For IRR purposes, VSB prefers a fixed rate loan. The bank can actually make the customer a floating rate loan and use a swap to convert it to a fixed rate loan.

Assume that the customer accepts a loan priced off of three-month LIBOR at a spread of 2.5%. VSB makes a $5 million, three-year loan at LIBOR + 2.5%. Interest is payable quarterly with all principal due at maturity. VSB simultane-

Exhibit 10.7 Victory Savings Bank Swap Transaction: Impact on Effective Loan Rate

	Asset		Rate
	3-year loan: $5 million		LIBOR + 2.5%
	Swap		Rate
	3-year swap: $5 million		Pay LIBOR; Receive 2%
Effective Loan Rate:		Receive:	Loan: LIBOR + 2.5% Swap: 2% Total: LIBOR + 4.5%
		Pay:	Swap: LIBOR
		Net Receipt:	4.5%

ously enters into a three-year Floating Rate Payer swap with the FHLB in which it agrees to pay LIBOR and receive 2% against $5 million in notional principal. As Exhibit 10.7 demonstrates, VSB has effectively converted the loan rate to a fixed 4.5%.

Regardless of whether LIBOR rises or falls, VSB receives a fixed 4.5% rate on the loan (ignoring default). There is still interest rate risk in this transaction because the borrower can repay the loan prior to maturity. If it were to do so, VSB would be left holding a swap that is no longer matched to any specific loan. It would have to find another loan or deposit to tie the swap to or needs to sell the swap position. This sale may generate cash or require a cash payment from VSB. For example, suppose that the borrower repays the loan in exactly one year. In terms of the timeline, there are eight remaining value dates ranging from 15 - 36 months from the present. The value of the swap will depend on prevailing LIBOR and what LIBOR is expected to equal for each future value date. Given the depth of the LIBOR swap market, VSB could readily sell the swap for the discounted value of the expected netted payments or receipts. If LIBOR was still below 2% and expected to remain low for two years, VSB would receive cash from the swap sale because the netted payments would reflect cash receipts to a floating rate payer. If, instead, LIBOR was expected to be well above 2%, on average, over the next two years, the netted values would project VSB swap payments (cash outflows) and VSB would pay the swap buyer. To offset this prepayment risk and set a value for selling the prepayment option to the borrower, VSB should write a make-whole clause into the loan agreement whereby the borrower is responsible for the required cash payment or receipt due from the swap sale.

Convert a fixed rate to a floating rate: Assume that Shore Bank (SB) is liability sensitive. Management expects interest rates to rise well above expected rates over the next three years. One of the bank's best business customers requests a $5 million, three-year fixed rate loan for expansion purposes. It wants the certainty of known loan payments as well as protection against rising rates. Interest will be paid quarterly with the $5 million principal due after three years. How might VSB make a fixed rate loan to the customer and use a prime rate swap to convert the loan to carry a floating rate?

The terms for a $5 million prime rate swap with a 3-year term are:

Fixed rate payer:	Pays: 1.95%	Receive: prime rate – 2%
Floating rate payer:	Pays: prime rate – 2%	Receive: 1.85%
Prime rate currently equals 3.75%		

If VSB makes the fixed rate loan, it will charge 5.25% and receive a fixed interest amount every quarter. In order to convert this receipt to a floating rate basis, it should enter into a fixed rate payer swap. Exhibit 10.8 demonstrates that, ignoring default risk, the combined transaction converts the 5.25% fixed rate loan to a loan priced at the prime rate + 1.30%. VSB gets the floating rate it wants and the borrower gets the fixed rate it wants. The loan agreement should contain a clause that requires the borrower to be responsible for the value of the swap at a sale prior to maturity if the borrower prepays the loan.

Exhibit 10.8 Shore Bank Swap Transaction: Impact on Effective Loan Rate

	Asset	Rate
	3-year loan: $5 million	5.25%
	Swap	**Rate**
	3-year swap: $5 million	Pay 1.95% Receive prime rate – 2%
Effective Loan Rate:	Receive:	Loan: 5.25%
		Swap: prime rate – 2%
		Total: prime rate + 3.25%
	Pay:	Swap: 1.95%
	Net Receipt:	prime rate + 1.30%

Derivatives are not necessarily bad. Virtually all banks are involved with mortgage-backed securities so they are familiar with these on-balance sheet derivatives. If a bank uses off-balance sheet derivatives, such as basic interest rate swaps, for hedging purposes, they provide a valuable tool to adjust a bank's IRR exposure. Community banks do not buy and sell derivatives for speculative reasons and do not act as dealers. Thus, there is a role in IRR management. Bank directors and managers must, however, conduct significant due diligence to ensure that they understand the risks and benefits associated with derivatives and have the appropriate policies and procedures to manage derivatives' use and control risks within acceptable limits.

Summary

In recent years, bank regulators have issued guidance regarding bank interest rate risk management. The impetus is a recognition that given the low rates prevailing currently, interest rates will rise at some point in the future. The intent of the guidance was to provide a framework for bank managers to better measure interest rate risk, manage it and monitor outcomes over time. Regulatory expectations vary with the complexity of a bank's on and off-balance sheet activities and the bank's overall risk profile. More complex institutions must conduct more rigorous interest rate risk analysis.

Most banks measure interest rate risk via models known as GAP analysis, earnings sensitivity analysis or income simulation, and economic value of equity analysis. Banks are encouraged to match their model's analytical power with the complexity of the bank's risk exposures. When risks are expected to be outside the bank's policies, management should take actions to mitigate risk. This chapter describes the framework that banks use to measure interest rate risk and the general guidelines that regulators suggest to help manage exposures over time. It emphasizes the importance of understanding the models and model output and how management might use the information to adjust a bank's interest rate risk profile. The true benefit comes from understanding interest rate risk and then using the information to make strategic decisions regarding the structure and pricing of loans and deposits.

Strategies for Achieving Competitive Advantage

CHAPTER 11
Taking Advantage of Competitive Opportunities

Since the onset of the financial crisis at the end of 2007, many banking organizations have taken a defensive posture. Senior managers and members of the board of directors have focused on reducing risk exposures and strengthening the balance sheet. This has generally taken the form of ensuring that lending is targeted at customers with a higher than normal likelihood of repayment and a loan portfolio that is appropriately diversified. Lenders are trying to reduce concentrations. Banks have improved liquidity by increasing core deposits, holding more short-term liquid assets and reducing reliance on wholesale or brokered funding. They have effective contingency funding plans in place to help identify potential net cash outflows that might present cash calls in the future. CFOs and the bank's ALCO have focused on better matching rate sensitive assets and liabilities in anticipation or rising rates. All managers and directors are paying increased attention to technology and operational risk along with legal and reputation risks. Finally, most banks have increased their Tier 1 capital by retaining more earnings and issuing common stock when possible. They have also focused on growing the portion of regulatory capital that is common equity. This has the benefit of lowering financial leverage and reducing the likelihood of failure in the event of future asset quality problems.

When viewed in total, these efforts have largely de-emphasized earnings and earnings growth. Building a Fortress Balance Sheet has the near-term impact of lowering current and expected earnings and return on equity. Strategies for value creation have instead focused on risk reduction and improving regulatory CAMELS ratings. While many banks have been in this "survival mode," it is now time to focus on how to prosper going forward. Managers and directors need to change their mindset to a proactive one of creating value by enhancing earnings relative to risk. They must shift from defense to offense.

Chapter 11

Strategies to Enhance Shareholder Value

Chapter 5 introduced key measures of shareholder value:

- Cash earnings per share (Cash EPS)
- Tangible book value of equity per share (TBVS)
- Core deposit funding

Managers and directors should change the mindset to implement strategies that will increase each of these metrics. Key decisions will address:

- Effective enterprise risk management (ERM)
- Contingency funding planning and balance sheet liquidity
- Effective loan migration analysis and a meaningful ALLL methodology
- Pre-purchase analysis of high quality investment securities
- Systematic assessment of loan and deposit customer demographics
- Effective use of technology
- Proactive critique of interest rate risk analytics and strategic opportunities
- Regular compliance reviews for safety and soundness, consumer services, fair lending and other risks

Enterprise Risk Management

For effective enterprise risk management, banks should integrate their periodic strategic planning efforts with budgeting and institution-wide risk identification, measurement and monitoring with putting controls in place. Managers should conduct regular internal stress tests to assess whether the bank faces unacceptable risks.[1] This involves forecasting performance in the future in the event of adverse economic conditions, rising loan losses, potential deposit outflows, etc. and evaluating the impact on key risk and profit measures. If done appropriately, it also allows management to assess how specific strategies, such as loan acquisitions, changes in deposit pricing, branch acquisitions or sales, capital raises and leverage strategies affect the bank's performance targets.

Contingency Funding Planning and Balance Sheet Liquidity

To best manage liquidity, banks should structure their balance sheets to reduce the likelihood of large cash outflows and hold sufficient amounts of saleable assets in the event that borrowing opportunities decline. Banks should be growing their balance sheets by increasing core deposit funding and judiciously targeting longer-term wholesale funding opportunities in anticipation of future rate increases. In terms of assets, banks should hold a reasonable amount of unpledged short-term securities, or at least securities currently priced at a gain, to cover potential cash outflows. To facilitate asset sales and improve borrowing opportunities, banks should allocate their loans and securities as collateral in the most efficient manner. This typically involves collateralizing borrowing from the Federal Reserve and FHLBs with qualifying loans while leaving securities for pledging against public deposits and future borrowings.

Banks must also regularly update their contingency funding plans in line with prevailing economic conditions. Effective plans will incorporate regular stress testing in which deposits are presumed to leave the bank in varying amounts with different levels of loan defaults and loan demand. This will ensure that the bank will be positioned to readily meet cash flow needs under adverse circumstances. Management and the board of directors should ensure that all policies have been updated to recognize the bank's current risk profile and targeted strategies. For example, do the policies allow for the use of appropriate amounts of rate-board deposits, FHLB advances, and so on?

Conduct Effective Loan Migration Analysis & Have a Meaningful ALLL Methodology

Banks should have a systematic procedure to regularly document shifts in the amounts of classified assets over time and track the expected cash flows associated with each individual loan or security. They should ensure that all loans are appropriately documented, that the information provided is comprehensive and clean and eliminates duplication and that appraisals are up-to-date. This will provide useful information as to when the banks can ultimately collect on loans that enter default.

Following the onset of the financial crisis, regulators forced banks to formalize and document their procedures for establishing the appropriate size of the *allowance for loan losses* (ALLL).[2] Guidance issued in 2006 requires banks to ensure that the ALLL is sufficient to cover estimated losses on individually evaluated loans impaired under ASC 310-10-5 (formerly FAS 114) and estimated credit losses on all other loans under ASC 450-20 (formerly FAS 5). Operationally, banks estimate losses in the latter case by evaluating groups of loans with similar risk characteristics. Most banks use a two-stage process. In the first stage, they estimate losses applying historical loan charge-off rates to the homogeneous pools of loans and then aggregating across loan pools. In the second stage, they attempt to estimate losses beyond historical experience attributable to 'environmental factors.'[3] Factors mentioned in the Interagency Policy Guidance (2006) include:

- Changes in lending policies and procedures
- Changes in economic and business conditions (global, national and local)
- Changes in the nature and volume of the loan portfolio and in loan terms
- Changes in management and staff experience, ability and depth
- Changes in the volume and severity of past-due loans, nonaccrual loans and classified and graded loans
- Changes in the value of the underlying collateral in collateral-dependent loans

The implication is that management should dedicate resources to the careful analysis of the ALLL and make periodic adjustments.

Pre-purchase Analysis of High Quality Investment Securities

Under Section 939A of the Dodd-Frank Act, banks are required to document that the investment securities they hold and acquire are the equivalent of investment grade securities and are safe and sound investments. They can no longer rely exclusively on ratings. Banks must have policies in place that authorize who can buy and sell securities, which instruments are allowable investments and what limits, if any, exist on specific portfolio allocations to avoid undue concentrations. These are essentially safety and soundness requirements. Banks also need to have a formalized approach to systematically conduct due diligence prior to making investment purchases. An effective approach will fulfill the following functions:

- Demonstrate an understanding of a security's general characteristics.
- Ensure that investments both exhibit low risk of default by the obligor and promise full and timely repayment of principal and interest over the life of the instrument.
- Ensure that the security fits within the bank's acceptable interest rate risk, liquidity risk and credit risk parameters.
- Confirm the obligor's capacity to meet debt service requirements by evaluating its operating and financial performance either through third party analysis or internal analysis.
- Confirm that the cash flows supporting an asset-backed security will be sufficient to meet debt service requirements, such that the bank must evaluate the underlying collateral.
- Confirm that the security's spread to a benchmark (usually U.S. Treasury securities) is consistent with spreads on bonds of similar credit quality.

This analysis is particularly valuable for municipal bonds and for structured securities with different tranches reflecting the priority of the investor's claim on cash flows in the securitization structure. To ensure ongoing equivalence to investment grade, a bank should perform periodic stress tests on parameters that might possibly alter value significantly. Given the costs of pre-purchase analysis and ongoing monitoring, once management identifies acceptable securities that meet both risk and return objectives, it should consider buying larger blocks as long as the bank remains within concentration guidelines. By investing a larger amount, a bank will need to buy and sell securities less frequently.

Assess Customer Demographics and Bank Use of Technology

In a survey of C-Level officers at small banking organizations by FIS, over 60% indicated that the primary value proposition of their institution was its focus on being a relationship leader.[4] Not surprisingly, the value of the relationship is tied to the level of perceived customer service. In order to deliver a high level of customer service, banks must understand what their customers want and then deliver it. Banks must believe and act as if they have the customers' 'best interests in mind.'

Bank managers must understand the institution's different customer segments, the range of products and services demanded by and offered to each segment and the associated customer behaviors in obtaining what is delivered. This requires that they understand who the bank's customers are and how they want services delivered. The bank must then offer the appropriate delivery channels at a reasonable price. While it is difficult to obtain precise estimates, the bank should attempt to estimate which customers are profitable and be able to explain why. Operationally, managers can then develop strategies that appeal to the different customer segments based on each group's value proposition. Such a comprehensive effort will allow the bank to remain relevant to its current customer base and attract new customers. It will grow and improve profitability.

Which customers should the bank target? To answer this question, management must address the following:

- Who are the bank's current customers according to age, income, wealth, current residence, deposit services used, loans outstanding, etc.?
- What product/service delivery channels do the customers in different segments use most actively?
- What new products and services are demanded by each customer segment?
- How profitable are customers in each segment?
- What target market(s) will the bank focus on going forward? Why are the markets identified the appropriate target markets?
- What strategies will the bank pursue to meet the demands for new products or services, expand delivery channels and increase customer profitability?
- What sales and marketing strategies are most relevant?

As expected, this assessment will eventually lead to a detailed analysis of how the bank currently uses technology and what technological improvements are necessary to maintain and improve the level of customer service? In actuality, such a technology review should be an ongoing strategic initiative.

In today's environment, many community banks are examining how they deliver their products and services. This often reduces to an assessment of the current status of bank branches and alternative branching strategies. Any substantive change in strategy, in turn, leads to alternative staffing utilization. Many community banks are experiencing (1) a decline in the number of people visiting physical branches, (2) an increase in account openings online, (3) an increase in the volume and number of online banking transactions and (4) an increase in the volume of mobile banking transactions (when available). This leads to a systematic reassessment of the effectiveness of all delivery channels and what future investments should be made.

Managers and directors must take a careful look at whether expansion of the number of brick-and-mortar branches is justified. Do not be enamored of the real estate if customers won't use the branch. Instead, management should assess whether the existing branch design and locations best meet customer demands and needs. Analyze the demographics of the current and expected customer base according to age and income and the mix of businesses, governments and nonprofits as customers. Conduct a branch profitability analysis and you may be surprised at the low volumes especially in markets where the bank has little market share and low public awareness. How can the bank consolidate brick-and-mortar and in-store branches and migrate existing customers who want the physical branch experience to other branches?

Is your bank's website up-to-date and does it meet customer expectations? Many potential bank customers get their first impression of a bank by viewing its website. Not only must it be visually attractive, it should be functional—offering all important information, products and services with a few clicks, and fast. Otherwise, the customer will look elsewhere. Does your bank allow customers to open new accounts and request loans online? If not, why not as this is in high demand by many customer segments? Does your bank offer mobile banking? The cost of processing mobile transactions is far below that of an ATM or live teller. Most surveys show that younger audiences demand effective mobile banking opportunities and have little interest in visiting anyone at a physical branch. While this may vary as they age, a bank that loses the young will not have first crack at being their primary banking relationship when they are older. Banks that do not offer mobile banking will eventually lose because mobile devices are becoming the most effective branch of the future. Finally, can business and individual customers deposit checks remotely? Or make and accept payments remotely? Does the bank offer easy to use personal financial management tools? These are increasingly popular and help tie customers to the institution. Take a look at what GoBank offers for its mobile bank account and how it prices the services (www.gobank.com) to see where the market is going. If not, why not?

Regularly Critique Interest Rate Risk Analytics and Reassess Strategic Opportunities

For banks under $1 billion, net interest margins are at a long-term low. Given the low level of interest rates in 2013, most market participants expect both short-term and long-term rates to rise over time. As such, many community banks have positioned their institutions to be asset sensitive. As rates rise, most community banks will observe the following:

- A gradual increase in NIM
- Higher yields on new loans and investments
- A rising cost of funds
- Declining market values of fixed-rate bonds and loans
- Loss of some 'core' deposits that were not truly core

To best prepare for rising rates, bank managers should actively conduct relationship reviews of all customers and reassess opportunities within the loan and securities portfolios and with wholesale funding.

Review Deposit Customer Relationships

A bank's deposit customers exhibit different degrees of sensitivity to changing interest rates depending on why they choose to bank with the organization. Management should identify the customers and balances that exhibit a high probability of staying with the bank as rates change. Conduct a detailed deposit analysis by identifying specific customers with a high degree of loyalty. These *core customers* are those with multiple accounts at the bank, who have been long-term customers, who live and/or work within the bank's trade area, who have a reasonable number of active transactions monthly and whose balances are fully-insured.

The detailed analysis involves evaluating how deposits will reprice as interest rates rise. Most ALM models incorporate beta coefficients and decay rates associated with different deposits in this analysis. *Beta* measures how much a bank will change a deposit rate relative to a change in some benchmark rate or index. For example, a bank that will change the rate on MMDAs by 0.50% when the federal funds rate rises by 1% is said to have a MMDA beta coefficient of 0.5. There will be a different beta for each different type of deposit account. Importantly, betas for core customers are lower than betas for noncore customers such that core customers are much more attractive than noncore customers and a bank can price the different customers accordingly.

Decay rates relate to the speed by which non-maturity deposits flow out of a bank. For example, a decay rate of 5% indicates that over a one-year period a bank would lose $5 per $100 in balances through withdrawals and account closings. Decay rates will vary depending on the interest rate environment. In 2013, banks were flush with liquidity and many presumably core deposits were actually held at banks because rates paid on alternatives were so low, not because of any strong relationship. Decay rates will likely be higher when rates increase in future years, but they will be lower for core customers.

Take Advantage of Strategic Opportunities

To fully understand interest rate risk, management must understand betas and decay rates and price deposits accordingly. A bank might reasonably pay the lowest rates to noncore customers and implement a strategy to sell these customers more products and services. It should also avoid marketing short-term CDs. As rates rise, some wholesale funds may become attractive. Management should initially ensure that the bank has the appropriate policies that allow the acquisition of wholesale funds going forward. It should evaluate potential benefits from creating a ladder of wholesale funding at different maturities (using FHLB advances or CDs) especially if the bank is faced with reasonable loan demand. In terms of securities, management should avoid bonds and MBSs with long durations and consider selling current long-term holdings carrying fixed rates.

Conduct Compliance Reviews

Banks are subject to multiple compliance examinations by regulators. The exams are intended to ensure that banks are meeting legal and regulatory requirements in lending, deposit gathering, advertising and operations which are quite extensive. The various banking areas include: Equal Credit Opportunity (Fair Lending), Truth in Lending, Home Mortgage Disclosure (HMDA), Mortgage Licensing (SAFE), Community Reinvestment (CRA), Bank Secrecy (BSA), Anti-Money Laundering (AML), and many others.

Well-run banks recognize that they must not only be knowledgeable about bank regulations and relevant laws, but they will better serve their customers and communities if they comply and exceed the minimum standards. Such performance signals that they truly value their customers and expect to grow the bank's business proactively. To accomplish this, banks must have effective compliance programs. While all individuals should be aware of the legal and regulatory requirements via regular training programs, specific individuals within each organization should be responsible for conducting internal compliance reviews or authorizing third-party reviews and implementing recommendations from the reviews as appropriate. Internal auditors should be truly independent of management and have a direct line to the board of directors.

The establishment of the Consumer Financial Protection Board (CFPB) demonstrates the increasing role that consumer compliance regulations will play in bank activities going forward. Management and the board must embrace this whether or not they agree with the new rules. This doesn't mean that they don't question and challenge the rules as appropriate. Instead, it means that they must dedicate the resources necessary to understand the rules and remain in compliance.

The U.S. Retail Payments System

With rapidly changing technology, how individuals pay for products and services is far different today than even a few years ago. How individuals and businesses receive payments has similarly changed. One significant change is that many U.S. government payments are now available only electronically. For example, effective March 1, 2013, all Social Security, Supplemental Security Income (disability), veterans' payments and retirement payments will be delivered electronically rather than be offered as checks.[5] Recipients can choose either direct deposit at their financial institution or payment via a prepaid card (Direct Express Card).

The most significant trend, however, is that nonbanks have become far more active. While banks still dominate in the areas of check processing, debit and credit card processing (networks), ATMs and clearinghouses, the presence and impact of nonbanks is growing rapidly. Consider the following nonbank competitors:

- *Square, Inc.* Square allows users (virtually any individual or business) to accept credit card payments via a mobile phone. The vendor attaches a small card reader (plastic device) via the phone's audio jack and simply swipes the card. The buyer signs digitally – or has set up an electronic account – which provides him or her with an electronic receipt. The cost to the vendor is 'only 2%-3%.'[6] Square offers the card reader free of charge to all users.

- *PayPal.* PayPal's business model involves many different aspects of e-commerce and serves primarily as an alternative to the use of cash, checks and money orders. The firm is a subsidiary of eBay where many buyers and sellers effect their transactions via PayPal. PayPal allows customers to transfer and receive funds electronically in over 30 currencies around the world. Individuals as well as businesses are discovering that they don't need to do business with a bank or via checks, debit and credit cards, if they have a PayPal account.

- *Dwolla.* Dwolla (created from dollar and web) is another e-commerce firm that offers a network that handles online and mobile payments. Dwolla's appeal is that it charges less to process payments, such as $0.25 per transaction, if the dollar value exceeds $10. Contrast this with the typical credit card charge of 3% to 4% of the payment amount.

- *Prepaid Cards.* Prepaid cards are essentially stored-value cards onto which someone (federal government, bank, parent, etc.) loads purchasing power. Once loaded, anyone can use the cards much like a credit or debit card as a vendor will accept payment up to the amount of funds loaded on the card. Government-issued prepaid cards have been available since the early 2000's as a means to distribute government benefits and tax refunds. Today, many employers use them as an alternative to direct deposit for customers who either don't have a bank account or don't want one. More recently companies such as GreenDot and NetSpend have aggressively marketed prepaid cards as an alternative to cash and retail stores sell prepaid gift cards to those who want to give cash. Prepaid cards are heavily used by the unbanked population in the U.S., which the FDIC identified in a 2009 survey as totaling 17 million adults, or 8% of U.S. households. Many large financial institutions have recognized the increasing attractiveness and potential profitability of prepaid cards and aggressively entered the marketplace. For example, American Express and Walmart jointly offer the prepaid Bluebird card. Consider these two firms as your competitors.

- *P2P Payment Systems.* P2P refers to person-to-person payments. The trend is for an increasing volume of transactions to involve digital payments rather than payments via cash or check.[7] The use of PayPal is an example involving a nonbank. At its formation, GoBank allowed new users to transfer $1 to a friend via its P2P system which encouraged future usage. Alternatively, an individual can work with a bank. For example, Popmoney is a bank-related firm that makes P2P payments between bank customers and noncustomers. It has over 1,300 participating banks. Several of the largest banks (Bank of America, JPMorgan Chase and Wells Fargo), in turn, formed clearXchange which allows their customers to make payments among each other via their individual bank websites.

The growth in these nonbank payment systems providers raises two important questions. First, these entities are not regulated as are commercial banks and other traditional payment providers.

What happens if and when a payments crisis emerges with one of the firms? Second, what is the long-term impact on the federal government's ability to control the effectiveness and strong reputation of the U.S. payments system if it does not have any real influence on these nonbank providers? Finally, what will the impact be on community banks if customers increasingly rely on nonbanks to handle financial transactions?

How many of your institution's customers are using these payment systems or payment alternatives and to what extent are they taking business away from you?

Financial Targets and Strategies that Will Increase Shareholder Value

The following offers specific targets for financial performance and general strategies to grow shareholder value. They center around the concept of building a fortress balance sheet and increasing cash earnings over time. They require specific strategies to grow core deposits, increase loans and other earning assets, grow noninterest income and control expenses and use technology wisely.

Key Financial Targets

As demonstrated in Chapter 5, the board of directors and management must know what to measure if they want to increase shareholder value. Pursuing the following financial targets will help achieve the goal. They should be addressed annually as part of the board and management's efforts to set strategy:

- 10% compounded annual return on tangible book value of stockholders equity over the next three years (no dilution of TBVS); 15% if publicly traded
- 8.5% tangible equity capital ratio at the holding company at the end of five years
- Increase the portion of holding company capital that is comprised of common stock; achieve a 60% target within five years
- Keep the ratio of nonperforming assets to total assets below 3%
- Have core deposit funding of at least 70% of assets
- Hold at least 2% of assets as short-term, unpledged securities
- Increase wholesale funding as a percentage of assets once interest rates are expected to rise substantially
- Sell unprofitable branches
- Grow cash earnings per share by 6% compounded annually over the next three years
- Pay cash dividends as appropriate
- Target a composite CAMELS rating of 2

Summary

Bank regulators expect members of the board of directors and senior management to have a firm grasp of bank strategies and a strong awareness of bank operations and risks. Board members are expected to be much more engaged today as evidenced by actions that define the institution's risk appetite. The board should ensure that the risk appetite and general strategies are communicated effectively within the organization and to regulators. Board members should be willing and able to challenge management as appropriate. This requires a better understanding of the complexity of bank operations and all risks. Given this environment, the board of directors must ensure that the bank's senior managers have the requisite expertise and ability to manage the bank effectively.

This chapter discusses core strategies to enhance shareholder value at community banks in the current environment. It offers specific financial performance targets that are consistent with growing cash earnings and tangible equity. These targets will change over time as the bank's competitive position changes and opportunities arise. Boards and managers that invest in the people and systems to effect strategies that will help achieve such performance targets will see their institutions grow and prosper.

CHAPTER 12
Building Value in Difficult Times: One Bank's Story

Banks cannot be successful long-term if they are always playing defense.
Actions such as reducing dividends to retain capital, tightening credit standards to slow growth and protect earnings, and selling securities at a gain to increase capital are relevant and valuable strategies during difficult times. However, they are designed to maintain the institution's competitive power in the near-term rather than build long-term value. Banks that successfully build value are proactive in assessing risks and profit opportunities. Being on offense requires that they conduct effective strategic plans within their ERM implementation. They determine what changes in business strategy and organizational structure are necessary and build a plan to implement the changes.

The arrival of the financial crisis in 2007, its severity and the subsequent competitive and regulatory pressures on community banks led many analysts to argue that the banking industry will consolidate. Of course, the number of banks will shrink—as it has for the past 30 years. Few new banks are being chartered while every year some banks disappear with mergers and acquisitions and failures. However, as Gunther and Klemme (2012) document, smaller banks had fewer problem loans, on average, when compared with larger banks from 2008 to 2012 except for banks in Arizona, Florida, Georgia, Illinois, Michigan and Nevada. This relationship held even for residential real estate loans. Still, the environment is becoming more challenging with the slow growth of the U.S. and global economies and increased regulatory hurdles.

This chapter tells the story of First Community Bank (FCB) based in Lexington, SC which was introduced in Chapters 4 and 5. The discussion documents the bank's performance during the crisis years and emphasizes FCB's key business strategies to enhance shareholder value in the future. Like many community banks, FCB saw its profitability and risk profile worsen during the crisis. However, the bank's board of directors and management team have been actively working through the problems they experienced and implementing different strategies to build value.

CHAPTER 12

A Brief History of First Community Bank

The city of Lexington, SC is a suburb of Columbia, SC, the state's capital. According to the 2010 Census, its population was around 263,000 with 13% aged 65 or over and 24% under age 18. The community is relatively stable with more than 85% of the population living in the same house for one or more years and an average homeownership rate of 75% from 2007 to 2011. The median income of residents was just under $53,000 during this same period with almost 12% of the population below the poverty level. Along with an active retail environment, the surrounding county is home to manufacturing plants for Michelin, FLP Foods, Flextronics and Akebono, among other firms, and is a hub for the shipping giant, United Parcel Service (UPS). Finally, agribusinesses support approximately 200,000 jobs in South Carolina with Lexington County a preferred location.

FCB opened for business in 1995 with offices in the heart of Lexington and in Forest Acres, a market near the business center of Columbia. The de novo charter followed the sale of Lexington State Bank, a community bank favorite for many years, to BB&T, which was part of a trend where regional banks were acquiring community banks across the Southeast. FCB's founding Chairman, Jim Leventis and President Michael Crapps, viewed the Lexington market as particularly attractive given the perceived need for a bank that focuses on small to medium-size businesses, individuals and emphasizes local community relationships. They formed a group of local businesses and community leaders with strong ties to Lexington and Forest Acres to serve as bank directors. The intent was to provide excellent service to local customers by local bankers. Leventis retired in 2009 after which he was named Chairman Emeritus. At formation, the bank had 17 founding Directors with the majority still members of the board of directors. At its opening, FCB's senior management team consisted of Mike Crapps (President), Robin Brown, (Director of H.R. and Marketing), Ted Nissen (Chief Operations Officer), David Proctor (Chief Credit Officer) and Joe Sawyer (CFO) all of whom are still with the bank. With its growth, FCB has added board members and both senior and junior level employees. These individuals know their community well and the community knows them. From 2008 to 2011 during the heart of the financial crisis, FCB was named one of South Carolina's Best Places to work by the South Carolina Chamber of Commerce. The composition of the board and management team along with the emphasis on employee satisfaction and targeted service to local customers is the essence of community banking.

The bank is part of First Community Corporation which has stock traded on NASDAQ under the symbol FCCO.[1] At year-end 2012, the bank had 11 branches with $603 million in total assets, $332 million in loans and $54 million in common equity. Net income available for common shareholders reached $3.3 million for the year with diluted EPS equal to $0.79. Exhibit 12.1 lists key profitability and risk ratios from 2010 to 2012. As with most banks, changes in the ratios reflect different economic and strategic impacts over the period. When FCB reported its results for the fourth quarter of 2012 and the entire year, it announced a one cent increase in the cash dividend to $0.05 per share reflecting the bank's greater profitability and strong capital position. The bank's stock closed at $8.39 at year-end. During the first 6 months of 2013, FCB earned $2.24 million in net income and raised its leverge capital ratio to 10.6%, while nonperforming assets (NPAs) fell to 1.39% of assets, which was well below peers.

Exhibit 12.1 Key Profitability and Risk Ratios: First Community Bank, 2010–2012

Ratio	2012	2011	2010
ROE	7.40%	7.98%	3.73%
Return on Tangible Equity	7.55%	8.16%	3.87%
ROA	0.55%	0.44%	0.20%
NIM	3.22%	3.33%	3.26%
Noninterest Inc./Oper. Revenue	31.2%	25.6%	17.5%
Efficiency Ratio	74.8%	75.6%	73.1%
EPS (diluted)	$0.79	$0.81	$0.36
Loans / Deposits	70.3%	70.6%	73.5%
NPAs/Total Assets	1.45%	2.16%	2.29%
Net Charge-off/Loans	0.17%	0.50%	0.54%
ALLL/NPAs	52.8%	35..85	37.4%
Tangible Equity/Tangible assets	8.88%	6.04%	5.00%
Leverage Capital Ratio	10.6%	9.40%	8.79%
Tier 1 RBC Ratio	17.3%	15.3%	13.7%
Total RBC Ratio	18.6%	17.3%	15.0%
Book Value Per Share	$10.37	$11.11	$9.41
Tangible Book Value Per share	$10.23	$10.83	$9.14

During its relatively brief 18-year history, FCB acquired two bank holding companies (in 2004 and 2006) in nearby communities, two financial planning/investment advisory companies (2008) and the assets of a residential mortgage company (2011).[2] Since its founding, it also opened seven de novo branches to where it now operates 11 branches in four counties in the middle part of South Carolina. FCB saw its total assets peak around $670 million in 2007 after which the bank's assets fell modestly until 2012. During the peak of the financial crisis, the bank reported net losses of $6.9 million and $25.9 million in 2008 and 2009, respectively. These losses were due largely to noninterest income of –$10.6 million in 2008 and noninterest expense of $44.3 million in 2009, which represented an increase of almost $30 million over 2008. Both losses sharply lowered stockholders equity. So, what is the bank's story during the crisis?

When FCB completed its acquisition of Newberry Federal Savings Bank (NFSB) in 2004, it created a company with over $425 million in assets. At the time of the transaction, NFSB had almost $240 million in assets with roughly two-thirds in investments. Compared with year-end 2003, FCB's assets increased from $215 million to $455 million and its investments increased from $59 million to $196 million. FCB added another $44 million in assets when it acquired DeKalb Bankshares in 2006.

Financial Results for 2007

While the nation's institutions were suffering the initial throes of the financial crisis, FCB announced record earnings for 2007. When describing FCB's 2007 results, Mike Crapps stated:

> *We are thrilled to be reporting record earnings for the second consecutive quarter led by a 42% increase in EPS...The 42% growth in fourth quarter EPS is the gratifying result of success in the execution of our plan for 2007. This includes the continued growth in our loan portfolio increasing our loan-to-deposit ratio from 66.3% to 76.3%. This accomplishment occurred while our long time commitment to credit quality and loan underwriting continued to pay off. The loan charge off ratio of 0.03% (excluding net overdraft charge-offs) and the nonperforming asset ratio of 0.22% are excellent compared to industry standards and especially impressive given the current economic conditions.*[3]

The bank further raised its quarterly dividend by a penny to $0.08 per share. FCB reported $4 million in net income for the year, $1.21 in diluted EPS and $573 million in average assets during the last three months. So how did the bank lose $7 million in 2008 and $27 million in 2009?

Problems with the Investment Portfolio

When FCB purchased NFSB, many analysts viewed the savings bank as a bond fund that also made 1-4 family residential mortgages. In performing its due diligence, FCB's financial team was well aware that NFSB owned a large portfolio of private-label CMOs and had a large investment in preferred stock issued by the Federal Home Loan Mortgage Corporation (Freddie Mac). It reviewed the entire block of securities selling those that did not meet the bank's investment policy guidelines and management's risk tolerance. In mid-2008, the Freddie Mac preferreds were paying their quarterly dividends (7% annualized) and were rated AA– by S&P and A1 by Moody's. FCB also subsequently decided to implement a leveraged investment strategy by which it borrowed via FHLB advances and brokered CDs and invested the proceeds in private-label mortgage-backed securities because of the attractive spreads. As of December 31, 2009, the bank owned $66 million in private-label MBSs. In addition, the bank purchased part of a pool of trust preferred securities issued by different community banks. In retrospect, these types of securities exhibited above-average default risk and the bank suffered from owning them.

On September 7, 2008, U.S. Treasury Secretary Hank Paulson announced that Treasury was placing Fannie Mae and Freddie Mac (Federal Home Loan Mortgage Corporation) into conservatorship. This action came as a surprise to many investors given the implied Treasury guarantee under which Fannie and Freddie operated as *government-sponsored enterprises* (GSEs). It was also a surprise when Treasury suspended dividend payments on both GSEs' outstanding preferred stock. Thus, the 7% annual yield that FCB was earning on its Freddie Mac preferreds since acquiring NFSB fell to zero. FCB wrote-off its entire $14.3 million holdings at an after-tax cost of $9.5 million. While this was a noncash impairment charge, it did lower the bank's reported capital and reduced the amount of dividend income that would be forthcoming in future years.[4] Who could have imagined that the U.S. government would stop paying dividends on preferred stock issued by Fannie and Freddie? Most market participants long believed that these GSEs carried an implied federal government guarantee in which the Treasury would use its borrowing power to make good on promised interest and dividend payments on these GSEs' outstanding debt and preferred stock. Curiously, during the early part of the decade, street talk had it that some representatives of the national bank regulatory agencies were actually recommending that community banks buy Fannie and Freddie preferred stock because the dividends were secure and the yields were attractive.

From 2008 to 2012, FCB routinely recognized *other-than-temporary-impairments* (OTTI) on its holdings of private-label mortgage-backed securities based largely on third-party evaluations. With the market disruptions, all firms found it difficult to value these instruments. Because most of the securities continued to pay interest and principal as promised, many banks argued that no write-down was necessary until an actual default occurred. However, accountants and regulators, with a "deer-in-headlights" perspective, routinely required write-downs because they could not determine 'true' market values. Thus, FCB's reported earnings were systematically lower even though its cash inflows were not adversely affected.[5]

FCB's financial performance for 2008 was underwhelming. For the year, the bank lost $6.9 million due primarily to the write-down of Freddie Mac preferred stock.[6] However, the bank's operating performance remained relatively strong. Loans grew by more than 7% with net charge-offs at 0.32% (UBPR peers' ratio was 0.52%) and nonperforming assets equaled 0.39% of assets (versus 1.72% for peers). FCB largely avoided the commercial real estate problems that plagued the Southeast. At year-end 2008, the bank reported $13.2 million in acquisition and development loans, or 3.9% of total loans, with one $3.2 million loan recognized as a potential problem loan. FCB did increase its provision for loan losses by $1.6 million during the year in anticipation of future charge-offs. During the year, core deposits grew by over 4%, the bank's operating income remained strong with operating earnings to average assets of 0.51%, NIM fell to a respectable 3.16%, all of the capital ratios exceeded the regulatory minimums and the bank continued to pay quarterly dividends at $0.08 per share. Still, given the difficult economic times and general concerns about banks, the bank's stock price fell to $6.31 at year-end when its reported tangible book value of equity was $8.57.

Capital Strategy – Part I

Remember the hectic days of 2008 when interest rates on some Treasury securities fell to zero and markets for nonfederal government securities dried up. Many market participants had little confidence that banks were reporting true financial results such that asset quality and capital ratios were likely overstated. Federal officials were concerned that the global financial system was on the verge of collapse. After several earlier plans failed, the U.S. Treasury created the Troubled Asset Relief Program (TARP) of which the Capital Purchase Program (CPP) was designed to inject capital into commercial banks. While all banks were eligible to sell preferred stock to Treasury under CPP upon approval by Treasury, banks with CAMELS ratings of 4 and 5 were effectively excluded. Qualifying banks could obtain up to 3% of risk-weighted assets. The appeal was that these issues would immediately add to the institution's Tier 1 capital thereby raising each of the three regulatory capital ratios. For healthy banks, the additional capital would serve as a buffer against future loan losses but also support new loans. For weaker banks, it was totally defensive and viewed as protection. The preferred stock paid a 5% annual dividend for the first five years after which the dividend rate jumped to 9%. Treasury also received warrants to buy each bank's common stock once the bank agreed to sell preferred stock to Treasury.

Given market uncertainty and its write-down of Freddie Mac preferred stock, FCB applied for and received authorization to sell $11.8 million in preferred shares to the U.S. Treasury under the CPP. It completed the transaction in November 2008, such that its year-end capital ratios were strong:

	First Community Bank Capital Ratios	
	December 31, 2008	Regulatory Minimum
Tier 1 Risk-Based Capital Ratio	13.1%	6%
Total Risk-Based Capital Ratio	14.3%	10%
Tier 1 Leverage Ratio	8.2%	5%

FCB obligated itself to pay $568,000 in dividends annually for five years on the preferreds and $1,022,400 afterward unless it redeemed the shares. In addition, FCB gave Treasury 10-year warrants for 195,915 common stock shares.[7]

Why would any bank issue TARP to Treasury? Mike Crapps stated:

> *While our company was well-capitalized prior to this transaction, this additional capital further strengthens our balance sheet and our capital structure…It is an understatement to say that 2008 was a very challenging year for the company as well as the entire industry. All indications are that there will not be a rapid economic recovery and as a result 2009 will present many challenges. With our capital strength, core deposit base, and overall loan portfolio quality, we are well positioned to meet these challenges and to take advantage of the opportunities we see in the market. In fact, it is interesting to note that the company experienced solid loan growth in the fourth quarter…We continue to aggressively seek sound lending opportunities with our many qualified borrowers.*

The stock issuance was defensive in the context that it built a buffer against potential future charge-offs and write-downs. It was offensive in the sense that it allowed the bank to continue growing its loan portfolio and otherwise meet the needs of its customers.

In addition to the required dividend payment, the obvious cost is that FCB added Treasury as a stockholder. In certain circumstances where a TARP bank didn't make its dividend payments, Treasury retained the right to put someone on the bank's board. In addition, Treasury can and did change the rules of the CPP program over time creating uncertainty about the future. Finally, many of the banks that sold stock to Treasury took a reputation hit as the general public believed TARP was a bailout of banks. In retrospect, only extremely troubled banks that have not been able to withstand the impact of the financial crisis appear to have benefited from having Treasury as a stockholder.

Write-Down of Goodwill

When a firm buys another firm for more than book value, it typically records a portion of the difference as an intangible asset labeled "goodwill." The dollar amount reported presumably represents value attributable to intangible elements of the acquired firm, such as brand value, going concern value, quality of management, and the like. The acquiring firm typically amortizes (takes annual noncash charges) such goodwill over time. However, under current accounting rules, the acquiring firm must annually evaluate the value of unamortized intangibles to determine whether the goodwill became impaired during the year. As the financial crisis worsened in 2009, FCB's management chose to take a $27.8 million goodwill impairment charge against all of its unamortized intangibles associated with its purchases of DutchFork Bancshares and DeKalb Bankshares. This appears as an increase in noninterest expense. Fortunately, the write-down of goodwill is a noncash charge that does not affect the bank's regulatory capital or current and future operating earnings. It is an accounting recognition that the bank paid more than the prevailing market value when it acquired the two firms. FCB's $26 million loss in 2009 largely reflects this charge, which can be compared to FCB's reported $2.5 million in operating earnings.[8]

In response to the extraordinary uncertainty facing banks and the U.S. economy in 2009, FCB's board of directors cut the quarterly dividend in half to $0.04 per share. While the bank's regulatory capital ratios remained strong, the dividend cut allowed the bank to retain as much common equity as possible.

Formal Regulatory Enforcement Action

In April 2010, FCB entered into a formal agreement with the OCC.[9] In the agreement, the OCC stated that it had found "unsafe and unsound banking practices relating to the management of the Bank's investment portfolio." Under the agreement, the OCC ordered the bank's board to do the following. Each of these requirements included a specific deadline for meeting the requirements as noted in brackets:

1. Adopt, implement and ensure Bank adherence to a written strategic plan incorporating objectives for its overall risk profile, earnings, growth, balance sheet mix, off-balance sheet activities, liability structure, capital adequacy, reduction in nonperforming assets and product line /market segments that the Bank intends to develop. [60 days]
2. Develop, implement and ensure adherence to a capital plan including a plan for cash dividends. [90 days]
3. Review and revise the Bank's investment policy, implement the policy and ensure adherence to policy. The policy was to include documentation on diversification

guidelines, concentration limits, approval procedures and incorporate due diligence commensurate with the risk associated with complexity of the instruments. [60 days]
4. Review all of the Bank's classified securities that are backed by nonagency mortgage collateral including an assessment of risk ratings, collateral, cash flow waterfall and valuations. [90 days]
5. Review, revise and adhere to a written Liquidity Policy that tracks expected cash inflows and outflows and sets limits on wholesale funding sources, FHLB advances and nonagency mortgage securities. It will also include a revised contingency funding plan. [60 days]
6. Establish systems to monitor compliance with lending policies and loan portfolio management, develop and adhere to the maintenance of an adequate ALLL and incorporate current independent real estate appraisal guidelines. [90 days]
7. Establish a compliance committee to ensure adherence to the terms of the Consent Order. [10 days][10]

It seems clear that the OCC did not like the bank's investment strategy. Prior to receiving the agreement, the bank owned Freddie Mac preferred stock which it wrote-down to zero. It also owned a healthy amount of private-label mortgage-backed securities that had been downgraded below investment grade by one or more of the rating agencies. These securities were difficult to value in the marketplace, especially when many mortgage market participants wanted nothing to do with anything other than agency mortgage product.[11] Finally, the bank also purchased portions of a pool of trust preferred securities issued by banks. Some of the banks in the pool of issuers were troubled and stopped paying dividends on their outstanding trust preferreds such that the value of FCB's investment fell over time. These securities were perceived as risky.

Due to problems that borrowers with mortgages underlying the private-label MBSs were having along with banks that stopped paying on their outstanding trust preferreds, FCB was taking OTTI write-downs on a quarterly basis over time. Private-label MBSs include those with terms that do not meet the criteria set by Fannie Mae, Freddie Mac and the Government National Mortgage Association (GNMA). These three agencies are GSEs that guarantee securities backed by mortgages that do meet the criteria. Such conforming mortgages have lower default risk and can be easily securitized such that agency MBSs can be readily bought and sold. Importantly, regulations limit the principal amount of a mortgage that the GSEs can guarantee. Loans in excess of this amount are labeled *jumbo mortgages*. Jumbo mortgages are not necessarily high risk, but unless the issuer purchases credit insurance, securities based on jumbo loans are backed only by the underlying borrower and value of the collateral. Private-label MBSs include such jumbo loans as well as mortgages tied to no doc or low doc loans and thus are riskier than agency MBSs.

A second interesting implication of the agreement is the impact of the tight time frames associated with the terms. Think of a bank's composite CAMELS rating. Banks must meet specific criteria to be rated high for their capital, asset quality, management, earnings, liquidity and sensitivity to market risk. Under the agreement, FCB was required to dedicate considerable resources to identify and implement policies and strategies to improve C, A and L—all within 60 to 90 days. When the order was made effective, FCB's asset quality ratios, capital and earnings were still better than peers, especially when you omit the noncash charges in 2008 and 2009. Imagine the difficulty in meeting terms of a consent order if the bank truly had serious asset quality and earnings problems.

Finally, when regulators place a bank under an enforcement action, it is costly to operate the bank. In a subsequent press release, FCB estimated the annualized cost of responding to the regulatory agreements at $450,000. Part of this incremental cost is increased FDIC deposit insurance. Other parts relate to hiring consultants to help meet the terms of the agreement.

When it signed the formal agreement, FCB reported the capital ratios listed below compared with the targets from the OCC's order. As such, it already met the capital thresholds:

	FCB Ratio – March 2010	Regulatory Target
Tier 1 Risk-Based Capital	11.55%	10%
Total Risk-Based Capital	12.60%	12%
Tier 1 Leverage	8.20%	8%
Tangible equity/Tangible assets	4.88%	

At the same time, nonperforming assets equaled 1.41% (UBPR peers was 2.99%), net loan charge-offs were 0.16% and the bank reported a first quarter profit of $423,000. Under the terms of the order, the OCC appears to also be concerned that the ALLL might be too low and that the securities might not have any real long-term value. In addition, the regulators did not look kindly on the leverage strategy whereby FCB used purchased liabilities to buy risky securities. Hence, part of the order required a review and policy assessment of liquidity funding and the bank's contingency funding plan.

Response to the Order

Given its business plan, which emphasized core deposit growth and modest additions to its loan portfolio, FCB was able to use cash inflows from maturing assets to completely eliminate funding from brokered deposits by the third quarter of 2010. As total assets fell slightly, FCB let maturing jumbo CDs and FHLB advances roll-off. FCB reported positive earnings in each quarter following the agreement such that it systematically increased its regulatory capital ratios over time. Contributing to the earnings was the systematic sale of securities at a gain. In addition, FCB dedicated resources to resolving problem loans. Problem loans increased to 2.2% of total assets, or $13.2 million, at year-end 2010 while the comparable ratio for peers was 4.5%. Net loan charge-offs also increased to 0.54% which was well below the comparable peer figure.

Investments and Loans

Exhibit 12.2 documents significant changes in FCB's loans and investments that are consistent with the OCC's required actions under the agreement. In an effort to restructure its investment portfolio, FCB moved all of its private-label MBSs and the trust preferred securities from held-to-maturity to available-for-sale. While this required the bank to report an unrealized loss, it improved the bank's capital ratios and allowed the bank to sell the securities outright. FCB held almost $66 million in nonagency MBSs at the end of 2009 including $43 million that were not investment grade. By June 2011, it had reduced its nonagency MBS portfolio to just $18.4 million of which $14.5 million were not investment grade. Both amounts were negligible by 2012. Interestingly, FCB sold 10 nonagency MBSs during the first six months of 2011 of which three carried investment grade ratings and seven were rated as junk realizing a combined gain of $110,000. The implication is that their value marks were reasonable. Not only did these actions help the bank meet the terms of the agreement regarding the investment portfolio but they had the added benefit of increasing risk-based capital ratios as the proceeds were used to purchase securities that carried lower (20%) risk weights. In general, FCB maintained the same basic size of investment portfolio, but changed the mix away from nonagency MBSs and other noninvestment grade instruments. The result is a bond portfolio with much lower default risk.

Data at the top of Exhibit 12.2 further suggest that FCB's nonperforming assets declined after 2010. While the bank continued to grow loans, those classified as special mention and substandard were relatively constant over time. The allowance for loan and lease losses remained around 1.4% of loans over the entire period. Thus, even during the difficult economic climate, the bank appears to have maintained its historical credit quality in the loan portfolio.

Exhibit 12.2 Selected Assets at FCB, 2009 – 2012 (millions)

Assets	2012	2011	2010	2009
Loans by Risk Rating				
Special Mention	$ 8.7	$ 8.5	$ 8.6	$ 5.0
Substandard	17.6	17.8	21.9	17.8
Doubtful	—	—	—	—
Pass	315.5	301.7	299.4	321.4
Total	$341.8	$328.0	$330.0	$344.2
Nonperforming Assets	$ 8.8	$ 12.8	$ 13.2	$ 8.3
ALLL to Loans	1.39%	1.45%	1.49%	1.41%
Investment Securities				
Nonagency MBSs		18.4*	51.4	65.8
Below Investment Grade				
Nonagency MBSs	1.7*	14.5*	37.1	42.9
Other Noninvestment Grade		1.9*	30.0	51.7
Total Noninvestment Grade		16.4*	67.1	94.6
Investment Grade		194.3*	129.1	101.2
Total	$206.0	$210.7*	$196.2	$195.8

*As of June 30

Liquidity and Funding

FCB responded quickly to terms of the agreement related to funding. As demonstrated in Exhibit 12.3, the bank increased core deposits and eliminated all brokered CD funding shortly after receiving the formal agreement in 2010. With ample liquidity in the marketplace, it continued to grow core deposits while simultaneously letting CDs and FHLB advances mature.[10] By the end of 2012, all CDs outstanding totaled $155 million down from $202 million in 2009, while advances were just one-half the $73 million outstanding in 2009. The bank's funding base became much more stable. It was also lower cost and less sensitive to changing interest rates.

Exhibit 12.3 Selected Liabilities & Capital at FCB, 2009 – 2012 (millions)

	2012	2011	2010	2009
Liabilities				
Total Pure Deposits	$319.5	$286.8	$259.8	$233.2
CDs < $100,000	92.0	107.4	122.3	122.4
CDs > $100,000	63.4	70.4	73.2	79.2
Brokered Deposits	0.0	0.0	0.0	14.9
Total Deposits	$474.9	$464.6	$455.3	$449.7
Customer Cash Mgmt	$ 15.9	$ 13.6	$ 12.7	$ 20.7
FHLB Advances	36.3	43.9	68.1	73.3
Capital				
Tier 1 Risk-Based Ratio	16.94%	15.12%	12.90%	12.41%
Total Risk-Based Ratio	18.19%	16.38%	14.15%	13.56%
Leverage Ratio	10.34%	9.27%	8.45%	8.41%
Tangible Common/Tangible Assets	8.88%	6.07%	5.00%	4.80%

During its entire history, FCB lost money in only two quarters—the ones where it wrote-down its Freddie Mac preferred stock and its unamortized goodwill from the two bank purchases. In every other quarter, even after being placed under the OCC's agreement, the bank reported positive profits. Annual profits were $1.2 million in 2010 which grew to $2.7 million in 2011 and $3.3 million in 2012. Combined with the bank's controlled asset growth and shift into less risky investment securities (carrying lower risk-based capital weights), the bank's regulatory capital ratios increased. Data at the bottom of Exhibit 12.3 show the systematic increase in all three regulatory capital ratios over time and the substantial excess above the OCC's targets in the formal agreement. The ratio of tangible common equity to tangible assets at 8.88% in 2012 far exceeds targets that most analysts and the regulators set as minimums. FCB has a strong capital base going forward.

Capital Strategy – Part II

Since the onset of the financial crisis, bank regulators have emphasized the role that capital plays in stabilizing financial institutions and the financial system. During the crisis, the perception was that no bank could have too much capital. It has also become clear that common equity is the preferred form of capital by regulators. Common stock is the best form because banks do not have to pay stock dividends to remain solvent and common stock protects the deposit insurance fund in the event of a bank failure.

In managing its capital, FCB pursued several dramatic actions. First, in 2008 it issued preferred stock to Treasury under the CPP program. Second, it controlled the bank's asset growth and shifted its portfolio into lower-risk assets thereby lowering required regulatory capital based on risk-weighted assets. Throughout the crisis, FCB's board members and management endeavored to pay cash dividends to stockholders. With the reported losses, the bank had negative cumulative retained earnings which under OCC rules prohibited the bank from paying dividends. Thus, just before the end of 2011, its third action was to issue $2.5 million in subordinated notes to officers and directors of FCB and other accredited investors using the proceeds to pay dividends on its common and preferred stock. FCB also benefited when the Federal Reserve Bank of Richmond terminated an MOU in 2011 that required FCB to get regulatory approval prior to paying dividends. This served to signal that the bank would likely make dividend payments going forward. By 2011, it seemed clear to FCB's management that the bank's financial condition had stabilized, it had met the terms of the formal agreement and it needed to get back to proactive banking.

Actions taken in 2012 created long-desired opportunities for future growth:

- In July, the firm sold $15 million in common stock to a mix of retail and institutional investors. The offering was over subscribed.
by three times the number of shares offered.
- In July, the firm repurchased one-third of the preferred stock owned by the U.S. Treasury.
- In August, it purchased another (approximate) one-third of its preferred stock at a Treasury auction.
- In September, it purchased the remaining outstanding preferred stock from various investors.
- In October, it purchased the warrants to buy FCB's stock from Treasury. Thus, it successfully exited the TARP CPP and eliminated the federal government as a stockholder.
- In November, it repaid the $2.5 million outstanding subordinated debentures it sold in 2011.

At this point, the bank had successfully restructured its capital to be composed almost entirely of common equity.

Termination of Formal Agreement and Charter Switch

The capital transactions in 2012 followed the OCC's termination of the formal agreement in the second quarter of the year. Shortly after the agreement was removed, FCB switched from its original national charter to a state of South Carolina charter. The switch changed the bank's primary federal regulator from the OCC to the FDIC with the South Carolina state banking department as the state regulator. The timing isn't coincidental. For one, only banks that are CAMELS rated 1 or 2 can switch charters.[11] A bank that is under an enforcement action (MOU, Formal Agreement, Consent Order) is probably rated at best a composite 3 such that it cannot change charters. In FCB's case, the termination of the formal agreement created the first opportunity to shift charters post-financial crisis. For another, there are significant cost differences between being regulated by the OCC versus the state. Depending on state charges, the cost savings can exceed six figures annually. Finally, many community bankers believe that state bank regulators are more sensitive to operating activities of the banks in the states where they live. They are likely more familiar with the communities in which the banks operate and have often met some of the bankers who work for the individual institutions. The perception is often that state bank regulators are willing to listen to explanations when performance is questioned rather than simply rely on numbers.

Building Shareholder Value at First Community Bank

Prior to the financial crisis, FCB's board of directors and management team recognized the need to rely less on net interest margin and more broadly diversify the firm's revenue stream. In 2008, FCB acquired two planning and investment companies to form First Community Financial Services, a division of the bank that offers a full-range of financial planning and retirement services along with asset management services. The transactions were structured such that the subsidiary's producers are largely paid on commission. Thus, while the transactions added some fixed costs, the risks associated with growing the business fall primarily on the subsidiary's employees. Of course, the returns to the employees also rise with the growth in volume of assets managed and financial plans implemented.

In 2009, FCB launched a five-step plan directed at helping customers work through the difficult economic times. Specifically, the bank implemented programs to help businesses better manage their cash flow and restructure debt and to help individuals better manage their personal finances. Of course, FCB now has a division that offers products and services to assist customers. One measure of success is that the bank opened almost 1,000 new core deposit accounts totaling $30 million, a 9.5% jump over 2008. It similarly grew loans by 3.4% with charge-offs higher at 0.84%, but still well below comparable peer figures. Another measure of success is that FCB's Financial Consultants grew assets under management by $24 million to $64 million during the year.

During the heart of the crisis, FCB took a step back from implementing its macro-level growth plans. Recognizing the recession's impact on individuals and businesses, the bank focused on maintaining its credit culture while it grew core deposits. Not surprisingly, Mike Crapps and Joe

Sawyer (CFO) expended considerable effort in responding to the regulatory agreement which had the benefit of helping the bank build a fortress balance sheet. The bank's other employees remained focused on implementing the bank's strategic plan. Thus, while these two senior officers and board members steered the bank through the regulatory maze, most employees were able to maintain the focus on customer service. Given the regulatory stress, it is a compliment to the management that FCB was named one of the best places to work throughout the financial crisis.

In 2011, the bank acquired Palmetto South Mortgage which offers mortgage banking services. As such, management expects the group and its legacy mortgage unit to become far more active in originating residential mortgages. If successful, FCB will realize larger amounts of noninterest income primarily through origination fees. The timing is especially fortuitous as the low interest rate environment has stimulated extensive refinancing across most of the U.S. Since the acquisition, FCB has seen mortgage origination fees jump. For example, during the fourth quarter of 2011, mortgage revenues reached $821,000 up from $343,000 in the fourth quarter of 2010 before FCB acquired Palmetto South Mortgage.

Exhibit 12.4 documents the trends in total noninterest income and its components for FCB from 2008 through 2012. Note that the chart omits extraordinary items such as securities gains or losses, OTTI charges and fair value adjustments. Clearly, total noninterest income really increased only in 2011 and again in 2012. The growth, in turn, is driven primarily by mortgage origination fees. While FCB operated a mortgage unit prior to its acquisition of Palmetto South Mortgage, the additional employees and low interest rate environment drove the higher mortgage revenues after 2010. Investment advisory fees have increased from a lower base at a much slower pace.

Exhibit 12.4 Trends in the Contribution of Noninterest Income at FCB, 2008-2012 (millions)

	2012	2011	2010	2009	2008
Noninterest Income*	$ 8.52	$ 6.52	$ 5.12	$ 5.14	$ 5.06
Net Interest Income	17.57	18.32	18.14	17.88	17.20
Total Operating income*	$26.09	$24.84	$23.26	$23.02	$22.26
Mortgage Origination Fees	$ 4.24	$ 1.97	$ 1.03	$ 0.75	$ 0.58
Investment Advisory & Nondeposit Commissions	0.65	0.77	0.50	0.50	0.33
Noninterest Income / Total Operating Income	32.7%	26.3%	22.0%	22.3%	22.7%

* Omits the components, other than temporary impairment, fair value gain or loss, loss on the early extinguishment of debt, and securities gains or losses.

Of course, the growth in noninterest income should not be viewed independently from changes in noninterest expense. For FCB, several employees of the mortgage banking and investment advisory/planning subsidiaries are paid on commission. As they book more business, both noninterest revenues and noninterest expenses rise from these sources. The true impact on FCB's bottom line is the difference between these two figures. Importantly, FCB benefits from the net, which is added to the bottom line, and the diversification of revenue streams as it has added two additional sources of potential profit. The bank's profits should grow along with production in these divisions.

Stock-Based Performance Metrics

First Community Bank's journey over the past few years has been adventurous to say the least. The bank entered the crisis with solid earnings and good momentum only to see its investment portfolio perform worse than planned and subject the bank to serious regulatory oversight. While it reported positive profits in all but two periods, its ROE and ROA were well below levels that appeal to investors in community banks. During the financial crisis, bank stocks in general suffered as many investors shied away from the sector. Not surprisingly, FCB's common stock price followed the industry trend with its lower performance during 2008–2011, but started to recover in 2012. For example, in March 2007, the stock price reached a high of $18.99 only to fall to $12.90 by year-end. In early 2009, the price reached a low of $5.05. Exhibit 12.5 shows year-end closing prices for subsequent years through 2012 when a share sold for $8.39. Investors who owned the stock over this period lost 55% of its stock price value from the peak in 2007. The bank also lowered its dividend in order to retain capital. FCB, like other banks, did not create shareholder value or generate a positive total return to long-term shareholders over this period. However, investors, in general, were exiting bank stocks including those of community banks over the same period. The KBW Bank Index was valued at 51.28 as of December 31, 2012, or 57% lower than its value on January 1, 2007. Thus, FCB's stock performed better than the index of bank stocks.

Exhibit 12.5 reports some of the stock-based measures introduced in Chapter 5 for FCB that analysts use to evaluate shareholder value. Remember that FCB issued a large number of common stock shares in 2012 and used the proceeds to exit TARP and repay outstanding subordinated debentures. Such a large capital issue serves to dilute earnings available for common stockholders in the near-term, particularly in this instance, as FCB replaced preferred stock with common stock. Thus, EPS and cash EPS both fell slightly in 2012. The same happened to both book value per share and tangible book value per share. To the extent the bank can grow earnings going forward, these measures should increase. Market participants appear to have recognized the positive aspects of the bank's risk profile and incorporated increased earnings and growth in TBVS in the future.

FCB used Raymond James when it sold stock in 2012. In April 2013, FIG Partners released an analyst report rating FCB's stock at outperform. At the time, a share was trading at $8.98 and FIG gave a price target of $11 per share. The rationale behind the recommendation was the firm's healthy dividend, positive loan growth, strong capital base, strong asset quality ratios, and the investment in new investment advisors was expected to grow wealth management revenues by 25% in 2013. Mortgage revenue was expected to be stable even with the slowdown in refinancing activity across the nation. The biggest concern was NIM compression as interest rates remain low. The report emphasized that FCB's revenue diversification should allow the bank to maintain its earnings better than peers. The report rationalized the $11 target price assuming that shares trade at 14× the EPS estimate and 103% of projected TBVS.

Exhibit 12.5 Stock-Based Measures of Value at First Community Bank, 2009–2012 (millions)

Measures	2012	2011	2010	2009
Earnings Per Share (EPS) – diluted	$ 0.79	$ 0.81	$0.36	- $7.95
P/E Multiple	10.6X	7.6X	16.1X	nm
Cash Earnings Per Share – diluted	$ 0.92	$ 1.10	$ 0.72	$ 1.10
P/Cash EPS Multiple	9.1×	5.6×	8.0×	5.7×
Book Value Per Share*	$10.37	$11.11	$9.41	$9.38
Tangible Book Value Per Share (TBVS)*	$10.23	$10.83	$9.14	$8.92
Stock Price to TBVS	0.82	0.57	0.63	0.71
Cash Dividends Per Share	$ 0.16	$ 0.16	$0.24	$0.32
Common Stock Share Price*	$ 8.39	$ 6.19	$ 5.78	$6.30

* Value at year-end.

Positioned for Prosperity

FCB's employees and stockholders cheered the bank's profile at year-end 2012. Regulators removed the formal agreement and the bank changed to a state bank charter. The bank paid-off its TARP preferred stock and subordinated debt. It issued common stock to achieve high capital ratios. It substantially reduced its holdings of noninvestment grade securities, saw core deposits continue to grow and increased its operating income by almost $2 million during the year with an increasing contribution from noninterest sources. Management and the board of directors believe that the bank is positioned to grow and thrive. Its success in doing so will be measured by its ability to grow cash earnings per share, increase tangible book value of equity and grow core funding. These metrics should improve if the bank follows the prescriptions for financial health introduced in Chapter 2 by focusing on customers, employees and its relationship with regulators along with meeting its targets for financial performance.

Many community bankers and analysts express concern that the community banking model is broken and community banks will find it difficult to excel in the future. Obviously, the competitive and regulatory environment is very challenging. However, now is the opportunity for proactive bankers to position their institutions for future prosperity. Much like the directors and management of First Community Bank, bankers should go on offense implementing growth strategies that will overcome the rising costs of meeting banking regulations.

Postscript

First Community Corporation to Merge with Savannah River Financial Corporation

As this book was going to print, First Community Corporation and Savannah River Financial Corporation (SRFC), with operations in Aiken, SC and Augusta, GA, announced an agreement to merge. Under terms of the agreement, FCCO would acquire SRFC at a current value of $33.6 million, roughly $11 a share for SRFC stock, with a 60% / 40% cash and stock split. The price amounted to approximately 112% of TBVS and 18 × EPS adjusted for estimated cost savings. The transaction will be immediately accretive to FCCO's earnings by an estimated 21%. The initial dilution in FCCO's TBVS will equal roughly 8% with an estimated payback of just under four years. The new company will have almost $800 million in assets, $635 million in deposits and 13 physical branches.

SFRC's banking subsidiary, Savannah River Banking Company (SRBC), was chartered in 2007 and had a reputation as a well-run, overcapitalized bank with a strong credit culture that produced low nonperforming assets and low charge-offs throughout the financial crisis. At the end of June 2013, SRBC had a loan-to-asset ratio of 70%, a core deposit-to-asset ratio of 78.4% and a Tier 1 leverage capital ratio of 13.61%. The bank's 2013 annualized ROE and ROA were 4.1% and 0.57%, respectively. At the announcement, SFRC's Chairman of the Board Paul Simon said "The Board of Directors of the SFRC, its Executive Officers, and I are pleased to recommend this merger opportunity to our shareholders and to join together with an excellent company that is well capitalized and has much forward momentum. This combination offers our shareholders a cash dividend and enhanced liquidity, as well as a premium on the capital they invested. We are excited about the future of this combined company."

Analysts at the two firms that actively follow FCCO, Raymond James and FIG Partners, maintained their ratings on FCCO's stock at Outperform. Analysts recognized the similar lending cultures and loan mix, strategic expansion in contiguous markets without overlap and low integration risk. Just prior to the announcement, FCCO's common stock was trading around $10.50 per share. Both Raymond James and FIG raised their price targets to $12 per share.

In October 2013, FCB announced that it was opening an office in downtown Columbia, the state capital. The bank's financial planning advisors and investment advisory firm will be located in the new facility along with its normal banking operations. The move reflects an aggressive step into the community's central business district and center of state government.

ENDNOTES

INTRODUCTION

[1] Some analysts label these firms as 'Too Connected To Fail' thereby emphasizing the large number of counterparties and volume of business any one firm has that would be disrupted by failure. Others label these firms as 'Too Big To Succeed' arguing that their business model encourages excessive risk taking without recourse by the government as ultimate guarantor. The reference to TBTF does not include firms such as General Motors and Chrysler that were similarly determined to be too big to fail.

[2] Much has been written about the roles that former Goldman Sachs' representatives played in the financial crisis of 2008 when Hank Paulson, U.S. Treasury Secretary, and senior executives of major U.S. financial institutions, such as Robert Rubin (Citigroup), John Thain (Merrill Lynch, now CIT), Ed Liddy (AIG) and Robert Steel (Wachovia), were friendly because they each once worked for Goldman Sachs. These relationships arguably influenced which firms failed and which firms acquired failing institutions. The criticism has continued with the role that Timothy Geithner (Treasury Secretary in 2009-2013) played in relation to his ties to former Goldman Sachs' executives Thomas Friedman and William Dudley at the Federal Reserve Bank.

[3] Under DFA, the Financial Stability Oversight Council (FSOC), which is chaired by the U.S. Treasury Secretary, is charged with identifying specific firms to designate at SIFIs including nonbanks. DFA officially designated all commercial banking groups with $50 billion or more in assets as SIFIs. SIFIs will presumably be supervised more closely going forward and may have to operate with different regulatory requirements.

[4] American Bankers Association, "Impact on Community Banks of the Regulatory Restructuring Bill," June 2010.

CHAPTER 1

[1] See the speech by Federal Reserve System Chairman, Ben Bernanke, on Community Banking and Community Bank Supervision to the Independent Community Bankers of America, Las Vegas, NV on March 8, 2006. Research from Federal Reserve Bank economists often designates community banks as those with less than $10 billion in assets. See Gilbert, Meyer and Fuchs (2013). In 2012, the FDIC published a comprehensive report on Community Banks. The FDIC designated institutions as community banks if they exhibited relationship lending, relied substantially on core deposits and focused on limited geographic markets. Most banks with less than $1 billion in assets met the criteria and 330 with assets between $1 billion and $10 billion met the criteria.

[2] The term "high touch" is typically attributed to John Naisbitt who, with Douglas Philips, wrote *High Tech High Touch: Technology and Our Accelerated Search for Meaning* (London: Nicholas Brealey Ltd., 2001) and is referenced in contrast to purely high-tech, or automated, experiences.

[3] A common criticism of subprime lending was that the risk models did not adequately consider the impact of stable or falling home prices. In addition, many lenders ignored standard credit scoring by making Alt A, or liar loans, in which the borrower did not provide detailed financial information, Instead, the borrower offered a "stated income" that would presumably support future payment obligations.

[4] Much like other mortgage originators, many community banks originate mortgages with the intent to sell them into the secondary market.

[5] The OTD emphasis has come back to bite many loan originators who were deemed not to have followed appropriate underwriting procedures. For example, many firms that originated large volumes of mortgages allowed "robo-signing" of documents. In March 2012, the federal government reached an agreement with Ally Bank, Bank of America, Citibank, JPMorgan Chase and Wells Fargo, who as a group contributed $25 billion to assist borrowers who lost their homes to foreclosure. The settlement agreement was based on the premise that employees of the lenders systematically signed documents without knowledge of the facts in the documents and without required notarization. In one notorious case, someone signed the name "Linda Green" to almost 1,300 documents over a few months in late 2010 and early 2011. The problem was that her position title changed frequently, the names were signed in more than 20 handwriting styles and the real Linda Green was thought to have left the mortgage industry in early 2010. (See Evann Gastaldo, "Fake Mortgage Signatures Still Rampant," *Newser.com*, July 19, 2011.)

[6] The process of recognizing loan losses and corresponding impact on earnings and equity capital is described in detail in Chapter 8. In terms of the current discussion, large loan losses could wipe out a bank's equity capital. In this situation, bank regulators will require that management obtain additional capital or the bank may fail. Remember that if a bank fails, the FDIC guarantees (or pays) insured depositors the full amount of their insured balances if necessary.

[7] In 2013, many politicians, regulators and banking analysts were arguing that large U.S. banking organizations should be required to operate with much higher capital to asset (leverage) ratios. For

example, Sherrod Brown (D-Ohio) and David Vitter (R-Louisiana) formally introduced the "Terminating Bailouts for Taxpayer Fairness" Act (TBTF Act), which would require banks with more than $500 billion in assets to have a minimum 15% capital to asset ratio while banks with $50 billion to $500 billion would need an 8% ratio.

[8] Imagine a bank with core operations in the Midwest that opens branches in Las Vegas, NV, Miami, FL or Phoenix, AZ. Its business model will change even with the greatest of intentions.

[9] The government allows related parties to count as a single stockholder such that the actual number of investors may well exceed 100.

[10] Philadelphia Savings Fund Society and Provident Institution for Savings were formed in 1816 and 1817, respectively.

[11] See American Bankers Association, "Mutual Savings Banks – A Primer," 2009.

[12] Under the Gramm-Leach-Bliley Act of 1999, firms could form financial holding companies with expanded powers in terms of the types of activities allowed. Few community banks choose this organization form.

[13] Private equity firms raise capital in the form of equity and debt and use the proceeds to buy individual securities or entire companies. They often have short-term investment horizons in which they attempt to improve an acquired firm's operating performance then take the firm public.

[14] The nine firms are Bank of America, Bank of New York Mellon, Citigroup, Goldman Sachs, JPMorgan Chase, Merrill Lynch, Morgan Stanley, State Street and Wells Fargo. Merrill Lynch was acquired by Bank of America in early 2009. Comprehensive data are provided in Cuomo (2009).

CHAPTER 2

[1] See Michael Porter, *Competitive Strategy: Techniques for Analyzing Industries and Competitors* (New York: The Free Press, 1980).

[2] Donna de St. Aubin, "10 Tips for Retaining Top Talent," *Scotsman Guide*, September 2008, http://www.scotsmanguide.com/default.asp?ID=3147.

[3] The term *corporate governance* refers to the establishment of authority and responsibilities by which the board of directors and senior management govern a bank. It encompasses setting strategy, risk tolerances, daily operating procedures and how to protect the bank's various constituencies (depositors, borrowers, stockholders and the insurance fund).

[4] Directors may be subject to personal liability if their actions or negligence harms the bank. However, the business judgment rule applies when directors have taken actions based on appropriate business judgment upon receiving full information and where there is no conflict of interest.

[5] Chapter 9 demonstrates that banks must now conduct effective pre-purchase analysis of individual bonds and not rely solely on credit ratings when buying and holding different securities.

[6] See the American Bankers Association, "Impact on Community Banks of the Regulatory Restructuring Bill," June 2010, http://www.aba.com/aba/documents/news/Listof30burdens52610.pdf; and "Dodd-Frank and Community Banks—Your Guide to 12 Critical Issues," 2012, http://www.aba.com/aba/documents/dfa/dfguide.pdf.

[7] Sarah Wallace, "The End of Community Banking," *Wall Street Journal*, June 29, 2010, http://online.wsj.com/article/SB10001424052748703964104575334611037072320.html.

[8] Don Musso of FinPro, Inc. provides an eight stage enterprise risk management framework that integrates planning, budgeting, asset and liability management modeling and stress testing which can be used to perform scenario analysis and thus make strategic decisions.

[9] Regulators also identify matters requiring immediate attention (MRIAs) that must be addressed immediately.

[10] It is less obvious that the number of insurance companies, finance companies, etc. will decline over time as they continue to be lightly regulated.

CHAPTER 3

[1] Banks fund the Deposit Insurance Fund (DIF) through premium payments to the FDIC. The DIF has never relied on taxpayer financing.

[2] You might note the number of institutions with the bank's name followed by N.A., which stands for "national association" and meets the OCC's requirement. The Office of Thrift Supervision (OTS), which once chartered thrift institutions, was effectively disbanded with the Dodd-Frank Act and rolled-into the OCC.

[3] Bernanke and the Fed have publicly stated that easy monetary policy will continue as long as the unemployment rate (U3) remains above 6.5%. As such, the Fed has pursued quantitative easing (QE1 through QE3 and now QE Infinity) whereby it systematically buys bonds and mortgages to keep long-term interest rates low and presumably stimulate borrowing and spending.

[4] There are other types of formal actions, such as Prompt Corrective Action (PCA) under the FDIC Improvement Act and the Termination of FDIC Insurance.

[5] The $250,000 limit was temporary through January 1, 2014, but was made permanent under the Dodd-Frank Act. Customers can have insured balances in excess of $250,000 at the same institution depending on how the accounts are titled and who has ownership.

[6] The Dodd-Frank Act changed the assessment base to total assets minus equity capital from an institution's total insured deposits. Because many large institutions finance a large portion of their operations with uninsured liabilities, such as federal funds, large CDs and brokered deposits, they previously did not pay insurance premiums against these debts. Yet, the financial crisis revealed that they were TBTF such that all liabilities were effectively insured. The move to net assets presumably shifts more of the insurance burden to these larger institutions. At year-end 2012, the DIF had a balance of $33 billion against insured deposits of $7.4 trillion.

[7] Banks are formally placed into categories based on their capital profile (well capitalized versus adequately capitalized, etc.) and CAMELS rating. These factors will be discussed in detail later in the chapter and text.

[8] Because of the government guarantee, issuers paid interest rates on the debt that were close to Treasury rates. The 75 basis point fee increased the effective cost of debt issuance which was still well below the rates prevailing on noninsured debt of the issuer outstanding at the time of issuance. The Wall Street Journal (2009) estimated that Citigroup and GE would save around $24 billion in interest expense on their outstanding FDIC-insured debt from 2008 to 2010. As an example, Goldman Sachs issued $5 billion in 2.5 year FDIC-insured debt at 3.25% at the same time that its outstanding three-year bonds were priced to yield 8.51%. The estimated interest savings on this issue amounted to $754 million while all of Goldman's outstanding FDIC-insured debt would produce estimated savings in excess of $2.3 billion.

[9] Gorton and Metrick (2012) describe the role that repurchase agreements (repos) played during the crisis and the corresponding problems that financial firms had with collateral requirements.

Discount window borrowings were used in many cases to replace short-term repo financing that lenders could not roll-over at maturity.

[10] Firms that borrowed from the Fed under duress had no alternative to obtain large amounts of financing on short-term notice. The extension of discount window credit prevented repo lenders from filing legal claims against the institutional borrowers. CEOs of institutions that received these emergency loans are incorrect to state that their firms were not bailed out. They were bailed out because they were perceived to be TBTF!

[11] Bob Ivry, Bradley Keoun and Phil Kuntz, "Secret Fed Loans Gave Banks $13 Billion Undisclosed to Congress," *Bloomberg*, November 27, 2011, http://www.bloomberg.com/news/2011-11-28/secret-fed-loans-undisclosed-to-congress-gave-banks-13-billion-in-income.html.

[12] Key elements that affect each factor rating are described in detail throughout the remainder of this book.

[13] The Federal Trade Commission Act formally identified certain acts as unfair, deceptive and abusive (UDAP) and gave bank regulators authority to enforce provisions on banks, thrifts and credit unions. The Dodd-Frank Act added "abusive" practices to the list and authorized the CFPB to take enforcement actions when violations occur. Under DFA, "abusive" means a practice materially interferes with a customer's ability to understand a term or condition and takes unreasonable advantage of the lack of understanding.

[14] See the testimony of FDIC Chairman Sheila Bair, "The State of the Banking Industry: Part II," before the Committee on Banking, Housing and Urban Affairs, U.S. Senate, June 5, 2008.

[15] Regulators offered guidance on commercial real estate lending in 2006. One key threshold was for banks to manage their concentrations carefully if they had more than 100% of equity capital in construction, land and development loans. You can see the potential problems for banks with ratios of 200% or higher.

[16] The federal Office of Management and Budget (OMB) decides which markets qualify as "rural." Preliminary indications are that the CFPB will allow a transition period in which banks can operate as if they are in a rural market while the final determination is made.

[17] *FDIC Compliance Manual*, IV. Fair Lending – Overview, Fair Lending Laws and Regulations, http://www.fdic.gov/regulations/compliance/manual/pdf/IV-1.1.pdf.

[18] U.S. Congress, "DOJ's Quid Pro Quo with St. Paul: How Assistant Attorney General Thomas Perez Manipulated Justice and Ignored the Rule of Law, Joint Staff Report," April 15, 2013, http://oversight.house.gov/wp-content/uploads/2013/04/DOJ-St-Paul.pdf,.

[19] The Financial Crisis Inquiry Commission concluded that the CRA did not adversely impact subprime lending and was not a significant factor in the financial crisis.

CHAPTER 4

[1] The format for the first page of data in a UPBR appears at the end of the chapter. This page reports select financial ratios for earnings, loans, liquidity, capital and growth. Go to www.fdic.gov, click the Quick Link 'Analysts,' then click Uniform Bank Performance under Data and Statistics and Search for a UBBR. You need to know the name of the institution, city and state or, alternatively, the bank's FDIC certificate number to access a specific institution's data.

[2] The summary page (01) reports data for the bank in question and the average value for a group of peer banks nationally in the same size group across several different profit and risk ratios.

[3] Provisions for loan losses is an expense item on the income statement as discussed in the next section.

[4] Coverage was permanently increased to $250,000 under the Dodd-Frank Act of 2010. The $100,000 figure has historically been used by regulators in determining what balances are labeled "brokered deposits." Banks that have a significant exposure to brokered deposits are penalized by paying higher deposit insurance premiums and are typically subject to greater regulatory scrutiny.

[5] Securities sold under agreements to resell are included in this category and effectively represent secured federal funds sold where the borrowing bank has to post collateral.

[6] The income statement reports interest income on a tax-equivalent basis by "grossing up" any tax-exempt interest to its pre-tax equivalent. The UBPR reports a bank's actual applicable income taxes based on taxable income then adds the amount of imputed taxes paid on the tax-sheltered interest. The tax figure cited for FCB represents applicable income taxes of $1.9 million and a tax-equivalent adjustment (imputed taxes) of $300,000.

[7] The reserves account is formally a contra-asset account reported on a bank's balance sheet. A bank lists the dollar amount of total loans outstanding from which it deducts the allowance (reserves) for loan losses to produce a net loans figure. First Community Bank reported $337.2 million in net loans in Exhibit 4.1 which actually represents $341.8 million in gross loans minus $4.6 million in the allowance for loan losses.

[8] The process is considerably more rigorous as demonstrated in Chapter 8. Banks essentially grade or rate each loan held in portfolio in terms of its presumed risk. Whether loans are performing or not, the rating system differentiates between loans with higher versus lower probabilities of default and expected losses in the event of default.

[9] The UBPR allows the user to identify a specific group of institution to construct peer data. Most banks select firms of similar size that operate with the same basic strategy and loan mix in similar geographic markets. Peer data in this chapter refer to national banks of similar size.

[10] Banks also focus on the economic (market) value of stockholders equity as a target measure of performance. Chapter 10 examines this framework for analyzing interest rate risk. Large banks that compete in global markets and have trading operations or take equity positions are also subject to market risk through unanticipated changes in foreign exchange rates and prices of securities, derivatives and businesses. These components are ignored here because most community banks are not subject to these risks.

[11] Precise definitions appear in Chapter 7.

[12] In reality, the denominator for the Tier 1 leverage ratio is an adjusted total assets figure which is less than actual total assets. This example is further simplified because it assumes no growth in assets over time.

[13] Basel Committee on Banking Supervision, "Regulatory Treatment of Operational Risk," September 2001.

[14] Colleen Long (2013) explains how the thieves stole the $45 million.

CHAPTER 5

[1] When comparing an income statement (flow) figure calculated over a period of time, such as one year, with a balance sheet (stock) figure calculated at a specific point in time, the balance sheet figure is measured as an average value over the same time period as the flow value. Thus, ROE and ROA compare net income (flow value for the year 2012) with average total stockholders equity and average total assets (stock values for the year 2012).

ENDNOTES

[2] FCB's peer group according to UBPR output is all insured commercial banks across the United States having assets between $300 million and $1 billion of which there were almost 1,200 in 2012. As will be discussed later, FCB has a different business strategy than many of these banks so ratio comparisons are not as meaningful as they might be for similarly-focused firms. Also, FCB had just under $600 million in average assets during the year which is much different from a bank with $1 billion in assets. Finally, FCB's trade area is central South Carolina an area that did not see the worst of economic conditions arising during the financial crisis, but which has also not seen strong growth as the state's unemployment rate has ranked among the highest in the nation.

[3] If you receive stock dividends, the share price may not have to increase to generate a positive return. You may instead find that the greater number of shares valued at a lower stock price still produces a value in excess of your $1,000 investment.

[4] Formally, the number of outstanding shares includes stock held by investors (public, company officers and insiders) and less-restricted stock held by the company. The ratio then adjusts the denominator further by adding dilutive shares associated with outstanding stock options, stock warrants and bonds convertible into stock.

[5] Operating cash flow can be estimated by adding noncash expenses, such as depreciation and amortization, to net income. Because provision for loan losses is a noncash expense, it lowers net income but does not directly lower cash inflows. It is reasonable to deduct a long-term average of provisions rather than a single period's provisions to get a more realistic estimate of net income. Similarly, it is reasonable to ignore one-time, extraordinary items that affect net income such as gains or losses from securities sales, bulk loan sales or sales of subsidiaries.

[6] Both figures assume that the share price remains at $10.

[7] Research demonstrates that investors, on average, respond favorably to the announcement of stock splits due to signaling benefits such that the share price initially rises above that reflecting no value change. In the bank stock example, the investor who paid $10 per share would mathematically expect the share price to fall to $2.50 per share if a 4-for-1 stock split were announced immediately after purchase. Research shows that, on average, the share price might initially be over $2.50.

[8] The multiple here is $10/$8 = 1.25×.

[9] The value of core deposits is recognized in accounting terms for branch and whole bank transactions via a *core deposit intangible* (CDI) that is calculated as the present value of the incremental cost advantage of core deposits compared with other sources of funds. The premium appears on an acquiring bank's balance sheet as an intangible asset.

CHAPTER 6

[1] According to the FDIC's Community Banking Study, December 2012, 1,092 of the 15,663 community banks that existed in 1984 failed by the end of 2011. The study defines community banks as banking organizations with less than $1 billion in combined assets and that operate in limited geographic markets with a limited number of banking offices.

[2] To qualify, customers must meet one of the following criteria: maintain a minimum balance of $2,500 in their checking or savings account; have a CD of $15,000 or more; or have at least $15,000 in investments at Raymond James with whom FCB has a financial relationship.

[3] IDC Deposits offers similar money market account funding for institutions that want to borrow or invest for shorter time periods.

[4] Loan fees are included in loan interest income.

[5] Data are from Moeb Services.

[6] "Loaded with Uncertainty: Are Prepaid Cards a Smart Alternative to Checking Accounts?" Pew Charitable Trusts, September 2012.

[7] Sheila Bair protested the preferential treatment that the Federal Home Loan Banks get because they make advances to banks that are fully collateralized. When a bank fails, the FHLBs get paid before the FDIC thereby increasing the loss to the DIF. On occasion, the FDIC and some members of Congress have proposed that secured lenders to banks take a haircut (loss) in the event that a bank fails. If implemented, this provision will increase the cost of borrowing because the FHLBs and other lenders recognize that their risks will have increased.

[8] Interestingly, the FDIC will have to pay the FHLB the prepayment penalty in the event that a failed bank has outstanding advances at the time of failure resolution.

[9] Remember that security prices for fixed rate instruments vary inversely with market interest rates. If rates fall, prices rise and a security trades at a gain when the price rises above the original investment. If rates rise, prices fall and a security trades at a discount when the price falls below the original investment. Selling a security for a gain effectively converts higher anticipated interest income over the life of the instrument into an immediate gain. Unfortunately, the government taxes the gain so the net benefit is reduced.

[10] The Federal Reserve Bank of Cleveland provides a sample contingency funding plan at http://www.clevelandfed.org/Banking/Documents/Sample_Plan.doc. It also provides an excel template to compare the potential erosion of funds with available sources of funds.

[11] The following information is based on presentations by Karl Nelson with KPN Consulting.

CHAPTER 7

[1] The discussion in Chapter 5 demonstrates that ROE equals ROA times the equity multiplier (assets divided by equity). The greater is the amount of debt financing, the greater are assets relative to equity such that EM is higher. A bank that generates a positive ROA will see its ROE increase the greater is its financial leverage. The reverse also holds as a bank that experiences a loss (ROA is negative) will see its ROE be a larger negative return.

[2] Regulators require at least a three-year plan which includes the bank's strategic focus, projected asset mix, funding mix and total assets at the end of the period. The initial capital contribution must be sufficient to support the projected growth. The plan should demonstrate what products the bank will emphasize, how they will deliver them (branches, Internet, etc.) and how they will differentiate themselves from competitors. In 2009, the FDIC extended the window to seven years under which de novo banks will be subject to greater scrutiny so plans should cover longer periods. Management is expected to stick with the plan.

[3] This characterization is simplistic in terms of the accounting, but is used to demonstrate the different components and role of capital. In practice, a de novo bank has expenses well in advance of receiving its official charter and these costs are covered by the initial capital raise.

[4] The term *retained earnings* is used interchangeably with *undivided profits*.

[5] Common stock generally has a par value of $1. In this example, the organizers sell shares for $10 thereby creating $9 in common stock surplus. Formal accounting rules record the initial $25 million in common stock that appears in Exhibits 7.1 and 7.2 as $2.5 million in common stock and $22.5 million in surplus.

⁶ The maximum amount is 1.25% of risk-weighted assets. This calculation will be demonstrated later in the chapter.

⁷ Most banks don't own equities (stocks) in other companies, but some hold mutual funds with equities.

⁸ The following definitions are not comprehensive but demonstrate the key components of capital at community banks. The largest institutions have more complex balance sheets and off-balance sheet activities and are subject to more complex capital regulations under international capital standards associated with the Basel Committee on Banking Supervision.

⁹ Intangible assets are not physical assets that can be touched or directly measured. Goodwill is typically generated when a firm buys another firm and pays more than the book value of equity. Mortgage servicing rights are the right to collect mortgage payments from borrowers, make the appropriate tax and insurance payments and pay holders of the mortgages the promised principal and interest. Deferred tax assets are amounts than may potentially be used to offset future tax payments to the government.

¹⁰ See Morgan Housel, "Which Banks Might Fail the Stress Test?" *The Motley Fool*, http://www.fool.com/investing/dividends-income/2009/02/12/which-banks-might-fail-the-stress-test.aspx.

¹¹ The Third Basel Accord (Basel III) was designed by the Basel Committee on Banking Supervision with guidelines to be introduced from 2013–2015. The guidelines are voluntary such that each country's banking authorities (Federal Reserve Bank in the United States) will propose specific and proposing specific rules for implementation in their home country. Because of widespread disagreement over the rules and their impact, few have yet been formally put in place in the United States.

¹² See his presentation to the International Association of Deposit Insurers, "Basel III Capital: A Well-Intentioned Illusion," 2013 Research Conference, Basel, Switzerland, April 9, 2013.

¹³ See the letter to the FDIC, OCC and Board of Governors of the Federal Reserve System dated October 17, 2012.

¹⁴ Earnings dilution refers to a transaction, such as issuing new shares of common stock, which lowers *earnings per share* (EPS). With dilution, existing stockholders have claims that generally fall in value with the transaction.

¹⁵ A firm's market capitalization equals the value of the firm measured as the number of common shares outstanding times the current price of a share of common stock. During financial crises, bank stock prices typically fall sharply as investors lose confidence in financial performance and the quality of financial information. They generally expect future earnings power to decline.

¹⁶ A paper by Gary Gorton and Andrew Metrick, "Securitized Banking and the Run on Repo," *Journal of Financial Economics*, 104 (2012): 425–451 suggests that global financial institutions, particularly shadow banks, experienced runs via the withdrawal of repurchase agreements such that liquidity problems and not limited capital were the primary catalyst.

¹⁷ Anat Admati and Marting Hellwig (2013) argue that the largest banks should operate with capital to asset ratios as high as 25% in order to eliminate TBTF. Imagine what this would do to expected return on equity at these institutions.

CHAPTER 8

¹ See Parzinger et al. (2004) for a summary of loan policy guidelines. This list also reflects suggestions from regulatory agencies. For example, "Insights for Bank Directors," Federal Reserve Bank of St. Louis offers suggested policy guidelines.

² Why should banks that follow such different business strategies be regulated in the same manner? At the extreme, managers intent on capturing market share typically grow assets (loans) very fast which often involves assuming increased credit risk. If so, shouldn't capital requirements be greater?

³ These rules vary by state and there are some exceptions.

⁴ See Concentrations in Commercial Real Estate Lending (2006).

⁵ Elizabeth Laderman (2008) found that roughly 90% of small business lending is from a bank with a physical presence in-market with the other 10% from banks with no office in the local market.

⁶ These factors are commonly referred to as the C's of Credit with the number of Cs varying with how comprehensive the analysis is.

⁷ See Donald Kummer, Nasser Arshadi, and Edward Lawrence, "Incentive Problems in Bank Insider Borrowing," *Journal of Financial Services Research*, 3, no. 1, (1989) "Insider Loans Distrusted by Bair as Georgia Failures Lead U.S.," Bloomberg.com (2009); and "Insider Loans Rife as Bank Collapsed," *Seattle Times*, January 30, 2013.

⁸ Peter Waldman, David Mildenberg, and Laurence Davidson, "Insider Loans Distrusted by Bair as Georgia Failures Lead U.S.," *Bloomberg*, December 8, 2009.

⁹ "Risk Management in Financial Institutions," speech, Annual Conference on Bank Structure and Competition, Federal Reserve Bank of Chicago, May 15, 2008.

¹⁰ If a mortgage borrower defaults soon after a loan is made, the loan originator may be required to buy the mortgage back which would happen at a loss. The originator may also keep in portfolio a portion of the collateralized securities (retained interests) such as residuals and interest-only or principal-only pieces, which are high risk. The terms of such "first payment default" mortgages, the risks with retained interests and the potential loss of servicing fees at least partially offset some of the originator's benefits from securitization.

¹¹ The acronym ARM refers to *adjustable-rate mortgage*.

¹² This example comes from a lawsuit filed in July 2008, *The People of the State of California v. Countrywide Financial Corporation*, Case No.: LC081846.

¹³ Many option ARMs included caps on the allowable amount of negative amortization. For example, once the outstanding principal exceeded 115% of the initial principal, the monthly payment would be immediately increased to the fully amortizing amount. Payment shock would occur before five years in this event.

¹⁴ See "Boundaries of the firm: evidence from the banking industry," *Journal of Financial Economics*, 70 (2003). Berger et al. (2005) find a similar result.

¹⁵ Net income is an accounting concept generally determined using accrual-based accounting such that it may differ substantially from cash flow from operations. Most basic accounting textbooks document the impact of accruals on cash flow versus reported net income or earnings.

¹⁶ Loans whose original terms have been changed to better facilitate repayments, by lowering the interest rate, extending maturity or reducing principal, are labeled restructured loans. *Other real estate owned* (OREO) equals real property that a bank owns which is not directly related to its normal business activity. It typically arises from foreclosures as a result of loan defaults in which a bank takes possession of collateral.

¹⁷ Gerard Cassidy and others related this ratio for Texas banks to the likelihood of failure during the 1980s recession. They concluded that Texas banks showed a higher probability of failure when the ratio exceeded 100%. Fajt (2010) reports that 60% of the 120 U.S. banks with a Texas ratio exceeding 100% at year-end 2008 failed by the end of the first quarter of 2010. There are several

versions of the Texas Ratio with some not including OREO in the numerator.

[18] The use of global cash flow versus projected NOI for commercial mortgages may produce different accept/reject decisions. DiLorenzo (2001) documents the different ratios and potential outcomes. See Brad Schaefer, "Global Cash Flow Analysis—Common Mistakes & Other Helpful Hints," May 5, 2011, www.sageworksinc.com/blog for a discussion of problems surrounding banks' use of cash flow.

[19] For example, accountants have been aggressive in forcing banks to write-down deferred tax assets. Deferred tax assets typically arise from prior period net losses. In their current interpretations, if management cannot reasonably project that the bank will generate earnings over the next year, it must write down (charge-off) a significant portion of its deferred tax assets which immediately depletes capital.

[20] Tom Brown (2009) provides an example using data for First Horizon in 2007 and 2008.

[21] Under FASB 15, a TDR may involve a transfer of receivables, real estate or other assets from the debtor to creditor, the conveyance of an equity interest from the debtor to creditor, and modification of credit terms. Financial difficulty is demonstrated by loan default, bankruptcy, the inability to service existing debt, and the lack of availability of other forms of credit.

CHAPTER 9

[1] These ratings are for long-term securities with original maturities beyond one year. The firms also assign ratings for short-term securities using the following standards for the top three categories: P-1, P-2 and P-3 (Moody's); A-1, A-2 and A-3 (S&P); and F1, F2 and F3 (Fitch).

[2] As part of the conservatorship, Treasury purchased mortgage-backed securities held by Fannie and Freddie, received $1 billion in preferred stock from each firm that paid a 10% dividend, and received warrants representing almost 80% ownership.

[3] In February 2013 the Department of Justice (DOJ) filed suit against S&P alleging that the firm intentionally mislead investors by "knowingly and with the intent to defraud, devised, participated in, and executed a scheme to defraud investors" in specific securities it rated. The suit asked for more than $1 billion in damages. S&P denied the accusations. Some market participants believe that DOJ was exacting revenge on S&P for its 2012 downgrade of U.S. Treasury debt and was favoring Moody's and others by not including them in the suit.

[4] Section 939A applies to banks, but not other investors in municipals such as property-casualty insurance companies, mutual funds and individuals. These investors can continue to rely on ratings and do not necessarily have to perform any due diligence. Thus, attractive new municipal issues will continue to sell quickly.

[5] Managers are generally averse to selling securities at a loss because they have to report the loss separately on the income statement and it lowers earnings. Selling at a loss may be the best financial decision based on the bank's tax position and how the funds can be invested, but managers often let reporting requirements drive the decision.

[6] Practically speaking, lenders disallow certain types of securities and impose large "haircuts" on the values that they credit toward meeting collateral requirements. Thus, a bank might have to post $1.2 million in mortgage-backed securities as collateral against a $1 million borrowing with the haircut representing almost 17% of the securities value.

[7] See *An Introduction to Option-Adjusted Spread Analysis: Revised and Expanded Third Edition of the OAS Classic by Tom Windax*, revised by Tom Miller, (New York: Bloomberg Professional Library, 2007) for details.

[8] Capital gains and losses on both tax-exempt and taxable municipals are treated as ordinary income for income tax purposes.

[9] "U.S. Municipal Bond Defaults and Recoveries, 1970–2011, *Moody's* March 2012. In contrast, Appleson, Parsons & Haughwout, "The Untold Story of Municipal Bond Defaults," Liberty Street Economics, Federal Reserve Bank of New York, August 15, 2012, conclude that both Moody's and S&P systematically understate the true number of municipal defaults. Their analysis, however, ignores nonrated municipals and the dollar amount of defaults, both important factors to consider when making investment decisions.

[10] Congress's decision regarding sequestration in 2013 further complicates the analysis because the subsidy rate on BABs was reduced to roughly 32% from 35%. If a BABs issuer is in financial difficulty, the lower subsidy will make it more difficult to meet debt service payments.

[11] The most significant fee is the servicing fee paid to the firm that collects the mortgage payments and pays escrow and guarantee fees to facilitate the securitization. The originating lender may or may not retain the servicing rights.

[12] It is possible that falling rates can lead to falling prices when the option is exercised (prepayments occur) at a faster than anticipated rate.

[13] PAC and TAC CMOs refer to Planned Amortization Class and Targeted Amortization Class CMOs, respectively. Each type creates a wide range of support tranches that absorb prepayments of principal until the bonds are paid off. They are complex and difficult to value given that prepayment speeds vary across the business cycle and are generally unpredictable.

[14] TruPS investments had the additional initial advantage of lower capital requirements due to their classification as debt instruments rather than equity. Still, when the rating agencies lowered their ratings below investment grade, the investing banks had to sharply increase required capital.

[15] Ed Krei, The Baker Group, frames his discussion of bank investments with these types of questions.

[16] Some banks buy agency step-up bonds that have variable coupons which increase (step-up) at predetermined intervals. The analysis of step-ups is beyond the focus of this discussion.

[17] This discussion reflects the standard analysis for the "Riding the Yield Curve" strategy. The typical analysis involves estimating the total return (coupon interest plus reinvestment income plus sale value) over the estimated three-to-four-year holding period.

CHAPTER 10

[1] A market maker holds an inventory of assets and agrees to either sell the underlying assets to willing participants or buy assets from them. The objective is to make a profit by selling at a higher price (ask price) than the price (bid price) paid for the asset. The market maker holds a specific asset for a short period of time but there is risk that the underlying asset may fall in price during the period held. Large banks also engage in proprietary trading in which they trade assets (stocks, bonds, commodities, currencies, etc.) using the firm's own resources in order to profit on the trades. They can either acquire (go long) or short the underlying assets.

[2] While this relationship normally holds, there are many situations where a bank can lose. For example, if the bulk of a bank's assets

are loans priced at the prime rate + 1% but each loan has a floor rate that is well above the current effective floating rate (floor loan rate equals 5% when the floating rate is prime (3.25%) plus 1%), an increase in the prime rate may not move the floating rate above the floor unless it jumps sharply. In this example, the rate on the loan is initially 5%, the floor rate, because prime + 1% equals just 4.25%. An increase in the prime to 3.5% changes the floating rate to 4.5%, which is still 0.50% below the floor rate. Small rate increases still raise the cost of liabilities so that the spread declines.

[3] The price or present value of a security equals the sum of the discounted values of each expected cash flow where the discount rate is the market rate on the underlying security. For bonds and loans, the cash flows are the expected principal and interest payments. When market rates change, prices change in the opposite direction for bonds and loans without options.

[4] For purposes of the example, interest is assumed to be paid for one-fourth of a year at 0.50% for the period.

[5] "Interagency Advisory of Interest Rate Risk Management, Frequently Asked Questions," January 12, 2012.

[6] A bank might also use derivatives, such as interest rate swaps, to reduce risk. Data for periodic GAPs can provide insight into the size (notional principal amount) of the derivatives position.

[7] Later discussion demonstrates that this type of policy limit isn't meaningful for banks with embedded options.

[8] With these assumptions, RSAs would increase from $149 million to $169 million with RSLs unchanged at $132 million.

[9] Some modified GAP models attempt to address these problems through the use of betas or *earnings change ratios* (ECRs). These parameters are estimates of the relative repricing sensitivity of a balance sheet item compared with changes in some index or driver rate. For example, a bank might use the prime rate as its benchmark, driver rate. Floating rate loans tied to prime will have an ECR of 100% or 1 indicating that when the prime rate changes the floating loan rate changes by the same amount. Treasury securities might have an ECR of 0.6 indicating that their yields increase by 60 basis points for each 1% increase in prime. At best, these models are rough approximations of reality. Given the low cost and ready availability of software that conducts sensitivity and simulation analysis, these more comprehensive models provide for better estimation of true IRR.

[10] With sensitivity analysis, the modeling incorporates specific interest rates for all balance sheet items recognizing that rates on individual assets and liabilities change by different amounts and at different times. In simulation analysis, the assumed interest rates and related balance sheet elements may be deterministic, that is, the model uses predetermined values that are not based on any specific probability, or stochastic where model values are drawn randomly from a pool of potential values reflecting the probability of occurrence. Community banks generally use deterministic modeling.

[11] When rates are low, the shock values will often be of lesser amounts, such as –0.5%, –1%, –1.5%. and –2%.

[12] Market capitalization refers to the total value of a company's stock measured by multiplying the number of shares of common stock outstanding by the current share price.

[13] Modified duration (DUR) equals Macaulay's duration divided by the current market interest rate. Readers can review the mathematical calculation of a bond's Macaulay's duration in any textbook on fixed-income securities with numerous examples or via a Web search.

[14] Note that an increase in MVL when rates fall simply recognizes that a bank would have to pay more to buy back its deposits if it is paying rates that are now well above current market rates. The bank has lost in the sense that its customers hold deposits paying rates higher than rates currently available.

[15] While generally true, there are balance sheet structures and off-balance sheet situations where these statements could be incorrect.

[16] The model incorporates estimates of effective duration that reflect an instrument's expected price sensitivity after taking account of cash flows that will change when interest rates change. For example, a bank that holds a fixed rate 15-year mortgage in portfolio will estimate cash flows under different rate environments recognizing that principal prepayments will be higher (lower) when interest rates are lower (higher). An effective duration measure will capture the resulting difference in price sensitivity when rates are expected to rise versus fall.

[17] Banks that actively manage the balance sheet in this manner are effectively taking a position that forward rates (market implied rates on future securities, loans and deposits) are either too low or too high compared with management's expectations. This recognition often motivates the use of off-balance sheet transactions such as interest rate swaps.

[18] Many banks got into trouble by buying private-label mortgage backed securities which are issued by banks, investment banks and other private institutions and do not carry any government guarantee. Many private-label MBSs experiences sharp reductions in value with the declines in real estate values in 2006–2010.

[19] The interested reader should reference FAS 133 and become familiar with "fair value hedges" and "cash flow hedges."

[20] In practice, floating rates are quoted on a money market basis using a 360-day year while the fixed rate is quoted using a 365-day year. The example uses similar rate quotes for each and thus approximates true cash payments and receipts. Note that the calculations are based on one-fourth the quoted rate times $5 million.

[21] In this example, the fixed rates would be set using forward rates from the yield curve. Discounting the expected cash flows derived from these rates would yield a zero net present value with a fixed rate of 2.025%. The swap dealer then adds 2.5 basis points to each position for the dealer spread.

CHAPTER 11

[1] The ERM model employed by FinPro, Inc. fully integrates planning and budgeting with all risk analytics, including interest rate risk modeling, in one model. Any bank can use the model to identify key performance measures it wants to achieve and conduct what-if analysis to assess how specific strategies might help achieve its performance targets.

[2] Regulators released an "Interagency Policy Statement on the Allowance for Loan and Lease Losses" in December 2006. This guidance requires that banks develop a methodology that provides a "comprehensive, systematic, and consistently applied process for determining the amounts of the ALLL and the provision for loan and lease losses." The guidance stipulates that the ALLL should cover (1) estimated losses on individual loans deemed to be impaired and (2) estimated losses inherent in the remainder of the loan and lease portfolio. Proposals currently being discussed suggest that the ALLL may also need to incorporate expected losses over the life of assets in the future.

[3] Wells and Gaskins (2010) identify problems often observed in regulatory exams regarding how banks identify and apply environment factors across different loan pools.

[4] Paul McAdam, "Can You Be a 'Relationship Bank' When Most Other Banks Are Too?," FIS Services, 2011.

[5] See Joe Valenti (2013) for a discussion of how the use of cash is declining.

ENDNOTES

[6] Many brick-and-mortar retail outlets balk at paying the transaction fees associated with a customer's use of VISA, MASTERCARD or American Express.

[7] Bradford and Keeton (2012) summarize trends in P2P activity including the availability on mobile devices.

CHAPTER 12

[1] FCB refers to the subsidiary bank but will be used to encompass both the bank and holding company, First Community Corporation, in the following analysis.

[2] Formally, the holding company for FCB acquired the holding company (DutchFork Bancshares) of NBSB. Holders of stock in Dutch-Fork Bancshares were given the option of taking 1.78125 shares in FCB's parent, then valued at $42 per share, or $42.74 per share in cash. The transaction was valued at $50 million, which amounted to 1.49× DutchFork Bancshare's book value and 12.8× its trailing 12-months EPS. The Bank of Camden (DutchFork Bancshares) had less than $50 million in assets when FCB acquired it.

[3] FCB Press Release dated January 16, 2008.

[4] Under accounting rules, the write-down is recorded as a reduction in noninterest income.

[5] FCB sold its entire portfolio of private-label mortgage-backed securities in 2011 to avoid the continual negotiations over value and write-downs. Ex post, the portfolio yielded approximately 2.4% annually from 2004 to 2011.

[6] As part of its leveraged investment strategy, FCB entered into a five year interest rate swap agreeing to pay a fixed-rate and receive a floating rate to hedge against a potential increase in interest rates. In 2008, FCB reported a fair value adjustment of –$788,000 on the swap given the decline in rates during the fourth quarter. If held to maturity, this fair value adjustment would be fully recovered.

[7] With warrants, Treasury would presumably capture some of the benefit of a bank that performed well as reflected in its common stock price over 10 years.

[8] In 2009 and 2010, 45% to 60% of the banks headquartered in South Carolina reported losses. In 2009, FCB also paid $300,000 for the special FDIC insurance assessment.

[9] See the Formal Agreement Between the OCC and Directors of First Community Bank, Lexington, SC, dated April 6, 2010, No. 2010-081. In June 2010, the Federal Reserve Bank of Richmond also put FCB's holding company under a memorandum of understanding (MOU) which required the bank to get regulatory approval before paying cash dividends.

[10] In its periodic earnings releases, the bank reported that the securities it owned were rated AAA at the time of purchase, but were downgraded by the rating agencies given the economic climate and general uncertainty around private-label MBSs.

[11] Remember that any firm that prepays FHLB advances prior to maturity must pay prepayment penalties in the event that rates have fallen. With lower interest rates, FCB would have been subject to substantial prepayment penalties on its advances so its plan was to let the advances run-off as they matured.

REFERENCES

Admati, Anat and Martin Hellwig, *The Bankers' New Clothes*, Princeton University Press, 2013.

Agarwal, Sumit, Benmelech, Efrain, Bergman, Nittai and Amit Seru, "Did the Community Reinvestment Act (CRA) Lead to Risky Lending?" National Bureau of Economic Research, working paper No. 18609, December 2012.

American Bankers Association, "Dodd-Frank and Community Banks – Your Guide to 12 Critical Issues," Washington, DC, 2012.

American Bankers Association, "Impact on Community Banks of the Regulatory Restructuring Bill," Washington, DC, June 2010.

American Bankers Association, "Mutual Savings Banks – A Primer," Washington, DC, 2009.

Anderson, Richard and Charles Gascon, "The Commercial Paper Market, the Fed, and the 2007-2009 Financial Crisis," *Review*, Federal Reserve Bank of St. Louis, Volume 91, No. 6, November/December 2009.

Appleson, Jason, Parsons, Eric and Andrew Haughwout, "The Untold Story of Municipal Defaults," Liberty Street Economics, Federal Reserve Bank of New York, August 15, 2012.

Bair, Sheila, "The State of the Banking Industry: PartII," testimony before the Committee on Banking, Housing and Urban Affairs, U.S. Senate, June 5, 2008.

Baker, Dean and Travis McArthur, "The Value of the 'Too Big to Fail' Big Bank Subsidy," Center for Economic and Policy Research, September 2009.

Barnes, Tom, "An Overview of Loan Workouts," Egbert & Barnes, P.C., at www.egbertbarnes.com, 2009.

Basle Committee on Banking Supervision, "Principles for enhancing corporate governance," Bank for International Settlements, October 2010.

Basel Committee on Banking Supervision, "Regulatory Treatment of Operational Risk," September 2001.

Berger, Allen, Molyneux, Philip and John Wilson, *The Oxford Handbook of Banking*, Oxford University Press, 2010.

Berger, Allen Miller, Nathan, Petersen, Mitchell, Rajan, Raghuram and Jeremy Stein, "Does function follow organizational form? Evidence from the lending practices of large and small banks," *Journal of Financial Economics*, 76, Issue 2, May 2005.

Bernanke, Ben, "Risk Management in Financial Institutions," Conference on Bank Structure and Competition, Federal Reserve Bank of Chicago, May 15, 2008.

Berndt, Antje and Anurag Gupta, "Moral Hazard and Adverse Selection in the Originate-to-Distribute Model of Bank Credit," *Journal of Monetary Economics*, July 2009.

Bhardwaj, Geetesh and Rajdeep Sengupta, "Where's the Smoking Gun? A Study of Underwriting Standards for US Subprime Mortgages, Working paper No. 2008-036C, Federal Reserve Bank of St. Louis, October 1, 2009.

Bhatt, Sanjay, "Insider Loans Rife as Bank Collapsed," *The Seattle Times*, January 30, 2013.

Bradford, Terri and William Keeton, "New Person-to-Person Payment Methods: Have Checks Met Their Match?" *Economic Review*, Federal Reserve Bank of Kansas City, Third Quarter 2012.

REFERENCES

Brickley, James, Smith, Clifford and James Linck, "Boundaries of the firm: evidence from the banking industry," *Journal of Financial Economics*, volume 70, 2003.

Bruggink, Maria, "Trust Preferred Securities: A capital-raising tool for community banks," *Northwestern Financial Review*, December 31, 2002.

Brown, Tom, "A Loan Loss Reserve Primer: Beyond Simplistic Ratios," Seeking Alpha, www.seekingalpha.com/article/128284, March 29, 2009.

Bruton, Garry and Carol Kinzer, "A Guide to Creating a Written Loan Policy," *Journal of Commercial Lending*, RMA, December 1987.

Buehler, Kevin, Mazingo, Christopher and Hamid Samandari, "A better way to measure bank risk," McKinsey on Finance, Number 35, Spring 2010.

Bunger, Daniel, "Bank Ownership Structure and Performance: An Analysis of Cooperative and Mutual Savings Banks," working paper, Hamilton College, August 27, 2009

Conference of State Bank Supervisors, letter to Robert Feldman, FDIC, Jennifer Johnson, Board of Governors of the Federal Reserve System and the OCC regarding the Notice of Proposed Rulemaking entitled *Regulatory Capital Rules: Standardized Approach for Risk-Weighted Assets; Market Discipline and Disclosure Requirements*, October 17, 2012

Congressional Oversight Panel, *June Oversight Report: The AIG Rescue, Its Impact on Markets, and the Government's Exit Strategy*, June 10, 2010.

"Concentrations in Commercial Real Estate Lending, Sound Management Practices," proposal No. 2006-01, OCC, Board of Governors of the Federal Reserve System, FDIC and OTS, January 2006.

de St. Aubin, Donna, "10 Tips for Retaining Top Talent," Graduate School of Banking at Colorado newsletter, December 10, 2008.

de St. Aubin, Donna, "Retention Strategies for an Increasingly Unengaged Workforce," St. Aubin, Haggerty & Associates, Inc., 2012.

Dev, Ashhish, Mingo, John and Jan Buckler, "Intrinsic Risk Measurement: A Model That Works," *The RMA Journal*, RMA, June 2009.

DiLorenzo, Frank, "Getting Behind the Numbers," *The RMA Journal*, RMA, September 2001.

"DOJ's Quid Pro Quo with St. Paul: How Assistant Attorney General Thomas Perez Manipulated Justice and Ignored the Rule of Law, 'Joint Staff Report, U.S. Congress, April 15, 2013.

Fajt, Marissa, "Texas Ratio, a '90s-Vintage Failure Predictor, Back in Vogue," *American Banker*, March 10, 2010.

FDIC Community Banking Study, December 2012.

FDIC Compliance Manual, IV. Fair Lending – Overview, Fair Lending Laws and Regulations, www.fdic.gov/regulations/compliance/manual/pdf.

FDIC Study of Bank Overdraft Programs, November 2008.

Federal Reserve System Report on Credit and Liquidity Programs and the Balance Sheet, Board of Governors of the Federal Reserve System, November 2009.

Fitzpatrick, Dan, "BofA Plans to Cut 10% of Branches," *The Wall Street Journal*, July 28, 2009.

French, George, "A Year in Bank Supervision: 2008 and a Few of Its Lessons," *Supervisory Insights*, FDIC, Vol. 6, Issue 1, Summer 2009.

Fuchs, James and Timothy Bosch, "Why Are Banks Failing?" *Central Banker*, Federal Reserve Bank of St. Louis, Fall 2009.

Gandel, Stephen, 'The Case Against Goldman Sachs," *Time*, May 3, 2010.

Gastaldo, Evan, "Fake Mortgage Signatures Still Rampant," www.newser.com, July 19, 2011.

Gilbert, Alton, Meyer, Andrew and James Fuchs, "The Future of Community Banks: Lessons from Banks That Thrived During the Recent Financial Crisis," *Review*, Federal Reserve Bank of St. Louis, March/April 2013, Volume 95, No. 2.

Goldman Sachs Earnings Reports, 2009 and First Quarter 2010.

Gorton, Gary and Andrew Metrick, "Securitized Banking and the Run on Repo," *Journal of Financial Economics*, Volume 104, March 2012.

Gorton, Gary, Metrick, Andrew and Lei Xie, "The Flight from Maturity," working paper, Yale School of Management, September 4, 2012.

Griffin, Lucy, "From UDAP to UDAAP to ??," *ABA Banking Journal*, March 6, 2012.

Guglielmo, Michael and Drew Boecher, "How 'Core' Are Your Deposits?, Darling Consulting Group, Inc., DCG Balance Sheet Management Conference, June 2012.

Gunther, Jeffery and Kelly Klemme, "Community Banks Withstand the Storm," 2012 Annual Report, Federal Reserve Bank of Dallas at www.dallasfed.org.

Gustini, Raymond, Spencer, Lloyd and Tiana Butcher, "Qualified mortgages vs. qualified residential mortgages," Regulated Financial Institutions Alert, Nixon Peabody LLP, February 26, 2013.

Hoenig, Thomas, "Basel III Capital: A Well-Intended Illusion," speech to the International Association of Deposit Insurers, 2013 Research Conference, Basel, Switzerland, April 9, 2013.

Housel, Morgan, "Which Banks Might Fail the Stress Test?," www.fool.com/investing/dividends-income/2009/02/12/which-banks-might-fail-the-stress-test.aspx, February 12, 2009.

"Insider Loans Distrusted by Bair as Georgia Failures Lead U.S.," *Bloomberg.com*, 2009.

"Insider Loans Rife as Bank Collapsed," Seattle Times, January 30, 2013.

Insights for Bank Directors, Loan Policy Guidelines, Federal Reserve Bank of St. Louis at www.stlouisfed.org

Interagency Policy Statement on the Allowance for Loan and Lease Losses, OCC, BOG of the Federal Reserve Systsem, FDIC, NCUA and OTS, December 13, 2006.

Interagency Advisory on Interest Rate Risk Management, OCC, BOG of the Federal Reserve System, FDIC, NCUA and State Liason Committee, January 6, 2010.

Interagency Advisory on Interest Rate Risk Management Frequently Asked Questions, OCC, BOG of the Federal Reserve System, FDIC, NCUA and State Liason Committee, January 12, 2012.

Ivy, Bob, Keoun, Bradley and Phil Kuntz, "Secret Fed Loans Gave Banks $13 Billion Undisclosed to Congress," Bloomberg, November 27, 2011.

Johnson, Steven, Sheely, Mark, Fitzgerald, Tracy and Charles Foster, "Managing Commercial Real Estate Concentrations," *Supervisory Insights*, FDIC, 2007.

Koch, Timothy and S. Scott MacDonald, *Bank Management*, 7th edition, Cengage-Learning, 2010.

Kummer, Donald, Srshadi, Nasset and Edward Lawrence, "Incentive Problems in Bank Insider Borrowing," Journal of Financial Services Research, 3, no. 1, 1989.

Laderman, Elizabeth, "The Quantity and Character of Out-of-Market Small Business Lending," *Economic Review*, Federal Reserve Bank of San Francisco, 2008.

Liberto, Jennifer, "Prepaid Cards are 'Risky' and Loaded with Fees, Pew Study Finds," CNNMoney, www.daily finance.com, September 10, 2012.

Long, Colleen, "Feds in NYC: Hackers stole $45 M in ATM card breach," Associated Press, New York, May 9, 2013.

Martin, Brian, "FCCO in SC: Strategic Market Expansion Produces Strong EPS Accretion with Modest Tangible Book Value Dilution," Research & Trading Thoughts: Aug 15, 2013, FIG Partners, August 15, 2013.

McAdam, Paul, "Can You Be a Relationship Bank When Most Other Banks are Too?," FIS Enterprise Strategy, August 2011.

Moody's Investors Service, U.S. Municipal Bond Defaults and Recoveries, 1970-2011, March 2012.

Moore, David, "Valuing Community Bank Stocks," AFG Research Summit Competition, 2009 at http://mch-inc.com/pdf/AFG%20Comp%20 Valuing%20Community Bank Stocks.

Onaran, Yalman and Jody Shenn, "Banks in 'Downward Spiral' Buying Capital in Discredited CDOs," *Bloomberg.com*, June 8, 2010.

"Panel: $182B AIG Bailout May Not Be Recouped," Associated Press, www.cbsnews.com, June 10, 2010.

Parzinger, Thomas, Wholeben, John and Brian Zeller, "The Importance of a Loan Policy "Tune-up," *FDIC Supervisory Insights*, Winter 2004.

People of the State of California v. Countrywide Financial Corporation, Case No.: LC081846 at http://ag.ca.gov/cms_attachments/press/pdfs/n1588_firstamendedcomplaint.pdf.

Peters, Andy, "Four Banks to Watch from the 2007-8 Startup Class," *American Banker*, January 2, 2013.

Pew Charitable Trusts, *Loaded with Uncertainty: Are Prepaid Cards a Smart Alternative to Checking Accounts?*" September 2012.

REFERENCES

Porter, Michael, *Competitive Strategy: Techniques for Analyzing Industries and Competitors,*" The Free Press, New York, NY, 2008.

Schaefer, Brad, "Global Cash Flow Analysis – Common Mistakes & Other Helpful Hints," www.sageworksinc.com/blog, May 5, 2011.

Sheshunoff, Alex, "Trust Preferred Securities: A Major Opportunity for Balance Sheet Management," *Bank Director Magazine,* 1st Quarter 2002.

Sidel, Robin and Alan Zibel, "Regulators Scrutinize Auto Lenders Over Add-Ons," *Wall Street Journal,* May 2, 2013.

Siems, Thomas, "The So-Called Texas Ratio," *Financial Insights,* DallasFed, Vol. 1, Issue 3, November 28, 2012.

Shorter, Gary, Bear Stearns: Crisis and "Rescue' for a Major Provider of Mortgage-Related Products," CRS Report for Congress, updated March 26, 2008.

Status of Dodd-Frank Act Rulemaking, *American Banker,* March 28, 2013.

Stewart, Jackie, "Regulatory Costs Keep Rising at Small Banks," *American Banker,* April 17, 2013.

Study on Core Deposits and Brokered Deposits, FDIC, July 8, 2011.

'Subordinated Debt,' Comptroller's Licensing Manual, Office of the Comptroller of the Currency, Washington, DC, November 2003.

Swift, Chris, "Two Empirical Essays on Mutual Thrift Conversions," Ph.D. Dissertation, University of Nebraska, December 2009

Sullivan, Richard, "Risk Management and Nonbank Participation in the U.S. Retail Payments System," *Economic Review,* Federal Reserve Bank of Kansas City, Second Quarter 2007.

Taibbi, Matt, "The Great American Bubble Machine," *Rolling Stone,* July 9-23, 2009.

"Troubled bank opportunities: What you need to know about FDIC-assisted transactions," Grant Thornton, March 8, 2010.

U.S. Congress, "DOJ's Quid Pro Quo with St. Paul: How Assistant Attorney General Thomas Perez Manipulated Justice and Ignored the Rule of Law, Joint Staff Report," April 15, 2013.

Valenti, Joe, "The End of Cash: The Rise of Prepaid Cards, Their Potential, and Their Pitfalls," Center for American Progress, April 4, 2013.

Wallace, Sarah, "The End of Community Banking," *The Wall Street Journal,* June 29, 2010

Waldman, Peter, Mildenberg, David and Laurence Viele Davidson, "Insider Loans Distrusted by Bair as Georgia Failures Lead U.S.," *Bloomberg.com,* December 8, 2009.

Wallace, William, "FCCO: Raising Price Target – Strategic Acquisition Should Boost Profitability," Raymond James Equity Research, August 15, 2013.

Wells, Sharon and Trevor Gaskins, "Qualitative Factors and the Allowance for Loan and Lease Losses in Community Banks," *SRC Insights,* Federal Reserve Bank of Philadelphia, Fourth Quarter 2010.

Whalen, Gary, "Recent De Novo Bank Failures: How Important is Supervisor Choice?" Office of the Comptroller of the Currency, working paper 2012-1, July 2012.

Whalen, R. Christopher, "What is a Core Deposit and Why Does it matter? Legislative and Regulatory Actions Regarding FDIC-insured Bank Deposits Pursuant to the Dodd-Frank Act," working paper, Networks Financial Institute, Indiana State University, June 2011.

Wilson, Gregory, "Bank Boards Beware," *American Banker,* February 7, 2013.

Windax, Tom, *An Introduction to Option-Adjusted Spread Analysis: Revised and Expanded Edition of the OAS Classic,* Tom Miller (revision), Bloomberg Professional Library, 2007.

Wright, Robert, "Governance and the Success of U.S. Community Banks, 1790-2010: Mutual Savings Banks, Local Commercial Banks, and the Merchants (National) Bank of New Bedford, Massachusetts," Business and Economic History, Vol. 9, 2011

Yerak, Becky, "Bank fails, family adjusts," *Chicago Tribune,* July 19, 2009.